# Engaging with
# Calvin

# Engaging with
# Calvin

Aspects of the
Reformer's legacy
for today

Edited by Mark D. Thompson

APOLLOS

APOLLOS (an imprint of Inter-Varsity Press)
Norton Street, Nottingham NG7 3HR, England
Email: ivp@ivpbooks.com
Website: www.ivpbooks.com

*First published 2009*

British Library Cataloguing in Publication Data
A catalogue record for this book is available from the British Library.

ISBN: 978-1-84474-398-8

Set in Monotype Garamond 11/13pt
Typeset in Great Britain by Servis Filmsetting Ltd, Stockport, Cheshire

Inter-Varsity Press publishes Christian books that are true to the Bible and that communicate
the gospel, develop discipleship and strengthen the church for its mission in the world.

Inter-Varsity Press is closely linked with the Universities and Colleges Christian Fellowship, a
student movement connecting Christian Unions in universities and colleges throughout Great
Britain, and a member movement of the International Fellowship of Evangelical Students.
Website: www.uccf.org.uk.

# CONTENTS

CONTRIBUTORS

**Peter Adam** is Principal of Ridley College, Melbourne. He is the author of *The Majestic Son: A Commentary on Hebrews* (AIO, 1992); *Speaking God's Words: A Practical Theology of Preaching* (IVP, 1996); *Hearing God's Words: Exploring Biblical Spirituality* (Apollos, 2004); and *Written for Us: Receiving God's Words in Scripture* (IVP, 2008).

**Colin R. Bale** is Head of Church History at Moore Theological College, Sydney. His special area of interest is Australian Church History. His doctoral research was on 'Australian War Graves Inscriptions on the Western Front of the Great War', with a particular focus on the language and imagery of the epitaphs.

**Andrew J. B. Cameron** is Lecturer in Christian Ethics at Moore Theological College, Sydney. He is the Chair of the Sydney Social Issues Executive and the author of numerous articles on various aspects of Christian living. He is married to Mary-Anne and they have two children.

**Oliver D. Crisp** is Reader in Theology at the University of Bristol. He is the author of *Divinity and Humanity: The Incarnation Reconsidered* (Cambridge University Press, 2007), and with Michael Rea has co-edited *Analytic Theology: New Essays in the Philosophy of Theology* (Oxford University Press, 2009).

**Robert C. Doyle** is a Research Fellow at Moore College, Sydney, the author of *Eschatology and the Shape of Christian Belief* (Paternoster, 1999). He has over the last 30 years moved from Calvin studies to trinitarian theology and back to Calvin. He is married to Roslyn, adores his grandchildren, and is in his third church plant.

**Martin Foord** is Lecturer in Systematic Theology and Church History at Trinity Theological College, Perth, Australia. He is an ordained Anglican minister and his research interests are in twelfth- to seventeenth-century theology.

**Paul Helm** is currently a Teaching Fellow at Regent College, Vancouver. He was J. I. Packer Chair of Philosophical Theology there from 2001 to 2005, and before that he held the Chair of the History and Philosophy of Religion at King's College, London (1993–2000). Recent books include *John Calvin's Ideas* (Oxford University Press, 2004) and *Calvin at the Centre* (Oxford University Press, forthcoming).

**David A. Höhne** is Lecturer in Christian Doctrine at Moore Theological College, Sydney. He is the author of *The Spirit and Sonship: Perfecting a Particular Person* (Ashgate, forthcoming). He is husband to Amelia and father of three children.

**Michael P. Jensen** is Lecturer in Christian Doctrine at Moore Theological College, Sydney. He is the author of *You: An Introduction* (Matthias Media, 2008).

**Peter F. Jensen** is Archbishop of Sydney and former Principal of Moore Theological College. He is the author of *The Revelation of God* (IVP, 2002) and *At the Heart of the Universe* (IVP, 1994).

**John McClean** is Lecturer in Systematic Theology at Presbyterian Theological Centre, Sydney. Prior to this he was the minister of the Presbyterian Church in Cowra in rural New South Wales. He is completing a PhD on 'Anticipation in the Thought of Wolfhart Pannenberg'. He is married to Elizabeth and they have two children, Michael and Brianna.

**Mark D. Thompson** is Head of Theology and Academic Dean at Moore Theological College, Sydney. He is the author of *A Clear and Present Word: The Clarity of Scripture* (IVP, 2006) and *A Sure Ground on which to Stand: The Relation of Authority and Interpretive Method in Luther's Approach to Scripture* (Paternoster, 2004). He is married to Kathryn and they have four young daughters.

# ABBREVIATIONS

*CC*    *Calvin's Commentaries*, 22 vols, repr. Grand Rapids, MI: Baker, 1989.

*CD*    K. Barth, *Church Dogmatics*, ed. G. W. Bromiley and T. F. Torrance, 4 vols in 14 parts, Edinburgh: T. & T. Clark, 1956–1975.

*CNTC*    *Calvin's New Testament Commentaries*, ed. D. W. Torrance and T. F. Torrance, 12 vols, various translators, Grand Rapids, MI: Eerdmans, 1960.

*CO*    *Ioannis Calvini Opera Quae Supersunt Omnia*, 59 vols, Brunswig/ Berlin: Schwatschke, 1863–1900 [Being volumes 29–87 of *Corpus Reformatorum*].

*CTJ*    *Calvin Theological Journal*.

*DHB*    *The Decades of Henry Bullinger*, ed. T. Harding, 4 vols, Cambridge: Parker Society, 1849–1852.

*IJST*    *International Journal of Systematic Theology*.

*Inst.*    J. Calvin, *Institutes of the Christian Religion*, ed. J. T. McNeill, trans. F. L. Battles, 2 vols, Library of Christian Classics XX, XXI, Philadelphia: Westminster, 1960.

*IPAC*    Thomas Aquinas, *In Omnes D. Pauli Apostoli Epistolas Commentaria*, Liege: H. Dessain, 1858.

*LPSS*    Gregory of Rimini, *Lectura super primum et secundum Sententiarum*, ed. D. Trapp and V. Marcoline, 7 vols, Berlin, 1979.

*LW*        *Luther's Works*, ed. J. Pelikan and H. T. Lehmann, 55 vols, St Louis/
            Philadelphia: Concordia/Fortress, 1955–1986.
MT          Masoretic Text.
*NPNF1*     *Nicene and Post-Nicene Fathers*, First Series, 14 vols, ed. P. Schaff, repr.
            Grand Rapids, MI: Eerdmans, 1978.
*NPNF2*     *Nicene and Post-Nicene Fathers*, Second Series, 14 vols, ed. P. Schaff
            and H. Wace, repr. Grand Rapids, MI: Eerdmans, 1982.
*OOSB*      *Opera Omnia S. Bonaventurae.*
*OTh*       *Guillelmi de Ockham Opera philosophica et theologica ad fidem codicum
            manuscriptorum edita*, St Bonaventure, 1976–1985.
*PL*        *Patrologiae, cursus completus series Latina*, ed. J. P. Migne, 221 vols, Paris:
            Migne, 1844–1864; *Supplementum*, ed. A. Hamman, Paris: Migne,
            1958.
*RTR*       *Reformed Theological Review.*
*ST*        Thomas Aquinas, *Summa Theologiae*, ed. C. Ernst, 61 vols, London:
            Blackfriars, 1964–1980.
*STAH*      Alexander of Hales, *Summa Theologica*, 6 vols, Quaracchi: Collegii S.
            Bonaventurae ad Claras Aquas, Grottaferrata, 1924–1979.
*Tracts*    J. Calvin, *Tracts and Treatises*, trans. & ed. H. Beveridge, 3 vols,
            Edinburgh: Calvin Translation Society, 1849.
*TS*        Peter the Lombard, *The Sentences, Book 1: The Mystery of the Trinity*,
            trans. G. Silano, Crescent East: Pontifical Institute of Medieval
            Studies, 2007.
VG          Vulgate.
*WTJ*       *Westminster Theological Journal.*

# INTRODUCTION

John Calvin was born on 10 July 1509. That is a long time ago. Yet the ideas of this French theologian continue to influence both churches all over the world and Western culture in general. He can legitimately lay claim to being one of the most influential of all Western thinkers. The very facts that during this 500th anniversary of his birth conferences have been planned all over the world to celebrate and theological bookshops have been inundated with new volumes analysing and evaluating his thought testify to his continued relevance.

The essays in this volume were prepared for one such conference, the 2009 Moore College School of Theology in Sydney, Australia. Moore College hosted speakers from all over Australia and around the world, who joined with its faculty to explore and appreciate Calvin's contribution. There was no requirement for the contributions to present a single homogenous perspective on Calvin. These were explorations rather than a coherent account of the Reformer's theology. Yet an interaction of perspectives is itself productive, challenging superficial thinking and expanding intellectual horizons. Of course, the differences are not themselves the focus of attention. They remain somewhat in the background. But from there they add depth to the issues which are being opened up for us in these pages.

Not every important facet of Calvin's thought is addressed in these essays. No attempt was made to cover every base or outline a Calvinian 'system'. More could be said on Calvin's doctrine of Scripture, his understanding of human nature and the devastating impact of sin upon every facet of our constitution, the cross of Christ, the necessity of regeneration together with the place of faith and repentance within it, or even the nature of Christian ministry. However, what is said in the stimulating essays which make up this collection amply demonstrates the importance of what Calvin had to say and its relevance for Christian life and thought in our very different time. What's more, the book was already quite large.

Calvin has always been a victim of caricature and misunderstanding. This was the case even within his own lifetime. There has been a quite robust industry of 'anti-Calvinism' operating over the past few centuries. Particularly in the wake of the Enlightenment, with its dramatic anthropological turn, Calvin's grounding of faith and life and hope securely in the person, action and will of a sovereign God has drawn considerable fire. Yet what unites these essays is a conviction that Calvin needs to be heard again, understood first on his own terms and then plundered as a theological resource for a new century.

A number of people have been instrumental in enabling this volume of essays to appear in the year of the Calvin 500th celebrations. Special thanks should be given to the Principal and faculty of Moore Theological College, who enthusiastically embraced the idea from the first moment it was suggested. The contributors willingly immersed themselves in Calvin yet again, in order to bring a fresh appreciation of and interaction with the great Reformer to the conference and the readers of this volume. Of particular importance, though, was the patience, assistance and encouragement of Philip Duce and all at IVP, who proved yet again to be a tremendous gift to evangelical scholarship. The contributors and the editor are immensely grateful.

There will, no doubt, be a plethora of articles and books on Calvin appearing in this year of celebration. If this particular collection encourages readers to move beyond the caricature and read Calvin for themselves with a more sympathetic disposition, but with no less determination to test all that they read against the Scriptures, then it will have fulfilled its purpose. For to read Calvin as he speaks about the knowledge of God the Creator and Redeemer — the God who thrilled him throughout his life and whom he was determined to serve with a singular devotion — cannot but mean that we will have our vision of God expanded and our love for God inflamed. And to him alone all glory is due.

Mark D. Thompson

# 1. 'PREACHING OF A LIVELY KIND' – CALVIN'S ENGAGED EXPOSITORY PREACHING

*Peter Adam*

John Calvin wrote to Protector Somerset of England in October 1548 that he heard there was 'very little preaching of a lively kind in the kingdom', and of his hope for preaching that would 'not be lifeless but lively, to teach, to exhort, to reprove', and for preachers who were well trained, for 'the Spirit of God ought to sound forth by their voice, so as to work with mighty energy'.[1]

I want to focus on Calvin's preaching. Let us place his sermons in their context. Calvin had three styles of published writing, each with its intended purpose, genre and audience. The first was his theological writing, most notably *The Institutes*. Here he addressed the universal church and responded to its issues. The genre was dense explanation of an outline of theological topics. The second style was exposition of the Bible texts in his *Commentaries*, which were his lectures to students or ministers in written form. These were also intended for the universal church.

The third style was that of his sermons. These were addressed to the congregations at Geneva, and responded to their issues. The genre was exposition and application of books of the Bible. This style was originally intended to

---

1. Quoted in T. H. L. Parker, *The Oracles of God: An Introduction to the Preaching of John Calvin* (London and Redhill: Lutterworth, 1947), p. 113.

be heard, rather than read. However, from 1549 his sermons were systemati-
cally recorded by shorthand and then published. So sermons designed to be
heard by the church at Geneva then became available for the wider people
of God.

It is this third style, that of Calvin's preaching, which is my focus. It is the
most significant, and the most neglected, of Calvin's styles. It is the most
significant, because the purpose of *The Institutes* and the *Commentaries* was to
prepare ministers to preach. Calvin's sermons indicate the kind of outcome
that he intended from these other writings. It is also the most significant
because Calvin knew that the great truths of Christian revelation were God's
gift to God's people, not primarily to theologians and pastors. Preaching, not
theology or Bible commentaries, is at the heart of ministry and church. The
Bible has its full effect only when it is heard by the church and by the world.
Calvin's preaching was well recognized in his day, but has been neglected since
that time. This may be because we instinctively undervalue oral communication. The opposite might well have been the case in Calvin's day.[2] It may be that
we have focused so much on Calvin's theology that we have undervalued his
practice of ministry. We have much to learn from Calvin the preacher. Calvin
had a specific style of communication in his sermons. It is that style I want to
commend.[3]

Calvin helped create a powerful pattern of vernacular expository preaching.
His aim was to let God have his say, to project God's eloquence, to help the
congregation to hear the voice of God. Calvin's sermons, heard in Geneva,
written down, published, translated and published again, helped to reform
Europe. We need to recover the health and vigour of engaged and lively
expository preaching for the maturity and usefulness of the people of God,
for the conversion of the world, for God's glory. We have much to learn from
Calvin's preaching.

Calvin preached on average five new sermons a week.[4] He also reordered
the church, worked to reform the society, provided pastoral care for individuals, taught in the Academy, oversaw gospel ministry in Geneva, with its three
parishes and large ministry team, and trained others in ministry. Yet it was
preaching 'which alone enabled the dogmatician to fashion the face of the

---

2. A. Hunt, 'The Art of Hearing: English Preachers & Their Audiences, 1590–1640'
   (unpublished PhD thesis, University of Cambridge, 1998), pp. 1–18.
3. R. A. Muller, *The Unaccommodated Calvin* (Oxford: Oxford University Press, 2000),
   pp. 140–158.
4. T. H. L. Parker, *Calvin's Preaching* (Edinburgh: T. & T. Clark, 1992), pp. 62–63.

city'.[5] Calvin was active in gospel ministry, and his preaching was a key ingredient in that ministry:

> [I]t was more through his preaching than through any other aspect of his work that he exercised the extraordinary influence everyone has acknowledged him to have had.[6]

There are five keys to Calvin's preaching: 1, Engage with the congregation; 2, Engage with God; 3, Engage with the Bible; 4, Engage with theology; and 5, Engage in training. Each one of these engagements is challenging. The genius of Calvin's preaching was his work at all five.

## Engage with the congregation

In preaching, Calvin engages in the heart of ministry: that of a local church. His sermons were primarily for a specific audience; his congregations at Geneva. So they were contextual and applied, with appropriate language and homiletic.

### *Contextual and applied*
This aspect of Calvin's preaching may come as a surprise:

> Many people would like me to preach with my eyes closed, not considering where I live, or in what locale, or in what time. As if those whose responsibility it is to proclaim God's message did not proceed the way it was done in the time of the apostles – as if the prophets did not apply the law of Moses to their day and time, as if the apostles did not follow the same practice![7]

Awareness of context needs pastoral wisdom:

---

5. J. H. Leith, 'Calvin's Doctrine of the Proclamation of the Word and its Significance Today', in T. George (ed.), *John Calvin and the Church: A Prism of Reform* (Louisville: Westminster John Knox Press, 1990), p. 206.

6. R. S. Wallace, *Calvin, Geneva, and the Reformation: A Study of Calvin as Social Reformer, Churchman, Pastor and Theologian* (Edinburgh: Scottish Academic Press, 1988), p. 17.

7. J. Calvin, *Sermons on the Acts of the Apostles*, trans. R. R. McGregor (Edinburgh/ Carlisle: The Banner of Truth Trust, 2008), p. 327.

[T]hose who have the responsibility of teaching in the church need to be endued with wisdom and discretion. For if their hearers behave themselves meekly, and are willing to be guided by the hand of God, they have no reason to thunder at them or speak roughly against them. But on the contrary if there appears any hardness of heart and stubbornness in them, or it be found by experience that it is but lost labour to speak gently to them . . . then the preacher should use greater vehemency.[8]

This reflects God's pastoral awareness in providing preachers:

We have the scripture preached to us, and by that means God allures us sweetly to him, that he could not do any more for us, except he should take us onto his lap. We feel that he takes account of our weakness, chews our food for us, and speaks to us like a nurse.[9]

God accommodates to us; so does the preacher:

A wise teacher has the responsibility of accommodating himself to the power of comprehension of those whom he undertakes to teach . . . imparting too much would only result in loss.[10]

God accommodates to his people in Scripture and in providing preachers and teachers.[11] This also expressed the humanist value of *decorum*: 'deliberate adaptation to one's audience for the sake of persuasion'.[12] For Calvin: 'Doctrine without zeal is either a sword in the hand of a lunatic, or lies cold and useless and serves a perverse ostentation.'[13]

It is not sufficient to utter timeless truths. The preacher must know the context, and craft the sermon to serve the people:

---

8. J. Calvin [1583], *Sermons on Deuteronomy* (repr. Edinburgh/Carlisle: The Banner of Truth Trust, 1987), p. 1104. All references modernized.

9. Calvin, *Deuteronomy*, p. 146.

10. *CNTC* 9, p. 66 (on 1 Cor. 3:1).

11. P. Adam, *Speaking God's Words: A Practical Theology of Preaching* (Leicester: IVP, 1996), pp. 137–145; and see F. L. Battles, 'God was Accommodating Himself to Human Capacity', *Interpretation* 31 (1977), pp. 19–38.

12. W. J. Bouwsma, *John Calvin: A Sixteenth Century Portrait* (New York/Oxford: Oxford University Press, 1988), p. 116.

13. *CNTC* 7, p. 144 (on Acts 18:25); translation as cited in Bouwsma, *Calvin*, p. 228.

> For it would be a cold way of teaching, if the teachers do not carefully consider the needs of the times and what is appropriate to the people, for in this matter nothing is more unbalanced than absolute balance.[14]

As van der Walt comments: 'Calvin's style of exegesis as revealed in his sermons is true homiletical exegesis, which means that it is not simply exposition but exposition and application.'[15] Application must be clearly expressed:

> We rightly divide the word of God when we give such lessons as the hearers are able to bear, and each one received a portion that he or she is able to receive. It is like a father feeding his children, when he gives each one the right amount.[16]

Calvin worked to transform the people of Geneva by entering their world, and by applying the Scriptures to their lives and community. To do so he used the right homiletic, including the right language.

### Language and homiletic
Homiletic is the art of preaching, *ars predicandi*, and language is a fundamental aspect of homiletic.

The Reformation was committed to use the vernacular, and vernacular expository preaching for the church created a new model of preaching. There were vernacular Bible translations and vernacular sermons before the Reformation.[17] The Franciscans and Dominicans revived preaching, including some biblical exposition, and some vernacular.[18]

---

14. *CNTC* 1, p. 120 (on Matt 3:7); translation as cited by Bouwsma, *Calvin*, p. 116.

15. A. G. P. van der Walt, 'John Calvin and the Reformation of Preaching', in *Our Reformational Tradition: A Rich Heritage and Lasting Vocation* [No editor named] (Potchefstroom: Potchefstroom University for Christian Higher Education, 1984), p. 195.

16. J. Calvin, *John Calvin's Sermons on Timothy and Titus*, trans. L. T. (facsimile edn, Edinburgh: Banner of Truth, 1983), p. 805. All references modernized.

17. G. W. H. Lampe (ed.), *The Cambridge History of the Bible*, vol. 2, *The West from the Fathers to the Reformation* (Cambridge: Cambridge University Press, 1969), pp. 338–491; and van der Walt, *Preaching*, p. 199.

18. H. O. Old, *The Reading and Preaching of the Scriptures in the Worship of the Christian Church*, vol. 3, *The Medieval Church* (Grand Rapids/Cambridge: Eerdmans, 1999), pp. 185–292, 341–440. Wycliffe used vernacular expository preaching: see G. W. H. Parker, *The Morning Star: Wycliffe and the Dawn of the Reformation* (Grand Rapids: Eerdmans, 1965), pp. 43–51.

Calvin knew that the right use of language was essential:

> And so it came to pass in Papistry, for there also every man changed his kind of
> speech, in so much that the Holy Scripture became as it were a strange language,
> which men call Divinity, not as doctrine common to all God's family, but as a craft
> or science for a few only. For what is true divinity? That which our Lord would have
> common to all his children both to small and great.[19]

For the Bible was addressed for the most part to the people of God, and
God expected the ordinary believers at Rome, at Corinth, at Thessalonica
and Ephesus to be theologians, able to understand the Scriptures, as he had
expected his people in Moab to receive Moses' preaching.

The language of preaching should be familiar. 'We always labour to make
the Scriptures familiar, so that we may know that it is God who speaks to us'.[20]
Preaching is 'familiar' when we know 'that *God* is speaking to *us*',[21] and uses
language that is accessible, simple and homely.[22]

For Calvin, vernacular included colloquial: the idioms of ordinary people.
In his sermons on Ephesians, Paul did not 'put the plough before the oxen' in
the wrong order,[23] and did not want us to 'swim under water' so as to avoid
detection,[24] nor 'howl with the wolves' so as to keep the world's approval.[25] He
used vivid images: 'We are in a boat, so we are always half a foot away from
death.'[26] He also articulated the kinds of responses he thought people might
make to the Bible.[27]

Calvin's preaching style was designed to be heard, not read: it was for ears,
not eyes. He had a rhetoric that he used for *The Institutes*,[28] and a different oral
rhetoric for his sermons. He preached to be heard, and usually preached for

---

19. Calvin, *Timothy and Titus*, p. 17.
20. Ibid., p. 15.
21. Parker, *Calvin's Preaching*, p. 139.
22. Ibid., pp. 139–149.
23. J. Calvin, *Sermons on the Epistle to the Ephesians*, trans. A. Golding, 1577 (Edinburgh: Banner of Truth, 1973), p. 692.
24. Calvin, *Ephesians*, p. 694.
25. Ibid., p. 695.
26. Calvin, *Timothy and Titus*, p. 105.
27. Adam, *God's Words*, pp. 150–153.
28. See S. Jones, *Calvin and the Rhetoric of Piety* (Columbia: Columbia Theological Seminary, 1995).

40 minutes.[29] He opposed grandiloquence that obscured the text, personal 'inspiration' that bypassed it, and misusing the text and so profaning it.[30]

One striking feature of his homiletic was that he used 'we' and 'us', rather than 'I' and 'you'.

> When we come to a sermon, if we do not understand all that is spoken to us, let us wait and, in the meanwhile, honour our God and reverence him in the things that are too high for our understanding to reach to.[31]

This meant that he and the congregation were joint recipients of God's words. This promoted solidarity with the congregation. He often used corporate monologue, in which he meditated with the congregation on shared experiences and struggles.

He used strong nouns and verbs, dialogue, direct speech, and the emotional intensity of simplicity, brevity, intellectual clarity, and biblical and theological rigour.[32] Calvin used the persuasive power of the Bible texts, including vivid contrasts, language and imagery. He used the power of the God who speaks, and the rhetoric that opens up truth so it can persuade.[33]

Calvin's homiletic was a comprehensive appeal to the mind, emotions, memory, will and actions.[34]

He appealed to the mind: he provided teaching and instruction; he challenged people to understand ancient texts; he continually asked what this text taught about God and ourselves, and why the Bible writer had written these words.[35]

He appealed to the emotions by pointing to the power of God among them, by uncovering the emotions of the text, by reminding them of the drama of the eternal consequences of their response, by warning of the enemies of God, by using metaphors, comparisons, and proverbial images that appealed to the imagination, by penetrating and challenging application,

29. Calvin, *Ephesians*, xv.

30. M. Anderson, 'John Calvin, Biblical Preacher', *Scottish Journal of Theology* 42.2, (1989), pp. 176–181.

31. Calvin, *Ephesians*, p. 237.

32. See Parker, *Oracles*, pp. 65–80; and Parker, *Calvin's Preaching*, pp. 131–149.

33. Leith, 'Proclamation', p. 221.

34. Here I have used R. C. Zachman, *John Calvin as Teacher, Pastor, and Theologian* (Grand Rapids: Baker, 2006), pp. 153–172.

35. M. Parsons, *Calvin's Preaching on the Prophet Micah: The 1550–1551 Sermons in Geneva* (Lewiston/Queenston/Lampeter: The Edward Mellen Press, 2006), p. 7.

and by encouraging emotional response within the sermon.[36] His doctrine was affective as well as cognitive.[37]

He appealed to the memory. He frequently referred to what the congregation had learnt in previous sermons, and worked to instil what he was teaching into the memory of the congregation.[38]

He appealed to their will and actions. His aim was their transformation in faith and obedience to God. He reminded the congregation that God intended this text for us: 'the doctrine which is contained in this epistle is directed and dedicated to us at this present day.'[39]

All this called for something more than the brief and plain style of the *Commentaries*. Calvin created and entered the rhetorical and imaginative world of Geneva.[40] Preachers should aim at vivid reality:

> Let those who want to discharge the ministry of the Gospel aright learn not only to speak and declaim but also to penetrate into consciences, so that men may see Christ crucified, and that His blood may flow.[41]

Calvin addressed his sermons to the people of God, the congregation, and not to individuals and their needs. In this he reflected the Scriptures, which are primarily addressed to the people of God, not to individuals.[42]

De Koster comments: 'The *living* text encounters the *living* expositor to receive a *living* interpretation conveyed to the *living* auditor in a *lived* experience, for *lived* obedience.'[43] Childs described Calvin's ability to relate the message of the Bible to his own time as: 'one of the most impressive aspects of Calvin's interpretation of Scripture'.[44]

---

36. Leith, 'Proclamation', p. 221.

37. P. Ward, 'Coming to Sermon: The Practice of Doctrine in the Preaching of John Calvin', *Scottish Journal of Theology* 58.3 (2005), p. 322.

38. Zachman, *Calvin as Teacher*, p. 167.

39. Calvin, *Sermon on Ephesians*, cited in Zachman, *Calvin as Teacher*, p. 166.

40. On Reformation rhetoric and imagination see P. Matheson, *The Rhetoric of the Reformation* (Edinburgh: T. & T. Clark, 1998) and *The Imaginative World of the Reformation* (Minneapolis: Fortress Press, 2001).

41. *CNTC* 11, p. 47 (on Gal. 3:1).

42. Ward, 'Coming to Sermon', pp. 328–330.

43. L. De Koster, *Light for the City: Calvin's Preaching, Source of Life and Liberty* (Grand Rapids/Cambridge: Eerdmans, 2004), p. 83.

44. Parsons, *Preaching*, p. 11.

Calvin engaged with his congregation, to serve them with God's words.

**Engage with God**

Calvin worked hard to help his congregation engage with God. He believed that God was powerfully and effectively present in the written words of Scripture and the spoken words of preachers.[45] It was a 'kerygmatic real presence'.[46] To preach was to help the congregation to engage with God, present and powerful in his words:

> It is certain that if we come to church we shall not only hear a mortal man speaking, but we shall feel (even by his secret power) that God is speaking to our souls, that he is the teacher. He so touches us that the human voice enters into us and so profits us that we are refreshed and nourished by it.[47]

So those who reject God's words are 'unable to taste God's goodness, which God's Word contains'.[48] For 'When we speak, behold God, who wishes to be heard in our persons.'[49] And 'He will have his Word to be his lively image'.[50] So God is present, and his words preached are an effective means of grace: 'Where there is preaching, there God's voice rings in our ears.'[51]

DeVries has shown that this idea was not common in the Roman Catholic church of Calvin's day.[52] Whereas for Augustine both Word and sacrament

45. See R. S. Wallace, *Calvin's Doctrine of the Word and Sacrament*, (Edinburgh/London: Oliver & Boyd, 1953), pp. 82–95; M. J. Beach, 'The Real Presence of Christ in the Preaching of the Gospel: Luther and Calvin on the Nature of Preaching', *Mid-American Journal of Theology* 10 (1999), pp. 77–134; and P. W. Butin, *Reformed Ecclesiology: Trinitarian Grace According to Calvin* (Princeton: Princeton Theological Seminary, 1994), pp. 20–22.

46. H. O. Old, *The Reading and Preaching of the Scriptures in the Worship of the Christian Church*, vol. 4, *The Reformation* (Grand Rapids/Cambridge: Eerdmans, 2002), p. 133.

47. Calvin, *Timothy & Titus*, p. 665.

48. J. Calvin, *Sermon on Micah*, as cited by Parsons, *Preaching*, p. 9.

49. J. Calvin, *Sermons on Job* (facsimile 1574 edn, Edinburgh: The Banner of Truth Trust, 1993), p. 575. All references modernized.

50. Calvin, *Job*, p. 574.

51. Calvin, *Deuteronomy*, p. 1206.

52. D. DeVries, *Jesus Christ in the Preaching of Calvin and Schleiermacher* (Louisville: Westminster John Knox Press, 1996), p. 14.

were effective means of grace, and the Word was also educative, by medieval times the sacraments alone were the means, and the Word was merely educative: 'The Preached word itself, so far from conveying the healing medicine of divine grace, was rather a prescription for the medicine that was only available in the sacraments'.[53] Whereas for Calvin: 'The gospel, in other words, is not only the announcement, but the actual gift imparting God's promised grace.'[54]

For Calvin the Word is effective, for it conveys what it promises. This is true of the Bible and true of preaching. Calvin wrote of the Bible that there we hear 'the actual tones of God's voice'.[55] This is the divine epiphany that occurs when the word of God is preached,[56] 'for it is as if God himself came to declare his favour to us'.[57]

So the Scripture functions as a pair of spectacles,[58] in a supernatural way: not only making things clear, but communicating God's powerful grace. 'Therefore, when the gospel is preached among us . . . is as much as if he came down to us himself.'[59] For God is present in power and majesty:

> When God's words be preached to us by men, let us receive it as if we saw his majesty face to face . . . we must not take the Gospel as a doctrine bred here below, but we must always have God's majesty before our eyes. [60]

The conviction that words can be a means of grace was also an issue for Protestantism. For Luther accused Zwingli of teaching that the words of Scripture were only signposts to the direct work of God in the soul.[61] This meant that the words of Scripture and the preacher would not convey God's grace and power, but only inform us about it.

Calvin's view was that God used words as an effective means of communication. God chose to exercise his power by means of the human words of Scripture and preacher. So human words are not bypassed so that God's grace only works

---

53. Ibid., p. 15.
54. Ibid., p. 16. See also A. Ganoczy, *Calvin Théologien de l'Eglise et du Ministère* (Paris: Cerf, 1964), pp. 330–333.
55. Parker, *Calvin's Preaching*, p. 3.
56. Leith, 'Proclamation', p. 211.
57. Calvin, *Deuteronomy*, p. 738.
58. *Inst.* 1.6.1.
59. Calvin, *Ephesians*, p. 376.
60. Calvin, *Deuteronomy*, p. 255.
61. Parker, *Oracles*, pp. 45–48.

through sacraments, as in Roman Catholic thought, or directly and independently of the words, as in the thinking of Zwingli.[62] So Calvin preached:

> [Y]et here God comes to call us . . . that is the way God has called us through the gospel like a trumpet calling us to assemble with his people.[63]

God is present in his powerful words in the Bible and in the preacher. Parker summarized Calvin's teaching:

> If the preacher faithfully hands on what he himself has learned in the school of God, then God himself 'presides' . . . he is 'in the midst' . . . as if he were showing himself visibly . . . or face to face . . . and his people are 'joined' to him . . . Our Lord Jesus Christ is present . . . and the Church is 'united' with him . . . The Pulpit is 'the throne of God, from where he wills to govern our souls'.[64]

For Calvin, the church is God's school, we are his students, and the true and perfect curriculum is the Bible.[65] God achieves this by his preachers:

> God speaks to us by the mouth of a man, and graciously shows himself here among us, and has a mortal man as his messenger.[66]

Or again: 'Thus the preaching of the Gospel is like a descent that God makes to come and seek us.'[67]

As we meet God, we will certainly meet Christ: 'If we obey the teaching of [Christ's] Gospel when men speak it to us it is as if he himself spoke to us.'[68] We are in Christ's school, and he is our master:

---

62. See discussions in Wallace, *Word and Sacrament*, pp. 82–95, and Parker, *Oracles*, pp. 49–56. Beach, 'Real Presence', pp. 130–132, relates this to a similar ambiguity about the relationship between the words of Scripture and the revelation of God in the theology of Karl Barth.

63. Calvin, *Acts*, p. 47.

64. Parker, *Calvin's Preaching*, p. 26.

65. Ibid., pp. 25–27; and R. W. Holder, 'Calvin as Commentator on the Pauline Epistles', in *Calvin and the Bible*, ed. D. K. McKim (Cambridge: Cambridge University Press, 2006), p. 232.

66. Calvin, *Timothy and Titus*, p. 269.

67. J. Calvin, *Sermon on 2 Samuel*, as cited in Parker, *Oracles*, p. 56.

68. Calvin, *Deuteronomy*, p. 256.

> The word of truth holds us bound: both the one who speaks and those who hear. For
> God will rule over us, and Jesus Christ alone will be our master. [69]

As we learn from Christ, so we see God:

> Therefore we must learn to see God when it pleases him to reveal himself to us,
> which he does as often as Jesus Christ is preached to us.[70]

Hearing sermons is worshipping Christ: 'such is the homage our Lord Jesus demands from us'.[71]

This work of God and of Christ is achieved within us by the Holy Spirit. The Spirit who caused the Scriptures to be written still speaks through them. The present secret work of the Spirit is to change us, not to make the Scriptures powerful. By the Spirit's power inherent in God's words and by the same Spirit's secret work within us, God effects hearing, faith, obedience and transformation:

> God works by his words that are preached to us. It is not a bare voice that sounds in
> the air and disappears. For God puts into his words the power of his Holy Spirit.[72]

We depend on God's immediate action: 'such wisdom from God . . . is incomprehensible unless it pleases him to reveal it to us by his Holy Spirit.'[73]

For Calvin, preaching meant engagement with God, not just with the Bible: '[God] calls us to him as if he had his mouth open and we saw him there in person.'[74]

**Engage with the Bible**

Calvin's aim was to hear God through his inspired words in the Bible. So he must read 'texts', and understand language, and help his congregation to do the same.

---

69. Calvin, *Timothy and Titus*, p. 804.

70. Ibid., p. 629.

71. Calvin, *Ephesians*, p. 363.

72. Calvin, *Timothy and Titus*, p. 665.

73. Calvin, *Ephesians*, p. 696.

74. *Sermon on Ephesians 4:11–12*, as cited in Parker, *Calvin's Preaching*, p. 42.

## Texts

Calvin's normal pattern of preaching was 'expository', accepting each book of the Bible as a 'text' and preaching that 'text' by expounding it from beginning to end. Bible 'texts' are the complete books of the Bible, not one or more verses used as a 'text'. In expository preaching in its strict sense, the 'text' defines the form and the content of the sermon. (There is a broader use of 'expository preaching', in which the Bible as a whole gives the content but not the form. This is expository of the Bible but not of the 'texts' of the Bible.)

Calvin practised expository preaching, rather than following the customary lectionaries, which did not follow books of the Bible.[75] On Sundays from 1549 to 1564 he preached Hebrews, Acts, Psalms, Thessalonians, Timothy, Titus, Corinthians, Galatians, Ephesians and the Gospels. On weekdays he preached Jeremiah, Lamentations, Micah, Zephaniah, Hosea, Joel, Amos, Obadiah, Ezekiel, Job, Deuteronomy, Isaiah, Genesis, Judges and Samuel.

Why did Calvin choose to preach books of the Bible? Calvin as a humanist respected texts.[76] So before he began his Christian ministry he expounded an ancient text. His first published work was a commentary on Seneca's *De Clementia*.[77] Battles and Hugo note Calvin's love of brevity, which helps focus on the text of Seneca, and his ability to paraphrase: to pick up 'the whole context and underlying spirit of Seneca's words'.[78] Wimpfeling, Geiler and Surgant, Christian humanists, were pioneers of an expository style that became common in Zürich, Strasbourg and Geneva.[79]

Calvin found examples of expository preaching in Augustine and John Chrysostom.[80] He planned to publish a collection of Chrysostom's expository

---

75. One sign of the Reformation in churches which retained lectionaries was to implement the sequential reading of books of the Bible. In England the *lectio continua* began to be adopted in the 1552 *Book of Common Prayer*, in which the Morning and Evening Prayer Lectionary covered the book of Psalms every month, the Old Testament once a year, and the New Testament three times a year.

76. I do not tackle the large and complicated question of Calvin's humanism. My point is that he made good use of the humanist respect for ancient texts and skill in understanding language.

77. F. L. Battles and A. M. Hugo, *Calvin's Commentary on Seneca's De Clementia, with introduction, translation and notes* (Leiden: Brill, 1969).

78. Battles and Hugo, *De Clementia*, p. 79.

79. Leith, 'Proclamation', p. 209.

80. Parker, *Calvin's Preaching*, pp. 79, 80.

sermons,[81] to provide biblical teaching for lay people and show expository preaching in the early church.[82] Expository preaching was also sometimes found in medieval monasteries. *Homilia* was used for verse-by-verse exposition of Scripture, *sermo* for popular preaching in which exegesis was insignificant.[83]

The Reformation had to undo the untold damage caused by the decision made by leaders of the Roman Catholic Church that the Bible was too difficult for ordinary people, and was reserved for scholars; and that instead of the Bible, the ordinary people would have statues and paintings, 'the bibles of the uneducated'.[84] Calvin said of those church leaders:

> Though they may kiss the closed copies of the Scripture as a kind of worship,
> yet when they charge it with being obscure and ambiguous they allow it no more
> authority than if not a single word of it existed in writing.[85]

This policy produced generations of people who knew Bible images, but had no idea what they meant.

Expository preaching in the early church died out for four reasons: the demands of theological controversy; the presence of many ignorant people requiring simpler sermons; more complex services meant that sermons had to be shorter; and low standards of clergy training meant that many were unable to preach biblical sermons.[86] The Reformers were dealing with centuries of neglect.

Calvin set aside the complicated thirteenth-century structure of the formal medieval sermon so that he could focus on the texts of Scripture and let them shape his sermons.[87]

Another source could have been the late medieval innovation of teaching

---

81. Zachman, *Calvin as Teacher*, p. 59.

82. There are also examples of expository preaching from Bernard, Anselm, Bonaventura and Thomas Aquinas. See Parker, *Calvin's Preaching*, p. 80.

83. A. G. P. van der Walt, 'Calvin on Preaching', in *John Calvin's Institutes: His Magnum Opus*, ed. B. J. van der Walt (Potchefstroom, S. Africa: Potchefstroom University for Christian Higher Education, 1986), p. 328.

84. *Inst.* 1.11.5.

85. *CNTC* 12, p. 225 (Dedication of *Commentary on 1 and 2 Peter*).

86. T. K. Carroll, *Preaching the Word*, The Message of the Fathers of the Church 11 (Wilmington, DE: Michael Glazier, 1984), pp. 63, 197, 206, 220.

87. Van der Walt, 'Reformation of Preaching', p. 198.

books of the Bible in universities.[88] Luther lectured for ten years at Wittenberg on Genesis, and Thomas Cranmer and other Reformers studied the Bible in this way.

Among Calvin's contemporaries, Zwingli was the first to preach through books of the Bible; he began his sermons on Matthew in Zürich in 1519.[89] What had been done in Latin in monasteries and universities was now being done in the vernacular in churches.

Why did Calvin choose to preach this way? Calvin wanted to convey God's words as clearly as he could, by preaching them in their biblical shape. This disciplined him and helped the congregation. He began his sermons on Psalm 119:

> I will frame myself to that manner and order which the Holy Ghost has here set down, [so] I shall enforce myself to follow as briefly as I can the plain and true meaning of the text and without continuing in long exhortations . . . For performance thereof I determine by the grace of God to finish eight verses apart in every sermon, and to hold myself within such compass, so that the most ignorant shall easily acknowledge and confess that I mean nothing else but to make open and plain the simple and pure substance of the text.[90]

In basing his sermons on the *lectio continua* of the Bible, 'Calvin's purpose in preaching was to render transparent the text of Scripture itself.'[91] Calvin wrote of the Bible commentator:

> It is almost his only task to unfold the mind of the writer whom he has undertaken to expound, he misses his mark, or at least strays outside his limits, by the extent to which he leads his readers away from the original meaning of his author.[92]

To expound a text of Scripture is to respect both the human author and God the author. Torrance commented:

> he has given up the rhetorical conception of *persuasion* beloved by the humanists, one that appeals to what is attractive and desirable, and substitutes for it a mode of

---

88. D. C. Steinmetz, 'John Calvin as an Interpreter of the Bible', in *Calvin and the Bible*, ed. D. K. McKim (Cambridge: Cambridge University Press, 2006), p. 289.

89. Parker, *Oracles*, p. 18.

90. *Sermon on Ps. 119:5*, as cited in De Koster, *Light for the City*, p. 81.

91. Leith, 'Proclamation', p. 214.

92. *CNTC* 8, p. 1 (Dedication of *Romans* Commentary to Simon Grynaeus).

*persuasion* which throws the reader back upon the truth itself and its inherent validity.[93]

Textual expository preaching was not his only style, as he preached special sermons for Christmas, Passiontide and Easter, and Pentecost, and for weddings.[94]

He wanted to avoid 'taking a text', in the sense of taking one or two verses of Scripture out of context. In his letter to the Seigneur of Piedmont, he warned of those preachers who have only 'snatched in a passing way a few words of Holy Scripture'.[95] He wrote in his *Commentary* on Acts 20:26: 'mortal man shall not be so bold as to mangle the Scripture and to pull it in pieces',[96] for 'When passages of Scripture are seized on rashly and no attention is given to context, it is not to be wondered at that errors often arise.'[97]

As Schreiner has shown, Calvin's 159 sermons on the book of Job are an excellent example of expository preaching, where his style of preaching serves the purpose of the book well.[98] She comments that in his preaching of the whole book 'Calvin had to respect the integrity of the complete text.'[99] This respect for the text must have strengthened his preaching. Zachman writes of Calvin as gathering meaning from context.[100] Expository preaching is a discipline which helps achieve this goal: 'The sermon respects the order of the text and develops it rather than tears it apart. The preacher gives the intention of the text.'[101]

Calvin showed his respect for Scripture by respecting its constituent texts, the sixty-six books of the Bible. Calvin knew that in Scripture we have the intention of God – *Dei consilium* – within the intention of the human author

---

93. T. F. Torrance, *The Hermeneutics of John Calvin* (Edinburgh: Scottish Academic Press, 1988), p. 148.

94. Parker, *Calvin's Preaching*, pp. 160–162, 165–168.

95. Wallace, *Calvin, Geneva, and the Reformation*, p. 171.

96. Leith, 'Proclamation', p. 213.

97. *Commentary on Isaiah 14:12*, as cited in Bouwsma, *Calvin*, p. 118.

98. S. Schreiner, 'Calvin as an Interpreter of Job', in *Calvin and the Bible*, ed. D. K. McKim (Cambridge: Cambridge University Press, 2006), pp. 57–59. See also S. Schreiner, 'Through a Mirror Dimly: Calvin's Sermons on Job', *CTJ* 21 (1986), pp. 175–193.

99. Schreiner, 'Interpreter', p. 58.

100. Zachman, *Calvin as Teacher*, pp. 103–130.

101. Leith, 'Proclamation', p. 217.

– *mens authoris*.[102] He recognized the moral duty of the reader and preacher: 'The Golden Rule, for hermeneutic and ethics alike, is to treat others – texts, persons, God – with love and respect.'[103] Calvin respected texts, because he respected their divine and human authors.

## Language

He also showed his respect for Scripture's divine origin and human presentation by understanding how human language functions. Calvin, as an evangelical humanist, knew how language works: how meaning functions; that usage rather than origin determines meaning; and that language communicates feeling.[104]

While Calvin rejected the traditional fourfold interpretation popular in the medieval church, his adoption of the 'literal meaning' did not indicate a lack of awareness of the subtleties of how words work. He knew that different languages have particular forms of speech,[105] and he recognized various forms of expression such as hyperbole, metaphor, metonymy, synecdoche and personification. He knew that in Scripture spiritual realities are communicated by physical types and symbols.[106] He explained in *The Institutes* why literal meaning is not always appropriate.[107] From his notion of God's accommodation to our understanding it follows that language about God and spiritual realities needs careful attention as to meaning.[108] Furthermore, his understanding of biblical theology meant that he read texts not only in their immediate context, but also in the light of the big themes and perspectives of the unfolding revelation in the Bible. However, his recognition that the literal meaning was a good place to start brought reality to his reading of Scripture, because it helped him focus on the historical reality of the texts,

---

102. Parsons, *Preaching*, p. 17.

103. K. J. Vanhoozer, *Is There a Meaning in this Text?* (Leicester: Apollos, 1998), p. 32.

104. Bouwsma, *Calvin*, pp. 115–118; Torrance, *Hermeneutics*, pp. 100–111; and R. C. Gamble, 'Current Trends in Calvin Research 1982–90', in *Calvinus Sacrae Scripturae Professor: Calvin as Confessor of Holy Scripture*, ed. W. H. Neuser (Grand Rapids: Eerdmans, 1994), p. 103.

105. Zachman, *Calvin as Teacher*, pp. 111–117.

106. R. M. Frye, 'Calvin's Theological use of Figurative Language', in *John Calvin and the Church: A Prism of Reform*, ed. T. George (Louisville: Westminster John Knox, 1990).

107. *Inst.* 4.17.21.

108. Battles, 'God was accommodating'.

rather than moving too quickly to their theological significance or application today.

Though he did not parade his learning in his preaching, that learning enriched and empowered his preaching. A comparison between his *Commentaries* and his sermons indicates how his broader study informed his preaching.[109]

Calvin entered the world of the Bible texts with sympathy and understanding, and helped his congregation to enter it as well. He helped people connect those two worlds. 'He moves constantly from text to meaning, from words to doctrine, and from doctrine to the contemporary problems of being a Christian in Sixteenth century Geneva.'[110]

Calvin's humanist training taught him four vital skills: to understand texts, to understand language, to think clearly, and to persuade others. To these skills he added a Christian understanding of God, a theologically informed ability to read the Bible, and a conviction that the purpose of understanding is to be able to teach the ignorant and uneducated.[111]

He used his skills to teach his congregation to read and understand the Bible; to engage with biblical texts and language.

## Engage in theology

Reading Bible texts is a theological, not merely a literary exercise. Leith comments:

> The sermons are powerful precisely because Calvin explicated and applied the
> Scriptures word by word, verse by verse, within the framework of a vision of the
> Christian faith as a whole.[112]

Calvin's preaching gained strength from his theological engagement with the texts, his general theological thinking, and his theological critique of the church and world. His theological engagement helped him avoid a superficial treatment of Scripture, and helped him to see the relevance of the texts for his people.

---

109. Zachman, *Calvin as Teacher*, pp. 149–163.
110. DeVries, *Jesus Christ*, p. 41.
111. W. S. Reid, 'Calvin and the Founding of the Academy in Geneva', in *Calvin's Work in Geneva*, ed. R. C. Gamble (New York and London: Garland Publishing, 1992), p. 255.
112. Leith, 'Proclamation', p. 224.

We should distinguish between biblical and systematic theology: both were present, and both brought depth to his preaching.

### Biblical theology

Biblical theology exposes the gradual unfolding of the biblical revelation. It expresses the shape and balance of the whole Bible, deals with its unity and diversity, and expresses its coherence. It is an account of the verbal revelation that accompanies salvation history. While the formal study of biblical theology did not occur until Gabler,[113] it is not possible to expound the Scriptures without some kind of biblical theology. Calvin developed a biblical theology which helped him interpret the Bible and also helped him to preach and apply it.

Calvin's biblical theology was based on four foundations: God's revelation; Christ's one Covenant; one People of God; and one Word of God.[114]

In his revelation God accommodates to our capacity: 'in descending among us by the exercise of His power and grace, He appears as near as is needful and as our limited capacity will bear.'[115] This revelation appears first of all in signs and symbols, and then in Christ. God also accommodates to our capacity in the Bible.

All knowledge of God is mediated through Christ, the one Mediator: 'God is comprehended in Christ alone.'[116] For there is only one God and one Mediator, so therefore the Old Testament believers 'had Christ as the pledge of their covenant, and put in him all trust of future blessedness.'[117] This knowledge of God is mediated in one Covenant, in two modes of dispensation. Calvin explains that the Old Covenant is really the same as the New. For all people, 'adopted by God into the company of his people since the beginning of the world were covenanted to him by the same law and by the bond of the same doctrine as obtains among us.'[118] For there is only one Mediator, Jesus Christ, and therefore all people relate to God in the same way, through Christ.

Calvin develops his theme of one Covenant, and how it appeared in two modes: 'The covenant made with all the patriarchs is so much like ours in substance and

---

113. M. Elliott, 'Gabler, Johan Philipp', in *Dictionary of Major Biblical Interpreters*, ed. D. K. McKim (Downers Grove: IVP, 2007).

114. P. Adam, *Hearing God's Words: Exploring Biblical Spirituality* (Leicester: Apollos, 2004), pp. 119–138. Here I use Wallace, *Word and Sacrament*.

115. *Commentary on Psalm 78:60*, as cited in Wallace, *Word and Sacrament*, p. 3.

116. *Inst.* 2.6.4.

117. *Inst.* 2.10.23.

118. *Inst.* 2.10.11.

reality that the two are actually one and the same. Yet they differ in the mode of dispensation.'[119] So those believers 'had and knew Christ as Mediator, through whom they were joined to God and were to share in his promises'.[120]

The people of God are one in every age, because God is one, and because God's people are all saved by the death and resurrection of Christ: 'the Old Testament was established upon the free mercy of God, and was confirmed by Christ's intercession.'[121] Calvin developed these ideas in his image of childhood and adulthood: 'The same church existed among them, but as yet in its childhood.'[122]

There is one Christ and one people of God, so there is one Word of God. The Bible is about Christ: 'the Scriptures should be read with the aim of finding Christ in them.'[123] For we have in the Bible the Covenant promises of God: 'We enjoy Christ only as we embrace Christ clad in his own promises.'[124] So the Word of God is not divided: it is one Word about Christ to the one people of God. The Word increases in clarity from shadow to substance, but its subject remains the same.

God's revelation is rooted in history, and is the accumulation of God's words over many generations, yet in it we hear God speaking to us in the present. When we hear the Bible read, we hear 'the public oracles of the Holy Spirit'.[125] It is easier to move between the world of the Bible text and the world of today, because we share in one Christ, one Covenant, and one Word of God.[126] Here is a universal image of God in his majesty speaking to his people and calling them to believe and obey, and God's provision of his grace in Christ for our salvation.[127]

Wilcox shows the centrality of the themes of the kingdom of Christ and the restoration of the church in Calvin's preaching of the prophets.[128] These also serve to help his application of the Old Testament to Geneva.

---

119. *Inst.* 2.10.2.
120. *Inst.* 2.10.2.
121. *Inst.* 2.10.4.
122. *Inst.* 2.11.2.
123. *CNTC* 4, p. 139 (on John 5:39).
124. *Inst.* 2.9.3.
125. *Inst.* 2.10.19.
126. For similar themes see P. Adam, *Written for Us: Receiving God's Words in Scripture* (Leicester: IVP, 2008).
127. See also Parsons, *Preaching*, pp. 12–17, 227–255.
128. P. Wilcox, 'Calvin as Commentator on the Prophets', in *Calvin and the Bible*, ed. D. K. McKim (Cambridge: Cambridge University Press, 2006), pp. 120–130.

## Systematic theology

Systematic theology is the exposition of the coherence of Christian thought, which expresses and develops biblical thought in topics, and shows the connections between those topics. It brings together what the Bible as a whole teaches on a topic, and shows the balance, shape, coherence and implications of that teaching. It analyses what the Bible teaches, and puts that teaching in the light of the intellectual history of the church and of humanity.

Calvin's focus was on knowing God and so knowing ourselves. As Parker has pointed out, he kept on answering the questions: 'Who is God?' 'What is God like?'[129] He functioned as a theologian.

Though Calvin did not write a biblical theology, he did write systematic theology in the successive editions of *The Institutes*. By investigating the shape and purposes of *The Institutes*, we can find what benefits for the preacher Calvin saw in the study of theology.[130]

*The Institutes* are a summary of the key topics of Christian theology: the knowledge of God the Creator; the knowledge of God the Redeemer in Christ; the way in which we receive the grace of Christ; and the external means by which God invites us into the society of Christ and keeps us there. He aimed to cover the broad outline or sum of Christianity, so that no essential topics were omitted, and key doctrines were given appropriate prominence.

He wrote briefly, 'lest this book, which I am anxious to prepare as a short textbook, burst all bounds'.[131] This brevity means that each part can be seen in the light of the whole and a sense of coherence retained by the reader, and what is important can be clearly seen.

He showed the foundations of both beliefs and practices. The word *Institutio* meant basic principles, or basic instruction. This was a matter of doctrinal clarity:

> Not all the articles of true doctrine are of the same sort. Some are so necessary
> to know that they should be certain and unquestioned by all men as the proper

129. Parker, *Calvin's Preaching*, pp. 95–100.

130. Here I use Zachman, *Calvin as Teacher*, pp. 77–102; and W. H Neuser, 'The Development of the Institutes 1536–1559', in *John Calvin's Institutes: His Magnum Opus*, ed. B. J. van der Walt (Potchefstroom: Potchefstroom University for Christian Higher Education, 1986).

131. *Inst.* 3.4.1.

principles of religion. Such are: God is one; Christ is God and the Son of God; our salvation rests in God's mercy; and the like.[132]

He wanted to compare Scripture with Scripture, to aid clarity of thought; to find fullness of teaching on a topic; and to use passages easier to understand to clarify passages that were more difficult. This *analogia Scripturae* was most conveniently done when writing theology, rather than by interrupting the flow of a Bible text in a Commentary or sermon.

He related Christian thinking to past and present Christian teaching, and also to past and present non-Christian thought.

*The Institutes* were originally written as 'a key to open the way for all children of God into a good and right understanding of Holy Scripture',[133] as also 'to prepare and instruct candidates in sacred theology for the reading of the divine Word'.[134]

Here are some of the ways in which Calvin thought that systematic theology was helpful, and especially how it could serve the task of preaching. 'The Institutes were written for the sake of the sermons, not the sermons for the sake of the Institutes.'[135] Their immediate purpose was to help people read Calvin's *Commentaries*, so he would not need to include long doctrinal discussions.[136] *The Institutes* served the *Commentaries*, and so helped preachers.

Steinmetz wrote: 'The Institutes uncovered the architectonic structures of the Bible, the underlying plan of the whole, that placed the details in their proper context.'[137] Systematic theology was fundamental to the power, relevance, and application of his preaching of the Bible.[138] Calvin's engagement with theology, both biblical and systematic theology, served his preaching well, and helped to train future generations of preachers.

Biblical and systematic theology helped to express the *analogia fidei*,[139] and

132. *Inst.* 4.1.12.

133. *Inst.* p. 7 ('Subject Matter of the Present Work', from the French edn of 1560).

134. *Inst.* p. 4 ('John Calvin to the Reader', 1559).

135. Leith, 'Proclamation', p. 219.

136. *Inst.* p. 5 ('John Calvin to the Reader').

137. D. C. Steinmetz, 'John Calvin as an Interpreter of the Bible', in *Calvin and the Bible*, ed. D. K. McKim (Cambridge: Cambridge University Press, 2006), p. 291.

138. Parker, *Calvin's Preaching*, pp. 87–88.

139. *Inst.* 4.16.4 and 4.17.32. See also H. Blocher, 'The "Analogy of Faith" in the Study of Scripture', in *The Challenge of Evangelical Theology: Essays in Method and Approach*, ed. N. M. de S. Cameron (Edinburgh: Rutherford House, 1987).

the *analogia Scripturae*. It brought unity to Calvin's exposition,[140] and also helped him apply the Scriptures to his congregation. He wanted his people to engage their minds to understand the texts of Scripture, and so know God.

## Engage in training

Calvin preached to transform his people, and also to train them. There were four aspects to this training: receiving sermons, reading the Bible, teaching and converting others, and participating in God's global gospel plan.

### Receive God's words in sermons

He had to train the congregation to hear sermons: '[w]e know the three marks which constitute Christ's church, namely, the proclamation of the word of God among us, the Lord's Supper, and our communion together in love.'[141] The wise believer will welcome the ministry of the preachers, and not despise it: 'Whoever . . . rejects the faithful teachers of the word, shows that he is a despiser of God himself.'[142] For to hear the preacher is to hear Christ:

> [I]t is the will of Christ to exercise his ministry as Prophet by the mouths of those whom he ordains to be ministers among the faithful.[143]

When so much had changed in church buildings, the pulpit remained:

> So the pulpit . . . has a prominent place in the church building, not only so that the preacher may be heard at a distance, but also so that the teaching which comes from the mouth of the preacher may be received with greater reverence, and everyone submit to it.[144]

Calvin wanted to train his people to hear God's words in sermons.

---

140. J. H. Leith, 'Reformed Preaching Today', *The Princeton Seminary Bulletin* 10.3 (1989), p. 230.
141. Calvin, *Acts*, p. 58.
142. J. Calvin, *Commentaries on the Prophet Jeremiah and the Lamentations*, trans. by J. Owen (repr. 5 vols; Grand Rapids: Eerdmans, 1950), III, p. 445 (on Jer. 29:18).
143. Calvin, *Deuteronomy*, pp. 674–675.
144. Calvin, *Timothy and Titus*, p. 243.

### *Read the Bible*

Calvin wanted to train ordinary people to read the Bible.[145] This represented one of the most significant changes achieved by the Reformation. Before the Reformation, as Calvin wrote to Cardinal Sadoleto:

> Among the people themselves, the highest veneration paid to the Word was to revere it at a distance, as a thing inaccessible, and abstain from all investigation of it.[146]

Calvin's aim was to ensure that lay people read and understood the Bible:

> When, therefore, we see that there are people from all classes making progress in God's school, we acknowledge His truth which promised a pouring out of his spirit on all flesh.[147]

He trained lay people to assess what they heard by the Scriptures:

> [T]herefore let this firm axiom stand, that no doctrine is worth believing except as we perceive it to be based in the Scriptures . . . which makes it all the clearer that individuals are called to read the Scriptures.[148]

The need for ordinary believers to know their Bibles is even more evident when we see that Calvin was training the congregation as a ministry team.

### *Teach and convert others*

Calvin wrote to Cardinal Sadoleto: 'It certainly is the part of the Christian man to ascend higher than merely to seek and secure the salvation of his own soul.'[149] Christians are to serve others in ordinary matters of daily life, and also in bringing them the words of eternal life.[150]

Calvin preached from Deuteronomy:

---

145. Here I use Zachman, *Calvin as Teacher*, pp. 55–76.
146. Ibid., p. 70.
147. Ibid., pp. 56–57.
148. *CNTC* 7, p. 101 (on Acts 17:11); Zachman, *Calvin as Teacher*, p. 70.
149. J. Calvin, *Calvin's Theological Treatises*, trans. J. K S. Reid (London: SCM Press, 1954), p. 228.
150. On Calvin's missiology, see P. Wilcox, *Restoration, Reformation and the Progress of the Kingdom of Christ: Evangelisation in the Thought and Practice of John Calvin, 1555–1564* (unpublished DPhil thesis, University of Oxford, 1993); and Parsons, *Preaching*, pp. 181–225.

> Although not all have the office of preaching the word of God, yet a private person who is a member of the church may beget spiritual children to God if he has the occasion and ability to win a poor soul and enlighten him with the faith of the gospel.[151]

He also warned of failing to take those opportunities:

> But when most people see that God provides an opening for them and a way to instruct the uninformed, they will remain silent, keep their mouths shut, and not say a word . . . He will be guilty of other people's sin because he had the means to admonish them and did not.[152]

So Christians are to know their Bibles, and be trained and active in teaching and exhorting others.

### *Take part in God's global gospel plan*
Calvin wanted the church in Geneva to have a global gospel vision, to take part in a strategy to convert the world to Christ, and to make provision for gospel ministry in the future: 'God places no higher value on anything than the preaching of the gospel for he wants his kingdom to be dominant in this world, and preaching is the way to lead men to salvation.'[153] And the church in Geneva should work with God: 'To draw the world to God and to build up the Kingdom of our Lord Jesus Christ that he may rule among us'.[154]

All believers have this responsibility:

> Will we have this treasure [the gospel] remain safe and sound in our custody? First of all let every man ensure that it is locked up safe in his own heart. Yet it is not enough for us to focus just on our own salvation. For the knowledge of God must be known through the whole world, and every one must share in it, and we must take pains to bring all that wander. And we must think not only of our own time, but also of the time after our death . . . we must labour to make God known throughout the whole world.[155]

The gospel will go to the world as churches are planted, and godly ministers are provided:

---

151. Calvin, *Deuteronomy*, p. 883.
152. Calvin, *Acts*, p. 337.
153. Ibid., p. 325.
154. Calvin, *Timothy and Titus*, p. 808.
155. Ibid., pp. 747, 749.

> The gospel cannot be maintained without the means of which Paul speaks, that there
> be ministers appointed in every town, for the means to maintain the church is by
> preaching . . . So the Church cannot but decay and perish unless it be maintained by
> the preaching of the word of God.[156]

Wilcox has documented Calvin's strategy and work in church planting in
France and providing pastors for those churches.[157]

What are the implications of this? Firstly, leaders should take great care in
the selection and appointment of ministers.[158] Secondly, people should think
strategically and sacrificially of the need for good ministers: 'But men have so
little care to serve God and his Church, that no man would have his son be a
Preacher.'[159]

The congregation should be aware of the need to train preachers, and what
kind of preparation was appropriate. This was important for their support
of their preachers, and for those who were thinking of becoming teachers or
pastors.

Future preachers need more training than they can receive in sermons.[160]
However, the sermons they hear in church begin that training.[161]

Preachers need gifts and humility:

> Choose out the ablest in the world, yet they must acknowledge that they cannot speak
> of God with such majesty and reverence, unless God govern them and give them
> new speech, altering and reforming their tongues so that they may not speak after the
> manner of men but may show that it is the Holy Spirit who rules them.[162]

Preachers must be students: 'No man shall ever be a good minister of
God's word unless he first be a student of it.'[163] They must be able to teach
and preach: 'For though a man walk uprightly and have great and excellent
virtues, yet if he does not teach, he may be a good Christian, but he is no

---

156. Ibid., p. 1064.

157. Wilcox, *Restoration*, pp. 13–81.

158. Calvin, *Timothy and Titus*, p. 244.

159. Ibid., p. 240.

160. On educating preachers, see Anderson, 'Preacher', pp. 176–181.

161. For the theme of preaching in the sermons on Micah, see Parsons, *Preaching*, pp.
147–180.

162. Calvin, *Deuteronomy*, p. 1105.

163. Ibid., 258.

Minister.'[164] They must be willing to face hardship and suffering: 'not only dili-gent and indefatigable in pursing the task of teaching, but . . . ready to undergo the danger of death for the defence of the doctrine.' [165] They must be able to rebuke sin: 'When the word of God is rightly applied, then there must be conflict and war against all vices.'[166] They must know how to serve people: 'We cannot serve God except by serving his people.'[167] They must avoid arrogance: 'One of the greatest virtues of those who have the charge of governing the Church and preaching the Word of God, is that they guard themselves from being puffed up and having a foolish arrogance which carries them away.'[168] They must be resilient enough to face the opposition of the world and of Satan: 'they cannot preach the word of God, but Satan on the one side will do what he can to hinder them, and the world will be in an uproar.'[169] They must show 'invincible constancy'.[170]

Calvin used his sermons to train his congregation to hear and receive God's words in the sermons, to read the Bible for themselves, to teach and convert others, and to take their part in God's global gospel mission.

### Concluding comments

If we want to find a good model of preaching, we will not imitate Calvin's *Institutes*, or his commentaries, but the style of his sermons. For it is here that Calvin demonstrates his costly commitment to the five demanding engagements of preaching: engaging with the congregation, engaging with God, engaging with the Bible, engaging with theology, and engaging in training.

Calvin influenced preaching and ministry by the people he trained and taught in Geneva, especially those training for ministry in France, and minis-ters who found refuge in Geneva and then returned home. Knowledge of his preaching spread through the publication of his sermons, especially in French and English. English publications included sermons on Job (1574), Galatians

---

164. Calvin, *Timothy and Titus*, p. 411.
165. *CNTC* 7, p. 54 (on Acts 15:26).
166. Calvin, *Timothy and Titus*, p. 59.
167. Ibid., p. 293.
168. Ibid., p. 289.
169. Ibid., p. 101.
170. Calvin, *Job*, p. 574.

(1574), Ephesians (1577), the Ten Commandments (1579), Timothy and Titus (1579), and Deuteronomy (1583).[171]

Calvin did not always meet the high standards that he set for himself. His sermon on 1 Timothy 3:16 loses the shape and content of the text and focuses entirely on the topic of the divinity and humanity of Christ.[172] When he expounds John's Gospel, he understands the phrase 'lifted up' when applied to Christ to refer to the preaching of Christ, and not to the crucifixion and resurrection/ascension.[173] In his series on Job, he cannot avoid the idea that after all Job must have sinned, and so favours Elihu that he is taken to speak as a Reformed believer.[174] I do not think that preaching from a Harmony of Matthew, Mark and Luke, as Calvin did for his Sunday sermons from 1559 to 1564, was the best way to present those three distinct texts. Sometimes Calvin moves so slowly through the text that its inherent momentum is lost in the detail. Yet it seems petty to throw stones, when Calvin preached so faithfully and effectively, and when he helped to set the standards by which we might now judge him.

Many have found it difficult to maintain the five engagements that Calvin exemplified. For it is possible to so engage with the congregation, or with God, or with the Bible, or with theology, or with training, that the other engagements are obscured or lost. In the history of preaching,[175] we have examples of the text being sidelined because theology and/or application dominate (in Puritan sermons, Doctrine and Uses). Sometimes the rate of exposition of the text is so glacial that the text itself is lost, and the sermons become a series of doctrinal expositions by word studies. Sometimes the sermon becomes an exercise in human communication, or has such a strong focus on the text, it is as though God is not present and powerful to save. Sometimes the focus is so strongly on the presence of God that the text, theology, and the congregation are obscured. Sometimes the sermon is so comprehensively applied that the text is lost. Sometimes the world of the text, or the world of the congregation is lost.

This is my version of 'Calvin against the Calvinists'. It is Calvin the preacher as a model for all preachers. I do not think that we should imitate his homiletic,

---

171. Parker, *Calvin's Preaching*, pp. 72, 108–127, 188–194.

172. Calvin, *Timothy and Titus*, pp. 321–333.

173. DeVries, *Jesus Christ*, p. 16.

174. D. W. H. Thomas, *Proclaiming the Incomprehensible God: Calvin's Teaching on Job* (Ross-shire: Mentor, 2004), pp. 105–110; and Schreiner, 'Interpreter', pp. 67–69.

175. I do not have the space to provide evidence for these rash assertions.

because that was adapted to his own congregation. I think we should preach theological and ethical topical sermons, not least to educate people in moving from the issues of daily life to a responsible use of the Bible. However, Calvin still provides a good model of engaged expository preaching.

Calvin's five engagements are essential. Each of the five requires gifts and hard work, and combining all five takes wisdom and fine judgment. The strength of these five engagements lies in participating in each, balancing them, and making the most of the interactions between them, so that the sermon is not an amalgam of disparate elements, but a powerful, coherent and convincing whole.

We need to recover the vitality of Calvin's engaged and lively expository preaching. May God in his mercy raise up such preachers in every land, and such preaching 'of a lively kind'.

© Peter Adam, 2009

## 2. FIGURING CALVIN: CALVIN'S HERMENEUTICS (ALMOST) FIVE CENTURIES ON

*Michael P. Jensen*

### Calvin's history and our history

On the final page of his authoritative work *The Unaccommodated Calvin*, Richard A. Muller writes: '[A] clever theologian can accommodate Calvin to nearly any agenda; a faithful theologian – and a good historian – will seek to listen to Calvin, not to use him.'[1] Professor Muller's warning is salutary, not least in the area of Calvin's hermeneutics. If anything, there has been since the 1960s a revival in interest in Calvin's interpretation of Scripture, owing to his emphases on narrative and Christology; and an indecorous rush to appropriate or 'accommodate' him to new hermeneutical models. In the light of the slow dismemberment of the text of the Bible by scholars who hunkered around it like vultures pecking at a carcass, what else was to be done? The problem is that while this clinging to our forebear is driven by motives that are indubitably noble, it is by no means clear that Calvin has been listened to, and not used.

That is all very easy to say. The honest truth is that it is by no means obvious

---

1. R. A. Muller, *The Unaccommodated Calvin: Studies in the Foundation of a Theological Tradition*, Oxford Studies in Historical Theology (Oxford: Oxford University Press, 2000), p. 188.

that listening to Calvin on the matter of hermeneutics is possible five centuries after his birth. According to the standard scholarly account, the providential unity of the historical and Christological senses of Scripture is no longer an assumption with which the contemporary interpreter can proceed. Stephen Edmondson voices the disquiet:

> These developments over the last four centuries have shut off any direct appropriation of Calvin's scriptural hermeneutic for contemporary interpreters concerned with the historical sense of the text. . . . it is problematic at this point to offer an historical reading of Scripture that is either unitive or generally theological, much less one that roots the unity of the narrative in a robust Christology. Calvin's history, then, is not our history.[2]

Though there are several things one might want to challenge here, Edmondson has framed the challenge for a contemporary reception of Calvin's hermeneutics very well. On the one hand, Calvin posited a single divine authorship to the Scriptures that was evidenced in its unity of voice and continuity of narrative; and that the text was a direct description of what actually happened in history explained in terms of cause and effect. In direct and mutually informing relationship with it, on the other hand, he held to a Christological theology of providence: the divine will shaped the events of history such that Christ was their consummation. Scripture's unity was history's unity. As Frei puts it,

> Calvin simply did not separate in principle the literal or for that matter the figural meaning of a text from its historical reference or from its religious use, not even for purposes of arguing that they belong together.[3]

If, first, the text could be shown to be not a united text but a plurality of competing texts, with an at best uncertain relationship to what actually happened in history; and second, if the view of the divine superintendence of historical events could be challenged and even discredited, then Calvin's reading of Scripture could be made to look very odd indeed. By the beginning of the nineteenth century both of these were held to have occurred; and

---

2. S. Edmondson, 'Christ and History: Hermeneutical Convergence in Calvin and Its Challenge to Biblical Theology', *Modern Theology* 21.1 (2005), p. 25.

3. H. W. Frei, *The Eclipse of Biblical Narrative: A Study in Eighteenth and Nineteenth Century Hermeneutics* (New Haven/London: Yale University Press, 1974), p. 23.

so Calvin's narrative reading of Scripture was 'eclipsed'.[4] 'History' just does not mean the same thing as it did in the sixteenth century. We have moved, as Charles Taylor puts it, 'from a society where belief in God is unchallenged and indeed, unproblematic, to one in which it is understood to be one option among others, and frequently not the easiest to embrace'.[5]

The responses of Hans Frei and Brevard Childs (both from Yale and both admirers of Calvin *via* Barth) to this conundrum have been, in their different ways and with some sophistication, to bracket out the history question. In this way they could, they imagined, recapture something of the force of the unity of Scripture that so enriched Calvin's exegesis. Not least, this meant a rediscovery of the witness of the Old Testament to Jesus Christ. A 'robust Christology' could once again be a central feature of Christian understanding of Scripture. Both authors were of course aware of the difficulty of what they were attempting. Nevertheless, the question of text and history remains a burr under the hermeneutical saddle. Are the virtues of pre-critical reading really available to a post-critical theologian?

Calvin's history not 'our' history? Muller's scepticism and Edmondson's hesitation are of a piece. The question of appropriating, using or listening to Calvin by those who would by self-description stand in his theological tradition mirrors the question of appropriating the narrative of Scripture by the Christian church. To be asked to write an essay in commemoration of someone's 500th birthday assumes, in one way or another, that it is worth envisaging *continuity* with him. It is not merely an antiquarian exercise. There is a pattern of resemblance, and a connection of sequence, it is held, between him and 'us'. In turn, Calvin's use of typology in his reading of Scripture makes an appropriation of the two Testaments of the Bible in a way that similarly traces the patterns of historical events and how they are replicated, and also connects them to the present by cause and effect. There is both a mimetic *and* a genealogical relation between the two instances, though the lines of connection are not necessarily always clear. However (and here the significance of the question becomes apparent), if Calvin's history is not 'our' history, then in what sense can Calvin be 'our' Calvin, at least *vis-à-vis* hermeneutics?[6]

I propose in this chapter to proceed firstly by providing an overview of

---

4.  This is substantially Frei's version of events: ibid.

5.  C. Taylor, *A Secular Age* (Cambridge, MA/London: Harvard University Press, 2007), p. 3.

6.  I leave aside the question of proprietorial rights over the Calvinian tradition, which is in itself one of the problems against which Muller rails.

Calvin's hermeneutics; and then by analysing an instance of Calvin's hermeneutics in the field, as it were, in his commentary on Psalm 2. These more descriptive sections will provide the grounds for a return to the question I have just outlined: in what sense can Calvin's hermeneutics inform contemporary hermeneutics and exegesis?

## Calvin's hermeneutics – an overview

Calvin was not so much a philosopher of hermeneutics as a reflective practitioner of the exegetical task. His method and practice of interpretation emerged from a combination of influences upon him and the needs of his times. If he is to be regarded as an innovator in any respect, it ought also to be recognized that he also had a great regard for the tradition of scriptural interpretation in which he stood.[7] Calvin's approach to the text of the Bible was, in important respects, not unlike those of his medieval predecessors. Primarily this is because Calvin read the text with the understanding that in it God was directing Christians in their faith, their hope and their love. This was the thoroughly theological instinct that had led to the development of practices of exegesis – the *quadriga* – whose aims Calvin shared even as he repudiated them as techniques. Muller writes:

> once it has been seen that Calvin consistently understood the 'literal' meaning of
> OT prophecies of the kingdom to be not only the reestablishment of Israel after the
> exile but also the establishment of the kingdom in the redemptive work of Christ,
> the furtherance of the kingdom in the reform of the church in the sixteenth century,
> and the final victory of the kingdom in Christ's second coming, it can also be seen
> that the 'literal' meaning of the text, for Calvin held a message concerning what
> Christians ought to believe, what Christians ought to do, and what Christians ought
> to hope for.[8]

---

7. See for example his letter to Grynaeus, in which he speaks of 'the ancient commentators, whose godliness, learning, sanctity and age have secured them such great authority that we should not despise anything which they have produced'. *CNTC* 8, p. 2.
8. R. A. Muller, 'Biblical Interpretation in the Era of the Reformation: The View from the Middle Ages', in *Biblical Interpretation in the Era of the Reformation: Essays Presented to David C. Steinmetz in Honor of His Sixtieth Birthday*, ed. R. A. Muller and J. L. Thompson (Grand Rapids/Cambridge: Eerdmans, 1996), p. 11.

In other words, though Calvin's practice of interpretation differed from that of his immediate forebears, his assumption that the meaning of the text of Scripture was ultimately focused on the doctrine, the ethics and the future hope of the Christian community was a point of substantial continuity with the mainstream tradition of biblical interpretation.

Though it was not alone his preserve, the change that Calvin in many ways embodied was the increased interest and attention given to the literal sense of the text, invited by the philological and rhetorical interest of humanistic learning. Calvin learnt to look *at* the text and not through it to some more spiritual reality. The text *in all its textuality* was now the medium of divine revelation; so close attention to its verbal and textual details was the means for deeper encounter with the speaking God. The mind of the divine author of Scripture was best discovered by rigorous study of the original languages, by an awareness of literary genre and rhetorical tropes, and by attention to matters of history, culture and geography.

Calvin combined aspects of scholastic and humanist thought because the combination both led him to his specific theological commitments and confirmed them. That is to say: what Calvin gained from his education was not in itself decisive for the development of his hermeneutics – at least not without his theological commitments to the inspiration of Scripture and its applicability to the present day. In the words of Brevard Childs:

> Calvin's humanistic training was joined to a profoundly theological stance which effected a radical shift in perspective from seeing the church as the source of the Bible's authority to that of the Bible itself. Scripture was self-authenticating (*autopistos*) because God himself was speaking through this vehicle.[9]

Scripture was self-authenticating; but tradition was not useless. Calvin was not ignorant of the opinions and interpretations of his predecessors; neither was he interested only in overturning them. The authority of Scripture was not to be practised in isolation from those other, earlier commentators. In fact, the wisdom of Augustine, Chrysostom and Bernard was to be gratefully received by later exegetes. This was, granted, a carefully selective rather than exhaustively comprehensive list of secondary authors: the point of the exercise was not to interpret the interpreters. Nevertheless, it was evidence that for Calvin the practice of scriptural interpretation was in a crucial respect dialogical, and itself located in a developing history.

---

9. B. S. Childs, *Biblical Theology of the Old and New Testaments: Theological Reflection on the Christian Bible* (London: SCM, 1992), p. 48.

For Calvin, it was Christ who was 'the scope' of Scripture. As he himself said:

> We must read the scripture with the purpose of finding Christ in it. Anyone who
> deviates from this may labour and study all his life, but he will not come to a knowledge
> of the truth. We must not think that we are wiser than the wisdom of God.[10]

The end point of Biblical interpretation is to find Christ. Not that this
resulted in Christ becoming an exegetical *deus ex machina*, produced at every
point, however fanciful.[11] In Calvin's exegesis of the Old Testament he is quite
restrained. It is the movement of salvation history in the biblical narrative that
points inexorably towards Christ.

Though Calvin believed that the literal and spiritual senses of Scripture
were in fact inseparable, this did not mean for him that he avoided figural readings. Far from it: what Calvin opposed was not allegory *per se*; it was allegory as
a speculative practice, ungrounded in the intentions of the author and the plain
reading of the text itself. As Frei wrote, 'his application of figural interpretation never lost its connection with literal reading of individual texts.'[12] It was,
rather, appropriate to read Scripture with an awareness of its uses of typology.
Scripture itself in its unity and in its Christological scope invites readings that
allow for typological comparisons.

The great literary critic Eric Auerbach described typological or figural
reading (as practised by Calvin) thus:

> Figural interpretation establishes a connection between two events or persons in such
> a way that the first signifies not only itself but also the second, while second involves
> or fulfills the first. The two poles of a figure are separated in time, but both, being
> real events or persons, are within temporality. They are both contained in the flowing
> stream which is historical life, and only the comprehension, the *intellectus spiritualis*, of
> their interdependence is a spiritual act.[13]

In other words, typology shows that two events or characters are part of
the one connected stream of history in a way that is not necessarily obvious

---

10. Cited in H.-J. Kraus, 'Calvin's Exegetical Principles', *Interpretation* 31 (1977), p. 17.

11. A great example of Calvin's restraint in this regard can be found in his commentary
    on Psalm 2, for which see following.

12. Frei, *Eclipse*, p. 31.

13. E. Auerbach, *Mimesis: The Representation of Reality in Western Literature*, trans. Willard
    R. Trask (Princeton: Princeton University Press, 1953), p. 73.

from mere analysis of causality. The prefiguring of one by the other is discerned by (or, perhaps better, revealed by the Spirit to) the reader. In Frei's words:

> In figural interpretation the figure itself is real in its own place, time, and right, and without any detraction from that reality it prefigures the reality that will fulfill it. This figural relation not only brings into coherent relation events in biblical narration, but allows also the fitting of each present occurrence and experience into a real, narrative framework or world. Each person, each occurrence is a figure of that providential narrative in which it is also an ingredient.[14]

Unlike allegorical reading, typological interpretation points to the embeddedness of the events in a common narrative framework governed by providence. These are 'real' or 'historical', at least in the sense that they gain their meaning from a relation to divine providence – the same providential narrative in which the reader of the text then in turn finds him or herself.[15] Calvin's use of typology, therefore, develops from the theological assertion that God works by theme and variations in the patterns he establishes in history.

For Calvin, typological interpretation gains its impetus from the New Testament's appropriation of the Old Testament. In fact, the very existence of the New Testament itself depends on a typological account that reads the story of Jesus Christ as continuous with, and indeed the fulfilment of, the salvation history narrated in the Jewish Scriptures. Examples of the New Testament writers employing typological readings are numerous, and Calvin expounded them in his commentaries: the Passion narratives in the Synoptics, for example, emphasize the correspondence *and* continuity of the events to significant events in the OT. Paul makes explicit use of the Greek word *tupos* in 1 Cor 10:11 as he compares the church with the Israelites in the wilderness; and in Romans 5, in comparing Adam with Christ. The argument of the Epistle to the Hebrews hinges on a typological account of the exodus and of the tabernacle. In each case, as Calvin observes, the rhetorical power of drawing the comparison is made more impressive by the salvation-historical link between the two events. They are, for Calvin, related thereby to the one overarching divine plan. The theological significance of 'history' for Calvin's hermeneutics becomes plain.

---

14. Frei, *Eclipse*, p. 153.

15. This is what Frei argued had been 'eclipsed' in all the debates about what it was to which the texts referred.

## Calvin' s hermeneutics in action: Psalm 2

Such is Calvin's approach to the interpretation of Scripture, seen in broad overview. What did this mean for Calvin's exegesis? Can we see his approach bearing fruit in his analysis of particular texts? I have chosen for this purpose to examine Calvin's commentary on Psalm 2. David Puckett agrees that this is a good choice because Calvin's comments here 'provide excellent examples of his method of exegetical reasoning as he tries to avoid the pitfalls often encountered by Jewish and Christian interpreters'.[16]

Psalm 2 is held by Christian interpreters to be one of the more obviously Christological psalms and it is frequently quoted in the NT. The psalmist sits in the point of view of the Davidic king as he is surrounded and assailed by his enemies. The anointing of David by God, his divine authorization, was, since he was subject to attack, not obvious – or at least in question. The psalm serves as a riposte to that questioning of the right of the Davidic king to rule, since his authority is so severely contested.

We can observe six things about Calvin's exegetical *modus operandi*. First, *for Calvin the type and the anti-type mutually inform one another*. The first exegetical issue that Calvin turns to is the identity of the enemies that surround David: as he says, '[I]t is not certain from the words, whether he speaks only of enemies in his own kingdom, or extends his complaints to foreign invaders'.[17] Admittedly, the plain reading of the text ('many nations') seems to give no option to the exegete; but nevertheless, Calvin proceeds as if this were a matter in need of clarification. To resolve this, he resorts in the first instance to the narratives of 2 Samuel, in which the cavils of David's own people *and* then the hostility of the surrounding nations were narrated in their turn. Yet, as if this were not enough evidence, he makes a further step:

> it agrees better with the completeness of the type [*quod figurae complement molius quadrat*] to suppose that different kinds of enemies were joined together; for we know that Christ had not only to do with enemies in his own country, but likewise with enemies in other nations: the whole world having entered into a common conspiracy to accomplish his destruction.[18]

16. D. L. Puckett, *John Calvin's Exegesis of the Old Testament*, Columbia Series in Reformed Theology (Louisville: Westminster John Knox, 1995), p. 120.
17. J. Calvin, *Commentary on the Book of Psalms*, trans. James Anderson (Edinburgh: Calvin Translation Society, 1845), p. 10.
18. Ibid.

The 'completeness of the type' is not in itself here decisive, but it is unmis-
takeable confirmation that the Gentiles as well as the Jews were included in the
enemies of Jehovah and his Christ – since Christ too was opposed by Jews and
Gentiles together. Calvin is happy to work back to the figural text from that which
it figures to clarify and confirm his reading of the text. However, he does not here
do so in a way which makes the pre-figuring of Christ utterly decisive: he only
introduces this element after establishing that the most likely reading is that which
is given in the original text itself. There is a kind of mutual illumination going on
between the type and anti-type, with each enriching and enlarging the other.

Secondly, Calvin emphasizes the incompleteness or unfulfilled nature of
the initial text, such that the *psalm itself invites a prophetic reading of itself as a literal
meaning of the text*. It cannot be read otherwise than as inviting a figural com-
pletion. In this was the literal which generates and justifies the figural reading.
Calvin is happy to ascribe knowledge of this to the first author. So, 'that David
prophesied concerning Christ is clearly manifest from this, that he knew his
own kingdom to be merely a shadow.'[19] David himself recognized that he had
been made King 'to be a type of the Redeemer', as an 'earnest to God's ancient
people of the eternal kingdom'. That is, David and his people saw the work of
God in anointing this earthly king for this earthly throne as presaging a greater
work that God as yet intended to bring to pass (for Calvin). Calvin insists that
this reading is not a matter of allegorizing or of making 'violent' and remote
connections between motifs, but rather a matter of true prediction *vis-à-vis*
Christ, intended in whatever remote way by the author. As Puckett writes:

> Calvin believes that the NT writer's use of Psalm 2 is an adequate demonstration that
> the psalm should be understood typologically. But apart from this explicit citation, it
> is still possible to prove that the psalm refers to Christ.[20]

The text itself, argues Calvin, points Christ-wards.

If the typological reading gains warrant from its literal sense, then (thirdly)
*it is further established by the practices of the apostles themselves*. And this reading of
the psalm is an apostolic reading. The apostles themselves have read David's
temporal kingdom as Christ's eternal one (see Acts 4:25–26).[21] The apostles,
'to place our faith beyond the reach of cavils', have explained how the things

---

19. Ibid., p. 11.

20. Puckett, *Calvin's Exegesis*, p. 120.

21. Curiously, Calvin does not make use of all the possible New Testament references
    to the psalm – a measure of his restraint, perhaps?

pertaining to David now pertain to Christ, so that Calvin is able to make application from the psalm directly to the believers of the first century, and with them, to his readers in the sixteenth century. The person of the Son of God – foreshadowed in David – is the decisive emblem and locus of God's rule over humankind. The psalm teaches, therefore, that to deny the command of Christ is to deny the authority of God himself.

Fourthly, then, *Calvin's pastoral desire to apply the text to the contemporary reader as a consolation and a warning leads him to make a second typological step in the direction of the present day.* This is a consoling truth for the present time, opened up for the reader by the figural reading. When opposition to Christ is observed today, it need only be recalled that this was predicted in this very text of long ago. The kingdom of Christ, like that of David, is peaceable in nature, but it provokes opposition. It does not appear without arousing disturbances against it. The hostility of the nations against the Messiah fall under the hand of divine providence – it is sad but not surprising.[22]

A further comfort comes from this observation:

> When we see Christ well nigh overwhelmed with the number and strength of his enemies, let us remember that they are making war against God over whom they shall not prevail, and therefore their attempts, whatever they may be, and however increasing, will come to nought, and be utterly ineffectual.[23]

Opposition to Christ – and by 'Christ' here Calvin means Christ embodied in the presence of the bearers of his true message – is futile and temporary, since it is opposition to God himself. We notice here that the type overflows onto the apostles as Christ's representatives. It is not only the person of Christ who is surrounded by enemies, but rather that 'this doctrine runs through the whole gospel'.[24] Calvin is not quite clear here, but he surely means that the attack of the enemies of the Messiah is not merely a prophecy of the crucifixion but also a type of the hostility with which the apostolic message is received in every age. In this way, then, Calvin reads the text as saying something *now*, and not just as having said something *then*.[25]

22. On this point see K. Greene-McCreight, '"We Are Companions of the Patriarchs" or Scripture Absorbs Calvin's World', in *Theology and Scriptural Imagination*, ed. L. G. Jones and J. J. Buckley (Oxford: Blackwell, 1998), pp. 51–62.

23. Calvin, *Psalms*, p. 12.

24. Ibid., p. 13.

25. R. A. Muller, 'The Hermeneutics of Promise and Fulfillment in Calvin's Exegesis

By the same token, Calvin reads the scornful laughter of God at the enemies arrayed against his Anointed One as having present significance: 'if God does not immediately stretch forth his hand against the ungodly, it is now his time of laughter'.[26] The point is this: if there is a delay in the final revelation of God's rule, it is only because of a purposed gap in the fulfilment of the holy plan. The establishment of the Son of God on the holy mountain ought to have been sign enough of the divine intention, and the security of his purpose in the anointing of the Davidic line for the consolidation of his rule. It is a reminder of the futility of the opposition – but also a prophecy concerning Christ, 'because at length, in God's own time, the truth of the prophecy was manifested and actually established by the solemn rite of his [i.e. Christ's] consecration.'[27]

Fifthly, *Calvin is markedly cautious in applying the Sonship of Christ in this psalm to the internal relations of the Godhead.* As Kraus says, 'Calvin always reveals himself as an unusually careful interpreter of the Old Testament when it comes to Christological interpretations'.[28] Even though Christ was indeed the 'scope' of Scripture, he was not held to be ubiquitous. While on the one hand he argues for the inadequacy of Jewish interpretations of the text, the language of 'begetting' is handled watchfully by Calvin: he does not want hastily to import intra-Trinitarian language, as other Christian exegetes have done.[29] To be 'begotten' in the first instance must indicate his anointing – God's election of him as kind: '[H]e is not said to be begotten in any other sense than as the Father bore testimony to him as being his own Son.'[30] The point of the declaration of the Christ as the Son of God was not to do with a change in his being, but was made as a declaration of his glory to the whole world. As Calvin says,

---

Footnote 25 *(cont.)*

of the Old Testament Prophecies of the Kingdom', in *The Bible in the Sixteenth Century*, ed. D. C. Steinmetz (Durham/London: Duke University Press, 1990), p. 76.

26. Calvin, *Psalms*, p. 22.

27. Ibid.

28. Kraus, 'Exegetical Principles', p. 15.

29. As Puckett puts it: 'He argues that the Jews are able to cite no adequate referent for the texts in OT times, and thus a Christological interpretation is necessary. Against fellow Christian exegetes he argues that one cannot tear a text out of its historical context in order to apply it to Christ': Puckett, *Calvin's Exegesis*, p. 124.

30. Calvin, *Psalms*, p. 18.

[T]his begetting ought not to be understood of the mutual love which exists between the Father and the Son; it only signifies that *He* who had been hidden from the beginning in the sacred bosom of the Father, and who afterwards had been obscurely shadowed forth under the law, was known to be the Son of God from the time when he came forth with authentic and evident marks of Sonship.[31]

In particular, the resurrection was this time (Rom. 1:4) – it is described by Calvin as its 'principal allusion'.

Sixthly, *Christ's royal rule – the 'sceptre of his power' – is the gospel.* Christ proved himself to have been called by God to the princely office by his demonstrations of the power of God – not only in his miracle-working but also by the preaching of the gospel itself. This, says Calvin, is the 'lawful power of God', now resounding through the whole world according to the apostolic testimony. The apostles and those after them 'bore testimony that Christ was made King by God the Father; but since they acted as ambassadors in Christ's stead, *He* rightly and properly claims to himself alone whatever was done by them.'[32] The preachers of Christ *are* Christ in another guise. What they do is attributable to him – it is *his* work. Even when it is broadcast by others, it is still his message and a message of his rule and authority. 'As often . . . as we hear the gospel preached by men, we ought to consider that it is not so much they who speak, as Christ who speaks by them'.[33] The corollary of this declaration is that Christ is a king above other kings. Psalm 2:7–8 means that the figure described is exalted even above angels. Calvin understands this figuratively: 'David, individually considered, was inferior to the angels, but in so far as he represented the person of Christ he is with very good reason preferred far above them.'[34] There is something singular and unique indicated about the Son in the psalm.

In his exposition of verse 8, Calvin is able to bring in the full extent of the work of the incarnate Christ. The Eternal Word of God was always exalted from the beginning; but the exaltation of the human nature of the Christ comes after his taking on of humble human flesh. The title of Son of God comes to him not only as God but as the 'whole person of the Mediator'.[35] David's career is insufficient to circumscribe adequately the prophecy of the

---

31. Ibid.
32. Ibid., p. 17.
33. Ibid.
34. Ibid.
35. Ibid., p. 19.

psalm. What was written here of David was not, for Calvin, fulfilled in him. His kingdom was, in relative terms, of modest size. Only Christ has 'subdued the whole world to himself'.[36] What is more, the call of the Gentiles in the evangelical preaching is foretold – the rule of Christ being extended in New Testament terms by the preaching of the gospel to the nations.

A crucial difference is the mode of rule. Christ *is* indeed given power and authority to rule *even* over those who reject him, but it is not by the sword that he now rules (unlike David). David is a 'specimen' of the unconquerable power of God in war. But Christ rules 'by the breath of his mouth'. Calvin probes the difference: how is it that the meek and gentle Lord is here seen as so austere and thunders against his enemies and destroys them? That is, the gospel of Christ itself is a judgment enacted by spiritual weaponry that is sufficient to cast down every proud thing.

Calvin has to explain, however, the historical disjunction: how is it that this breaking down of the high and mighty is not an experienced reality? In fact, it is the church which is seen as the vulnerable and fragile entity. For Calvin, the gospel with its judgments is a foretaste of the destruction which is to come upon the ungodly – the exposure in the ungodly of their own true nature is part of the judgment's impact. The point Calvin draws is this: 'that all who do not submit themselves to the authority of Christ make war against God'.

We can see in this example from Psalm 2 how Calvin applied his herme-neutical principles: privileging the literal sense but, with Christ as the 'scope', able to frame the psalm within the narrative of the whole Scripture. We can see how vital, then, a sense of the continuity of history was for him – a continuity discernible through the typological patterns made available to the Spirit-led and attentive reader. It was in this that the unity of the Scriptures consisted for Calvin – the continuity of the history recorded in the Bible finding its fulfilment in the gospel of Jesus Christ. This unity in the text was correlation of the theological unity of the divine authorship. Unity did not mean univocity, but it did mean continuity and correspondence. The unity of the Scriptures was in the first place a theological determination, granted; but we can see from the care and the reserve with which Calvin proceeded in practice, that this unity was not just something he asserted over them by an act of will, trimming its awkward loose ends to produce a smooth finish, but was something he allowed to emerge from the texts themselves, as the individual texts of Scripture invite the reader to consider them within the context of a greater whole.

------------

36. Ibid.

## Whose book is the Bible? Hermeneutics and Calvin today

Having offered both an overview of Calvin's hermeneutics and a sample of
its application in exegesis, it is now opportune to return to the questions I
posited in the opening section. I asked in what sense it might still be possible
for contemporary interpretation of Scripture to trail in Calvin's wake, given
the differences between then and now. Are the virtues of a pre-critical interpretation available in a post-critical environment? We live in the aftermath
of historical criticism. We have become used, in the last two centuries, to
understanding 'history' as a reconstruction of the facts in as objective and
disinterested a manner as possible. While, like Calvin, we understand the need
to trace the causes of events, it is not a matter of connecting analogous events
by resort to a doctrine of providence; modern practice has been to scrape away
at the evidence, removing the accrued layers of interpretation and bias, until
the causes of events are laid bare, to be linked in a great chain to other causes
and other events. We live, too, on the other side of the era in which the Bible
itself has become the subject of academic study, rather than exclusively the
book of a people of faith – read in the seminar as much as the sanctuary, in
the service of that great encyclopaedic vision that built the modern university.
Hans-Joachim Kraus writes:

> the Geneva Reformer, for all his significant and effective approaches, was yet bound
> by a doctrinal mindset that was oriented to the unity and inner harmony of Scripture.
> Nonetheless, the recognition of this limitation should be not merely an occasion for
> criticism, but an occasion for raising the question we must never neglect, the question
> whether and by what means we can, in view of the progress of historical-critical
> methodology, still search for the unity of the Word of God in the Scriptures.[37]

However, this is exactly where Calvin's pre-critical hermeneutics start to
offer possibilities for post-critical interpreters (despite Kraus's pessimism). As
we have seen, Calvin approached the Bible believing that it was saying something for the contemporary believer. He was an exegete in the service of the
believer and of the church – because he believed that the Bible was speaking
to those people today. This was the proper context of biblical interpretation.
He was not part of an independent academy, beholden only to the principles
of higher learning. It was to believers that the Bible was addressed – and so the
interpreter's task was to show how what the ancient text said was now God's

---

37. Kraus, 'Exegetical Principles', p. 18.

word for the present time. This message was not to be located *behind* the text, or by dismembering the text; it was not something to which the text referred. It was gleaned from reading the text itself.

The endeavours of historical critics cannot be merely set aside. However, interpretation in the service of the church and its members is never merely an analysis of the text and its (alleged) provenance. It is always an exercise of *listening* to the voice of God in the text. Calvin positions himself as the servant of the text, and not its master. This posture is not an empty rhetorical move, or a false humility on the part of the exegete (which in time turns out to have been a power-play over the text and its readers). It was for Calvin – and remains today for those who would honour him – actually a decisive condition for biblical interpretation if it is to be interpretation of *the Bible*, and not of some other thing to which the Bible is apparently a conduit.

If Calvin was always aware of the context in which he carried out his biblical interpretation, then we should not be embarrassed as his putative heirs to discover that our context is somewhat different – and that our task as interpreters, even if we would stand in his tradition, therefore has a different shape. That is: if in Calvin's day he read the Scriptures as addressed to the sixteenth-century reader, so then we might read the Scriptures as if we are being addressed in our time. How is that different? The believer of the twenty-first century lives in a context in which even belief in God is not at all a given. The 'Secular Age', as Charles Taylor calls it, is in some ways the step-grandchild of Calvin's thought.[38] The task of biblical interpretation now takes place in a context in which its value as a task is very much under question. The authority of Scripture is not taken for granted by our contemporaries, or even those within the churches.

There is, then, a need for greater awareness of the *evangelical* heart of the Scriptures. 'Christology' in abstract is not sufficient as a hermeneutical key, unless it is understood as a soteriological motif – this much Calvin clearly knew. The motifs of promise and fulfilment, so prominent in Calvin's exposition of the text, need to be understood afresh as propelling the missiological task of the churches of Jesus Christ. Calvin was aware of this, of course; but he could not have been aware of the extent to which secularism would roll back Christian belief five centuries after his birth, nor indeed of how full the earth would be of the extraordinary diversity of peoples who need to hear the message of the Christ of the Scriptures. Exegesis must not be an intramural activity; and hermeneutics must insist on this. Its sphere of reference cannot

---

38. See Taylor, *Secular Age*, pp. 77–80.

be ecclesial only – because the message of the Bible is not merely addressed to the church, but also to the world.[39]

Futhermore, Calvin's awareness of the work of providence in history leads him to be a remarkably supple reader of the text, in ways that anticipate contemporary hermeneutical debates. The human author's intentions, as far as we can reconstruct them, are only for Calvin the hermeneutical first step. Because the Bible coheres as history coheres, and because the text may be fulfilled in ways unforeseen by the first human author(s) – as we can plainly see from Psalm 2 – the text will mean a great deal more than what its author intended. If anything, it was the Enlightenment obsession with origins that meant that authorial intention became the interpretational maximum. The emphasis for Calvin is not on the reconstruction of the world of the first author, though that is not unimportant or without value; these intentions ought to be acknowledged and respected. In fact, as we have seen, he is cautious in applying figurative senses – and infuriated by speculative readings. But because of the way promise and fulfilment works in the narrative of salvation history, the text commonly overflows the bounds set for it by its original author's intentions. Scripture could not otherwise have a Christological wholeness. This does not however mean an interpretational free-for-all: the authorial intention and the Christological centre of Scripture provide interpretational parameters. But Calvin shows how meaning is generated by Scripture at a number of levels, not strait-jacketed by putative reconstructions of authorial intent.[40]

---

39. Francis Watson is making much the same point when he writes: 'Participation in the church, within the world, is the context within which this text seeks to be read. Only here does it show itself to be truth rather than non-sense, truth not only in itself but also in its ability to make sense of that which is otherwise senseless. In speaking of the risen Christ's commission to the apostles and to the church to proclaim a message of repentance and forgiveness to all nations, the text refers us to the reality and the hope of new modes of human community, stemming from the life, death and resurrection of Jesus Christ and moving towards the eschatological perfecting of community': F. Watson, *Text, Church and World: Biblical Interpretation in Theological Perspective* (Edinburgh: T. & T. Clark, 1994), p. 293.

40. David Jasper makes the rather cheeky claim that, in insisting on the priority of the text for interpreting the text rather than authorial intent, Calvin's hermeneutics anticipate those of Jacques Derrida: D. Jasper, *A Short Introduction to Hermeneutics* (Louisville: Westminster John Knox, 2004), p. 61. Of course, the decisive difference between them is that Calvin posits a divine author, where Derrida posits none. This amounts to all the difference in the world, whatever the purported similarity.

What is more, because of the divine superintendence of the historical process, Scripture does not have an abstract universal message regarding eternal timeless truths. It relates to a divine history with the world. It claims that it narrates a divinely ordered history, and then speaks into that history. It even has its own history! This means on the one hand that the grand narrative of Israel and the world that binds Scripture together has a decisive interpretational role. Calvin pre-empts the late-modern revival of interest in narrative, and in biblical narrative in particular. However, it also means that the text of Scripture, if it is to be taken seriously, can never be treated as a self-enclosed and self-referencing entity only. It addresses a world outside of itself and needs to be read in the context of that world which it claims it is describing. It ought to make sense in and of that world.

Awareness of the context of our reading allows us also to undermine the apparent dominance of the historical-critical approach. If contemporary interpreters must be aware of the way in which the intellectual and political context shaped Calvin's reading of Scripture, then we must also be aware of the way in which intellectual and political history shaped historical-critical readings – and, indeed, shape ours. These intellectual decisions about the meaning and nature of history were no less determined by historical context and cultural forces than in Calvin's time, and in ours. This is not to reduce ideas *to* their historical contexts, or so utterly to historicize them as to empty them entirely. But the point has particular force, given the claims to objectivity and universality that attend historical-critical scholarship.[41] The apparent threat to the unity and historicity of the Bible by that particular construal of history, once so dominant, is itself not above proper contextualization.

The proof of the pudding is in the discovery that its ingredients taste good in combination. Is Calvin's exegesis, which treats Scripture as a unity, but does not ignore the human differences between authors, convincing? Is it rash or speculative? Having taken a Pascalian wager on the unity of Scripture, it is readily apparent that the coherences and correspondences between its different parts proceed to flow. Calvin's exegesis is a reminder that the unity of Scripture is a theological discernment in the first instance, and only secondarily a literary one; but we need not suppose that the diversity and plurality of the human voices of Scripture threaten it. On a literary or textual level, Scripture may indeed present us with a number of valid and Christological ways of conceiving of its own unity. Calvin's lesson for modern interpreters, which

---

41. This point is made by Stephen Edmondson: see S. Edmondson, 'Christ and History'.

Kraus notes well, is that the presumption that Scripture is unified remains for us the basis on which theological interpretation of Scripture for the people of God – and for the world – may properly proceed.

© Michael P. Jensen, 2009

## 3. CALVIN AND PHILOSOPHY[1]

*Paul Helm*

We may distinguish philosophy as process from philosophy as product. The use of inductive and deductive logic, the making of distinctions of reason, the analysis of concepts, the definition of terms – these are among the procedures that have to do with philosophy as an intellectual ratiocinative process. The reality of the external world, the non-naturalness of ethics, the theory of Forms, scepticism, fatalism, body–mind dualism, the existence of God – these all may be regarded as among the products of philosophy – philosophical conclusions, or philosophical theses, rather than philosophical procedures. I do not say that procedures may not be fairly decisive as to philosophical products; nevertheless they are distinct. I admit, too, that some procedures are primed for the establishing of a certain type of substantive philosophical doctrine. Take, for example, the Verification Principle espoused by Logical Positivism. Accepting this Principle predetermines what for you can count both as a philosophical problem and a philosophical doctrine. Nevertheless, ragged-edged though the distinction between philosophy as process and philosophy as product may be, I think it is useful for the present

---

1. Some of the examples used in this paper are taken from my *John Calvin's Ideas* (Oxford: Oxford University Press, 2004) and *Calvin at the Centre* (Oxford: Oxford University Press, forthcoming.)

purpose: that of assessing the character and extent of a thinker's engagement with 'philosophy'.

When people, particularly professional philosophers, talk about 'doing philosophy' they chiefly have the process in view. But when other people, usually not, these days, professional philosophers, but pundits of some kind or other, talk about having a philosophy, or a philosophy of life, or a world view, or refer to 'my philosophy', then they are referring to philosophy as product. Philosophy as product usually has philosophy as process as one of its contributors, but it may have other factors or forces too: these days, science, or religion, or politics, or ethics.

## Calvin as a product philosopher

My thesis, briefly, is that John Calvin was not a process-type philosopher, or very rarely so, but he was most definitely a product philosopher. It is true that he had a healthy respect for consistency and the elimination of self-contradiction, and he utilized the ordinary processes of inductive and deductive reasoning for the gathering of evidence and drawing conclusions from it. Nevertheless Calvin did not usually appeal to reason or to nature in a way that did not already presuppose some elements of the Christian faith. However, as a Christian theologian he unashamedly utilized the products of philosophy, particularly of the philosophy of the ancient world, though he did so eclectically, putting these products to the service of Christian theology or to what he preferred to call 'true religion', as and when he judged that this service was either useful or necessary.

John Calvin lived 500 years ago. Augustine of Hippo lived 1,600 years ago. Seneca and Cicero lived 2,000 years ago, and Plato and Aristotle about 2,500 years ago. Calvin is, in years, nearer to us than he was to any of these others. But in another sense he is much nearer to them. For he was much more a part of ancient culture than he is of modern culture. He is nearer to Paul's encounter with the Stoics and Epicureans on Mars Hill than, say, to Charles Hodge or Karl Barth or Wolfhart Pannenberg or John Frame or Donald Macleod or John Webster – even though each of these is a theologian in 'the Reformed tradition'. When people presently seek to appropriate Calvin, to have him on their side for this or that issue, or to vilify him, they should remember that fact. In the remarks on Calvin and philosophy that are to follow, I am not only going to try to bear it in mind, but to attempt to make something of it. For Calvin is situating the Christian religion in what, for us, is 'ancient culture', but for him is simply culture, and especially, I shall argue, culture informed by the ancient view of philosophy. Why do I say this?

We cannot fail to note that at the head of the *Institutes*, not only of the 1559 edition but earlier, he claims that almost all the true and sound wisdom that we possess consists in the knowledge of God and of ourselves. Here he is, quite self-consciously, in the key of much ancient philosophy, the injunction to 'Know thyself'. You may think that this is sufficient to place him firmly in the tradition of philosophy of process: the process of knowing oneself and the wisdom and enlightenment that success in this endeavour brings with it. So is he not a philosopher after all: a philosopher with both a process and a product? To this I say 'Yes and no', but mostly 'No'. That is, 'No' not only from our vantage point of 500 years later, but 'No' from his own vantage point as well.

There are two reasons that disqualify Calvin from being a philosopher of process. The first is that he is a Christian theologian. According to Calvin, not only in the first few sentences of the *Institutes* but as this theme recurs in that work, true and sound wisdom is acquired by gaining the knowledge of God and of ourselves. So if the injunction 'Know thyself' is a keynote of ancient philosophy, the prescription that Calvin offers is not. For at its heart his recipe for true self-knowledge is a theological or religious one, not a recipe that relies upon human reason alone, or that centres upon the human person alone, and which merely allows references to God or 'the gods' as concessions to those who speak the language of popular mythology.

Calvin's references to God, his dominant key in making these references, are also somewhat disappointing for the philosopher. For unlike a philosopher, Calvin does not have a theoretical, detached interest in who God is, in the existence and nature of God, or whatever. Certainly not. He is dead set against such a project because, as he repeatedly says, it leads to opinions about God that merely 'flit in the brain' and which do not affect the heart.

Does this apply also to Calvin's attitude to natural theology? Perhaps it does. It is hard to say. Scholars have battled over the question of whether Calvin is a friend or a foe of natural theology: this battle is a good example, in my view, of the tendency of thinkers to want to have Calvin on their side as an ally to strengthen the *bona fides* of one or more of their projects. Certainly natural religion, in its original and its distorted and corrupted senses, is very important for Calvin in connection with his belief, no doubt derived from Paul, that the natural man is accountable for his rejection of God because God clearly reveals himself in the natural. Whether or not Calvin sees such beliefs as basic in some Plantingian sense, he believes that they are natural to us in more than one sense and that we are accountable for them and for what we do with them.

But what of natural theology? It obviously does not suit Calvin's religious purpose in the *Institutes* to dwell on arguments for God's existence; in addition, it may be that because natural theology was not an issue in the Reformation conflict Calvin simply waved it through. (There is one rather enigmatic reference in the *Institutes* to the 'common proofs' which suggests both Calvin's approval of them but relative lack of interest in them).[2] But this relative lack of interest hardly strengthens the case for Calvin as a philosopher; as a producer of philosophy, some one who 'does philosophy', as we say.

Hence also his resolute opposition to theological speculation, to asking and to chasing up 'What if?' questions. Further, if we wish to keep to the spirit of Calvin here, then we need to be wary even of the word 'theology' in connection with Calvin's thought. Calvin rarely uses that word. When he does use it, it is often as a term of contempt. For Calvin the 'theologians' are the speculative thinkers; especially the *Sorbonnistes* of his own day, who attempt to distract attention from and to disrupt the progress of the Reformation in France by their own 'blasphemous inventions' (as Calvin frequently dubbed them) about God. Calvin's characteristic term was not *theologia* (a word which, after all, was the invention of Aristotle), but *religio*, which bespeaks the binding of the self to God. For Calvin true religion has to do, intrinsically, with the knowledge of God and of ourselves in relationship with God.

Where did Calvin get the idea of this kind of knowledge of God from? Where did the emphasis that this wisdom is to be found in the knowledge of God and of ourselves arise? One obvious suggestion is that he simply took it from Scripture: from its depiction of Christ as the wisdom of God; from its warnings against the wisdom of this world; from the 'wisdom literature', for example from the eighth chapter of Proverbs, and especially from the Psalms. Perhaps this is the correct suggestion. But there are other possibilities, too, not incompatible with this. Suppose we ask from where does the emphasis on the twofold knowledge, of God and of ourselves, *in this particular formulation*, emerge? I suggest that it was one of the very many things that Calvin learned from Augustine. The supreme importance for Augustine of this twofold knowledge, of God and of ourselves, is found vividly, for example, in the *Confessions*. The whole work is prefaced by a meditation on the interrelation between the two. And in his wonderful discussion of memory in Book X he says, addressing the Lord, 'to hear you speaking about oneself is to know oneself', and 'what I know of myself I know because you grant me light'.[3] The fundamental point is stated with deliberate plainness and rather more

2.  *Inst.* 1.6.1.

3.  Augustine, *Confessions*, trans. Henry Chadwick (Oxford: Oxford University Press, 1992), X.3.3, X.5.7.

formality in the *Soliloquies*. 'God and the soul, that is what I desire to know. Nothing more? Nothing whatever'.[4] Calvin was acquainted with both works.

That's the first point. In the central place that he gives to the knowledge of God in our search for true wisdom, as well as the knowledge of ourselves, Calvin is certainly in the tradition of Augustine, and half in the tradition of ancient philosophy.

It is clear from what we have seen already (I hope) that for Calvin the knowledge of God is not the knowledge of something that does not affect us, that we can take or leave as we see fit. This is the 'frigidity' of the scholastics, which repels him. However, he does not reject the entire philosophical tradition, even at this point. For Calvin believes that some philosophers, particularly Plato, saw a necessary connection between the true knowledge of God and an appropriate affective response to him.

> This did not escape the observation even of philosophers. For it is the very thing which Plato meant when he taught, as he often does, that the chief good of the soul consists in resemblance to God; i.e. when, by means of knowing him, she is wholly transformed into him.[5]

Plato's is another case where the knowledge of God affects the state of the knower by a kind of immediate reflex. Plato's account of the connection of true knowledge to the affections is in sharp contrast to that knowledge which merely 'flits in the brain'. In fact, for this reason Calvin can scarcely bring himself to call this knowledge.

We can discover the second reason for thinking that Calvin is not a philosopher of process as well as of product by reflecting a little further on how the motif of the knowledge of God and of ourselves occurs in the *Institutes*. This motif, set out in the first few chapters of the *Institutes*, recurs in chapter 15 of Book 1, as well as on the opening page of Book 2, and elsewhere. Calvin tells us that the trouble is not with the precept 'Know thyself', but with the philosophers who think that it is a recommendation for us to discover what fine people we are. We are, by nature, inclined to admire ourselves. But (once more) this is

---

4. Augustine, *Soliloquies*, I.7 (*NPNF1*, VII, p. 539).
5. *Inst.* 1.3.3. See, for example, Plato, *Theaetetus*, 176. See also *CNTC* 5, p. 245 (on 1 John 2:3): 'Plato, though groping in darkness, yet denied that "the beautiful" which he imagined, could be known, without filling man with the admiration of itself; so he says in his *Phaedrus* and other places. How then is it possible for thee to know God, and to be moved with no feeling?' Compare *CNTC* 12, p. 258 (on 1 Pet. 2:3).

not true knowledge, but self-deception. To start with, nothing we have is our own, however excellent; it is the gift of God himself. But secondly, we must recognize that in 'our miserable condition since Adam's fall, all confidence and boasting are overthrown, we blush for shame, and feel truly humble.'[6]

So what is the reason for saying that Calvin does not approach the task of self-knowledge exactly as a pagan philosopher would, even though he is in the world of pagan philosophy? One prominent reason that Calvin provides is that we approach the project of knowing God and ourselves as those who are fallen knowers. The pagans were ignorant of the doctrine of the fall. Consider these sentences, drawn from various parts of the *Institutes*.

> Come, then, and let them show me a more excellent system among philosophers, who think that they only have a moral philosophy duly and orderly arranged. They, when they would give excellent exhortations to virtue, can only tell us to live agreeably to nature. Scripture derives its exhortations from the true source, when it not only enjoins us to regulate our lives with a view to God its author to whom it belongs; but after showing us that we have degenerated from our true origin – viz. the law of our Creator, adds, that Christ, through whom we have returned to favour with God, is set before us as a model, the image of which our lives should express.[7]

> These, I say, are the surest foundations of a well-regulated life, and you will search in vain for anything resembling them among philosophers who, in their commendation of virtue, never rise higher than the natural dignity of man.[8]

As part of this mistake, the philosophers think that our reason is sufficient to motivate us.

> They give the government of man to reason alone, thinking that she alone is to be listened to; in short, they assign to her the sole direction of the conduct. But Christian philosophy bids her give place, and yield complete submission to the Holy Spirit, so that the man himself no longer lives, but Christ lives and reigns in him (Gal. 2:20).[9]

So the knowledge that we are to seek is not that which flatters, in which we are credulous about the superiority of our gifts.

---

6. *Inst.* 2.1.1.

7. *Inst.* 3.6.3.

8. Ibid.

9. *Inst.* 3.7.1.

Hence, independent of any countenance from without, general credit is given to the very foolish idea, that man is perfectly sufficient of himself for all the purposes of a good and happy life . . . Accordingly, in every age, he who is most forward in extolling the excellence of human nature, is received with the loudest applause . . . Whosoever, therefore, gives heed to those teachers, who merely employ us in contemplating our good qualities, so far from making progress in self-knowledge, will be plunged into the most pernicious ignorance.[10]

Adam, therefore, might have stood if he chose, since it was only by his own will that he fell; but it was because his will was pliable in either direction, and he had not received constancy to persevere, that he so easily fell. Still he had a free choice of good and evil, and not only so, but in the mind and will there was the highest rectitude, and all the organic parts were duly framed to obedience, until man corrupted its good properties, and destroyed himself. Hence the great darkness of philosophers who have looked for a complete building in a ruin, and fit arrangement for disorder. The principle they set out with was, that man could not be a rational animal unless he had a free choice of good and evil. They also imagined that the distinction between good and evil was destroyed, if man did not of his own counsel arrange his life. So far well, had there been no change in man. This being unknown to them, it is not surprising that they throw everything into confusion. [11]

We must now explain what the power of human reason is, in regard to the kingdom of God, and spiritual discernments which consists chiefly of three things – the knowledge of God, the knowledge of his paternal favour toward us, which constitutes our salvation, and the method of regulating of our conduct in accordance with the divine Law. With regard to the first two, but most properly the second, men otherwise the most ingenious are blinder than moles. I deny not, indeed, that in the writings of philosophers we meet occasionally with shrewd and apposite remarks on the nature of God, though they invariably savour somewhat of giddy imagination . . . Besides, how many monstrous falsehoods intermingle with those minute particles of truth scattered up and down in their writings as if by chance. In short, no one of them even made the least approach to that assurance of the divine favour, without which the mind of man must ever remain a mere chaos of confusion. To the great truths, what God is in himself, and what he is in relation to us, human reason makes not the least approach.[12]

---

10. *Inst.* 2.1.2.

11. *Inst.* 1.15.8.

12. *Inst.* 2.2.18.

The trouble is that pagan philosophers have no conception of the fallenness of human nature.

Calvin adds, 'These, I say, are the surest foundations of a well-regulated life, and you will search in vain for anything resembling them among philosophers who, in their commendation of virtue, never rise higher than the natural dignity of man.' As part of this mistake, the philosophers think that our reason is sufficient to motivate us.

> They give the government of man to reason alone, thinking that she alone is to be listened to; in short, they assign to her the sole direction of the conduct. But Christian philosophy bids her give place, and yield complete submission to the Holy Spirit, so that the man himself no longer lives, but Christ lives and reigns in him (Gal. 2:20).[13]

There is one further element in the opening words of the *Institutes* which heralds a major theme in Calvin's theology but which also limits what philosophy can do as regards product.

When Calvin says that almost all the true and solid wisdom that we possess consists in the knowledge of God and of ourselves, it is well to note certain features of what he states, as well as what he is not saying. First, we note the emphasis on wisdom. Acquiring the knowledge of God and of ourselves offers the method of possessing true and sound wisdom. Here Calvin taps into one medieval emphasis, religion as *sapientia*, and he implicitly rejects another, that theology chiefly has to do with theoretical understanding and certainty, *scientia*. In this sense Calvin is a Franciscan rather than a Dominican. Theology does not provide us with more knowledge in the form of more explanations, as nuclear physics and history and criminal detection do, but with wisdom. It has to do with the *knowledge* (*notitia*) of God, certainly, but religion is not a matter simply of acquiring enough information of the right kind. Nonetheless, religion has a clear cognitive basis in beliefs about God and ourselves expressible in propositional form. The knowledge of God is not, say, simply a matter of adopting a set of rules, moral rules or rules for spiritual exercises. Further, the knowledge that true religion requires should lead us to enjoy the favour and presence of God, and to bring us to our everlasting home. It is an exaggeration to say that for Calvin the knowledge of God is mere know-how, but there is nevertheless more than a germ of truth in this. Here is one place at least where the affinity of Calvin's thought is more with John Bunyan's *Pilgrim's Progess* than it is with Aquinas's *Summa Theologiae*.

---

13. *Inst.* 3.7.1.

There are numerous places in his writings in which Calvin thinks that in thinking about God we are up against mystery. It is not a complete black hole, but a failure to comprehend in the technical and literal meaning of that term; a failure to get our minds around the essence of God, to encompass it, to understand God with the understanding that God himself has. Calvin repeatedly uses the words 'incomprehensibility' and 'ineffability' to characterize this: in his doctrine of God *in se*, in his Trinitarian character, in the Incarnation of the Logos, and in the relation of God's election, predestination and reprobation in relation to human powers and to human equity.

## Calvin on the Supper

Another, less familiar, area in which Calvin recognizes the presence of mystery – in the sense of a state of affairs that is unfathomable to the human mind – is in his teaching on the Supper. It might be worth examining this a little.

In his numerous, lengthy and repetitive discussions about the mode of Christ's presence in the Supper, he maintains (principally against the Lutherans) that Christ's glorified body is localized in heaven, and that such localization is necessary in view of the nature of a human body. To respect the reality of Christ's continued human embodiment is fundamental to Calvin's idea of Christ's real presence at the Supper. In his debates with the Lutheran Joachim Westphal (c.1511–1574) he pours scorn on the Lutheran idea of the ubiquity of Christ's flesh, arguing that it is both incompatible with the teaching of Scripture and contrary to the nature of things, to the nature of bodies. Here is one rare instance where Calvin supplements the strength of biblical data by an independent metaphysical argument.

Lutheran ubiquity must be false since it flouts the essential nature of bodies.

> [T]hey flee to their ordinary pretext, that God is not bound by physical principles. I admit he is not, except in so far as he has so ordained. They rejoin, that this order takes effect only in the common course of nature, but not at all in theology. That is true, unless indeed part of theology be the very order of nature, as it is in the present case. For we do not simply assert that Christ's body is in one place, because it is natural, but because God was pleased to give a true body to his Son, and one finite in its dimensions, and he himself was pleased to sojourn for a time on earth under the tabernacle of this body, and with the same body to ascend into heaven, from whence he bids us look for him.[14]

---

14. J. Calvin, 'Last Admonition to Joachim Westphal', in *Tracts*, II, 444.

Calvin extends the point about localization to the entire human nature of Christ. And this is not surprising, since he holds that Christ took on not a modified human nature, but real human nature, and that human souls are bounded, as bodies are. Bounded not in the sense that they take up space, but they are nonetheless non-materially present with one body at once, and 'accompany' that body on its various travels even as they animate it to travel, in accordance with a person's beliefs and desires.

Perhaps this emphasis on the necessarily local character of the human body is the nearest that Calvin ever comes to asserting and defending a metaphysical principle by an appeal to reason. But even here he enters an amusing caveat, though he certainly does not intend to make us smile. 'The body with which Christ rose is declared, not by Aristotle, but by the Holy Spirit, to be finite, and to be contained in heaven until the last day'.[15] Yet perhaps it would not be stretching things too much to say that he takes the Holy Spirit to be making a modal point about body and place every bit as much as did Aristotle.

Despite the confidence with which he asserts all this, his account of the Supper fills him with awe. His language is lyrical, almost ecstatic, as he seeks to convey the nature of Christ's presence at the Supper, all the while recognizing that he will inevitably fail to do so. For example:

> If, indeed, it be lawful to put this great mystery into words, a mystery which I feel, and therefore freely confess that I am unable to comprehend with my mind, so far am I from wishing anyone to measure its sublimity by my feeble capacity. No, I rather exhort my readers not to confine their apprehension within those too narrow limits, but to attempt to rise much higher than I can guide them. For whenever this subject is considered, after I have done my utmost, I feel that I have spoken far beneath its dignity. And though the mind is more powerful in thought than the tongue in expression, it too is overcome and overwhelmed by the magnitude of the subject. All then that remains is to break forth in admiration of the mystery – which it is plain that the mind is inadequate to comprehend, or the tongue to express.[16]

The 'great mystery' is the nature of full communion with Christ. As we have noted, Calvin frequently refers to the mysteries of the faith, and to the incomprehensibility of the divine essence and will, but this language is, by his usual standards, extraordinary.

---

15. *Inst.* 4.17.26. Further instances may be found at 4.17.16, 4.17.24, and 4.17.28–30.
16. *Inst.* 4.17.7.

## Philosophical anthropology

We have seen that Calvin is somewhat scathing in his attitude to the philosophers in the area of ethics, noting that they are far too optimistic about the ethical powers and prospects of the natural man, because they lack a doctrine of the fall. I think it is fair to say that, in general, he is less scathing of them in the areas of metaphysics, especially philosophical anthropology. Though even here there is a certain hesitancy.

For instance, in the *Institutes* Calvin is somewhat ambivalent with respect to the value of philosophical discussions about the soul. On the one hand he characteristically wishes to avoid anything that is subtle or speculative, but on the other hand he does not think that philosophical discussions about the soul are worthless. Subtle questions are the province of the philosophers, yet they are not to be entirely repudiated.

> But I leave it to the philosophers to discuss these faculties in their subtle way. For the upbuilding of godliness a simple definition [of the soul] will be enough for us. I, indeed, agree that the things they teach are true, not only enjoyable, but also profitable to learn, and skilfully assembled by them. And I do not forbid those who are desirous of learning to study them. Therefore I admit in the first place that there are five senses.[17]

Despite his reservations about including philosophical discussion in the *Institutes*, he does nevertheless commit himself to certain philosophical conclusions. There are five senses. In addition, there is

> fantasy, which distinguishes those things which have been apprehended by common sense; then reason, which embraces universal judgment; finally understanding, which in intent and quiet study contemplates what reason discursively ponders. Similarly, to understanding, reason, and fantasy (the three cognitive faculties of the soul) correspond three appetitive faculties: will, whose functions consist in striving after what understanding and reason present; the capacity for anger, which seizes upon what is offered to it by reason and fantasy; the capacity to desire inordinately, which apprehends what is set before it by fantasy and sense.[18]

---

17. *Inst.* 1.15.6. This underlines Calvin's view that theology's importance does not imply that other sorts of study, such as philosophy, are worthless.
18. *Inst.* 1.15.6.

This makes clear that despite his disavowal of a philosophical approach to the soul, Calvin endorses quite a complex picture of it; yet he goes on to say that such complexity ought to be passed over in favour of a much simpler set of distinctions. He prefers a fairly simple account of the soul for a theological and practical reason – namely, the need to choose 'a division within the capacity of all'.[19]

Calvin often used platonic language to characterize the body–soul distinction, repeatedly calling it a 'prison house'.[20] He would never have dreamt of using such language to describe the human mind, even when it is considered in its fallen state. However, it would be an exaggeration to use such expressions as evidence of commitment to a full-dress Platonism. There is no suggestion of a pre-embodied existence of the soul, and Calvin is a resolute upholder of the biblical and especially the Pauline doctrine of the resurrection of the body. It would, I believe, be more faithful to Calvin to understand this use of platonic language as his own vivid way of referring to the biblical reference to the body as a 'tabernacle'.[21] A favourite text is the reference in Job 4:19 to 'houses of clay': 'For what is our bodie? What foundation hath it? What firmnesse soever seemeth too be in it: there needes but one little shoure or raine to washe it quite away.'[22] In his *Commentary* on 2 Corinthians 5:1 where Paul refers to his body as a 'tabernacle' (Calvin refers to it in French as *luge*, 'hut'), he draws the inference that the believers know that 'they are here shut up in the body as in a prison'.[23]

His fondness for 'prison house' may also have an autobiographical source, as in these evidently heart-felt expressions:

> For if we reflect that this our tabernacle, unstable, defective, corruptible, fading, pining and putrid, is dissolved, in order that it may forthwith be renewed in sure, perfect, incorruptible, in fine, in heavenly glory, will not faith compel us eagerly to desire what nature dreads?[24]

---

19. Ibid.

20. The phrase is from Plato's *Phaedo*. There are numerous reference to the body as a prison in the *Institutes*: e.g. 'bound with the fetters of an earthly body' (2.2.19); 'a prison' (3.9.4); 'imprisoned in the body prison house' (3.25.1); 'a tabernacle' (3.25.1); 'the prison of the body' (4.17.30).

21. 2 Pet. 1:13; 2 Cor. 5:1.

22. J. Calvin, *Sermons of Maister John Calvin upon the Book of Job*, trans. Arthur Golding (London, 1574, repr. in facsimile, Edinburgh: Banner of Truth Trust, 1993), p. 73.

23. *CNTC* 10, 67 (on 2 Cor. 5:1).

24. *Inst.* 3.9.5.

Through excessive study and the effect of malnutrition, for much of his adult life Calvin was afflicted by numerous illnesses, which had a near-crippling effect on him. But if this is consciously autobiographical, it is extremely unusual for Calvin to bring himself into theological exposition.[25]

In the *Institutes* he has more to say about the inadequacy of philosophical discussions of the soul. 'In ancient times philosophers discoursed, and even debated with each other, concerning the chief good; none, however, except Plato acknowledged that it consisted in union with God. He could not, however, form even an imperfect idea of its true nature'.[26] 'And hence, while many of the philosophers maintained the immortality of the soul, few of them assented to the resurrection of the body. Although in this they were inexcusable, we are thereby reminded that the subject is too difficult for human apprehension to reach it'.[27] This reference to the resurrection of the body is probably a reference to the ancient belief in transmigration of the soul, whether or not the idea was held by Plato.

## Human action

Calvin has, I believe, a more positive relation to the philosophical products of the Stoics, mediated to him through Cicero and Seneca, than has been generally recognized. It is true that he scathingly rejects the idea of Stoic fate. Nonetheless, there is an interesting coincidence, and some direct evidence of influence, in the area of human action.

Neither Calvin nor the Stoics hold the view that the future is fixed irrespective of what men and women desire that future to be, and what they intend and bring about. For the Stoics, a person is fated to enjoy or suffer something not irrespective of their desires and intentions, but through their operation. That is to say, most events are not fated in isolation, but co-fated in a causal and in some cases a teleological sequence.

For the Stoics co-fatedness had a varied character. Some events are causally necessary and sufficient for others. If Laius is fated to have a son, then he is fated

---

25.  See the fascinating account in John Wilkinson: J. Wilkinson, *The Medical History of the Reformers: Luther, Calvin and John Knox* (Edinburgh: Handsel Press, 2001). Note also Calvin's letter to the physicians of Montpellier, 8 February 1564 (Calvin, *Selected Works*, 4, 358).

26.  *Inst.* 3.25.2.

27.  *Inst.* 3.25.3; 3.25.6.

to have intercourse with the son's mother-to-be.[28] Sometimes they are logically necessary. If Milo is fated to wrestle, then he is fated to have an opponent to wrestle with, since it is logically impossible to wrestle without having someone to wrestle with. So Laius cannot be 'simply' be fated to produce a son, or Milo to wrestle. Doing either involves other people, and so the fact that Laius is fated to become a father (if he is) cannot be a recipe for idleness, as opponents of Stoicism claimed. But the relation of the elements that are co-fated may be weaker than such a necessary causal connection; it may involve the existence of general but not universal connections. In order for me to recover from my illness it may be necessary for me to consult the doctor, and necessary that I know this; but I may consult the doctor and still not recover. It may in general be necessary for me to take care if I am to cross the road safely, but I may on some occasions be careless and still make it to the other side. As Susanne Bobzien says,

> For the 'efficiency' of the refutation of the Idle Argument (which after all is applied to particular situations, since actions are particulars), the existence of an empirically accessible, universal relation of necessary condition is not required and no causal theory with universal laws of nature has to be presupposed. For a non-futile action it is sufficient that there is a chance that the action matters for the outcome in that there is a probability that it is a necessary condition for triggering or preventing a prospective cause from being active and thus furthers a certain envisaged result.[29]

Calvin shares this general outlook. Because the order of things is a causal, teleological order, and though it is all, down to the last detail, under the providential governance of Almighty God, we cannot be idle or imprudent if certain of our goals are to be achieved. So the Stoics reject the Idle Argument that if the future is fixed then there is nothing that we presently do that can affect or influence it. And Calvin follows them in this.

Transposing the Stoic outlook into Calvin's theism, since it was eternally ordained by God (let us suppose) that Joe climbs the ladder, his decree that he does so is a necessary condition of the truth of 'Jones climbed the ladder'. But it is not by itself sufficient, because the decree has also to take effect in time. In ordaining that Joe climb the ladder God must also ordain that there is an available ladder, that Joe is not too frightened to climb it, that he has an objective for which ladder-climbing is necessary, the desire to climb, and so

28. S. Bobzien, *Determinism and Freedom in Stoic Philosophy* (Oxford: Clarendon, 1998), p. 201.
29. Bobzien, *Determinism*, pp. 225–226.

forth. For this sort of scenario to be a cure for Joe's idleness then he must want
to climb the ladder, knowing or believing that it is (probably) connected with
something further that he wants to achieve. Such factors have to be ordained
in the correct causal and teleological order and to 'fall out' thus.

Further, this co-fatedness is what explains why Joe uses the ladder, in the way
that merely to assert 'he was fated to climb the ladder' does not.[30] 'Whatever
you do it was fated that you do it' offers no guidance as to what you should do.
To the question 'Why are you turning on the television?' 'Because I am fated
to turn it on' or 'God has decreed that I do so' are not justifying reasons for
that action in the way that 'Because I want to see the match this afternoon' is.
For (for Stoicism) everything is fated and (for Calvin) everything is divinely
decreed. But it's not a reason for me doing what I do because (according to
Stoicism) I am fated to do everything I do, or (according to Calvin) everything
I do is decreed by God. Further (in general), I have no epistemic access to
the future. All I know (by past experience in some fashion) is that in order
to watch the match this afternoon I have normally to take the necessary steps
to do so. I might not take those steps, but still, by a series of unintended coin-
cidences, see the match that I intended to see. But this is no way to live. Effort
is causally contributory to an envisaged end. Calvin is assuming, of course, that
for the most part God does not disclose the future to us until it becomes the
present. So he is saying that, at the human level, action causally contributes to
what occurs, and so having reasons to do a certain action and to refrain from
doing another sort of action are explanations of why I act or forbear to act.
Nevertheless, what I do is necessitated by the divine decree.

Of course, both Stoic fatalism and Calvin's appeal to the divine decree
impose fixity on the sequences of events. Yet if the type of fatalism (for
the Stoics), or providence (for Calvin) were that sometimes called logical or
'simple' fatalism, such that Joe is fated to climb the ladder whether he wants to
or not, or perhaps even though he does not want to, and particular events are
fated in abstraction from any particular causal nexus, then his wanting or not
wanting to climb the ladder does not explain anything about how it comes to
be climbed. Nothing explains that except fate, or the God of such fate. Calvin
cites Cicero's *De Fato* on the connectedness of means and ends.[31]

In the *Institutes* Calvin's appeal to co-fatedness (he does not use the term
*confatalia* as far as I know) occurs in a variety of contexts. His use of it to reject
the Idle Argument occurs in his discussion of the use to which the doctrine

---

30. See the detailed discussion of this point in *Inst.* 1.18.2.

31. *Inst.* 1.17.4.

of providence ought to be put. Those convinced of the doctrine should view their lives and the lives of others not only in terms of secondary causes, which he here calls 'means', but in terms of God's will, the primary cause. But in referring to the primary cause, they should also not forget or neglect the place of secondary causes.

> For he who has fixed the boundaries of our life, has at the same time entrusted us with the care of it, provided us with the means of preserving it, forewarned us of the dangers to which we are exposed, and supplied cautions and remedies, that we may not be overwhelmed unawares. Now, our duty is clear, namely, since the Lord has committed to us the defence of our life – to defend it; since he offers assistance – to use it; since he forewarns us of danger – not to rush on heedless; since he supplies remedies – not to neglect them. But it is said, a danger that is not fatal will not hurt us, and one that is fatal cannot be resisted by any precautions. But what if dangers are not fatal, merely because the Lord has furnished you with the means of warding them off, and surmounting them? See how far your reasoning accords with the order of divine procedure. You infer that danger is not to be guarded against, because, if it is not fatal, you shall escape without precaution; whereas the Lord enjoins you to guard against it, just because he wills it not to be fatal.[32]

Such immanent causation, the order of secondary causes, coincides with part of the Stoic view, the considerations used to rebut the Idle Argument. Where it differs is that for Calvin God is at work through these chains of immanent causation; that is, they have a transcendent causal source and not, as with Stoicism, a merely immanent source. What happens is the result of God's decreeing of means to achieve his ends. If I am destined to post the letter, then I am destined to use the appropriate means to post it. If I want, as a general rule, to cross the road safely, then I must be alert to the traffic.

## Universal belief in God

I have already mentioned Cicero as providing for Calvin one route to ancient philosophical ideas. Better-known is Calvin's reference to the views of Cicero

---

32. *Inst.* 1.17.4. It is here that Calvin cites Cicero's *De Fato*, at a point where Cicero cites Chrysippus' appeal to co-fatedness with approval. For a similar expression of this outlook, see J. Calvin, *Concerning the Eternal Predestination of God* (1552), trans. J. K. S. Reid (London: James Clarke, 1961), p. 171.

in articulating his view of the *sensus divinitatis*, and also Cicero's *The Nature of the Gods* is one of the main ancient sources for what is known as the Argument from Universal Consent for the existence of God. 'The crux of the matter is known to all men everywhere. From their birth it is inscribed upon their minds that gods exist.'[33] Similar words are found in Seneca's *Epistolae Morales*.

> We are accustomed to attach great importance to the universal belief of mankind. It is accepted by us as a convincing argument. That there are gods we infer from the sentiment engrafted in the human mind; nor has any nation ever been found, so far beyond the pale of law and civilization as to deny their existence.[34]

Calvin appeals not only to the universality of belief in God, but also to its 'proleptic' character. This universal belief in God is not acquired, but is a pre-conception, from which a disposition to believe in God arises naturally. It is a 'common notion'. But it is doubtful whether he himself believed that he took the very idea from such sources, for it is surely more likely that he believed that the apostle Paul taught it in the first two chapters of his letter to the Romans.

But what is Calvin's estimate of the idea that this view of the proleptic character of belief in God is accompanied by the argument for the existence of God from universal consent? Are we to conclude that Calvin subscribes to a version of the argument from consent, and that the appeal to the *sensus divinitatis* encapsulates such an argument?

Despite the allusions to Cicero, this would be a rather hasty conclusion to draw. In fact there is more reason to think that Calvin subscribes to what one might call an inverted form of the argument from consent. For he writes the *Institutes* as a Christian man and a theologian. For him (and, he trusts, for his readers) it is a fundamental fact that God exists, for this is known through their own experience and is affirmed by the self-authenticating character of Scripture. One gains the impression, reading the *Institutes*, that Calvin would not have been greatly ruffled in his faith were, say, out-and-out atheism to have been widespread. But in that case why does he insist upon the fact of the universal *sensus divinitatis*? Presumably because he believes that the apostle Paul teaches it, and Cicero teaches it.

---

33. Cicero, *The Nature of the Gods*, trans. H. C. P. McGregor (London: Penguin Books, 1972), p. 128.

34. Cited in P. Edwards, 'Common Consent Arguments for the Existence of God', in *The Encyclopaedia of Philosophy*, ed. Paul Edwards (London: Macmillan, 1967), vol. 2, pp. 147–155.

Cicero's endorsement of it is a further reason why Calvin appeals to him and to what might reasonably be called 'empirical sources' to support his belief that there is a universal or near-universal *sensus divinitatis*, because Cicero's is independent evidence. Calvin held that the presence of such a sense is clearly taught by Paul in the first two chapters of the Letter to the Romans. For example, in commenting on Romans 2:14 Calvin claims that 'there appeared in the Gentiles a natural light of justice which did supply the place of the law . . . a certain discretion and judgment . . . certain seeds of justice abiding in their wit'. Calvin goes on:

> It is not to our purpose to inquire what sort of God they imagined him to be, or how many gods they devised; it is enough to know that they thought that there is a God, and that honour and worship are due to him.[35]

That is, they possess a *sensus divinitatis*. It might be thought that to cite such passages would be sufficient for Calvin to establish the fact. But this procedure would be self-defeating, because it would (in effect) be an appeal to special revelation to ground the reality of general revelation. Such an appeal would clearly nullify such a grounding. So Calvin does not believe in the universality of the *sensus divinitatis* only (or perhaps primarily) because it is taught by Paul, but because there is, as a matter of plain observation, a universal *sensus divinitatis*, as Cicero and other informed writers from outside the circle of special revelation testify.[36] To retain the integrity of this appeal Calvin must make it a matter of direct report, not a report mediated by Scripture. Though it should, consistently with his position, be endorsed by Scripture.

The widespread, near universal belief in God or the gods is offered by Calvin as empirical support for the thesis that God is known to all men, a proposition which he believes is taught in the Bible. It is not that Calvin argues (in the manner of the Argument from Universal Consent) that there is widespread or universal belief that God exists, therefore God exists; but the opposite. Given that he, John Calvin, knows that God exists, experience confirms

---

35. *CNTC* 8, 48 (on Rom. 2:14–15).

36. T. H. L. Parker makes a similar point: 'Calvin's argument is that all men have this innate knowledge of God's existence. If that is so, then the heathen philosophers must also have such a knowledge and express it in their writings. Hence, merely to be able to make legitimate use of these writings is a confirmation of the argument': T. H. L. Parker, *Calvin's Doctrine of the Knowledge of God*, 2nd edn (Edinburgh: Oliver & Boyd, 1969), p. 35.

that this knowledge is universal, though universally corrupted. Calvin appeals to Cicero, it is true, but he turns Cicero's argument from consent upside down; he uses it not to establish that God exists *ab initio*, but to provide confirmatory evidence for what he already knows.

## Christ's presence

Earlier I tried to make a distinction between philosophy as process and philosophy as product. But, as I hinted there, it is sometimes not easy to separate the two. The last example that I shall refer to is a case of this. It is philosophical distinction taken from writers within the Christian church, Peter Lombard, perhaps Aquinas, and probably going back as far as Augustine: the *totus–totum* distinction. In fact a key element in Calvin's discussion of the sense in which the whole Christ may be present at a place, though not physically present there (since his human nature is localized in heaven), is his use of this distinction between two kinds of presence, or two understandings of presence: *totus ubique, sed non totum*. In one place Calvin refers to it as a 'trite' distinction.

In discussing the simplicity of God, Thomas Aquinas considers the objection that if God is simple it must be possible to comprehend him, since what is simple, having no parts, must be understood as a whole. 'Therefore, if he were simple, he would be attained as a whole by the blessed, but what is attained as a whole is comprehended.' But of course it is fundamental that the creature cannot comprehend the Creator, and therefore, the objection runs, God cannot be simple. To which Aquinas responds by deploying the *totus–totum* distinction. The blessed attain to the whole God, but not wholly. The argument is to grant that since he is simple, God does not have parts, but nevertheless since he is infinite, that simplicity cannot be comprehended by the creature. 'It should be said that the whole God is attained by the mind of the blessed but not wholly, because the mode of the divine knowability infinitely exceeds the mode of created intellect.' This application of the distinction is rather different from Calvin's, who is arguing that although Jesus Christ has parts, the whole Christ is nevertheless present at the Supper even though 'all that is Christ', his human nature, and particularly his human body, is not and cannot be present.[37]

---

37.  T. Aquinas, 'On the Divine Simplicity, Disputed Question of the Power of God, 7', trans. Ralph McInerny, in *Thomas Aquinas: Selected Writings* (London: Penguin Books, 1998), pp. 291–294.

Reference to the distinction occurs quite frequently in Calvin's discussions of the Supper, and though he may consider it to be trite it nevertheless plays a critical role in his defence of his own views,[38] as in this paragraph from his Introduction to his *Commentary on Jeremiah*.

But Christ, it is said, sits at the Father's right hand, which is to be taken as meaning, everywhere, confined within no limits. I indeed allow that God's right hand is unlimited, and that wherever it is there is the kingdom of Christ; which is metaphorically represented in Scripture by the term sitting: for whatever is declared of God is beyond controversy to be now ascribed to Christ; and therefore to sit, which means to govern the world, is what Christ has in common with the Father; and still more, as the Father by him sustains the world, rules all things by his power, and especially manifests the presence of His grace in governing His Church, He may be said, strictly speaking, to reign in His own person. It hence follows, that He is in a manner everywhere; for He can be limited by no place who sustains and protects all parts of heaven and earth, and rules and regulates by His power all things above and below. When now I name Christ, I include the whole Person of his only-begotten Son, as manifested in the flesh. He, I say, God and man, is everywhere as to His authority and incomprehensible power, and infinite glory, according to what the faithful experience by evident effects, as they know and feel His presence. It is not then without reason, that Paul declares, that he dwells in us. (Eph. 3:17) But to distort what is said of His infinite power, which is evident in His spiritual gifts, in the invisible aid which he affords, and in the whole of our salvation, and apply it to His flesh, is by no means reasonable or consistent.

I wish that many of those who are with little reason angry with us, were at least to recall to mind that common and notable saying used in the Papal Schools, "Christ is whole everywhere, but not altogether" (*Christus ubique totus est, sed non totum*). They may reject it as it is in the barbarous language of Peter Lombard, which is not pleasant to their tender and delicate ears. It is yet wisely expressed, from whomsoever it may have come, and I willingly adopt it.[39]

The basic distinction is conveyed by the use of the masculine and neuter forms of *totus*, 'the whole', and it is used to highlight two ways in which Christ

---

38. E.g. *Inst.* 4.17.30; J. Calvin, 'Last Admonition', pp. 418, 488; J. Calvin, 'True Partaking of the Flesh and Blood of Christ', pp. 496–572 in *Tracts*, vol. 2, at pp. 514–515.

39. J. Calvin, *Commentaries on the Book of the Prophet Jeremiah and the Lamentations*, trans. J. Owen (repr. in 5 vols; Grand Rapids: Eerdmans, 1950), pp. xix-xx. See also *Inst.* 4.17.30.

may be referred to: as he is the whole Christ, and as he is wholly Christ. The whole Christ (*totus*) is God and man understood concretely, a person with two natures. The whole Christ is everywhere, and so it is possible that by his Spirit he is really present in the Supper. The whole Christ was wholly present during his earthly ministry. But the whole Christ is not now wholly present at any place on earth, since his body is located in heaven. Nonetheless, according to the distinction, although the whole Christ cannot be present, nevertheless Christ may be wholly present.

### Conclusion

I have tried in this chapter to provide a fair sample of Calvin's attitude to philosophy viewed as both a process or processes of human reasoning and the products of such processes. I have argued that Calvin uses theological rather than philosophical processes, but in his theological conclusions he sometimes embodies philosophical products. The evidence that I have provided is, I believe, representative of his outlook, but it is only a sample; I have said little or nothing about, for example, Calvin's use of the Aristotelian fourfold causal schema; or his strong defence of logical consistency as a necessary condition of truth; or his use of non-biblical analogies and his wariness of the same; or his commitment to the Augustinian 'grammar' of God to which God's immutability, simplicity and timelessness are central. I have said nothing about his alleged 'Scotism', nor the mysterious fact that although Calvin scarcely ever refers directly to Thomas Aquinas, his outlook time and again reflects that of the Angelic Doctor.

In his paper '*Ad fontes argumentorum*' Richard Muller has drawn attention both to the need to interpret the Reformed orthodoxy of the seventeenth century within its own context, and, where the use and influence of philosophy on that tradition is concerned, he has pointed to the eclecticism of the theologians.[40] What we do not find, he argues, is a degeneration into 'scholasticism' or 'Aristotelianism' or 'rationalism', but a nuanced selection of philosophical tools and doctrines to be put to work in the service of Christian theology in its encounters with its cultured despisers. I hope that I have shown that the same pattern is visible in one of the fountainheads of the Reformed tradition: in none other than John Calvin himself. Calvin's theological achievement was

---

40.  R. A. Muller, in *After Calvin: Studies in the Development of a Theological Tradition* (New York: Oxford University Press, 2003), pp. 47–62.

not received by him fully formed from heaven, nor was it the fruit of a 'purely biblical' exegesis, nor devised as a pure 'theology of the Word'. Rather, it is a fascinating and in some respects a perplexing mix. Calvin picked and chose among the philosophical offerings of antiquity and medievalism as he saw fit, and we best appreciate him when we respect this selectivity and wrestle with the inevitable methodological untidiness that it brings to his 'system'.

© Paul Helm, 2009

## 4. STRATEGIES AND CONSEQUENCES IN CALVIN'S TEACHING ON THE TRINITY

*Robert C. Doyle*

With the wealth of writing on the doctrine of the Trinity we have had over the last sixty years, we might ask what is the value of investigating the doctrine in the company of John Calvin? As well as seeing how Calvin handled the Eastern tradition associated with the Nicene Creed and the Western anchored in Augustine, the discipline he brought to bear on the doctrine still raises fruitful questions concerning the method, content and limitations of all trinitarian reflection. In Calvin's hands, how do notions like 'begottenness', '*principium*' and 'order' illuminate our understanding of the triune God?

Calvin's trinitarian writings span his career from 1536 to 1560. Much takes the form of concentrated and relatively brief explanations in the context of broader expositions of the Christian faith. They were always in the context of discussing salvation and personal piety. Although the most rounded treatments are in the various editions of the *Institutes*, he also deals with trinitarian questions in tracts, treatises, catechisms, letters and his commentaries. Across this diversity, and development of his ideas, there is remarkable consistency. By the 1559 *Institutes* we have in the short compass of one chapter (chapter 13, book 1) a well-integrated and mature presentation of his thought. It does not exhaustively contain all Calvin's trinitarian ideas, but it contains most, and appears to be representative of all.

There is a history of interpretation which offers help in appreciating Calvin. Three studies particularly stand out and may be regarded as magisterial: B. B.

Warfield, 'Calvin's Doctrine of God' (1909) and 'Calvin's Doctrine of the Trinity' (1909);[1] T. F. Torrance, 'Calvin's Doctrine of the Trinity' (1990);[2] and most recently, the first two chapters of Paul Helm's book, *John Calvin's Ideas* (2004).[3]

## Basic strategies (*Institutes* 1.13.1–6)

In sections 1 to 6 of chapter 13, Calvin lays a foundation, characterized by a strong epistemological concern, yielding an 'anti-theory' stance.[4] After a brief review of these foundations, the main concern of our study will be to examine the strategies Calvin pursues in articulation of trinitarian doctrine beyond the basics. But the basics are important, for they set the foundations which help determine what follows.

In order to safeguard us against idolatry, Calvin is seeking 'proper limits' for thinking about God.[5] He reminds us that God's essence, about which God only 'speaks sparingly', is incomprehensible. From our experience of God's actions in the world ('how he is towards us'), which we meet in Holy Scripture, we are able to discern attributes of his nature. God's nature 'announces' his otherwise unknowable essence. Prior to chapter 13, Calvin has already identified a limited number of what we would call communicable attributes: kindness, goodness, mercy, justice, judgment and truth.[6]

Now, at the beginning of chapter 13, he uses two incommunicable attributes to describe God's essence: infinity and spirituality. As befits descriptions of God's essence, they are apophatic or negative identifications: God is not

---

1. Both articles are reprinted in B. B. Warfield, *Calvin and Augustine*, ed. S. G. Craig (Philadelphia: Presbyterian & Reformed, 1980), pp. 133–284.

2. T. F. Torrance, 'Calvin's Doctrine of the Trinity', *CTJ* 25 (1990), pp. 165–193.

3. P. Helm, *John Calvin's Ideas* (Oxford: Oxford University Press, 2004), pp. 11–57.

4. A point well made by Paul Helm, amongst others.

5. Staying within the limits of the simplicity of Scriptures is a theme of his 'Prefatory Address to King Francis' (*Inst.* pp. 18–23).

6. '[L]et us observe that his eternity and his self-existence [i.e. his essence] are announced by that wonderful name twice repeated [Yahweh]. Thereupon his powers are mentioned, by which he is shown to us not as he is in himself, but as he is toward us; so that this recognition of him consists more in living experience than in vain and high-flown speculation. Now we hear the same powers enumerated there that we have noted as shining in heaven and earth: kindness, goodness, mercy, justice, judgment and truth.' *Inst.* 1.10.2.

limited but infinite, not material but spiritual. Then, to these two classic attributes, Calvin adds a third:

> But God also designates himself by another special mark to distinguish himself more precisely from idols. For he so proclaims himself the sole God as to offer himself to be contemplated clearly in three persons. Unless we grasp these, only the bare and empty name of God flits about in our brains, to the exclusion of the true God.

And Calvin makes it clear he is still speaking about the one, simple, undivided essence of God.

We note immediately that unlike the first two attributes of essence, this one is not primarily apophatic; it is kataphatic, a positive description. Yes, it also serves an apophatic function, stopping us from falling into idolatry, for it anchors our notion of God so that it is no longer a 'bare and empty name', which 'flits about'. B. B. Warfield may have been the first in English-language Calvin studies to note this third attribute in Calvin's understanding of the divine essence. Quite rightly, he is excited by it. Not only is God's essence inherently and irreducibly *personal*, but there can be no proper or true human idea of God which is not triune. Warfield thus encourages us to surmise that if humankind had not suffered the fall, our innate idea of God would have had in it 'triunity', or at least the idea that the differentiation in God's oneness is a personal differentiation.[7]

This approach yields three results. First, as already indicated, in our theological construction we may have only a modest expectation for explaining the triunity of the one essence, which in itself is 'incomprehensible'. Even Scripture is an 'accommodation' to the gap between us and God due to 'his loftiness' and 'our slight capacity'.[8] Both Hilary and Augustine highlight the fact that such is the poverty of human speech that we only use terms like hypostasis (subsistence), 'not to express what it is, but only not to be silent on how Father, Son, and Spirit are three'.[9] There is in Calvin, Paul Helm points out, not quite the same high view held by many modern theologians of the continuity of knowledge between the economic Trinity (God as he is towards us in the economy of salvation) and the immanent Trinity (God as he is in himself in eternity).[10] Calvin certainly affirms an identification, but he holds it at the modest end.[11]

---

7. Warfield, 'Trinity', pp. 189–192.
8. *Inst.* 1.13.1.
9. *Inst.* 1.13.5.
10. Helm, *Ideas*, pp. 46–50.
11. Paul Helm does not use the word 'identification' for Calvin, but 'consistency'.

Second, working out from the 'simple and undivided essence', Calvin offers us his own 'short and easy definition': there are in God three distinct persons or subsistences.[12] A '"person" is a "subsistence" in God's essence, which, while related to the others, is distinguished by an incommunicable quality'.[13] Because of their common bond in the one, simple essence 'the Father expresses himself wholly in the Son', except for his own incommunicable quality as Father.[14]

Thirdly, Calvin moves to affirm the traditional terms found in Nicene theology and Augustine. 'Essence' or 'substance', 'person' or 'subsistence', and 'consubstantial', although forced upon us by the poverty of human speech, are shown to be both necessary and useful in explanation and defence of God's triunity. Non-scriptural terms are permissible because they express the teaching of Holy Scripture and unmask false trails. 'Say that in the one essence of God there is a trinity of persons; you will say in one word what Scripture states, and cut short empty talkativeness'.[15] In keeping with his anti-speculative stance and his belief in liberty of expression, Calvin's own preferred definition is uncomplicated as well as irenical:

> Indeed, I could wish they were buried [the traditional terms and the strife about them], if only among all men this faith were agreed on: that Father and Son and Spirit are one God, yet the Son is not the Father, nor the Spirit the Son, but that they are differentiated by a peculiar quality.[16]

But it would be a mistake to think that Calvin's broad adoption of the teaching and terminology of Nicaea is merely a concession in order to repel heresy. To God we ought and may give right worship. Baptism is an initiation into the 'faith and worship (*religionem*)' of the one God, who shows himself 'with complete clarity in the Father, the Son, and the Spirit'. This must be articulated as, 'in God's essence reside three persons in whom one God is known'.[17] Within the limits and reserve placed on all talk about God's essence, Calvin's appraisal of the traditional terms is, it seems to me, a robust affirmation of them. The honour he accords the

---

12. *Inst.* 1.13.2.
13. *Inst.* 1.13.6.
14. *Inst.* 1.13.2.
15. *Inst.* 1.13.5.
16. Ibid.
17. *Inst.* 1.13.16.

Fathers is genuine.[18] He is certainly not asking us to trade Nicaea for his own definition.[19]

In his basic approach unfolded in sections 1 to 6, Calvin has added tri-unity to a limited number of incommunicable attributes that describe God's essence. He has thus allowed the metaphysical truths of Christian theism to exert a fruitful control over our theological thinking. Such is the nature of God's one, united simple essence that *of course* the Son is God through and through. The strategy also alerts us to the need to keep our conceptions modest. It is important that we recognize that at this point Calvin is not arguing in an *a priori* way. We come to understand God *in se* from how he is towards us.

## Further elaboration (*Institutes* 1.13.7–29)

In the rest of the chapter Calvin builds on what has gone before, further elab-orating on the deity of Christ and the Spirit (sections 7–15), and then engages in a protracted treatment of the oneness, threeness, differentiation and rela-tionship of the three persons immanently, within the eternal Trinity.

### *Our questions*
We come to Calvin not only to understand his exposition on its own terms, but also with our own questions concerning the deeper levels in knowledge of the triune God.[20] How may we discern and express the trinitarian relations

---

18.  Responding to the rather heterodox and confused questions from yet another peripatetic priest, Giorgio Biandrata, who had lodged himself in the Italian congregation in Geneva, Calvin wrote: 'It would take too long to examine all the ways of speaking used by the ancients. Human words will never properly explain this ineffable mystery in accordance with its dignity. Each has his own way of speaking, and despite the fact that one speaks differently from another, they are in the closest of agreement': refer J. Tylenda, 'The Warning that went Unheeded: John Calvin on Giorgio Biandrata', *CTJ* 12.1 (1977), p. 62.

19.  Paul Helm expresses it differently: 'A doctrine of the Trinity, then, that mentions neither "trinity", nor "person" nor "substance", nor the begetting of the Son nor the procession of the Spirit, is what Calvin in principle favours': Helm, *Ideas*, p. 41.

20.  T. F. Torrance's observation of three conceptual levels in our knowledge of the triune God is helpful here: see Torrance, *The Christian Doctrine of God, One Being Three Persons* (Edinburgh: T. & T. Clark, 1996), pp. 82–111.

that exist in God *himself*? In thinking through the nature of the persons and their relations in eternity, what are we to make of terms like 'coinherence' ('the divine mutual indwelling', or 'perichoresis'), 'begottenness', and 'procession'? How may we use the Bible? How, if at all, may we move from statements about the relations between the Persons we see in the economy to their relations immanently? May we speak of an 'order' between the Persons? What are we to do with the submission we see of the incarnate Son to the Father during his earthly ministry? When we have made our decisions about terms and concepts, just how much explanatory power may we expect, and have, from the concepts we adopt?

Scholarly appraisal is not uniformly positive. T. F. Torrance sees Calvin's most important contribution to the trinitarian doctrine of God to be his account of the intra-trinitarian relations: that is, the relations between Father, Son and Holy Spirit in the eternity of God's own being.

As well as his interest in theological epistemology and language, Paul Helm also examines Calvin's presentation of the incommunicable distinctions between the Persons of the Trinity and his safeguarding of them from speculation by his appeal to *autotheos*, the notion that the Son is 'God in his own right'. By application of the notion of God's united, simple essence and its conceptual cognate, *autotheos*, Calvin is able to pare down or restrict the meaning of key words or concepts in order to exclude error. This method is applied to the Nicene concept of the eternal generation of the Son, so that Calvin accepts it, but in a modified way which safeguards the true divinity of the Son. But, Helm asks, what meaning is left to the begottenness of the person of the Son from the person of the unbegotten Father? What truth is safeguarded by asserting the Son's begottenness?[21] In a context where some in English-speaking Reformed theology wish to move away from the notion of eternal generation, the question is pressing.[22] If we keep it, what truth of God's own triune being may it elucidate?

So we might expect that Calvin will make a very important contribution to our understanding of the relations in the immanent Trinity, but it will have limits.

––––––––––––––––––

21. Helm, *Ideas*, pp. 55–57.

22. E.g. Robert Reymond believes there is no biblical warrant for it, and will only use it parenthetically to describe the truth that the person of the Father precedes the person of the Son by reason of order: Reymond, *A New Systematic Theology of the Christian Faith* (Nashville: Thomas Nelson, 1998), pp. 323–335.

### Eternal deity of the Son (7–13)

In these (7–13) and the following sections (14–15) Calvin is concerned 'to demonstrate the deity of the Son and of the Spirit . . . and how they differ from each other.'

Demonstrating the divinity of the Son is a major concern in Calvin's writings on the Trinity. The greatest part of the interchange between Calvin and the anti-trinitarian heretic Servetus is devoted to Christological questions.[23] If Christ is not God, then his mediatorial work will not be saving:

> Moreover, if apart from God there is no salvation, no righteousness, no life, yet
> Christ contains all these in himself, God is certainly revealed.[24]

Trinitarian reflection on the deity of Christ, then, is the necessary prolegomenon to his later exposition of Christ as Mediator.

Calvin's explanation has two focal points: to show the eternal deity of the Son, and the evidence for it from the Old and New Testaments.

Because the Word has perpetually resided in God, 'his eternity, his true essence, and his divinity are proved'.[25] It is notable that Calvin follows the Nicene tradition by defining the divinity of the Son from the Father: 'begotten before time', 'the substantial Word of the Father'. Later, in reflecting on the relations of the immanent Trinity, Calvin will further develop his exposition of Christ's divinity by advancing his distinctive theologoumenon that Christ is also *autotheos*, God in his own right. The question we face then is: does Calvin at this point depart from the Nicene tradition of defining the Son from the Father?

With respect to the scriptural evidence, Calvin highlights the fact that in the Old and New Testaments the name and titles of Yahweh (Jehovah) are applied to the Christ.[26] He also appeals to the theophanies, apostolic statements, the Son's participation in functions that are God's alone, and his miracles. He concludes by emphasizing that Christ's divine power is power to save. Since the name of Christ is invoked for salvation, and it is only by the name of Yahweh that we are saved (Joel 2:32), it follows that Christ is Jehovah.[27]

---

23. The interchange is contained in 'Refutatio Errorum Michaelis Serveti' (1554), *CO* 8, pp. 453–518. The three leading questions Servetus poses to Calvin are to do with the person and work of Christ and the sacraments which flow from it.

24. *Inst.* 1.13.13.

25. *Inst.* 1.13.8.

26. *Inst.* 1.13.9–13.

27. *Inst.* 1.13.13.

Again, as he analyses the scriptural presentation, Calvin follows Nicene theology in identifying Christ's divinity by reference to the Father. However, at the end of section 13 he drops a hint of another approach: the Father and Son have a 'mutual participation in power'. We are to think also of the divinity and the attributes of the divinity of both Christ and the Father against something else they mutually share in common. In constructing Christology, Calvin will show us the propriety and fruitfulness of thinking-out from the divine essence in which the two Persons have a common bond. This is a return to the strategy with which he opened the chapter.

### Eternal deity of the Spirit (14–15)

The divinity of the Spirit is demonstrated in his work. The Spirit 'everywhere diffused, sustains all things, causes them to grow, and quickens them in heaven and in earth ... in transfusing into all things his energy, and breathing into them essence, life, and movement, he is indeed plainly divine. So the Spirit 'resides hypostatically in God'.

Unlike his treatment of the divinity of Christ, in the sections which follow the nature of the Spirit's hypostatic existence is not developed much further. But in keeping with the Western patristic tradition with its distinctive *filioque* clause ('and the Son'), the relation of the Spirit to the Father and the Son is to be conceived of as 'procession' from both Persons:

> the Son is sent forth from the Father alone; the Spirit, from the Father and the Son at the same time.[28]

Calvin passes by the difficult task of investigating and articulating the differences between the notions of 'eternally begotten' with respect to the person of the Son and 'eternal procession' with respect to the Spirit. Indeed, he is happy to say that the Son also is 'sent forth'. In the light of the precision of the Nicene Creed and its theology, it is a loose statement. This is a little puzzling, for quite frequently and positively Calvin refers to the Son's eternal generation or begottenness as defining his person. Paul Helm is undoubtedly right: here against Nicaea, Calvin's language is 'muffled'.[29] It is at least clear from what immediately follows that Calvin's main aim is to reinforce the notion of 'the utterly simple unity of God'. After all, the Father and the Son share the same Spirit (18 and 19).

---

28. *Inst.* 1.13.18.
29. Helm, *Ideas*, pp. 54–55.

### Distinction and unity (16–28)

The first part (16–20) is a closely argued statement of the oneness, threeness, differentiation and relationship of the three persons. The second part (21–28) amounts to a testing of these truths against anti-trinitarian heresies which say otherwise. In this way, Calvin investigates and draws conclusions about the immanent relations.

The central contention which Calvin is developing and defending is 'that in God's essence reside three persons in whom one God is known'. Seven movements or components in his thought are of particular interest:

1. the frame of mind appropriate to thinking trinitarianly;
2. God's acts in the economy structure our understanding of the personal distinctions;
3. the three persons in their distinctions and relations are to be understood against 'the utterly simple unity of God';
4. Augustine's construct is adopted: the distinctions are to do with the relations of the three hypostases, *not* to do with the essence in which they have a common bond;
5. thus, the Son is *autotheos*: 'the downright deity and aseity of the Son';[30]
6. 'begottenness' needs to be understood to refer to the Father as the source or fountainhead of the person of the Son, but *not* his divinity;
7. appropriate use of texts which speak of the relations in the economy.

### 1: Thinking trinitarianly

In the task of differentiating between the persons, Calvin knows that the basic data we work with are the distinctions set forth in Scripture. But it is not straightforward, for 'the greatness of the mystery warns us how much reverence and sobriety we ought to use in investigating this.' He then commends to us a particular trinitarian mindset: a habitual way of thinking trinitarianly.

> That passage in Gregory of Nazianzus vastly delights me: I cannot think on the one without quickly being encircled by the splendour of the three; nor can I discern the three without being straightaway carried back to the one. Let us not, then, be led to imagine a trinity of persons that keeps our thoughts distracted and does not at once lead them back to the unity.[31]

---

30. To use T. F. Torrance's phrase: Torrance, 'Calvin's Doctrine', pp. 180–186.
31. *Inst.* 1.13.17; Gregory of Nazianzus, 'Oration on Holy Baptism', 41 (*NPNF2*, 7, p. 375).

So, in order to use Scripture aright in thinking about the threeness we ought move recursively from 'the splendour of the three' to 'the one' and back again. The one, simple essence, which is characterized by triunity, will control our interpretation, but this essence is only understood aright in the light of the three Persons.

*2: Using the economy to understand the distinctions: begottenness, procession and order*
Second, while thinking with this habit of mind, Calvin appeals to God's acts in the economy of salvation to inform our understanding of the distinctions. That they are assigned different roles in the economy first shows that 'the Son has a character distinct from the Father.' Use is made of John's Gospel: the Son has his glory with the Father; he bears witness to the Father; the Father creates through the Son; it is the Son not the Father who was sent forth and died. The conclusion Calvin draws about the distinctiveness of the Son is short, efficient and straight out of Nicaea: he is and always has been 'the only-begotten "in the bosom of the Father"'. The same in briefer compass is done for the Spirit: 'the Holy Spirit proceeds from the Father'.[32]

What does Calvin think is the value of begottenness in delineating distinction? Immediately in the next section, he continues to discuss difference.[33] On the grounds of inadequacy, he distances himself from those who used analogies. He will stay with scriptural expressions.

To the Father is attributed the beginning of activity, fountain and wellspring of all things.

To the Son is attributed wisdom, counsel, and the ordered disposition of all things.

To the Spirit is attributed the power and efficacy of that activity.

That is, there is an order.

*3: Order understood from the simple unity*
Third, immediately Calvin directs us back to the united essence: 'the eternity of the Father is also the eternity of the Son and the Spirit'. Therefore, 'we must not seek in eternity a *before* or an *after*, nevertheless the observance of an order is not meaningless or superfluous'.[34] Why? How? At this point Calvin directs

---

32. *Inst.* 1.13.17.
33. *Inst.* 1.13.18.
34. *Inst.* 1.13.18.

us *not* to God in himself, the immanent relations, but to God as he is towards
us. The value of the order is that it helps us see that it is God acting from first
to last in our salvation. That, I take it, is the import of the next sentence: 'For
the mind of each human being is naturally inclined to contemplate God first,
then the wisdom coming forth from him, and lastly the power whereby he
executes the decrees of his plan.' What Calvin has done, then, is not so much
demonstrate the explanatory power of the creedal 'begottenness', but to use
the notion of order inherent in the Son coming 'forth from the Father alone'
and 'the Spirit from the Father and the Son at the same time' to stabilize our
perception of what is happening in the economy of salvation. It is truly God
as Father, Son and Holy Spirit who is dealing with us.

Calvin returns to the question of the immanent distinctions.[35] The distinctions do not contravene 'the utter simple unity of God'. On the contrary, by
privileging the simple unity we may prove 'that the Son is one God with the
Father because he shares with the Father one and the same Spirit; and that
the Spirit is not something other than the Father and different from the Son,
because he is the Spirit of the Father and the Son.' Because of the priority
we assign to the one, undivided essence, 'in each hypostasis the whole divine
nature is understood', and without extinguishing their individual distinctive
qualities. Without further delineating these distinctive qualities, in following
the logic of each hypostasis having the whole divine nature, in words echoing
John 14:10, Calvin makes a statement about the divine mutual indwelling or
coinherence: 'the Father is wholly in the Son, the Son wholly in the Father'.
Calvin has arrived at this point by thinking into each other 'the united, simple
essence' and the 'three hypostases'.

*4, 5 and 6: Augustine's construct,* autotheos *and what 'begottenness' means and does not
mean*
Calvin now returns to the question of the distinctive properties of the Persons
by identifying and then adopting a central construct of Augustine's trinitarian
theology. The names Father, Son and Holy Spirit set forth the unique qualities
of each hypostasis, *and* these characteristic qualities are to do with their mutual
relations as persons, and *not* the one simple essence 'by which they are one'.
In making this point, Calvin gives us another theological rule that highlights
the difference in how the concepts of the 'one essence' and the 'three persons'
work and places more conceptual distance between them: 'the simple name of
God admits of *no relation*, nor can God be said to be *this* or *that* with respect to

---

35. *Inst.* 1.13.19.

himself'.[36] So, Calvin is implying, although triunity is alongside immensity and spirituality an attribute of the simple essence, such triunity does not immediately or easily carry with it the notion of three subsistences or Persons. We will return to this problem later.

Augustine's construct allows Calvin to make further sense of order between the Persons. Calvin believes the order is real, but how may we best understand it? The problem is that unspecified Church Fathers have left us with two contrary statements about the relation of Father and Son: 'sometimes, indeed, they teach that the Father is the *principium* (beginning or ground) of the Son; sometimes they declare that the Son has both divinity and essence from himself, and thus has one *principium* (beginning, ground) with the Father [i.e. the essence itself]'.[37] The Latin word *principium* translates the Greek word *monarchē*, which can mean beginning or source and, depending on context, rule. Often in discussions of 'beginning' or 'source', the notion of 'rule' is not far away. Asserting that there is but one *principium* or *monarchē* protects the oneness of God and overcomes any incipient tendency towards tritheism in thinking about the economic Trinity.

Thus Augustine's construct is invoked. The Father is indeed the *principium* of the Son (begotten of the Father), but that is to do with their relations as the divine Persons, not the essence. Augustine 'speaks as follows: "Christ with respect to himself is called God, with respect to the Father, Son."' 'Christ with respect to himself is called God' is the *autotheos*, or 'the downright deity or aseity of the Son', as Torrance expresses it. The Son (and the Spirit) is 'God in himself', God *in se*.

Warfield regards as 'epochal' Calvin's steady insistence and exposition of Christ as *autotheos*. Until Calvin, many theologians, following a tradition from Origen, had reserved the concept (if not the term) for the Father as the 'fount of divinity'; although several recognized that it also rightly applied to the Son.[38] Within Calvin's theology, and the Reformed tradition that followed, Warfield judges that *autotheos* drives off any inchoate subordinationism lying in

---

36. *Inst.* 1.13.20 (emphasis mine).

37. *Inst.* 1.13.19.

38. In the *Institutes* (1559), Calvin cites a passage from Irenaeus to support the notion: 'the godly man insists on this one thing, "that he who in Scripture is called God in an absolute and undifferentiated sense is in truth the only God, and that Christ indeed is called God in an absolute sense"' (*Inst.* 1.13.27). In his 'Defence against the calumnies of Peter Caroli' (1545), Calvin appeals to Cyril of Alexandria's *Thesaurus*. Refer to Warfield, *Calvin*, pp. 239–241.

the Nicene formularies and the writings of the Nicene Fathers. We will return to this later.

On the basis of the *autotheos*, Calvin draws a conclusion which will act as a firm interpretative principle for understanding the immanent relations:

> Therefore, when we speak simply of the Son *without* regard to the Father, we well and properly declare him to be of himself (*a se esse*); and for this reason we call him the sole beginning (*unicum principium*). But when we mark the relation that he has with the Father, we rightly make the Father the beginning (*principium*) of the Son.[39]

Calvin returns to this in dealing with a heresy introduced into the Italian-speaking congregation at Geneva by John Gentilis Valentinus. Gentilis seems to have held inconsistent propositions: the Father alone was the *Monarch*, the one true God; and that there are in the Trinity three eternal Spirits, each of which is by itself God: that is, tritheism.[40] From Calvin's treatment of Gentilis in the *Institutes*, it appears that in order to make his erroneous point that the Father alone is God, Gentilis drew on an understanding amongst some of the Fathers that the statement 'begotten of the Father' refers to the being or essence as well as the Person of the Son. The Father is eternally the *principium* or beginning of *both* the Person and the being of the Son. What this construct is intended to do is both secure the oneness of God (against any tendency to tritheism) and also affirm the true divinity of the Son (the stress is on *eternally* begotten, alongside the thought that the Father could only be truly the divine Father if his Son was fully divine too). What Gentilis does, though, against the grain of Nicaea, is take the proposition that the Father is the *principium* of both the being and Person of the Son and declare the Father the *sole* God. The Son is thus less than fully divine; that is, ontologically subordinate.

Calvin did not have had at hand the range of writings from the patristic period we have, and thus may not have been fully informed of why and how several Fathers advanced the idea that the Father was *principium* of both the Person and being of the Son. Nevertheless, in order to undercut the onto-logical subordinationism of Gentilis and others, Calvin now invokes and applies Augustine's rule. The Father is *not* the 'essence giver' or *Essentiator* of the Son.[41] The three Persons have the one essence in common. Christ is certainly to be

---

39. *Inst.* 1.13.19 (emphasis mine).

40. J. H. Blunt, *Dictionary of Sects, Heresies, Ecclesiastical Parties and Schools of Religious Thought* (London: Rivingtons, 1874), p. 37, fn. 2.

41. *Inst.* 1.13.23.

differentiated from the Father with respect to his Person, but there is no differentiation from the Father with respect to his being or essence. Because the name Yahweh is applied to Christ, 'it follows that with respect to his deity his being is from himself (*autousias*).' The Son's 'being (*essentia*) is without *principium*, while the *principium* of his Person is God [the Father] himself'.[42] In other writings, citing Augustine's works, Calvin stresses this by stating that with respect to the essence, the Father and the Son together must be thought of as *principium* (*pater et filius sint simul principium*); nevertheless, this does not mean that there are two *principia*, but only one *principium* (*neque duo sunt, sed unum principium*).[43]

How intelligible is this understanding of the notion of *principium* in God? The question needs to be asked from two different points of view. Yes, in the essence there are not two *principia* or beginnings, but only one. In the essence, that is with respect to their divinity, the Father and Son share the one *principium*. But with respect to their personhood, the Father is the *principium* of his Son. That is, with respect to their relations, they do not share the one *principium*, for the Father is 'unbegotten', without beginning or source, without *principium*. So, in a sense we have two different types of *principium*: a shared one in the essence and another not shared in the relations between Persons.

For now, we note that the use of Augustine's construct allows Calvin to recognize order amongst the Persons in the immanent relations without implying any diminution of their true divinity and the unity of God. The order pertains to the relations, not to their common essence. Augustine's construct also allows the preservation of the *monarchē* or the priority of the Father in the relations. Section 20 presents a succinct summary of the results of Calvin's thinking:

> When we profess to believe in one God, under the name of God is understood a single, simple essence, in which we comprehend three persons, or hypostases. Therefore, whenever the name of God is mentioned without particularization, there are designated no less the Son and the Spirit than the Father, but where the Son is joined to the Father, then the relation of the two enters in; and so we distinguish among the persons. But because the peculiar qualities in the persons carry an order

---

42. *Inst.* 1.13.25.
43. J. Calvin, 'Epistle 474' (May 1543), *CO* 11, p. 561. I have used Torrance's summary: Torrance, 'Calvin's Doctrine'. Here, and where it reappears again in his 1545 *Ad. Caroli* (*CO* 7, p. 324), Calvin states that he is following Augustine's 'Homily 39 on John's Gospel' (see *NPNF1*, 7, pp. 222–223) and 'Homily on Psalm 109 [110 in English Bible]' (see *NPNF1*, 8, p. 542).

within them, e.g., in the Father is the beginning and the source, so often as mention is made of the Father and the Son together, or the Spirit, the name of *God* is peculiarly applied to the Father. In this way, unity of essence is retained, and a reasoned order is kept, which yet takes nothing away from the deity of the Son and the Spirit.

### 7: A rule for interpreting the relations seen in the economy

T. F. Torrance observes another important strategy in Calvin's exposition of trinitarian doctrine, a strategy that takes up one of Torrance's own concerns. Against Arianism and other forms of ontological subordination, Calvin interprets the famous 'test verse', John 14:28, soteriologically. 'My Father is greater than I' refers to the economy of salvation, to Christ's mediatorial work in bringing us to the Father. This is in line with the patristic tradition's interpretation. On Jesus' statement in John 14:28, Calvin writes: 'he does not attribute to himself merely a secondary divinity so that he is inferior to the Father with respect to eternal essence; but because endowed with heavenly glory he gathers believers into participation in the Father'.[44]

Torrance draws the general conclusion: 'in other words, the subordination of Christ to the Father in his incarnate and saving economy cannot be read back into the eternal personal relations and distinctions subsisting in the Holy Trinity.'[45] Torrance further develops the principle in his *Christian Doctrine of God*: 'the subjection of Christ to the Father in his incarnate economy as the suffering and obedient Servant cannot be read back into the eternal hypostatic relations and distinctions subsisting in the Holy Trinity.'[46] This principle then qualifies another theological truth which operates in all Torrance's writings on the doctrine of God: God is in himself as he is towards us in Jesus Christ. There are two reasons advanced for the qualification. First, it avoids any vestige of ontological subordinationism. Second, the economic Trinity is not an end in itself, but is a true revelation of the ontological Trinity.

> [T]hrough the oneness in Being and Act of the Son and of the Spirit with the one eternal God, the economic Trinity cannot but point beyond itself to the theological or ontological Trinity, otherwise the economic Trinity would not be a faithful and true revelation of the transcendent Communion of Father, Son and Holy Spirit which the eternal Being of God is in himself.[47]

---

44. *Inst.* 1.13.26.
45. Torrance, 'Calvin's Doctrine', pp. 185–186.
46. Torrance, *God*, p. 180.
47. Ibid., p. 92.

At least, this means that we cannot collapse the ontological Trinity into the economic Trinity, for that would be to deny God's transcendence. But it also means that we must interpret the economic Trinity as it arises in Scripture in a way that does not compromise the transcendence of God's eternal being. A qualification on 'God is in himself as he is towards us' is warranted. There are issues here that we will revisit.

Calvin's handling of other texts indicating relational subordination in the economy of salvation supports Torrance's observation on John 14:28: John 8:42; 12:49; 17:21, 25; 1 Cor. 11:3; 15:24–28. In each case Calvin interprets these in a soteriological way. They pertain to the mediatorial work of the incarnate Word, the Christ. However, when identifying the particular aspect of trinitarian doctrine which is at stake, he does not refer to relations, but to essence. For example, on John 8:42, 'for I came forth and am come from God; for neither have I come of myself, but he sent me':

> He says: 'I did not come of Myself. You cannot discover anything in Me that is against God. In short, you will find nothing earthly or human in My teaching or in the whole of My ministry.' For he is not speaking of His essence but of His office.[48]

In commenting on these texts, with respect to the question of the relations in eternity Calvin is silent. Torrance, though, quite explicitly sees Calvin as applying his hermeneutical rule to the 'eternal hypostatic relations and distinctions subsisting in the Holy Trinity'.[49] Despite the evidence not quite supporting this, Torrance's appeal to Calvin remains appropriate, because Calvin insists on interpreting the texts soteriologically, and not essentially, and although silent on the question of the interpretative principle itself, he does in fact not read subordination texts back into the immanent Trinity in order to elucidate the relations of the Persons.

*Consequences*

Calvin's treatment of the distinctions and the unity of the Trinity has exposed a rich vein of disciplined and fruitful theological thought. It has led us into our questions concerning the deeper level of knowledge of God. How may we discern and express the trinitarian relations that exist in God himself? How may we use the Bible? What are we to do with the

---

48. *CNTC* 4, p. 226 (on John 8:42).
49. Torrance, *God*, p. 180.

submission we see of the incarnate Son to the Father during his earthly ministry? How much explanatory power may we expect, and have, from the concepts we adopt?

I will highlight two areas where Calvin offers us useful strategies, yet raises questions to pursue further: *autotheos* and order in the relations; and the twofold *principium*.

## *Autotheos* and order in the relations

Warfield observes that Calvin's construction of the trinitarian distinctions is 'equalization rather than subordination'. Calvin does use 'the old language of refined subordinationism' of Nicene theology, 'and he expressly allows an "order" of first, second and third in the Trinitarian relations.' But Warfield stresses that it is the 'principle of equalization' which is the leading principle in Calvin's exposition of the immanent relations.[50] That is, Warfield is inviting us to see 'order' only parenthetically. Several others in their exposition of Calvin have taken this route. Gerald Bray observes that what 'distinguishes the theology of the Reformers is their belief that *the persons of the Trinity are equal to one another in every respect.*'[51] Others have argued that the order that Calvin explains in chapter 13 is operational or functional, and 'he intimates that this order applies only to what is revealed in the economy'.[52]

However, it is clear that Calvin does talk about order in the immanent Trinity. Of course, one can posit the nature of the immanent relations only by moving from the way God has revealed himself in the economy. As Calvin often stated, we know no Christ except Christ clothed with his gospel.[53] So in all Calvin's discussions of the immanent Trinity, near at hand is some reference to how God has operated in the economy of salvation. Calvin deals with order as he articulates what are the distinctive properties of each Person, explaining the nature of God's triunity, which is an attribute of his essence. In the one, single essence we 'comprehend three persons, or hypostases'. The distinctions between them become evident when the relation of the Persons is on view; and in that context,

---

50. Warfield, *Calvin*, p. 230.

51. G. Bray, *The Doctrine of God* (Leicester: IVP, 1993), p. 200 (his emphasis).

52. K. Giles, *Jesus and the Father: Modern Evangelicals Reinvent the Doctrine of the Trinity* (Grand Rapids: Zondervan, 2006), p. 164. Unfortunately, Giles's polemical concerns skew his readings of both Calvin and the Fathers.

53. *Inst.* 3.2.6; *Sermon on Job*, 19:26–29; *Commentary on Isaiah*, 25:19.

the peculiar qualities in the persons carry an order within them, e.g., in the Father is the beginning and the source, so often as mention is made of the Father and the Son together, or the Spirit, the name of *God* is peculiarly applied to the Father. In this way the unity of essence is retained, and a reasoned order is kept, which takes nothing away from the deity of the Son and the Spirit.[54]

Paul Helm's criticism of Gerald Bray's observation is accurate. Since there is an order among the Persons, 'they are not equal in every respect, since in virtue of this order each bears a unique relationship to the others.'[55] The question remains, however, how may we best articulate this order and uniqueness?

Calvin's *autotheos* is a great achievement because he has set it in the context of his adoption of Augustine's construct. Calvin applies the *autotheos* to the one essence, not to the relations. This allows him, along with Augustine, to recognize the distinctive properties of each Person, including their immanent order, without leaving the door open for subordinationism. In the one essence the Father and the Son and the Spirit share the one *principium*, and therefore the Son is indeed *autotheos*, not only the Father, as with the tradition from Origen. But between the three persons exists an order in which the Father alone is the *principium*. In this way Calvin is able to avoid modalism, tritheism and Arian subordinationism as he affirms the personal triunity of God. Modalism is avoided, for each Person has a distinctive property which is not communicable to the others. So too tritheism, for in the one, simple and united essence, in their common bond the Persons share the same *principium*, and in their relations there is only one *principium*, the Father. Any Arian-like ontological subordinationism is avoided because of the way Calvin gives priority to the one, simple essence of God.

Calvin speaks of this immanent distinctiveness and its order in terms of derivation: the Son is eternally begotten, the Spirit proceeds. He does not directly speak of it in terms of authority: that is, the Father is also the fount of the divine authority. With safeguards against ontological subordinationism, the Nicene tradition will centre the one *monarchē*, understood as 'rule' and not only 'source', on the Father. It is an authority that the Father shares with the Son and the Spirit, and so in that way it is the authority or rule of the whole Godhead.[56] Athanasius, for example, centres God's authority on the Father in

---

54. *Inst.* 1.13.20.

55. Helm, *Ideas*, p. 45.

56. For a contemporary statement of this in the context of a dialogue between Greek Orthodoxy and the Reformed Churches of Europe, see Torrance, *Trinitarian Perspectives: Toward Doctrinal Agreement* (Edinburgh: T. & T. Clark, 1994), pp. 119–120.

order to battle polytheistic tendencies, for if there are three equal centres of authority in the Godhead, then there is more than one God.[57]

There is also a tradition of reading the obedience and submission of the Son in the economy against the immanent relations with careful qualifications. As already noted, this is a movement that Torrance eschews and Calvin exemplifies. However, in his anti-Arian writing 'Answer to Maximus', Augustine states: 'It was not fitting that the Begetter be sent by his Son, but that the Son be sent by his Begetter. This is not inequality of substance, but the order of nature; it does not mean that one existed before the other, but that the one has his origin from the other.'[58] In the light of Paul Helm's observation that Calvin's pared-down version of eternal generation leaves us wondering just what truth of God's own triune being it elucidates, Augustine's conclusion gives quite explicit explanatory power to begottenness. The submission of the only begotten Son in the economy is appropriate to the immanent relations, to the 'order of nature': he is sent by the Father and comes into the world. In the modern period, both Karl Rahner[59]

---

57. [Against polytheism] 'For we must not think there is more than *one ruler and maker* of Creation: but it belongs to correct and true religion to believe that its *Artificer is one* . . . Who then might this Maker be? . . . the God we worship and preach is the only true One, Who is Lord of Creation and Maker of all existence. Who then is this, save *the Father of Christ*, most holy above all created existence, Who like an excellent pilot, *by* His own Wisdom and His own Word, *our Lord and Saviour Christ, steers and preserves and orders all things*, and does as seems to Him best?' (*Against the Heathen*, paragraphs 39–40 [*NPNF2*, 4, pp. 24–25], emphasis mine). In context, Athanasius is speaking about the eternal Trinity. Athanasius says that there is only '*one* ruler', whom he clearly identifies as the Father, but the Father works *by* the Son, while still remaining the 'one ruler'. See also *Against the Heathen*, paragraphs 6–7 (*NPNF2*, 4, pp. 6–7); also *Defence of the Nicene Definition*, paragraphs 26, 30–31 (*NPNF2*, 4, 167–168, 170–171); and *On Luke* 10:22 (*NPNF2*, 4, pp. 87–90).

58. Augustine, 'Answer to Maximus', 2.14.8, in *Arianism and Other Heresies*, trans. R. J. Teske, ed. J. E. Rotelle (New York: New City Press, 1995), pp. 285–286. Compare Augustine, 'On the Holy Trinity', 2.3 (*NPNF1*, 3, p. 38); also M. R. Barnes, 'Augustine in Contemporary Trinitarian Theology', *Theological Studies* 56 (1995), p. 248.

59. In thinking through the identity between the economic and immanent Trinities, Rahner strongly insists that the Father could *not* die. What happened in the economy of salvation is rooted in the eternal differentiation of the three Persons. If every divine member of the Trinity could become man, become incarnate, that would 'create havoc with theology' and 'go against the whole sense of holy

and Karl Barth[60] also observe a propriety between the economic obedience and the immanent relations which define the Persons. If we will permit ourselves to think by way of analogy, 'begottenness' may be taken to indicate a real Father in eternity who has a real Son in eternity, for, at least at the human level, it is appropriate that fathers send and sons be sent. This strategy is not without potential pitfalls, and the concerns of both Calvin and Torrance are no doubt legitimate. But without some recognition of its propriety, the notion of the priority of the Father can be so apophatically or negatively expressed that one wonders if there is sufficient particularity left to the Father.[61] We ought not to make room for nominalism.

There is one place in chapter 13 of the *Institutes* where Calvin indirectly states a consistency between the Son's obedience in the economy and the immanent order:

> The passages we have already cited show that the Son has a character distinct from the Father, because the Word would not have been with God unless he were another than the Father, nor would he have had his glory with the Father were he not distinct from the Father . . . Furthermore, it was not the Father who descended upon the earth, but he who went forth from the Father; the Father did not die, nor did he arise

---

Scripture': K. Rahner, *The Trinity* (1970; repr. New York: Crossroad, 1997), p. 28.

60. Against those who would limit Christ's obedience to his manhood, Barth first insists that the submission must be read up into the Father–Son relation, and then into God himself. He insists that in this expression of differentiation, the Father is one with the Son through their eternal love and fellowship in the Spirit. This oneness with the Son does not, however, obviate the distinction between the Father who disposes and the Son whose begottenness means his part in the majesty and disposing of the Father is compliance. K. Barth, *CD* IV/1, pp. 202–210.

61. In the context of affirming that the monarchy of God is of the whole Trinity, Torrance can only speak apophatically of the Father as 'Principle': he is not the Source (*Archē*) or Cause (*Aitia*) of the divine Being of the Son and the Spirit, he is Unoriginate, or Father. And because we are here speaking about the Father as Principle, we must also express the meaning of 'Father' negatively: 'in respect of his not being a Son, although all that the Son has the Father has except Sonship': Torrance, *God*, p. 180. Colin Gunton has expressed concern that this leads to a loss of particularity: C. E. Gunton, 'Being and Person: T. F. Torrance's Doctrine of God', in *The Promise of Trinitarian Theology: Theologians in Dialogue with T. F. Torrance*, ed. E. M. Colyer (Lanham: Rowman & Littlefield, 2001), pp. 120–121, 130–131.

again, but rather he who had been sent by the Father. Nor did this distinction have its beginning from the time that he assumed flesh, but before this also it is manifest that he was the only-begotten 'in the bosom of the Father'.[62]

From the fact that salvation is Father-centred, Calvin notes that the order and activities of Father and Son in the economy are appropriate to the relations in the immanent Trinity, where the only-begotten is 'in the bosom of the Father'.

We may note that the tension amongst the heirs of Calvin over how far to delineate the immanent order continues. Robert Reymond, who is firmly in the tradition of Christ's and the Spirit's *autotheos*, is quite rightly cautious about attempts by the Nicene Fathers to explain 'how' the Son is generated or the Spirit processes. Nevertheless he affirms that the economic activities 'flow' from the distinguishing marks of the Persons. 'It is unthinkable that the Son would have sent the Father to do his will.'[63] T. F. Torrance also affirms that the order we see in the economic mission 'is governed by the irreversible relation between the Father and the Son intrinsic to them in which, while the Father "naturally" comes first, the Son is nevertheless everything the Father is except being Father.' Torrance and Reymond, then, explain the congruity of the economic order with God in himself by reference to the incommunicable properties which distinguish each Person. Torrance also affirms the priority of the Father in the monarchy of the whole God on the same grounds: 'the Son is begotten of the Father, not the Father of the Son.'[64]

### Intelligibility of a twofold *principium*

The notion of a single *principium* or *monarchē* functions in trinitarian theology to protect the oneness of God and overcomes any incipient tendency towards tritheism in thinking about the economic Trinity. It has been used in two ways.

In Nicene theology, the unbegotten Father is the *principium* or *monarchē* and his eternally begotten Son (and the Spirit) come to share in the Father's monarchy. In this way we may speak of the monarchy of the whole Godhead, but the priority remains with the Father.[65] Gregory of Nazianzus states that

---

62. *Inst.* 1.13.17.

63. R. Reymond, *Systematic Theology*, pp. 340–341.

64. Torrance, *God*, p. 176.

65. E.g. Gregory of Nazianzus, while recognizing the priority of the Father, emphasizes that the *monarchē* is of the one, undivided Godhead: Gregory, *Orations*, 29.2–3, 31.14 (*NPNF2*, 7, pp. 301–302, 322). Athanasius does the same, and quite

the Son has his being from the Father, but safeguards this from an ontological subordinationist interpretation by straightaway stating that this is 'beyond all time, and beyond all cause'. By this type of reasoning he is able to claim that 'their being itself is common and equal, even though the Son receive it from the Father.'[66] However, the Nicene Fathers' arguments are not all unalloyed. Their seeking to articulate how the Son and the Spirit are begotten and proceed from the Father muddied the waters. The Cappadocian answer to the 'how' question could look like a chain of causality, patent of intrusion by ontological subordinationist thinking.[67]

The other approach was that of Augustine, an approach which Calvin adopted. With respect to the essence, the Father and the Son share the same *principium*. With respect to the relations, the Father alone is the *principium* of the Son. Both Augustine and Calvin deny that this means that there are four things in God: Father (the *principium*), Son and Spirit, and the one essence (the *principium* of which the Father and the Son) the three come from. There is no quaternity, both Augustine[68] and Calvin argue, because the one, simple essence has the attribute of triunity:

> they falsely and calumniously charge that we have set up a quaternity, for they falsely and calumniously ascribe this fiction of their own brain to us, as if we pretended that three persons came forth by derivation from one essence. On the contrary it is clear from our writings that we do not separate the persons from the essence, but we distinguish among them while three remain within it.[69]

That is, we must conceive of the relation between the essence and the three persons not in terms of 'from' but 'in', and 'in' in such a way that Christians

pointedly against polytheism: Athanasius, *Against the Arians*, 1.14, 3.15 (*NPNF2*, 4, pp. 314–315, 402).

66. Gregory of Nazianzus, *Orations*, 30.11 (*NPNF2*, 7, p. 313).

67. Torrance, *God*, pp. 239–240, 319–320.

68. 'It remains for us to believe that the Trinity is of one substance and that the essence is nothing else than the Trinity itself': Augustine, 'Epistle 120', 3.17, cited from L. Ayres, '"Remember that you are Catholic" (Serm. 52.2): Augustine on the Unity of the Triune God', *Journal of Early Christian Studies* 8.1 (2000), p. 71. Similarly, 'there is both said to be and is one God, nor is that Trinity in one God, but it is one God . . . the Highest Trinity itself is three persons': Augustine, 'On the Holy Trinity', 15.23.43 (*NPNF1*, 3, p. 222).

69. *Inst.* 1.13.25.

cannot properly conceive of the simple essence of God without at the same time conceiving of it as trinitarian through and through.

But the notion of the *principium* or *monarchē* of God viewed in two different ways and with two different specifications does somewhat reduce the work it usually does, for it is God's *one principium* that upholds the notion of monotheism. The notion does the work Calvin wants it to do only because he makes what Roger Beckwith has called 'a difficult abstraction' in distinguishing between 'the Son, regarded as God, and without reference to Person'.[70] I grant Calvin the gains he has made by this abstraction, for it secures real order in the immanent relations without subordinationism, but it 'disguises the fact that the Son is *divine* Person.' Beckwith's conclusion is judicious: 'to think of him as God but not as Son is as unreal as it is to think of him as Son and not as God.'[71]

Both the approach of the Nicene theology and that of Calvin and Augustine are open to criticism, the former for leaving open the door to ontological subordinationism, the latter for a potential division between the essence and the persons. My own preference is for the Nicene approach, with due safeguards against subordinationism: eternal generation, *God* of God, *light* of light. Its use must certainly not allow discussions of 'how' these things are so. It seems to me that Nicaea more intelligibly honours the priority of the Father that we see in Scripture, and that the name 'God' is regularly applied to the Father (e.g. 1 Cor. 8:6; Col. 1:3), and even occasionally 'Father' applied to the whole Godhead (Eph. 4:6; 1 Pet. 1:17; Jas 1:27). However, Calvin's approach has the strengths already mentioned, and it also fosters thinking of the one true God of Israel in terms of one, simple essence which has triunity as an attribute. This staple of classical or metaphysical Christian theism gives good results, as I hope our investigation of Calvin has shown. The priority of this one, simple shared essence forestalls tritheism, as well as any ontological subordinationism with respect to the three Persons.

What we have reached, I think, are the boundaries of our theological conceptions. Recognition of the limits of the explanatory power of our concepts honours God. This triune God in his incomprehensible being will always remain a mystery, though we are able to apprehend him truly without detracting from who he really is because of his self-revelation in Christ. Consequently, we have been enabled to confess and proclaim the gospel of this God before

70. R. Beckwith, 'The Calvinist Doctrine of the Trinity', *Churchman* 115.4 (2001), pp. 310–311.

71. R. Beckwith, 'Trinity', p. 311.

the world, that we might return and live in union with him. Nicene theology, Augustine and Calvin have all contributed to our understanding in ways which have stood the test of time, and for that we are rightly thankful.

On the broader question of the relation between the 'one God' and the 'three Persons', between the one substance and the three subsistences, it helps to keep in mind that although we may from time to time give priority to one or the other in our thinking, in reality both essence and Persons arise together. Neither have ontological priority; that is why Calvin's reminder to us of Gregory Nazianzen's dictum is so helpful:

> I cannot think on the one without quickly being encircled by the splendour of the three; nor can I discern the three without being straightaway carried back to the one.

## Appreciating Calvin

There is much to appreciate in Calvin's exposition of the doctrine of the Trinity. By way of concluding summary, I draw attention to one item in particular that emphasizes both the nature and the success of Calvin's work.

In considering Calvin's elaboration on his foundations, and especially his investigation of the immanent relations, we have already observed the stress he places on thinking recursively from the unity to the Persons, and Person to Person, and Persons to unity. I believe it is that habit, in support of which he cites Gregory of Nazianzus, which accounts for the richness of insight and balance in his treatment. In this we find ourselves in profound agreement with T. F. Torrance, who sees Calvin's account of the immanent relations as his great achievement:

> Calvin's account of the manifold interpenetrating personal relations or subsistences within the one indivisible Godhead . . . is in many respects his most significant contribution to the doctrine of the Triunity of God. Here it becomes clear that his biblical approach has led him to offer a more unreserved account of the Deity of the Son and of the Spirit both in their distinguishing properties and in their consubstantial relations with God the Father than that offered by most of his theological predecessors. Yet even here Calvin does not take his feet off biblical ground.[72]

© Robert C. Doyle, 2009

-------------------

72. Torrance, 'Calvin's Doctrine', p. 176.

## 5. CALVIN ON THE MEDIATOR

*Mark D. Thompson*

'The whole Gospel is contained in Christ.' So writes John Calvin, commenting on Romans 1:3. 'To move even a step from Christ means to withdraw oneself from the Gospel. Since Christ is the living and express image of the Father, it need not surprise us that He alone is set in front of us as the One who is both the object and centre of our whole faith.'[1] This was no isolated comment, tied to the exegesis of a particular biblical text and easily forgotten. Though he did not leave us a treatise on Christology, the generally Christocentric character of Calvin's theology has long been recognized.[2] So too has been his Christological

---

1. *CNTC* 8, p. 15 (on Rom. 1:3).
2. E. g. F. Wendel, *Calvin*, trans. Philip Mairet (London: Collins, 1963), p. 215; S. Edmondson, *Calvin's Christology* (Cambridge: Cambridge University Press, 2004), x. It is, however, quite right of Richard Muller to advise caution in the use of the term 'Christocentric'. While the assumption that 'saving knowledge of God is knowledge of God in Christ is a major structural principle of Calvin's *Institutes*', we must be careful not to impose twentieth- or twenty-first-century categories on this sixteenth-century theologian. 'Calvin's "Christocentrism" is not the "Christocentrism" of Barth': R. A. Muller, 'A Note on "Christocentrism" and the Imprudent Use of such Terminology', *WTJ* 68 (2006), pp. 259, 258.

approach to the 'plain sense' of Scripture.[3] He took very seriously the character of Scripture as a testimony to Christ and just as seriously the discipline of ensuring that everything Christians say about Christ is properly and securely anchored in the teaching of Scripture. Commenting on John 5:39 in 1553, he remarked,

> Again, we are taught in this passage that the knowledge of Christ must be sought from the Scriptures. Those who imagine what they like about Christ will ultimately have nothing but a shadowy ghost in His place. First, then, we must hold that Christ cannot be properly known from anywhere but the Scriptures. And if that is so, it follows that the Scriptures should be read with the aim of finding Christ in them.[4]

Calvin's Christocentricity is, at one level, entirely unremarkable. Christian theology, precisely because it is *Christian* theology, is profoundly oriented to the person and work of Jesus Christ. At the centre of God's purposes for all creation is the beloved Son by whom, through whom and for whom all things were created (Col. 1:11–16). However, the pursuit of inter-faith relations in the last decades of the twentieth century and the escalation of religiously motivated terrorism at the beginning of the twenty-first have raised serious questions about such a sharp focus on this one figure and, in particular, the claims for uniqueness surrounding him. How useful is this emphasis of Calvin in our very different global context? In fact, does our new situation suggest that such an insistence upon the centrality of Jesus Christ is in reality nothing more than a Christian cultural imperialism? Perhaps we cannot blame Calvin for not noticing it. After all, he was every inch a sixteenth-century man, one who lived and taught in a period in which the Christian faith still dominated most aspects of life in the West. Nevertheless, his approach might appear to some as hardly serviceable at the beginning of the third millennium. Is it time to recognize it as entirely determined by his historical and cultural environment and leave it behind?

Or, just perhaps, Calvin's teaching about Jesus Christ might still challenge

---

3. S. R. Holmes, 'Calvin on Scripture', in *Calvin, Barth and Reformed Theology*, ed. N. B. MacDonald and C. Trueman (Milton Keynes: Paternoster, 2008), p. 155. For more on the Christological dimensions of Calvin's approach to biblical interpretation, see Michael Jensen's contribution to this volume.

4. *CNTC* 4, p. 139 (on John 5:39). Earlier, in 1549, he remarked, 'In dealing with everything that has to do with Christ we must scrupulously observe that we do not accept anything that is not from the Word of God': *CNTC* 12, p. 89 (on Heb. 7:3).

us about our own preoccupations. Calvin's work in this area was never simply a slavish rehearsal of the tradition or the ideas of his contemporaries. At a number of points Calvin's treatment is fresh and invigorating, reflecting his extensive engagement with the teaching of Scripture and a willingness to face tough questions. Calvin might yet provide us with the resources to resist a new slide into anthropocentric theology – a theology dominated by our interests, our questions and our priorities, and constrained by the necessities of a larger cultural and political agenda – without retreating into a mere repetition of old mantras. But if this is to be the case, more attention and not less will need to be given to the nature of Calvin's teaching about Jesus Christ and the contexts in which it occurred.

## The controversial contexts of Calvin's Christological reflection

Calvin was involved in extended reflection upon Christological questions throughout his teaching ministry, due not least to an almost continuous series of debates over the nature of Christ's Sonship and what it meant for him to be the one Mediator between God and the human race. In 1537, not long after Calvin settled into his first period in Geneva, he was accused of entertaining the Arian heresy by Pierre Caroli of Lausanne. Caroli had noticed what Karl Barth would later describe as 'the strangely unemphatic and "loveless" position that the doctrine of the Trinity occupies in the *Institutes* and the catechism'.[5] It was even erroneously suggested that Calvin had deliberately avoided the terms 'trinity' and 'person' in his teaching about God.[6] As far as Caroli was concerned, his objections to Calvin's teaching were vindicated when, during the disputation convened to discuss Caroli's concerns held at Lausanne in February 1537, Calvin refused to subscribe to the three symbols or creeds. The reason was never quite explained, it seems. Most assume that Calvin was guarding the principle of Scripture alone and that he believed subscription at

---

5. K. Barth, *The Theology of John Calvin*, trans. G. W. Bromiley (Grand Rapids: Eerdmans, 1995), p. 312.

6. Barth, *Calvin*, p. 318. As Barth notes, Caroli was right to observe these terms were not used in Calvin's catechism (though Calvin himself believed articles 31 and 33 affirmed the truth denoted by those terms), but they were used in chapter 2 of the 1536 edition of the *Institutes*: J. Calvin, *Institutes of the Christian Religion 1536 Edition*, trans. F. L. Battles (Grand Rapids: Eerdmans, 1975), p. 44. Caroli's charge would, nevertheless, be repeated by the Senate of Berne in August: Calvin, Epistle 73 (*CO*, 10/2, p. 118).

this point would have implied his previous teaching was defective, which no doubt is precisely how Caroli would have portrayed it.[7] Calvin's report of the proceedings to the pastors of Geneva included a reminder that the Athanasian Creed had never actually been officially endorsed by the church.[8] He added, in a subsequent letter to the pastors of Berne, that he was not accustomed to recognizing anything as the word of God without properly weighing it.[9] Whatever his reasons, sufficient heat was generated by Calvin's exchanges with Caroli that a further disputation was held in Berne two weeks later and two synods were held in May that same year (again one in Lausanne and one in Berne). This dispute may have appeared formally as a re-run of ancient trinitarian debates; however, in common with those which came after it, the central issue was in fact the nature of Christ's Sonship.[10]

In this regard at least, Calvin's second stint in Geneva began much as the first had done. Within two years of returning to Geneva from Strasbourg, in May 1543, Calvin was again accused of unorthodox views on Christ, this time by two of the pastors in Neuchâtel, Jean Courtois and Jean Chaponneau. Their particular concern was Calvin's insistence that Christ, as the eternal Son, was self-existent. In a series of articles drawn up by these men, they anathematized anyone who taught 'Christ as he is God, is *a se ipso*'. While they were willing to grant that self-existence could be predicated of the Father, they insisted that the Son, precisely because he is of the substance of the Father, cannot properly be spoken of in the same way.[11] As Calvin summarized their case nearly two years later, they argue that the Son 'has a principium from the Father' – an explanation that was confused at best, a dangerous diminution of Christ's divinity at worst.[12] Calvin's response was to make a highly significant

---

7. B. Thompson, *Humanists and Reformers: A History of the Renaissance and Reformation* (Grand Rapids: Eerdmans, 1996), p. 490; Barth, *Calvin*, p. 319.

8. J. Calvin, Epistle 49 (*CO* 10/2, pp. 83–84).

9. J. Calvin, Epistle 50 (*CO* 10/2, p. 86).

10. 'Under the head, therefore, of the trinity Calvin speaks of the relation of the Son to the Father': R. A. Muller, *Christ and the Decree: Christology and Predestination in Reformed Theology from Calvin to Perkins*, Studies in Historical Theology 2 (Durham, NC: Labyrinth, 1986), p. 30.

11. J. Calvin, Epistle 474 (*CO* 11, p. 560).

12. J. Calvin, Epistle 521 (*CO* 11, p. 652). A helpful summary of the controversy, including quotations of extracts from Calvin's letters concerning it, is to be found in B. B. Warfield, 'Calvin's Doctrine of the Trinity', reprinted in *Calvin and Augustine* (Phillipsburg: Presbyterian & Reformed, 1980), pp. 237–239.

distinction between the Person and the essence of Christ: 'since the Person has a cause, I confess that He is not *a se ipso*. But when we are speaking, apart from consideration of the Person, of His divinity or simply of the essence, which is the same thing, I say that it is rightly predicated of him that He is *a se ipso*.'[13]

Christological controversy just would not leave Calvin alone. The most notorious case was that of Miguel Serveto (Servetus), a convinced anti-trinitarian and internationally renowned as the first European to describe the function of the circulation of blood through the lungs.[14] Servetus' Christology was decidedly adoptionist: he denied the pre-existence of Christ and argued that the Word of God should simply be understood as the seed of Christ.[15] In 1546 Servetus wrote to Calvin with three questions, one of which concerned Jesus' identity as the Son of God and what were the implications of Calvin's contention that Jesus was crucified as the Son of God. Reviewing the exchange years later, Calvin responded to this question by insisting 'we truly believe and confirm Jesus Christ, that man who was crucified, to be the Son of God'.[16] As is well known, Servetus eventually made his way to Geneva in August 1553, by then an escapee from Inquisitorial justice, only to be arrested and eventually executed by the City Council.[17]

Sometime between Servetus' first approach to Calvin and his arrival in

---

13. J. Calvin, Epistle 607 (*CO* 12, p. 16).

14. Wilhelm Niesel made the observation that although Calvin's dispute with Servetus is usually understood as a debate over the doctrine of the Trinity, his 1554 work *Defensio orthodoxae fidei de sacra Trinitate, contra prodigiosos errores Michaelis Serveti Hispani* 'does not so much propose to defend the orthodox doctrine of the Trinity as to refute the Christology of Servetus with its soteriological presuppositions and inferences': W. Niesel, *The Theology of Calvin*, trans. H. Knight (Philadelphia: Westminster, 1956), p. 56.

15. Calvin included a collection of propositions taken from Servetus' work in his *Defensio orthodoxae fidei de sacra Trinitate* (*CO* 8, pp. 502–507).

16. Ibid. (*CO* 8, p. 482). Our chief source for the questions, Calvin's response and Servetus' refutation remains Calvin's report of them in this work (*CO* 8, pp. 482–495).

17. One of the more balanced accounts of Calvin's involvement in all of this, one which takes seriously the limits of Calvin's influence with the Council at that particular time, is that of Alister McGrath: A. E. McGrath, *A Life of John Calvin: A Study in the Shaping of Western Culture* (Oxford: Blackwell, 1990), pp. 114–120. A more traditional account, documented from Calvin's own letters, can be found in W. de Greef, *The Writings of John Calvin: An Introductory Guide*, trans. L. D. Bierma (Grand Rapids: Baker, 1993), pp. 173–176.

Geneva, Calvin became aware of the insistence of Andreas Osiander that the incarnation was not bound of necessity to the human need of redemption.[18] Osiander argued that the eternal Son would have become incarnate even if Adam had not sinned, since the first man and woman were made in the image of God and the incarnation was always intended to demonstrate the fullness of this image. He was, it appears, reflecting the teaching of Duns Scotus, who argued against Anselm that the necessity of the incarnation was not determined by events external to God but rather was the result of God's covenanted will.[19] In addition, Osiander held to a kind of Christ-mysticism, including the suggestion that the human nature of Christ was simply the bearer of his divine nature, a proposal that led to a controversially participationist view of justification.[20] Calvin would respond in the 1559 edition of the *Institutes* by pointing out that 'the only reason given in Scripture that the Son of God willed to take our flesh, and accepted this commandment from the Father, is that he would be a sacrifice to appease the Father on our behalf'.[21] He also provided an extended refutation of Osiander's doctrine of 'essential righteousness'.[22]

In the mid- to late 1550s Calvin was once again challenged on his teaching about Christ by members of the Italian congregation in Geneva, most notably Giovanni Valentino Gentilis and Giorgio Biandrata. Gentilis insisted on an essential distinction between the Father and the Son that raised serious questions about Christ's divinity. Calvin appears to have been quoting him when he wrote 'For certain rascals, to escape the invidiousness and shame of Servetus' impiety, indeed confessed that there are three persons; but they added the provision that the Father, who is truly and properly the sole God, in forming the Son and the Spirit, infused into them his own deity. Indeed, they do not refrain from this dreadful manner of speaking: the Father is distinguished from the Son and the Spirit by this mark, that he is the only "essence giver".'[23] In this connection it would appear that it was Gentilis who introduced Calvin to the term *autotheos*, a term which Gentilis restricted to the Father but which Calvin

18. Osiander's argument was published in his 1550 work, *An filius Dei fuerit incarnandus*.

19. D. C. Steinmetz, *Reformers in the Wings* (Grand Rapids: Baker, 1981), p. 96. See also R. A. Muller, *The Unaccommodated Calvin: Studies in the Foundation of a Theological Tradition* (New York and Oxford: Oxford University Press, 2000), p. 54.

20. Steinmetz, *Reformers*, pp. 96–97.

21. *Inst.* 2.12.4.

22. *Inst.* 3.11.5–12.

23. *Inst.* 1.13.23. See also his 'Expositio impietatis Valentini Gentilis (1561)', *CO* 9, pp. 374, 380 (cited in Warfield, 'Trinity', p. 234).

would insist must be affirmed of the Son if he is to be genuinely divine. Calvin understood the need to distinguish the Father and the Son – 'there must be some mark of differentiation in order that the Father may not be the Son' – but insisted, 'even though we admit that in respect to order and degree the beginning of divinity is in the Father, yet we say that it is a detestable invention that essence is proper to the Father alone, as if he were the deifier of the Son'.[24] After being forced publicly to burn his own writing on the subject, Gentilis left Geneva in 1558 and was eventually executed as a heretic by the authorities in Berne in September 1566.

Biandrata first sent a series of questions to Calvin some time in 1557. In the light of subsequent events it seems clear that though he presented himself as a confused inquirer, he had already committed himself to an anti-trinitarian position which denied the divinity of Christ on 'rational' grounds. His first question gives the tone of his inquiry:

> Since Jesus never revealed to the world a God other than his Father, and since he told the Jews (who worshipped that one God according to Moses' clear words, 'Your God is one God'), 'He whom you say is your God, is my Father', and since the Apostle speaking especially of the one God says, 'for us there is one God, who is the Father from whom are all things', and elsewhere, 'one Lord, one faith, one baptism and one God, the Father of all', and inasmuch as he always began his letter with 'God the Father', or 'God and Father', and frequently with 'the God and Father of our Lord Jesus Christ', the question could be put this way: Are we to look for a God other than the Father of our Lord Jesus Christ, and how are we to understand the words of Christ and the apostles when they speak of the Father?[25]

Biandrata's other questions asked whether it was permitted to invoke God directly and without a mediator; whether it is right to pray to Jesus; and whether 'the Word of God in the Godhead [is] something substantive and essential'.[26] The brief and almost staccato nature of Calvin's reply has long been noted:

> When we profess a belief in one God, we understand by the word God the one simple essence in which we include the three persons or hypostases. Therefore, as

---

24. *Inst.* 1.13.23, 24.
25. *CO* 17, p. 169, translated in J. N. Tylenda, 'The Warning that Went Unheeded: John Calvin on Giorgio Biandrata', *CTJ* 12.1 (1977), p. 52.
26. *CO* 17, p. 170; Tylenda, 'Warning', p. 53.

often as the name of God is used without qualification, we believe that it designates the Son and the Spirit no less than the Father. However, when the Son is added to the Father, then a relationship intervenes, and hence we distinguish the persons . . .

As for the form of prayer, the ordinary one is the one prescribed for us in the gospel, directing our words to the Father in the name of Christ . . . Besides, it would be sacrilegious and rash on anyone's part to condemn the other forms which the apostles used under the guidance of the Holy Spirit . . .

Hence it must be held that the Word is essentially God, but at the same time it denotes the person, for the person subsists in the essence itself . . .

The name Christ belongs not to the man alone but to God made manifest in the flesh; the anointing, on the other hand, is properly referred to the humanity. The Mediator, God-man, is truly the Son of God according to both natures by reason of their union; but it is properly referred to the divinity, because the Word was born of the Father before all ages.[27]

In May the next year (1558) Biandrata fled Geneva and, after a few years in Poland, spent most of the rest of his life in Transylvania.

Around the same time Calvin was drawn into the debate generated by Menno Simons' writing on the nature of the incarnation. As early as 1544, Menno had denied that Jesus received any part of his humanity from Mary: 'he did not become flesh *of* Mary, but *in* Mary'.[28] He had a number of concerns. In the first place, if Jesus shared the sinful flesh of his mother this could only mean that he would stand guilty before God the Father on his own account. How then could he act as the redeemer of humanity?[29] Furthermore, given the then prevailing view that the essentially procreative element in the union of a husband and wife came from the man – 'a child takes its origin in the father and not in the mother' – the traditional view of the incarnation had an even

---

27.  *CO* 9, pp. 325, 329, 330, 332; Tylenda, 'Warning', pp. 54, 59, 61, 62.

28.  Menno Simons, 'Brief Confession on the Incarnation (1544)', in *The Complete Writings of Menno Simons c.1496–1561*, trans. L. Verduin, ed. J. C. Wenger (Scottdale, PA: Herald, 1956), p. 432 (emphasis added).

29.  Menno Simons, 'The Incarnation of our Lord (1554)', in *The Complete Writings of Menno Simons*, p. 807. See also his public reply to an attack on his teaching by Martin Micron, from 1556: 'it is plainly shown that He is not of Mary's flesh, which was also concluded under sin; but that the Father's most glorious Word, which knew no sin, became flesh': M. Simons, 'Reply to Martin Micron (1556)', in *The Complete Writings of Menno Simons*, p. 870.

more basic difficulty.[30] Was all talk about a genuine humanity mere sophistry if there was no genuinely human seed? Even if it could be argued that the mother contributed as much to the life of her child as the father, Menno conceded, 'Christ would be but half a man'.[31] For these reasons Menno argued for Christ's unique, heavenly humanity: 'For Christ Jesus, as to His origin, is no earthly man, that is, a fruit of the flesh and blood of Adam. He is a heavenly fruit or man'.[32] Calvin responded both in advice to Martin Micron (who had taken the lead in the debate with Menno) and in a number of important statements in the 1559 edition of the *Institutes* (though these do not mention Menno by name).[33] Menno's severing of the connection between Christ and Adam raised its own questions about Christ's true humanity. Just as importantly, in doing so he also severed the link between Christ's humanity and ours, a critical part of Paul's argument in 1 Corinthians 15 and elsewhere. As the Fathers had put it, what is not assumed is not healed.[34] There were other ways to secure the sinlessness of Christ, as Calvin would go on to argue.[35]

Finally, in the last years of his life, Calvin was faced with the teaching of Francesco Stancaro, an Italian whose theological opinions had been troubling the Reformed churches in Poland. In 1559 Peter Statorius wrote to Calvin seeking his assistance in responding to 'a most quarrelsome individual' who was teaching that 'the human nature of Christ is the only mediator between God and men and that the divine nature has nothing to do with it'.[36] This wasn't the first time Calvin had heard this name and the teaching that went with it.[37] Nor was the teaching itself entirely novel. Stancaro would appeal to the sixth ecumenical council (Constantinople III 680–681).[38] There were also echoes in the writings of Augustine, though later evidence suggests the

---

30. Simons, 'Incarnation', p. 793. See again the 'Reply to Martin Micron', p. 867: 'That the woman has no procreative seed is as clear as day'.

31. Simons, 'Incarnation', p. 792.

32. Simons, 'Confession', p. 437.

33. *CO* 10/1, pp. 167–176 and *Inst.* 2.13.1–2.

34. Gregory of Nazianzus, *Ep. CI* (*NPNF2*, 7, p. 440).

35. *Inst.* 2.13.4.

36. J. N. Tylenda, 'Christ the Mediator: Calvin versus Stancaro', *CTJ* 8.1 (1973), p. 9. (Tylenda's name appears as 'Tylanda' at the head of this article.)

37. A report from Melanchthon had been relayed to Calvin by Francis Dryander in 1552: Tylenda, 'Christ the Mediator', pp. 8–9.

38. *CO* 18, p. 262. See also J. N. Tylenda, 'The Controversy on Christ the Mediator: Calvin's Second Reply to Stancaro', *CTJ* 8.2 (1973), p. 137.

development of his thought in another direction.[39] Calvin and the pastors of
Geneva, able to cite precedents of their own, responded to Stancaro's ideas
with the insistence: 'a union of both natures is required for the office of mediator, but whatever pertains to the mediator's role should not be indiscrimi-
nately ascribed to either nature'.[40] There is no threat to Christ's divinity when
his mediatorial role is located in his person. On the contrary, the gracious gift
of adoption as God's children depends on it.

It is evident that Calvin was engaged in an extraordinary series of intense
exchanges over the nature of Christ as the eternal Son and Mediator. Retracing
that series demonstrates both the persistence of these questions and the carefully considered responses which Calvin repeatedly made. In this light we can
certainly argue that Christological issues were never far from his theological
consciousness. This lifelong series of debates, together with his exegetical
work on the text of Scripture and its Christological affirmations, and his
regular refining of the argument and content of the *Institutes*, ensured Calvin
gave this subject careful attention. So just what was it that he taught about the
person of Christ?

## Calvin's overarching Christological category: the Mediator

The location of Calvin's discussion of Christology in the overall architecture
of the *Institutes* is instructive. Calvin turned to discuss the purpose of the incarnation (and in so doing to refute the arguments of Osiander) immediately after
his treatment of the similarity and difference of the Old and New Testaments.
It is the unfolding history of redemption which provides the context for
Calvin's Christological comments in this carefully structured presentation
of his theology. This has the effect of keeping Christology and soteriology
together from the outset: 'We enjoy Christ only as we embrace Christ clad in
his own promises'.[41] As one important study puts it,

> Calvin's Christology . . . is neither a traditional 'Christology from above' nor a
> modern 'Christology from below' but a Christology developed out of the historical

---

39. David Fink contrasts *Confessions* 10.43 from around 397–401 with *Sermon* 47.21
    from around 410 in his review of Edmondson's book *Calvin's Christology* in *Trinity
    Journal* 27 (2006), pp. 331–332.
40. *CO* 9, p. 353: translation in Tylenda, 'Controversy', p. 150.
41. *Inst.* 2.9.3.

line of the covenant-promise which points, as by a soteriological necessity, to the concrete, historical person of the God-man'.[42]

Calvin will fill out the nature of Christ's mediation in terms of his three-fold office as prophet, priest and king. The three anointed offices of the Old Testament each find their fulfilment in the Messiah, who has come in these last days. Once again the significance for Calvin of the Bible's redemptive history is apparent. The one true Mediator between God and humanity reveals God and his purposes as both prophet and himself the prophetic message; provides in his own flesh the only truly effective propitiation and expiation as priest; and sovereignly directs the universe towards its goal as king. Calvin may have learned this way of thinking from Bucer, who published his *Enarratio in Evangelis* in Strasbourg in 1536, prior to Calvin's stay in the city. However, Calvin substantially developed the scheme and made it his own. It helped him to bring together the Bible's teaching on Christ's person and biblical teaching about his work in a most productive way.[43] What is not always noticed is the way its impact is heightened by the placement of Calvin's Christology imme-diately following his account of the relation of the testaments.

Another important effect of this placement is to underline Calvin's insist-ence that the work of Christ, even as the Mediator, does not simply begin with the incarnation but is a feature of the Old Testament as well. It remains true that the language of mediation is best suited to the redemptive activity of the incarnate Christ. Nevertheless, it has an even wider application. Calvin can speak of our need of a Mediator simply because we are creatures. We have always been too lowly to reach God without a Mediator.[44] Calvin had developed this idea elsewhere. In a sermon on Daniel 8:16–27 from 1552 he remarked that Christ was Mediator even before his manifestation in the flesh.[45] In his second reply to Stancaro in 1561 he went further: 'since Christ was head of angels and men in the still innocent state of things, he is rightly consid-ered the mediator whom the elect angels even now see and acknowledge'.[46]

---

42. Muller, *Christ*, p. 29. This important context and its indissoluble connection to soteriology is explored in detail in Edmondson, *Christology*, pp. 84–88.

43. See my 'Calvin and the Cross of Christ', in *John Calvin and Evangelical Theology: Legacy and Prospect*, ed. S. W. Chung (Louisville: Westminster John Knox, 2009), pp. 107–127.

44. *Inst.* 2.12.1.

45. *CO* 41, p. 504.

46. *CO* 9, p. 350: translation in Tylenda, 'Controversy', p. 147.

Certainly Calvin sees differences between the Old Testament and the New. While Christ is always the only Mediator between God and humanity, there is a point at which he takes up the task entrusted to him by his Father and is made manifest in the flesh. The Old Testament mediatorial work of Christ always has the character of promise. In the person of the incarnate One we are faced with the fulfilment of that promise.[47]

The category of 'Mediator' lies close to the centre of Calvin's Christology for these reasons. Calvin does not begin the section of the *Institutes* on Christology with a discussion of the two natures or the hypostatic union, but with an exploration of the need for a mediator arising out of the redemptive history he has just outlined. However, as we have already seen, while Calvin acknowledges the universal need of a mediator if we are to be properly related to God, he is careful to avoid suggesting an absolute necessity to the incarnation determined by factors outside of God's own character and will. He will distance himself both from Osiander and from Anselm at this point. 'If someone asks why this is necessary', Calvin begins, 'there has been no simple (to use the common expression) or absolute necessity. Rather, it has stemmed from a heavenly decree, on which men's salvation depended. Our most merciful Father decreed what was best for us.'[48] This is not simply an expression of Calvin's voluntarism or of a dependence upon the thought of Duns Scotus (despite the obvious resonances).[49] While it undoubtedly locates Calvin firmly in the Augustinian tradition, this is not the full explanation either. Rather, it arises directly out of the structure and content of redemptive history. Throughout that history the momentum has come not so much from the reality and profundity of the human predicament as from God's loving determination to fulfil his purpose for humanity. The incarnation is fully and finally an act of divine love.

Calvin insisted that Christ is the Mediator not simply in his human nature

---

47. 'From the beginning of the world He has performed the office of Mediator, but as all this depended on the final revelation, it is right that at the end as in His new Person He puts on the title *Immanuel*, when as Priest He comes onto the scene, to expiate the sins of men by the offering of his body, at the cost of His blood to reconcile them to the Father, altogether to fulfil the whole calling of human salvation': *CNTC* 1, p. 69 (on Matt. 1:23).

48. *Inst.* 2.12.1.

49. Derek Thomas thinks otherwise and draws attention to the work of Dewey Hoitenga on Calvin and the will: D. W. H. Thomas, 'The Mediator of the Covenant', in *Theological Guide to Calvin's Institutes: Essays and Analysis*, ed. D. W. Hall and P. A. Lillback (Phillipsburg: P & R, 2008), p. 207.

but in his person. His fullest defence of this position is found in his responses
to the teaching of Stancaro, but the affirmation is present in the *Institutes*:
'those things which apply to the office of the Mediator are not spoken simply
either of the divine nature or of the human'.[50] It is the person of Christ who
is the Mediator. To argue otherwise risked a rupture of the hypostatic union
and the error of Nestorius. Calvin was no doubt aware that this issue had been
subject to debate in the medieval schools. Others before Stancaro had insisted
that Christ is Mediator 'according to the human nature only'.[51] According to
such thinking, the divine nature could not be spoken of as mediating between
God and human beings without applying considerable strain to the *homoousion*.
How could the Son, who is of one being with the Father, be considered the
mid-point (*medium*) between God and his creatures? How could he intercede
with himself? If Calvin was concerned with the danger of Nestorianism,
Stancaro would hit back at Calvin with a very different but uncomfortably
familiar charge: 'O Calvin, what devil has seduced you to join Arius against
the Son of God?'[52] Calvin insisted that there is no suggestion of a distinction
in the essence of the Father and the Son:

> As long as Christ is placed in this medial position this is not a question of his essence,
> nor do we subtly dispute about what it is; we should rather direct our attention to the
> divine counsel which the ancients have called economy and dispensation . . . These
> two facts, that the *Logos* and eternal Son of God is equal to the Father and that the
> mediator is less than the Father are no more incompatible than these two, that the
> *Logos* by itself and separately is a divine person and, nevertheless, that the one person
> of Christ the mediator is constituted by two natures.[53]

Calvin points out that Scripture does not present us with extensive discussions of the work of Christ according to each nature. When Christ is spoken

50. *Inst.* 2.14.3.

51. Gabriel Biel, *Collectorium* III, d. xix, 1. unica, art. 3, dubium 4, quoted in Muller,
    *Calvin*, p. 53. Muller also quotes Duns Scotus in this regard: 'unde tandem
    concludit quod Christus dicitur mediator non secundum divinam sed secundum
    humanem (Finally, from this it is argued that Christ is called mediator, not
    according to [his] divinity but according to [his] humanity)'. Duns Scotus, III. *Sent.*
    d. 19, q. unica (Muller, *Calvin*, p. 210).

52. F. Stancaro, *De Trinitate et Incarnatione atque Mediatore adversus Iohannem Calvinum
    Genevensis ecclesiae Pastorem* (1561), quoted in Tylenda, 'Controversy', p. 141.

53. *CO* 9, pp. 353, 355 (Tylenda, 'Controversy', pp. 150, 153).

of in the New Testament we are presented with one complete person, though constituted by two natures.[54] Just so, the mediatorial office of Christ should not be located in either nature alone but in the one person who is 'God manifest in the flesh'.

This is all the more obvious, according to Calvin, when Christ's mediatorial *work* is examined more closely:

> Christ offered himself as the price of redemption; he reconciled all things in his suffering flesh; he is the lamb who takes away the sins of the world; he is our propitiator through faith in his blood. Although he accomplished all this in his human nature it is not to be concluded, therefore, that he is mediator in this sole respect, because Christ did not fulfil all the duties of his office by expiation and sacrifice. What does it mean to overcome death? To rise in the power of the Spirit and receive life from oneself? To unite us to God and to be one with God? Without doubt, these will not be found in Christ's human nature apart from the divinity, yet they do come into consideration when it is a question of the mediator's office.[55]

Here is the reasoning behind the simple statement with which Calvin begins the Christological discussion of the *Institutes*: 'Now it was of the greatest importance for us that he who was to be our Mediator be both true God and true man.'[56] There are aspects of Christ's mediatorial work that can take place only because he is genuinely human. Nevertheless, it is as the one Christ, both human and divine, that this is accomplished: 'neither as God alone could he feel death nor as man alone could he overcome it'.[57] Again, it is highly significant that Calvin unfolds his treatment of Christ's work in the closest possible relation to his identity as anointed prophet, priest and king.

Christ has always been the one Mediator between God and the human race. Yet is this something we can expect to continue into eternity? Will he continue to be the Mediator on the other side of the judgment? Calvin, reflecting upon 1 Corinthians 15 in the *Institutes*, suggested he might not:

> Let this, then, be our key to right understanding: those things which apply to the office of the Mediator are not spoken simply either of the divine nature or of the

---

54. *CO* 9, p. 351 (Tylenda, 'Controversy', p. 148).

55. *CO* 9, p. 355 (Tylenda, 'Controversy', p. 153).

56. *Inst.* 2.12.1. 'He would certainly be no true Mediator if there were not in Him an undivided bond of each nature to tie men to God': *CNTC* 1, p. 69 (on Matt. 1:23).

57. *Inst.* 2.12.3.

human. Until he comes forth as judge of the world Christ will therefore reign, joining
us to the Father as the measure of our weakness permits. But when as partakers in
heavenly glory we shall see God as he is, Christ, having then discharged the office
of Mediator (*tunc perfunctus Mediatoris officio*), will cease to be the ambassador of his
Father, and will be satisfied with that glory which he enjoyed before the creation of
the world.[58]

Was Heinrich Quistorp right to conclude that, according to Calvin, the
humanity of Christ 'recedes' following the judgment?[59] If so, does Calvin
envisage a time when Christ's humanity will 'lose its significance'?[60] As we
might expect, Calvin's treatment of 1 Corinthians 15:27 in his commentary
serves to illumine the point he is making in the *Institutes*. Calvin begins his
comment by acknowledging the tension this verse introduces to the biblical
teaching that Christ's kingdom is an eternal one (e.g. 2 Pet. 1:11). His resolution
of the difficulty is quite subtle:

Of course we acknowledge that God is the Ruler, but His rule is actualized in the
man Christ (*sed in facie hominis Christi*). But Christ will then hand back the Kingdom
which He has received, so that we may cleave completely to God. This does not
mean that He will abdicate (*abdicabit*) from the Kingdom in this way, but will transfer
(*traducet*) it in some way or other (*quodammodo*) from His humanity to His glorious
divinity, because then there will open up for us a way of approach, from which we are

---

58. *Inst.* 2.14.3.
59. 'The humanity of Christ which now mediates to us the knowledge of and
    communion with God is yet a limitation which hinders perfect union with God. In
    the final consummation it will no longer stand between us and God. For the
    humanity of Christ is a veil (*velum*) in which God clothes Himself in order to draw
    near to us. But in eternity this will no longer be necessary . . . As the humanity of
    Christ in which He performed His special work as Mediator and Governor recedes,
    He will Himself become ultimately subject to the Father after subjecting all things
    to Him. That does not mean that His reign ceases but rather that in truth it is
    consummated in the communion which He has with His own': H. Quistorp,
    *Calvin's Doctrine of the Last Things*, trans. Harold Knight (Richmond, VA: John Knox,
    1955), pp. 168, 169.
60. Quistorp, *Last Things*, p. 170. Quistorp quotes (and translates) E. Emmen at this
    point: 'Here the mission of Christ (as God-man), which the fall had rendered
    necessary, is completed': E. Emmen, *De christologie van Calvijn* (Amsterdam: Paris,
    1935), p. 109.

now kept back by our weakness. In this way, therefore, Christ will be subjected to the Father, because, when the veil has been removed, we will see God plainly, reigning in His majesty, and the humanity of Christ will no longer be in between us to hold us back from a nearer vision of God.[61]

Calvin's recognition that the teaching of Scripture doesn't answer every question is indicated by his use of 'in some way or other (*quodammodo*)'.[62] We are limited in what we can say. What is clear, though, is that while Christ's rule continues, it takes a different form once the judgment is complete and his mediatorial work of reconciliation is fulfilled. Further, the change that takes place at that time is primarily related by Calvin to our eschatological perception of God as he is: 'a nearer vision of God'. There is an important parallel here to Calvin's understanding of the emptying (*kenosis*) that took place in the incarnation, as explained in Philippians 2. Just as there was no lessening of divinity in the incarnation but rather a 'concealment' of it under the conditions of genuine humanity, so in the fulfilment of all things 'the veil is removed'.[63] As Richard Muller puts it: 'The changes noted here are epistemological, not ontological. Human nature does not pass away – it simply no longer impedes perception.'[64]

The importance of these observations is threefold. In the first place, they confirm that the mediatorial work of Christ has a trajectory. There is a point at which all that Christ has set out to fulfil for us has been fulfilled. He remains our Mediator at the end, since nothing has been accomplished apart from his work, and yet that work will then have been completed. Secondly, genuine humanity is not simply a temporary acquisition of the eternal Son. Just as Christ did not shed his humanity either in the resurrection or in the ascension, he retains his humanity on the other side of the consummation of all things. The hypostatic

---

61. *CNTC* 9, p. 327 (on 1 Cor. 15:27).
62. Robert Doyle refers to this as 'the adverb of eschatological inexactness': R. C. Doyle, 'The Context of Moral Decision Making in the Writings of John Calvin: The Christological Ethics of Eschatological Order' (unpublished PhD thesis, University of Aberdeen, 1981), p. 321.
63. Compare with the comments on 1 Corinthians 15:27 quoted above, Calvin's comments on Philippians 2:7, *CNTC* 11, pp. 248–249. See also *Inst.* 2.13.2.
64. R. A. Muller, 'Christ in the Eschaton: Calvin and Moltmann on the Duration of the *Munus Regium*', *Harvard Theological Review* 74.1 (1981), p. 37. Muller later speaks of 'a change made possible not by an alteration of Christ's person but by the removal of human *infirmitas*' (p. 47). I am grateful to my colleague David Höhne for drawing my attention to this stimulating article.

union of divinity and humanity is not dissolved at the end. Finally, the real and wonderful change that does take place involves both knowing 'fully . . . as I have been fully known' (1 Cor. 13:12) and seeing Christ 'as he is' (1 John 3:2). Muller puts it well: 'Calvin's teaching, in the passage under examination, implies no alteration of the union of natures in Christ's person, but rather an alteration of the relation of the believers to God and therefore to Christ'.[65]

## The genuine humanity of our Mediator

It should already be evident that Calvin placed particular emphasis on the genuine humanity of Christ. His insistence that the incarnation resulted in a real participation in our humanity, a 'fellowship of nature' as he puts it, stands in explicit contrast to the ancient reservations of the Manichees and Marcion and to his contemporary Menno Simons' suggestion of Christ's uniquely 'celestial flesh'.[66] 'God's natural Son fashioned for himself a body from our body, flesh from our flesh, bones from our bones, that he might be one with us [*ut idem nobiscum esset*].'[67] This truth had profound implications for Calvin's understanding of salvation: 'He offered as a sacrifice the flesh he received from us [*carnem quam a nobis accepit*], that he might wipe out our guilt by his act of expiation and appease the Father's righteous wrath.'[68]

Calvin was absolutely determined that the genuine humanity of Christ should not be compromised. He daringly insisted that Christ's humanity should be understood in the fullest possible sense:

> Jesus Christ was not only man as to his body but as to his soul also. He was subject to passions, fears and sorrows, as we see him to have been. And since he thus willed to take a human soul, why should he not have had the qualities that pertain to the nature of souls?[69]

---

65.  Muller, 'Eschaton', p. 48.

66.  *Inst.* 2.13.1–2.

67.  *Inst.* 2.13.2. Note Heiko Oberman's conclusion: 'The eternal Son, appointed as Mediator before the beginning of the world, has in the Incarnation not diluted or compromised the reality of our humanity; he has identified himself with it by becoming "flesh of our flesh"': H. A. Oberman, 'The "Extra" Dimension in the Theology of Calvin', *Journal of Ecclesiastical History* 21.1 (1970), p. 62.

68.  *Inst.* 2.12.3.

69.  Sermon on Luke 2:50–52 (*CO* 46, pp. 487–488), cited in Wendel, *Calvin*, p. 217.

Calvin's earliest writing on the doctrine of Christ, chapter 2 section 12 of the 1536 edition of the *Institutes*, already stakes out this position on the genuine humanity of Christ, a humanity which characterizes not only Christ's earthly life but his heavenly session as well. No doubt he does this in full knowledge of the medieval disputes over the nature of Christ's continuing humanity. Gabriel Biel had famously written that 'Christ reigns at the right hand of the Almighty Father not as pure man (*homo purus*) but as God-man (*deus homo*)'. This led Biel to insist upon the necessity of Mary's intercession since she, unlike Christ, is present in heaven as one who shares our 'own simple nature'.[70] A lack of emphasis on Christ's humanity had in this way contributed significantly to the quest for other mediators, a development Calvin wholeheartedly deplored. The biblical insistence that Christ is our faithful high priest, one who is able both to sympathize and to help us in our weakness (Heb. 4:15–16; 2:17–18), had become obscured by the suggestion that the union of divine and human natures in Christ made his human nature different to ours.

Yet didn't Scripture itself testify to at least one critical difference between Christ's humanity and ours? He was made like us in every way, 'yet without sin' (Heb. 4:15; Rom. 8:3–4). If sin is part of the inheritance we all receive from Adam, can Christ be without sin and still share our humanity in any meaningful way? The sinlessness of Christ, particularly when tied to the absence of a human biological father in his case, raised challenging questions. Menno and others had abandoned any suggestion that Christ shared *our* human nature on precisely this ground. In response, Calvin was emphatic:

> For we make Christ free of all stain not just because he was begotten of his mother without copulation with man, but because he was sanctified by the Spirit that the generation might be pure and undefiled as would have been true before Adam's fall. And this remains for us an established fact: whenever Scripture calls our attention to the purity of Christ, it is to be understood of his true human nature, for it would have been superfluous to say that God is pure.[71]

This appeal to the work of the Spirit should not be read as indicating a Spirit-Christology in the classic sense. Calvin was not proposing that Jesus

---

70. G. Biel, *Sermones de Festivitatibus B. V. M.*, sermo 25 A, cited in Oberman, 'Extra', p. 58. Biel also spoke of greater hope of our own resurrection arising from 'the Resurrection of the Virgin who possessed a purely human nature, not hypostatically united with the divine' (sermo 18I, cited in Oberman, 'Extra', p. 58).

71. *Inst.* 2.13.4.

Christ was simply a man animated by the Holy Spirit.[72] Nor does he anticipate later, more carefully nuanced Spirit-Christologies. He does not, for instance, suggest the Spirit's involvement in the incarnation reflects an eternal mediation of divine personhood. The Spirit does not constitute the person of the Son from eternity. Calvin insists that the Son's *essence* is 'self-existent (*ex se ipso esse*)' while his *person* 'exists from the Father (*esse ex Patre*)'.[73] However, it has often been noted that Calvin's presentation of the person and work of Christ makes constant reference to the Spirit.[74] Once again this is an indication of Calvin's determination to discipline his Christological reflection by the explicit teaching of Scripture. The Bible itself testifies that Jesus' miraculous birth was the result of a secret working of the Spirit (*per arcanam Spiritus operationem*) in Mary's womb.[75] He is anointed by the Spirit at his baptism and gives the Spirit without measure.[76] The ascended Christ 'pours out' the Spirit on the gathered disciples in fulfilment of the Father's promise.[77] In this passage from the *Institutes*, Calvin is similarly focused on the economy rather than on eternity. The sinlessness of Christ's genuine humanity was secured by the sanctifying work of the Spirit. It is not the result of a divine reluctance to be fully human, nor does it suggest his humanity was essentially different from ours. It is by the Spirit that the Son is able to share our humanity in the fullest sense and yet without sin.

It is this concern to ensure the Christ's humanity is not compromised that leads Calvin to define more carefully the way the divine attributes are predicated of Christ. The Lutheran use of the ancient concept of a 'communication of the attributes [*communicatio idiomatum*]' risked precisely the kind of compromise Calvin was seeking to avoid.[78] How could Christ's human nature be spoken of as ubiquitous, for example, without ceasing to be a genuine

---

72. E. D. Willis, *Calvin's Catholic Christology: The Function of the So-Called Extra Calvinisticum in Calvin's Theology* (Leiden: Brill, 1966), pp. 82–83.

73. *Inst.* 1.13.25.

74. W. Krusche, *Das Wirken des Heiligen Geistes nach Calvin* (Göttingen: Vandenhoeck & Ruprecht, 1957), p. 151; Willis, *Extra Calvinisticum*, p. 82.

75. Luke 1:35; Matt. 1:18. The expression 'secret working of the Spirit' is Calvin's, from the same section of the *Institutes* (2.13.4).

76. Mk 1:10; John 3:34.

77. Acts 2:33.

78. The concept, if not the terminology, can be found in the work of Tertullian, Eustathius of Antioch, Athanasius, Gregory of Nyssa and Cyril of Alexandria amongst others. See A. Grillmeier, *Christ in the Christian Tradition*, vol. 1, *From the Apostolic Age to Chalcedon (451)*, trans. J. Bowden (Atlanta: John Knox, 1965), pp. 122, 297, 313, 376, 452.

participation in our humanity? The transfer of attributes from one nature to another in this way is fraught with difficulty. After all, Calvin wanted to avoid the heresy of Eutyches as well as that of Nestorius.[79]

Calvin does not reject the idea of a communication of attributes but adds two very important qualifications. The first is to identify this as a biblical 'figure of speech [*tropus*]':

> Thus, also, the Scriptures speak of Christ: they sometimes attribute to him what must be referred solely to his humanity, sometimes what belongs uniquely to his divinity; and sometimes what embraces both natures but fits neither alone. And they so earnestly express this union of the two natures that is in Christ as sometimes to interchange them. This figure of speech is called by the ancient writers 'the communicating of properties'.[80]

According to Calvin, this is a way of speaking which is intended to underline the union of the two natures in Christ rather than suggest a transformation of either nature. Bruce McCormack has criticized Calvin at precisely this point: 'What Calvin has done is to reduce the *communicatio* to a mere figure of speech . . . Missing in this account is any sense that the exchange of properties on a verbal level is only possible (and necessary!) because it has already occurred on the level of reality.'[81] But can this criticism really be sustained? After all, a page later in the *Institutes* Calvin concludes:

> But the communicating of characteristics or properties consists in what Paul says: 'God purchased the church with his blood', and 'the Lord of glory of crucified'. John says the same: 'The Word of life was handled'. Surely God does not have blood, does not suffer, cannot be touched with hands. But since Christ, who was true God and true man, was crucified and shed his blood for us, the things that he carried out in his human nature are transferred improperly, although not without reason [*improprie, licet non sine ratione, transferuntur*], to his divinity . . . because the selfsame one was both God and man, for the sake of the union of both natures he gave to the one what belonged to the other [*alteri dabat, quod erat alterius*].[82]

---

79. Calvin explicitly rejects both in *Inst.* 2.14.4.

80. *Inst.* 2.14.1.

81. B. L. McCormack, 'For Us and Our Salvation: Incarnation and Atonement in the Reformed Tradition', *Studies in Reformed Theology and History* 1.2 (1993), pp. 8–9.

82. *Inst.* 2.14.2. It is noteworthy that the examples Calvin chooses at this point are all examples of the attribution of a human attribute to the divine and not the other way around.

In what sense is this transfer 'improper'? Is this really nothing more than an inexact 'hermeneutical device', a biblical 'accommodation to our capacity' (to use one of Calvin's favourite expressions), with no clear grounding in what has actually happened?[83] Calvin does, after all, believe that the language is used 'not without reason'. However, in keeping with Calvin's more general theological temperament, he holds back from extensive speculation about the relation of the natures that might take him beyond the testimony of Scripture. There are genuine boundaries between what we may properly affirm and what has not been revealed to us. As Stephen Edmondson summarizes, 'The *communicatio idiomata*, in other words, is a means to express Christ's unity, not to explain it'.[84] Yet this is only part of the reason for Calvin's suggestion of a certain impropriety.

Calvin's second qualification to the use of the *communicatio idiomatum*, though only hinted at in the texts which touch upon the subject, does take us further. The transfer effected is not, strictly speaking, an application of the attributes of one nature to the other; rather it involves applying the attributes of either nature to the one Person. It is a *communicatio in concreto* not a *communicatio in abstracto*, an indirect exchange rather than a direct one.[85] If it were otherwise, the integrity of each nature would indeed be compromised. This, of course, is precisely Calvin's complaint about the Lutheran use of the concept to argue for the ubiquity of Christ's body and blood. The result of such a move was to transform Christ's humanity into something other than *our* humanity. In the preface to his 1563 commentary on Jeremiah, Calvin warned, 'Both Christ himself and His Apostles clearly show that the immensity of God does not belong to the flesh; a personal union is what they teach; and no one, except *Eutyches*, has hitherto taught, that the two natures became so blended, that when Christ became man, the attributes of Deity were communicated to his human nature'.[86]

Calvin was thoroughly and explicitly committed to the Chalcedonian

83. F. L. Battles, 'God was Accommodating Himself to Human Capacity', *Interpretation* 31 (1977), pp. 19–38.

84. Edmondson, *Christology*, p. 216. Wendel writes of Calvin's 'much hesitation' in discussing the communication of the idioms: Wendel, *Calvin*, p. 222.

85. Oberman, 'The "Extra" Dimension', p. 57. '[I]n the communication of properties, an attribute of one nature is affirmed of a subject or person, named indicated or denominated by his other nature': J. N. Tylenda, 'Calvin's Understanding of the Communication of Properties', *WTJ* 38.1 (1975), p. 61. Tylenda draws attention to the same idea in John Damascene and Leo the Great (p. 60).

86. J. Calvin, *Commentaries on the prophet Jeremiah and the Lamentations*, trans. J. Owen (repr. Grand Rapids: Eerdmans, 1950), xviii (*CO* 20, p. 73).

Definition with its affirmation of 'one and the same Christ, Son, Lord, Only-begotten recognized in two natures, without confusion, without change, without division, without separation, the distinction of natures being in no way annulled by the union, but rather the characteristics of each nature being preserved and coming together to form one person and subsistence'.[87] Here he recognized the teaching of Scripture.[88] As a consequence, Calvin was determined that in all his debates on the topic, in the *Institutes* and in his commentaries, nothing should be allowed to compromise the genuine and continuing humanity of Christ.

### The full, unqualified and unconstrained deity of the Mediator

Yet Scripture and Chalcedon bound him just as clearly to an unambiguous and unqualified affirmation of Christ's divinity: 'at once complete in Godhead and complete in manhood, truly God and truly man, consisting also of a reasonable soul and body; of one substance with the Father as regards his Godhead, and at the same time of one substance with us as regards his manhood'.[89] Calvin took the *homoousion* seriously. He would not countenance any suggestion of a distinction in essence between the Father and the Son, just as he would not countenance any distinction between Christ's humanity and ours.[90]

As we have seen, Calvin was challenged on just this issue by Pierre Caroli in 1537. He was accused of being Arian; of suggesting that the Son is subordinate to the Father in essence. Calvin reflected on the issues involved in the dispute in correspondence with Simon Grynee, Rector of the Academy in Basle. He affirmed both the unqualified divinity of the Son and an eternal order of relation between the Son and the Father.

> Certainly, if the distinction between the Father and the Word be attentively
> considered, we shall say that the one is from the other. If, however, the essential

---

87. Calvin describes the theological decisions of the Council as containing 'nothing but the pure and genuine exposition of Scripture' (*Inst.* 4.9.8) and carefully echoes the language of the Definition (*Inst.* 2.14.1).

88. *Inst.* 4.17.30.

89. *The Creeds of Christendom*, ed. P. Schaff; rev. D. S. Schaff (3 vols; Grand Rapids: Baker, 1983), p. 62.

90. More extensive reflection on Calvin's trinitarian thinking can be found in Robert Doyle's contribution to this volume.

quality of the Word be considered, in so far as He is one God with the Father, whatever is said concerning God may be also applied to Him, the second person in the glorious Trinity . . . Nothing, indeed could have been set forth more plainly than the statement in our Confession, that Christ is that eternal Word begotten of the Father before all time.[91]

A similar affirmation is found at the other end of his teaching career, in his reply to Biandrata from 1557: 'In this way the unity of essence is retained and the order of relationship is set forth; this, however, does not take anything away from the divinity of the Son or of the Spirit'.[92] It is clear that Calvin sees no contradiction between an eternal unity which secures Christ's full and unqualified divinity and an eternal relational order within the Trinity which distinguishes the person of the Son from the person of the Father and of the Spirit. Yet this can only be the case when these two truths are carefully correlated:

> Indeed, although the eternity of the Father is also the eternity of the Son and the Spirit, since God could never exist apart from his wisdom and power, and we must not seek in eternity a *before* or an *after*, nevertheless the observance of an order is not meaningless or superfluous, when the Father is thought of as first, then from him the Son, and finally from both the Spirit.[93]

Calvin goes on to endorse Augustine's judgment in his comment on Psalm 110: 'Christ with respect to himself is called God; with respect to the Father, Son', and then to insist 'the peculiar qualities in the persons carry an order within them'.[94] This gives a depth to Calvin's affirmation of Christ's unqualified divinity which is once again reminiscent of the doctrinal settlements of Nicaea and Chalcedon. In post-Rahnerian terms, he is trinitarian and not simply monotheistic.

It is in this light that Calvin's insistence upon the self-existence of the Son in

---

91. J. Calvin, 'Letter 15 — To Simon Grynee' (May 1537), in *Letters of John Calvin*, trans. D. Constable, ed. J. Bonnet (Edinburgh: Thomas Constable, 1855), pp. 31–32 [Epistle 64 in *CO*, 10/2].

92. *CO* 9, p. 325 (Tylenda, 'Warning', p. 55); compare *Inst.* 1.13.20. Richard Muller boldly observes in Calvin 'a subordination in order described by the generation of the Son and by the procession of the Spirit but no subordination relating to divinity or essence': Muller, *Christ*, p. 30.

93. *Inst.* 1.13.18.

94. *Inst.* 1.13.19, 20.

terms of his essence should be understood, an affirmation at the heart of his debate with Caroli in 1537 and with Gentilis in 1558. His concern in speaking like this was undoubtedly to deny that the Father in any sense confers deity upon the Son, since this would entail a difference at the critical point: the Son would not be God in the same way the Father is. No, Calvin insists: just as the Father is self-existent in terms of his essence, so is the Son. The relational order, in which the Son is begotten of the Father and not vice versa, operates at the level of the Persons rather than the essence.

> Therefore we say that deity in an absolute sense exists of itself; whence likewise we confess that the Son since he is God, exists of himself, but not in respect of his Person; indeed, since he is the Son, we say that he exists from the Father. Thus his essence is without beginning; while the beginning of his person is God himself.[95]

All of this explains why Calvin's preferred designation for Christ is one which echoes 1 Timothy 3:16 – 'God has been manifested in the flesh (*deus in carne manifestatus*)'.[96] All that is true of God is true of him. His pre-existence is affirmed in the face of Servetus' denial. He was manifested at a certain time in human history, but we should not confuse manifestation with origination. 'The Word existed long before . . . the power of the Word emerged and stood forth'.[97] His intimate engagement with the history of Israel has a particular emphasis. In the first place, as we have noted, Calvin's treatment of the person and work of Christ in the *Institutes* immediately follows his treatment of the redemptive historical framework which unites the Old and New Testaments. More than that, Calvin explicitly speaks of the activity of Christ in the Old Testament. Figures such as 'the angel of the Lord' indicate that 'even though the time of humbling had not yet arrived, that eternal Word nevertheless set forth a figure of the office to which he had been destined'.[98]

So what actually happened at the point of the incarnation, and what impact does this have on Christ's divine nature? After all, the New Testament itself testifies to some kind of 'emptying' (Phil. 2:7). Calvin is insistent that the Son's

---

95. *Inst.* 1.13.25.

96. *Inst.* 1.13.11. McCormack calls this 'the heartbeat of Calvin's thought': McCormack, 'Incarnation', p. 7.

97. *Inst.* 1.13.8. In his commentary on John 1:10 Calvin insists 'Christ was never so absent from the world that men ought not to have been awakened by His rays and to have looked up to Him': *CNTC* 4, pp. 15–16.

98. *Inst.* 1.13.10.

divinity has not been diminished in any way. As he comments on John 1:14 he remarks,

> Again, since he distinctly attributes the name of the Word to the man Christ, it
> follows that when He became man Christ did not cease to be what He was before
> and that nothing was changed in that eternal essence of God which assumed flesh.
> In short, the Son of God began to be man in such a way that He is still that eternal
> Word who had no temporal beginning.[99]

The incarnation involves an addition, not a subtraction: the Word takes on a human nature but remains no less divine. At this point Calvin's argument follows that of the orthodoxy which led to the Chalcedonian Definition. Paul Helm's summary is apposite: 'if the Incarnation is truly the Incarnation of the Son of God, then it must preserve the divinity of the Son of God unaltered or unimpaired. For otherwise it would not be a true incarnation of the Son.'[100] In Philippians 2, Calvin argues, Paul is not so much teaching 'what Christ was' but 'how he conducted himself': 'He took the image of servant, and content with such lowness, allowed his divinity to be hidden by a veil of flesh'.[101] Calvin was apparently untroubled by how Docetic this sounds, most likely because this comment in the *Institutes* is in fact part of his argument against the denial of Christ's genuine humanity by Marcion and Mani. A reading of Philippians 2 which suggested the incarnation was merely formal and external, or else an elaborate illusion, was an abusive reading. Calvin's commentary on Philippians 2 makes his meaning plain:

> Christ, indeed, could not renounce His divinity, but He kept it concealed for a time,
> that under the weakness of the flesh it might not be seen. Hence He laid aside His
> glory in the view of men, not by lessening, but by concealing [*supprimendo*] it.[102]

The divine nature of Christ retains all that is proper to it, uncompromised by its union with our humanity. The *kenosis* consists in the taking of a genuine

---

99.  *CNTC* 4, pp. 20–21 (on John 1:14).

100. P. Helm, *John Calvin's Ideas* (Oxford: Oxford University Press, 2004), p. 62. Later
     (p. 64): 'Nothing could happen to make the humanity of Jesus Christ other than
     true humanity or his deity other than true deity.' Similar observations are made by
     McCormack, 'Incarnation', p. 7.

101. *Inst.* 2.13.2.

102. *CNTC* 11, p. 248 (on Phil. 2:7).

humanity, not in the reducing Christ's genuine divinity: 'even though he emptied himself, he lost not his glory with the Father which was hidden to the world'.[103]

The same point is being made in Calvin's few enigmatic references to the divine nature of Christ 'resting', most of which refer to the exercise of omniscience.[104] Representative is Calvin's comment on Matthew 24:36, 'But concerning that day and hour no one knows, not even the angels of heaven, nor the Son, but the Father only':

> As to the first objection, that nothing is unknown to God, the answer is easy. We know that the two natures in Christ were so conformed in one Person that each retained what was proper to it: in particular the Divinity was silent [*praesertim vero quievit divinitas*] and made no assertion of itself whenever it was the business of the human nature to act alone in its own terms in fulfilment of the office of Mediator. So there was nothing absurd for Christ, who knew everything, to be ignorant of something as far as man could understand. Otherwise He could not have met grief and anxiety, or have been like us.[105]

There is no suggestion that at moments such as this the divine nature of Christ is altered in any way. Christ is no less divine than at other times. However, the person of Christ has both a divine and a human nature, and it is in the union of both that his participation in what we suffer is possible. God may well be omniscient, but as the God-man Christ chooses not to know all things. God as God cannot die, but as the God-man Christ the Mediator embraces death for us. This is part of what it means for the Son to humble himself and take the form of a servant. Another similar passage, John 12:27 – 'Now is my soul troubled . . .' – provided Calvin with the opportunity to comment on this aspect more fully:

> Nor was it absurd that the Son of God should be troubled like this. For His divinity was hidden [*Divinitas enim occulta*], did not put forth its power [*neque vim suam exserens*] and, in a sense, rested [*quodammodo quievit*], that an opportunity might be given for making expiation. But Christ put on not only our flesh but also human feelings. It is true that in Him these feelings were voluntary. For He feared, not because He was

---

103. *Inst.* 1.13.26.
104. I am indebted to the Revd Geoff Broughton for drawing my attention to this aspect of Calvin's teaching on Christ.
105. *CNTC* 3, p. 99 (on Matt. 24:36); *CO* 45, p. 672.

forced to, but because of His own accord He had subjected Himself to fear. Yet we must believe that it was not in pretence but in truth that He feared.[106]

Once again, it is not that the Son's divinity disappears but rather that this aspect of his mediatorial work gives a special prominence to his genuine humanity: real anguish, real suffering and a real death which expiates sin.[107] Nevertheless, it is difficult to reconcile Calvin's very strong distinction between Christ's humanity and divinity at these points with a full-orbed understanding of the hypostatic union. The language Calvin uses, though heavily qualified ('*in a sense* rested'), raises questions about the inseparability of the natures in Christ. These questions are perhaps intensified by one final aspect of Calvin's account of Christ.

Just as Christ's genuine humanity must not be compromised by what we say about the incarnation, so too his full and unqualified divinity. This theological commitment leads Calvin to insist that Christ's divinity is not constrained by its union with humanity in Christ's person. The Son never ceases to be the one who 'upholds the universe by the word of his power' (Heb. 1:3). What would come to be known as the *extra Calvinisticum* (a term first used by those who opposed the idea in the seventeenth century) is first expressed as Calvin outlines the nature of Christ's true humanity:

> For even if the Word in his immeasurable essence united with the nature of man
> into one person, we do not imagine that he was confined therein. Here is something
> marvellous: the Son of God descended from heaven in such a way that, without
> leaving heaven, he willed to be born in the virgin's womb, to go about the earth, and
> to hang upon the cross; yet he continuously filled the world even as he had done from
> the beginning![108]

---

106.  *CNTC* 5, p. 39 (on John 12:27).

107.  Fred Graham has misrepresented Calvin's thought at this point by suggesting
      'Calvin saw God as withdrawn from man at man's worst moments': W. F.
      Graham, *The Constructive Revolutionary: John Calvin and His Socio-Economic Impact*
      (Richmond, VA: John Knox, 1971), p. 182. At points Graham's portrayal of
      Calvin's theology more generally is extraordinarily unsympathetic and tantamount
      to a caricature.

108.  *Inst.* 2.13.4. Similar ideas emerge amidst Calvin's rejection of the Lutheran
      argument for the real presence of Christ in the Lord's Supper: the body of Christ
      lies hidden under the form of the bread in the Supper by virtue of God's promise
      and the ubiquity of Christ's body (*Inst.* 4.17.30).

The basic idea is not original to Calvin. It can be found in Athanasius, Augustine, Thomas Aquinas and others.[109] What is more, it is not developed at any length in the *Institutes* or elsewhere by Calvin himself, though it will form an important part of the exchanges between Reformed and Lutheran thinkers over the sacraments in the next two generations. What is evident from the context here in the *Institutes* is that Calvin wants to insist both that the incarnation truly 'expresses the divine essence without exhaustively revealing it' and that the Son's divinity can be united to a genuinely human nature without distorting it.[110] As one thorough study of the concept puts it, the distinctive mark Calvin makes on Christology at this point is that

> he keeps in the foreground the assertion that the Incarnation was not the Eternal Son's abdication of his universal empire but the reassertion of that empire over rebellious creation. This continuity of gracious order over creaturely attempts at discontinuity depends on the identity of the Redeeming Mediator in the flesh with the Mediator who is the Eternal Son of God by whom, and with whose Spirit, all things were created according to the Father's will.[111]

Even during Calvin's lifetime, opponents of this way of speaking about the divine nature united to humanity in Christ sensed the danger of Nestorianism, in which the two natures are separated to the point of division. Was it not possible under this rubric to speak too boldly about 'the Word without flesh [*Logos asarkos*]'? And yet isn't some such concept inevitable if we are not to fall into the opposite danger of Eutycheanism, where the two natures are so blended that neither retains what is proper to it? Neither God nor his human creation is diminished by the incarnation.

## Unplundered riches in Calvin's Christology

Calvin's Christology is worth renewed consideration. Not only are the sources more extensive than is usually recognized, but a number of his insights can

---

109. Willis, *Extra Calvinisticum*, pp. 34–60. A brief but helpful treatment of the idea and the debate between Reformed and Lutheran thinkers surrounding it can be found in T. F. Torrance, *Incarnation: The Person and Life of Christ*, ed. R. T. Walker (Milton Keynes: Paternoster, 2008), pp. 216–221.

110. Helm, *Ideas*, p. 64.

111. Willis, *Extra Calvinisticum*, pp. 99–100.

challenge truncated accounts produced in our own very different context. He is certainly not beyond challenge. Bruce McCormack is right to ask whether, for all his clear determination to affirm the contours of the Chalcedonian Definition, his concern to preserve the integrity of each nature threatens to compromise their union. More needed to be said at this point, especially in the light of the tantalizingly brief mention of the so-called *extra Calvinisticum*.[112] Yet Calvin's determination to avoid a one-sidedness in his presentation of Christ is salutary: 'those who despoil Christ of either his divinity or his humanity diminish his majesty and glory or obscure his goodness'.[113] Contemporary accounts of the Christology do well to follow Calvin's lead at this point.

At a time when exclusive claims about Jesus are seen as impediments to inter-faith dialogue or incentives to religious violence, the profound uniqueness of the incarnate Son, 'God manifested in the flesh', resists all human attempts to marginalize him. Similarly, our preoccupation with ourselves, which is as much a problem in theology as elsewhere – witness the avalanche of books on how *we* do theology – is challenged by Calvin's robust reminder that at the centre of God's purposes for the entire creation stands Jesus Christ.

However, perhaps it is Calvin's most enduring contribution to Christology which might prove to be the most effective counter both to heavily metaphysical accounts of Christ's person and the all-too-persistent tendency to paint Christ in our own image. Calvin's use of the biblical category of 'Mediator' as an organizing principle, and the way he develops this in terms of the threefold office of prophet, priest and king enables him to deeply integrate his presentation of the person of Christ and of the work of Christ. It also gives Christology a context in the unfolding drama of redemption. Calvin does not so much abandon a 'natures Christology' in favour of an 'office Christology'.[114] After all, as we have seen, Calvin is certainly not averse to speaking about the divine and human natures of Christ. However, he refuses to treat Christ in abstract. The object of our consideration in Christological discussion is the eternal Son, whom we always know as our Redeemer. It is this

---

112. McCormack, 'Incarnation', pp. 8–9. See also Helm, *Ideas*, pp. 63–67. Note the caution implied in Karl Barth's observation: 'Self-evidently Calvin did at times make it possible for others to exaggerate some aspect of his teaching': Barth, *Calvin*, p. 311.

113. *Inst.* 2.12.3.

114. Heiko Oberman, it must be admitted, spoke only of a 'shift of accent' and did suggest a convergence towards a 'Mediator-theology': Oberman, 'Extra', p. 60.

perspective which embraces Christological reflection, not just as a necessity, but as an opportunity to rejoice.

> outside of Christ there is nothing worth knowing, and all who by faith perceive what he is like have grasped the whole immensity of heavenly benefits.[115]

---

115. *Inst.* 2.15.2.

# 6. JOHN CALVIN AND PETITIONING GOD

*Oliver D. Crisp*

John Calvin's discussion of prayer in the final edition of his *Institutes* is second in length only to the chapter on faith. It is situated immediately prior to his discussion of divine election in Book Three. And in it, he has much to say that is of value in contemporary discussion of the theology of prayer. Calvin deals with a range of issues clustered around prayer as petition and prayer as thanksgiving, and ends up with a careful exposition of the Lord's Prayer as a pattern for the Christian life – an earlier version of which can be traced right back to the first edition of the *Institutes* in 1536. In this chapter I will not attempt to expound Calvin's doctrine of prayer as a whole, or as it developed in the different editions of the *Institutes*. Instead, I will focus on one besetting problem for petitionary prayer or impetration (I shall use the two terms interchangeably). This has to do with whether or not such prayer is pointless or redundant, given the nature and purposes of God. At first glance, such a concern may seem rather more narrowly philosophical than the sort of issues Calvin is engaged with in the *Institutes*, his biblical commentaries, or even his controversial works. However, this issue raises important pastoral and practical concerns for a theology of the Christian life. What is more, the particular form Calvin's doctrine takes make the concern about the apparent redundancy of impetration particularly pressing. For these reasons, the resources Calvin's doctrine can bring to bear on this particular problem with what we might call the metaphysics of impetration actually serve the sort of practical purpose with which Calvin's theology is deeply concerned.[1]

The argument falls into three parts. In the first, I situate the Calvinian doctrine within a broader account of the doctrine of God.[2] I then consider what a Calvinian notion of impetration amounts to. In the course of this scene-setting section, I introduce the pointlessness problem. The second section examines the contribution Calvin makes to the resolution of this problem, as part of his doctrine of prayer. The third section offers a defence of a Calvinian doctrine of impetration against the pointlessness problem.

## Three problems for impetration

### Situating the Calvinian doctrine

If God is essentially omniscient, he knows all that will come to pass. (*How* he knows all that will come to pass was not a problem Calvin seems particularly concerned with.) To co-opt the language of scholastic theology for a moment, via his natural knowledge God knows all that is necessary and possible in all possible worlds. And via his free knowledge, he knows all that will happen in this world, the world that obtains as a consequence of God's creative fiat.[3]

---

1. Charles Partee observes that Calvin treats prayer as a given rather than a problematic. 'Nevertheless, if Calvin is not regarded as developing a *complete* doctrine of prayer, his teaching on the subject seems to constitute a distinctive view which may be called, not improperly, a doctrine': C. Partee, 'Prayer as the Practice of Predestination', in W. H. Neusner (ed.), *Calvinus Servus Christi* (Budapest: Presseabteilung des Raday Kollegiums, 1988), p. 246. I will be treating impetration as a problem, using Calvin's doctrine to see whether it has the resources to overcome the apparent pointlessness of petitioning God. This is not improper because, as I shall argue, Calvin presents a distinctive doctrinal contribution to a theology of prayer that has an important bearing on the question of the pointlessness of impetration.
2. In this chapter I use the term 'Calvinian' to designate any view that takes up the particular concerns of Calvin himself. This seems preferable to 'Calvinist', which is a broader term, associated with the theological tradition that looks to Calvin as its fountainhead. In this chapter I am not primarily concerned with that tradition, but with the ideas of Calvin himself and how they might be put to use in a theology of prayer.
3. For a very clear exposition of the distinction between divine natural and free

Through similar conceptual distinctions, school theologians of the medieval and post-Reformation period sought to express the exhaustive nature of divine knowledge. Thus, an omniscient God will know what we desire before we pray, and will know what is best for us in every possible circumstance, all things considered. In which case, and from the point of view of a theology of impetration, God knows the content of a given petition directed to God in prayer in advance of its being uttered by the petitioner (Ps. 139:4).[4] What is more, whether or not granting that petition is a good idea all things considered is known prior to any petition we make (Prov. 16:33; Isa. 46:10; Jer. 29:11; Jas 1:17). God knows what we want and what we need, and his knowledge of these things is not affected one whit by our petition.

Still, knowing what a person desires and what is best for that person, all things considered, is not the same as having the power to bring about what is best for that person all things considered. So we need to add essential divine omnipotence to essential divine omniscience.[5] Calvin does not really offer a

Footnote 3 (*cont.*)

  knowledge, as well as the concept of 'middle knowledge' first articulated by the sixteenth-century Spanish Jesuit divine Luis de Molina, see T. P. Flint, *Divine Providence* (Ithaca: Cornell University Press, 1991), ch. 1. I shall not delve into divine middle knowledge here, since it is a development that postdates Calvin.

4. In his commentary on Ps. 139:4 Calvin allows two possible meanings of the verse: God knows what we are about to say before we say it; or God knows our secret intentions even if we try to keep them from him. 'Either rendering amounts to the same thing', says Calvin; 'it is of no consequence which we adopt.' For, says Calvin, on both renderings of the verse the net result is the same: God knows the thoughts of our hearts as intimately as we do. But this is not strictly true. If God knows our secret intentions logically or temporally *prior* to our knowing them, then he knows my thoughts before I know them. But if he knows our secret intentions despite our trying to hide them from him, this does not imply that God knows such intentions in advance of, or prior to, our knowing them. So the first rendering of the verse has an important consequence for divine knowledge that the latter rendering does not. See Calvin, *Commentary on the Book of Psalms, Vol. V*, trans. James Anderson (Edinburgh: Calvin Translation Society, 1845), p. 209.

5. In fact, as we shall see, in light of his doctrine of divine providence, it seems that Calvin, like a number of other Augustinian theologians, maintains that God's knowledge is causal. It brings about what is the case according to his divine power. This is one way in which a traditional doctrine of divine simplicity bears upon this

philosophical definition of divine power, preferring instead to refer to God's 'ceaseless activity' whereby he brings about all he ordains.[6] But he does speak of divine omnipotence as being that 'power ample enough to do good' that exists 'in him in whose possession are heaven and earth'.[7] Interestingly, this is commensurate with a much weaker account of divine power than is found in some contemporary analytic philosophical discussions of omnipotence.[8] But it is consistent with the idea that God has the power to bring about what we desire and what is best for us all things considered, as well as knowledge of what we desire and what is best for us all things considered, which is sufficient for present purposes.

Now, petitioning a being who has the knowledge and power requisite to bring about what is best for us all things considered may not be pointless. Such a being may or may not have the motivation to do what is best for us all things considered. So we need to add essential benevolence to the list of divine attributes under consideration. If God is essentially benevolent as well as omniscient and omnipotent, then he desires the best for us, and will only

---

particular aspect of the divine nature. Each of God's attributes implies all the others, on the classical, traditional account of divine simplicity. See *Inst.* 1.13.2. There Calvin says 'the essence of God is simple and undivided'.

6. *Inst.* 1.16.3.

7. Ibid. A related issue here has to do with the medieval distinction between the absolute and ordained power of God, which Calvin makes reference to in a number of places in the *Institutes* and his commentaries. Some Calvin commentators, such as David Steinmetz, think Calvin denies this distinction – see, e.g., D. C. Steinmetz, 'Calvin and the Absolute Power of God', in *Calvin in Context* (Oxford: Oxford University Press, 1995), pp. 40–52. But recently Paul Helm has persuasively argued that Calvin endorses this distinction. See P. Helm, *John Calvin's Ideas* (Oxford: Oxford University Press, 2004), ch. 11.

8. What Calvin actually says on the matter in the *Institutes* seems, on the face of it, to be consistent with something like Peter Geach's account of divine power in terms of God being 'almighty' rather than 'omnipotent'. See P. Geach, *Providence and Evil* (Cambridge: Cambridge University Press, 1977), pp. 3–28. There has been considerable dispute about the definition of omnipotence in recent analytic philosophy. But usually the discussion turns on how to construe the idea that God can do, bring about, or otherwise actualize all that is logically possible – whether states of affairs, actions, events, or whatever. Calvin is not interested in this sort of definition of omnipotence. His is the concrete language of piety rather than the abstract problems faced by philosophical reflection on this topic.

bring about what is best for us, all things considered.[9] (Bringing about the best for us all things considered is not inconsistent with permitting certain evils to obtain, such that we suffer. Some measure of suffering might be for the best, all things considered – compare Luke 22:42.) Indeed, if we do petition God then doubtless he will only bring about our petition if it is in accord with what he already knows is best for us, all things considered. However, presumably God will bring about what is best for us regardless of our petition – he is not free to act contrary to his essentially benevolent nature in this regard. But then it looks as if God will bring about what he wills to bring about regardless of my prayer (Job 1:21; Jon. 4).[10] And what he wills to bring about is, given the foregoing, the best for his creatures, all things considered.[11]

---

9.  At one point, as he discusses the necessity of prayer, Calvin remarks that by praying 'we invoke the presence both of his providence, through which he watches over and guards our affairs, and of his power, through which he sustains us . . . and of his goodness, through which he receives us . . . in short, it is by prayer that we call him to reveal himself as wholly present to us . . . We . . . rest fully in the thought that none of our ills is hid from him who, we are convinced, has both the will and the power to take the best care of us': *Inst.* 3.20.2. Note in this passage the appeal to divine providence – which, for Calvin, includes divine knowledge of all that comes to pass – divine power, and divine benevolence.

10. It might be argued that this is a good reason for preferring non-essential divine benevolence. If God is not essentially benevolent but must be impetrated to act in a benevolent way, this might be a motivation for prayer. But I presume that only an essentially benevolent deity is trustworthy and perfect. A non-essentially benevolent God hardly comports with Calvin's doctrine. See, for example, *Inst.* 2.16.3.

11. 'The best for his creatures all things considered' does not entail that this is the best of all possible worlds (which is a term that becomes important after Calvin, with the theodicy of Leibniz). I am using this phrase as shorthand for 'the best that God has in mind for us consistent with divine benevolence'. It may be that there are other logically possible maximal states of affairs which have a different distribution of good and evil and which have a total objective moral value equal to, or commensurate with, the world that does obtain (i.e. with this world). And it may be that there are numerous possible worlds that have an objective moral value beyond some particular threshold, which makes such worlds one of a set of 'best possible' or 'most valuable'. It may also be that there are worlds whose objective moral value is incommensurable with one another, such that we cannot assess which world, if any, is a best possible world. There may be other metaphysically possible options in

But is that quite right? Provided God is essentially omniscient, omnipotent and benevolent – three essentials of Christian theism endorsed by Calvin – impetrating God may seem problematic in circumstances where what the petitioner asks for is not actually what is the best for her all things considered.[12] But commitment to these three components of traditional, classical theism does not *entail* the pointlessness of impetration. For it seems conceivable that there are situations in which God could bring about one of two or more circumstances each of which has an equal objective moral value. He knows what will obtain in each circumstance. He has the power to bring about each circumstance. And the bringing about of each circumstance would be consistent with his essential benevolence. But perhaps God has ordained that a believer impetrates him to bring about one, and only one, of the possible outcomes in question. And perhaps God desires that his creatures express their desires to him in prayer and that, other things being equal, where there is a circumstance in which a human creature impetrates God for one amongst several possible outcomes all of which have an equal objective moral value, God will grant the petition of his creature. Then, given such a state of affairs, it may be that the fact that a human creature impetrates God for one, and only one, of the situations in question gives God reason to bring about that state of affairs over the other, equally objectively moral states of affairs he could have brought about.

Yet this is itself not unproblematic. God ordains and brings about this world. He decides which of the myriad possible worlds that might obtain will obtain. Where there are two possible states of affairs that could obtain, both of which have the same objective moral value, where there are no other overriding moral or metaphysical reasons for bringing about one or other of these states of affairs, why would God choose one over the other? The idea here is that God has no good reason to strongly actualize one over the other state of affairs. Both would suit his purposes, such that there is a sort of axiological stand-off: the value of either state of affairs is equivalent in the divine economy, all things considered. And God has no overriding reason to strongly actualize one or other of the two states of affairs before his mind's eye, as it

the neighbourhood. All we need here is the notion that God's best for his creatures in this world, all things considered, has the right objective moral value to be consistent with his essential benevolence, whether or not he could have brought about other worlds with an equal or commensurate objective moral value.

12. An example: St Paul prays three times that God will remove his 'thorn in the flesh'. But God does not. Eventually, Paul realizes God refrains from granting this petition because it is for the best, all things considered (see 2 Cor. 12:7–10).

were. Might human impetration provide a reason for God to bring about one, rather than the other, state of affairs, provided the human petitions God for only one of the two otherwise axiologically equivalent states of affairs? The problem here is that this will only have metaphysical purchase if the act of human impetration is free in a libertarian sense. God may have reason to bring about one rather than the other state of affairs in our imagined scenario if the human act of impetration is not ordained by God – is not determined by his divine decree. But Calvin would not allow this. He thinks God determines all that comes to pass. According to Calvin's way of thinking, it is unhelpful to speak of human 'free will' because this presumes that the one willing has some innate power to choose between a good and a bad option (or between any option) without divine ordination. The 'illusion' is thereby generated that the human will 'has both good and evil within its power, so that it can by its own strength choose either one of them.'[13] But Calvin maintains this is not the biblical way of thinking about human free will. Instead, in his treatise on free will directed against his opponent Pighius, he offers the following by way of explaining what he means by 'free will':

> We say that it [i.e the human will] is self-determined when of itself it directs itself in the direction in which it is led, when it is not taken by force or dragged unwillingly . . . We allow that man has choice and that it is self-determined, so that if he does anything evil, it should be imputed to him and his own voluntary choosing . . . We deny that choice is free, because through man's innate wickedness it is of necessity driven to what is evil and cannot seek anything but evil. And from this it is possible to deduce what a great difference there is between necessity and coercion. For we do not say that man is dragged unwillingly into sinning, but that because his will is corrupt he is held captive under the yoke of sin and therefore of necessity wills in an evil way.[14]

The problem is this: if God determines all that comes to pass, including acts of human free will, then it is difficult to see how impetrating God – an act that is itself ordained by God – should, in and of itself, give God reason to actualize one state of affairs over another state of affairs, other things being equal. Or to put it another way, the reason God has for actualizing one over the other state of affairs is not do to with the fact that a particular human creature impetrates

---

13. Calvin, *On the Bondage and Liberation of the Will*, trans. G. I. Davies, ed. A. N. S. Lane (Grand Rapids: Baker, 1996), p. 68 (II.279–280).

14. Ibid., p. 69. Cf. *Inst.* 2.2.2–11.

God to do so. For this act is itself ordained by God as part of the unfolding of his divine plan in the created order. The reason God brings about one state of affairs rather than another must be sought elsewhere.

With this in mind, we turn to consider two complications to the account of the divine nature outlined thus far that do in fact yield the pointlessness problem that Calvin faces. These are that God is essentially immutable and that he is the determiner of all that comes to pass. Most traditional, classical Christian theologians have thought God was both immutable and the one who ordains all that comes to pass. So adding these two complicating factors into the mix is really only a matter of including as aspects of the problem of pointlessness two divine attributes that are very much part of much historic Christian theology, including, as we shall see, the theology of Calvin.

Now, if God is immutable, then he cannot change. There are different ways in which one can parse this claim.[15] Here I assume a traditional, classical notion of divine immutability, according to which God is immutable if, and only if, he is essentially unchanging. That is, he cannot change in any substantive way whatsoever.[16] Calvin seems to agree with this view. For instance, in his commentary on Malachi 3:6, he says that

> God continues in his purpose, and is not turned here and there like men who repent of a purpose they have formed, because what they had not thought of comes to their mind, or because they wish undone what they have performed, and see new ways by which they may retrace their steps. God denies that anything of this kind can take place in him, for he is *Jehovah*, and *changes not*, or is not changed.[17]

---

15. For discussion see, for example, R. Creel, *Divine Impassibility: An Essay in Philosophical Theology* (Cambridge: Cambridge University Press, 1986), *passim*; K. A. Rogers, *Perfect Being Theology* (Edinburgh: Edinburgh University Press, 2000), ch. 4; and R. Swinburne, *The Coherence of Theism*, rev. edn (Oxford: Oxford University Press, 1993), ch. 12.

16. I take it that this is consistent with Scripture, although it may not be the only way one could read Scripture. So, for instance, when God says 'I am the LORD, I do not change; therefore you are not consumed, O sons of Jacob' in Mal. 3:6 (NKJV), this is consistent with the notion that God is immutable in the strong sense intended here. But it is also consistent with something metaphysically weaker, such as that God's character remains the same.

17. J. Calvin, *Commentary on the Minor Prophets*, vol. V, *Zechariah and Malachi*, trans. John Owen (Edinburgh: Calvin Translation Society, 1847), p. 579.

One sort of change that *can* be ascribed to God on this sort of view is what philosophers these days call a 'merely Cambridge change'. These are relational changes that involve no alteration to the subject in question. An example of such change occurs when at a particular moment in time I begin to be shorter than my son, having previously been taller than him at some earlier time. I have not changed at all; my son has grown, so that the relation of his height to mine has altered over time. Such 'mere Cambridge change' may obtain with respect to God. But the change needed for God to respond to my petition, altering his plans accordingly, is ruled out on this understanding of divine immutability, because this would constitute a substantive change to what God has ordained will obtain.

Add to this divine determinism: roughly the thesis according to which God ordains all that comes to pass, and nothing comes to pass without God's determining it (Deut. 29:29; Prov. 16:33; 21:1; Isa. 45:7; Amos 3:6; Mal. 1:2–3; Matt. 10:29–31; Rom. 8:28–30; Eph. 1 – 2). If God determines all that comes to pass, then, coupled with his omniscience and omnipotence, nothing can frustrate the divine will. Necessarily all things that take place occur according to divine ordination. But if this is so, then not only is it the case that impetration is redundant, because God will bring about what he wills to bring about regardless of my prayer, in accordance with his benevolence, omniscience and omnipotence; it transpires on this expanded view that *necessarily* impetration is redundant, because God will bring about what he wills to bring about regardless of my prayer, and my petition can have no effect upon what God wills because he is immutable.[18]

----

18. Further to the earlier citation from Calvin's *The Bondage and Liberation of the Will*, it is interesting to consult *Inst.* 2.3.5, where, in dealing with the sin of human beings, Calvin distinguishes between necessity and compulsion. The idea is that through the fall humans are morally depraved, sinning from necessity of nature – the noetic effects of sin having fundamentally warped the moral nature of fallen humans. Nevertheless, that sin is voluntary, not compelled. This is one indication of Calvin's adherence to a doctrine of theological compatibilism, according to which divine determinism is consistent with human freedom provided this means a liberty of spontaneity (very roughly, freedom to act as I desire, choosing on that basis; not freedom to choose between alternative possibilities open before me, any one of which is a live option as far as my choice is concerned, prior to actual volition). It is worth noting that Francis Turretin, one of Calvin's successors in the Academy in Geneva, who regarded his own theology as an extrapolation of a basically Calvinian position, explicitly aligns himself with theological compatibilism, in his

The first, more theologically modest account of the divine nature which we examined requires only that God is essentially omniscient, omnipotent and benevolent. This, as we have seen, is commensurate with the idea that God may factor human impetration into the bringing about of certain states of affairs that are for the good, all things considered. But such an account also implies that God is mutable and does not determine all that takes place. But if God is mutable, then, presumably, he can change his mind. And if he does not determine all that comes to pass, then at least some things that come to pass may be the result of the significantly free actions of created moral agents. For this reason, and for want of better terms, I shall refer to the former, more modest view as the *non-determinist account of the divine nature*, and the latter, expanded view as the *determinist account of the divine nature*. As is well known, Calvin's understanding of the divine nature is a version of the determinist account:

> To sum up, since God's will is said to be the cause of all things, I have made his providence the determinative principle for all human plans and works, not only in order to display its force in the elect, who are ruled by the Holy Spirit, but also to compel the reprobate to obedience.[19]

Although Calvin is set against what he calls 'bare permission' – as if God merely permits certain events or actions to occur, rather than bringing them about – he is willing to concede that there are different 'levels' of causal activity in particular acts. God is the one who brings about a particular action, but he may use mediate causes to achieve his ends, such as his use of Satan to test Job's faith. Only in this sense can we speak of divine permission, according to Calvin:

> The Lord permits Satan to afflict His servant; He hands the Chaldeans over to be impelled by Satan, having chosen them as His ministers for this task . . . Satan is properly said, therefore, to act in the reprobate over whom he exercises his reign, that is, the reign of wickedness. God is also said to act in His own manner, in that Satan himself, since he is the instrument of God's wrath, bends himself hither and thither at His beck and command to execute His just judgments. I pass over here the universal activity of God whereby all creatures, as they are sustained, thus derive the energy to do anything at all. I am speaking only of

---

*Institutes of Elenctic Theology*, trans. G. M. Giger, ed. James T. Dennison Jr (3 vols, Philipsburg: Presbyterian & Reformed, 1992–1997), I, pp. 665–683.

19. *Inst.* 1.18.2.

that special action which appears in every particular deed. Therefore we see
no inconsistency in assigning the same deed to God, Satan and man; but the
distinction in purpose and manner cause God's righteousness to shine forth
blameless there, while the wickedness of Satan and of man betrays itself by its
own disgrace.[20]

'In a word', as Calvin puts it elsewhere in his treatise on predestination,
'when inferior causes, like veils, withdraw God from our sight, as they usually
do, we must penetrate higher by the eye of faith, so as to discern God's hand
working in these instruments.'[21] Although his view is not equivalent to Stoic
fatalism, as has sometimes been asserted, it is clear that Calvin does believe
that God ordains all that comes to pass, saying things like 'For he is deemed
omnipotent . . . because, governing heaven and earth by his providence, he so
regulates all things that nothing takes place without his deliberation.'[22] This
is consistent with his approval of the notion that God is timeless, ordaining
all that comes to pass eternally. He observes, 'When we attribute foreknow-
ledge to God, we mean that all things always were, and perpetually remain,
under his eyes, so that to his knowledge there is nothing future or past, but
all things are present. And they are present in such a way that he not only
conceives them through ideas . . . but he truly looks upon them and discerns
them as things placed before him.'[23] Moreover, as we have already had cause
to note, it is clear that Calvin believes God is essentially immutable. In this
way, Calvin's doctrine of impetration, being a species of the determinist
account of the divine nature, does yield the pointlessness problem that we
were in search of.

---

20. *Inst.* 2.4.2. Compare *Inst.* 1.16.2, where Calvin denies that there are fortuitous
    events, claiming of animate and inanimate objects that 'These are, thus, nothing
    but instruments to which God continuously imparts as much effectiveness as he
    wills, and according to his own purpose bends and turns them to either one action
    or another.'

21. J. Calvin, *Concerning The Eternal Predestination of God*, trans. J. K. S. Reid (London:
    James Clarke & Co., 1961), p. 168 (X.6).

22. *Inst.* 1.16.3. See also Calvin's definition of predestination in *Inst.* 3.21.5. On the
    relationship between Calvin's determinism and Stoic fatalism, see C. Partee, 'Calvin
    and Determinism', *Christian Scholars Review* 5 (1975), pp. 123–128, which refutes the
    charge that Calvin's position is indistinguishable from Stoicism.

23. *Inst.* 3.21.5; cf. *Inst.* 1.10.2. See also similar comments with respect to the Trinity in
    *Inst.* 1.13.18.

## A Calvinian understanding of impetration

We are now in a position to turn to the concept of impetration itself. I take it that impetration is that aspect of prayer which has to do with petitioning God. Plausibly, when one petitions God in prayer, one aims to ask God to do something that *would not otherwise obtain.* That is, it looks like a prayer only counts as a petition (and thus, as impetration) if the one praying asks God for something that, as far as she is aware, will not come about without such petition.[24] Impetration, then, is not merely expressive of a desire one might have; it is prescriptive of what one wants to happen.[25] One does not ask God to grant things that one thinks of as inevitable, or impossible. Thus I would not ask God to change the date of the Battle of Hastings to AD 1106, or to make $1 + 1 = 5$. Or, if I did, these would be pretty peculiar requests. And at least part of the reason we would think them peculiar is because we have the intuition that one cannot change events that are wholly in the past and one cannot change the modal status of necessary truths. Nor would it make much sense to ask God to grant something that is inconsistent with the divine character, such as the instantaneous and entirely gratuitous death of a rather irritating, but otherwise harmless relative. Some requests may be within the bounds of metaphysical possibility, not inevitable, and not inconsistent with the divine nature, and yet theologically dubious: for instance, magical or superstitious requests that are forbidden by divine fiat (Deut. 18:10–12). I suppose God would not normally grant this class of requests either, though for rather different reasons.[26]

---

24. The caveat 'as far as she is aware' has to do with the epistemic limitations placed upon any act of impetration. As far as I am aware, my friend will not recover from terminal cancer without divine intervention. So I might pray God heals her in the hope that my petition is answered. It may be that in certain circumstances, the limited epistemic vantage of the one praying renders the prayer ineffective or beside the point: e.g. praying that my friend will be healed of the condition he suffers from when he has been prescribed a course of drugs that will cure him regardless of my prayer, as the drugs take effect. Hence, epistemic limitations are an important consideration when assessing the effectiveness of a particular instance of impetration.

25. Compare P. T. Geach, *God and the Soul* (London: Routledge, 1969), p. 87; and V. Brümmer, *What Are We Doing When We Pray?* (London: SCM Press, 1984), pp. 29–30.

26. And yet, God does appear to permit the successful prosecution of at least some magical acts. See, for example, the story of the Witch of Endor, whose necromancy summons up the shade of Samuel for a disobedient King Saul in 1 Sam. 28:3–25.

Closely related to this understanding of petitioning God (in the recent analytic philosophical literature at least) is what several contemporary philosophers have called a *two-way contingency*. Take, for instance, the Roman Catholic logician Peter Geach. He maintains that 'if we are to be justified in saying that a state of affairs S came about from somebody's impetratory prayer, then at the time of the prayer S must have had two-way contingency: it could have come about, it also could not come about.'[27] That is, God may or may not grant the request made in impetration. My request does not compel God to act one way or another. It is not a sufficient condition for God's action or apparent inaction. But might a given act of impetration be a necessary condition for God acting one way rather than another? Consider the following homely example. My son asks me to play a game of chess with him when I am reading a book. His request is, we might think, a necessary condition for my deciding to put down the book and pick up the chessboard, though it does not compel me to act in one way rather than another. I might have refused my son's request. Perhaps I am a selfish parent, or the book is too interesting to put down, or my son is supposed to be doing his homework rather than playing board games. I might ignore his request, which, though distinct from refusing his request, has the same effect. But if I comply with his request, I do it because he has asked me to do so.[28] In which case, his request is an insufficient but necessary condition of my putting down the book and beginning to play chess with him. Complying with his request or refusing it constitutes a two-way contingency of the sort philosophers like Peter Geach seem to have in mind.

There are numerous biblical examples of petitions made by human agents that fall within the bounds of what is metaphysically and theologically permissible, given the foregoing, and which appear to depend on something like a two-way contingency. To take just one example, King Hezekiah is told via the prophet Isaiah that he is going to die from an illness. He petitions God. 'Remember, O LORD, how I have walked before you faithfully and with wholehearted devotion and have done what is good in your eyes' (2 Kgs 20:3, NIV). God hears and sends Isaiah back to Hezekiah to tell him he will recover and have another fifteen years of life. But this raises the following question: did God change

---

27. Geach, *God and the Soul*, p. 89.

28. Or, at least, I may comply with my son's request largely because he has asked me to do so. I may have other reasons for complying with his request in addition to this one, of course. For instance, wanting to spend time with my son, wanting to be a good parent, wanting to impress my spouse, wanting to encourage my son's burgeoning chess skills in the hope that one day he will become a grandmaster, and so on.

his mind in response to the impetration of Hezekiah? On the face of it, this seems like a plausible explanation of the data. The advocate of the indeterminist account of the divine nature may find this conducive. For on that account, God can change his mind. Still, even if God can change his mind, it seems odd to think he requires the petition of some created agent in order to bring about a particular action. God does not need prompting to do the right thing. Unlike the example of the chess game, he knows every thought before it is on our lips (Ps. 139). He does not need to be asked to know what we need. And he has the power and motivation to ensure that we are provided with what he thinks we need, all things considered. If God is immutable and determines all that comes to pass, it is even harder to see how to make sense of Hezekiah's request. For then God has determined all that takes place according to his immutable will, and Hezekiah is either asking for what will inevitably take place, or asking for what cannot obtain, given what God has determined upon. So, whichever of the indeterminist or determinist accounts one opts for (if one opts for either of them), the example of Hezekiah shows that there is a serious problem with the apparent pointlessness of impetration as I have just characterized it.

One means by which the pointlessness problem can be ameliorated is to deny one or more of the aspects of the divine nature with which we began. This is a popular manoeuvre in the recent philosophical literature on impetration. Few Christian philosophers today are willing to stand by the claim that God determines all that takes place, though it has been the majority view in the tradition. Alongside this concern, a number of recent philosophers and theologians have argued that the doctrine of divine immutability must be circumscribed or redefined – perhaps even rejected – in order to avoid problems raised by the fact that an essentially unchanging God cannot *respond* to the actions of his creatures. For such a response would constitute a change in God that the traditional doctrine of divine immutability could not countenance.[29]

---

29. There are all sort of reasons for these revisions to the divine nature, and I am not suggesting that theologians and philosophers have opted to make these revisions simply because of the problems they raise for petitioning God. But the idea that God is responsive is an important consideration for many who have made such changes. To give just two examples, see J. Moltmann, *The Crucified God* (London: SCM Press, 1970), *passim*; and N. Wolterstorff, 'Suffering Love', in *Philosophy and the Christian Faith*, ed. T. V. Morris (Notre Dame, IN: University of Notre Dame Press, 1988). For a response to this sort of objection from a Calvinist point of view, see P. Helm, 'Prayer and Providence', in *Christian Faith and Philosophical Theology, Essays in Honour of Vincent Brümmer*, ed. M. Sarot, G. van den Brink and L. van den Brom (Kampen: Kok Pharos, 1992).

Such revisions to the doctrine of God do have the consequence that at least some human petitions may not be pointless after all. But this is not a cost Calvin would have tolerated. He thought his own position had the theological resources to avoid having to make such a concession.

## John Calvin on impetration

Thus far, we have seen that the task of making sense of impetration in Calvinian terms is that much harder than it would be for a defender of a doctrine of God without commitment to immutability and determinism. What does Calvin have to say by way of addressing this pointlessness problem for impetration?

Interestingly, Calvin raises this matter early on in his discussion of prayer in Book III of the *Institutes*. He puts it like this:

> But, someone will say, does God not know, even without being reminded, both in what respect we are troubled and what is expedient for us, so that it may seem in a sense superfluous that he should be stirred up by our prayers – as if he were drowsily blinking or even sleeping until he is aroused by our voice?[30]

To which he responds that 'they who thus reason do not observe to what end the Lord instructed his people to pray, for he ordained it not so much for his own sake as for ours.'[31] He then goes on in the same section of the *Institutes* to adduce six reasons for petitionary prayer. These are,

1. That our hearts may be 'fired with a zealous and burning desire ever to seek, love and serve him' and to flee to him in time of need.
2. That our hearts become trained so as to refuse to entertain wishes that we should be ashamed to make of God a witness. In this way we will learn to lay all our desires before the plain sight of God.
3. That we be prepared to receive his benefits 'with true gratitude of heart and thanksgiving' – all of which come 'from his hand'.
4. That having been granted that for which we petitioned God, we should be drawn to meditate upon his goodness in granting our desires.
5. That we 'embrace with greater delight those things which we acknowledge to have been obtained by prayers'.

---

30. *Inst.* 3.20.3.
31. Ibid.

6. That our experience may confirm divine providence, whereby God 'promises never to fail us' as well as that 'he ever extends his hand to help his own, not wet-nursing them with words but defending them with present help'.

God may appear not to respond to our petitions, but, says Calvin, this is simply a means by which he intends to train us 'to seek, ask, and entreat him for our great good'.[32] Calvin castigates those who 'with excessive foolishness' 'prate' that petitioning God for what he will gladly bestow upon us anyway renders such prayer otiose. For, according to Calvin, prayer is an opportunity for the exercise of faith.

This, I suggest, offers us a rather different perspective on the nature of impetration than that favoured by philosophers like Geach. Calvin suggests that what is important in petitioning God is that our faith is exercised and that the desires of our hearts are brought into conformity with the desires of God. Paramount among his concerns here is the divine will, not what we may desire. For, as a consequence of our fallen state, what we desire may not necessarily be for our good all things considered. It is also worth noting that God's desire to encourage the believer in prayer is, in fact, part and parcel of this concern with what we might call a theocentric account of impetration. At root what is important is that petitioning God be seen primarily in terms of God's aims and objectives, rather than mine.[33] This is reinforced by Calvin's exposition of the third petition of the Lord's Prayer later in the same section of the *Institutes*. There he says things like the following:

> We are therefore bidden to desire that, just as in heaven nothing is done apart from God's good pleasure . . . the earth be in like manner subject to such a rule, with all arrogance and wickedness brought to an end. And in asking this we renounce the desires of our flesh for whoever does not resign and submit his feelings to God opposes as much as he can God's will, since only what is corrupt comes forth from us. And again by this prayer we are formed to self-denial so God may rule us according to his decision . . . In consequence, our wish is that he may render futile and of no account whatever feelings are incompatible with his will.[34]

---

32. Ibid.

33. It also looks as if this Calvinian account of impetration means that the impetrator has to have a belief that God would not, or might not, perform what he is praying for without his prayer for it. In other words, it may be that the impetrator has to have a different reason for offering his prayer than God does for ordaining it.

34. *Inst.* 3.20.43.

The first three petitions of the Lord's Prayer are concerned with God's glory, says Calvin, not with our own advantage, which 'though it amply accrues from such a prayer, must not be sought by us here'. Yet, 'even though all these things must nonetheless come to pass in their time, without any thought or desire or petition of ours, still we ought to desire and request them.' The reason being that we should desire God's greater glory in all we do because 'this is what we owe our Lord and Father'.[35] So our petitions are both ordained by God, and yet also an obligation that is enjoined upon all believers, as an exercise of faith.

Even when approaching the last three petitions of the Lord's Prayer that are specifically to do with our human needs, Calvin warns that we should 'seek nothing for ourselves without the intention that whatever benefits he confers upon us may show forth his glory'.[36] We are 'bidden to ask [sic] our daily bread that we may be content with the measure that our Heavenly Father has deigned to distribute to us, and not get gain by unlawful devices'.[37]

In effect, throughout his discussion of the Lord's Prayer, impetration functions as a corollary of his doctrine of divine providence. God will provide what he knows we need; we are enjoined to pray earnestly for what God wills for us in accordance with his grace, not what we desire from the sinfulness of our hearts; to which God will respond in his own good time. When faced with the prospect of answers to prayer deferred or apparently withheld after prolonged impetration, Calvin responds by saying that the Christian should take heart because God will not forsake his people, even if circumstances suggest, on the face of it, that he has. God may well test the faith of the one praying, often driving his people 'to extremity', allowing them, so driven, 'to lie a long time in the mire before he gives them any taste of his sweetness'.[38] Hope and patience in prayer are, it seems, as important for Calvin as the fact that prayer is the outworking of faith.

There is no appeal to a two-way contingency here. But that should come as no surprise, since Calvin endorses divine determinism. Every event that comes to pass has been ordained by God for his own glory, but also for the good of his people, all things considered. In which case, my impetration is part of the plan of God. He has ordained that I pray as I do for the things that I do, although I do this of my own volition, not of compulsion, but (in

---

35. Ibid.
36. *Inst.* 3.20.44.
37. Ibid.
38. *Inst.* 3.20.52.

some sense) of necessity, as a consequence of divine ordination. This raises a
further, subsidiary problem for Calvin's doctrine of petitioning God, related
to the matter of its apparent pointlessness. This is, whether impetration boils
down to something therapeutic – whether, in fact, it helps me to accept God's
will, but really changes nothing.

## In defence of a Calvinian account of impetration

In the recent philosophical literature on impetration, Paul Helm has come to
the defence of a determinist account of the divine nature, arguing that acceptance of this picture of God does not render impetration redundant. He offers
the following response to this sort of objection:

> In the case of the prayer for rain one would have to say that God did not only ordain
> 'from the beginning' the meteorological sequence that included rain on Thursday, but
> that he also ordained that at least one phase of the sequence (the 'rain on Thursday'
> phase) was to follow prayer for rain on Thursday, and also that he ordained the rain
> *because* of the prayers.[39]

On this way of thinking, talk of God ordaining all that comes to pass,
impetration included, need not render such prayer pointless. If God ordains
every event, then he ordains the petition uttered on Wednesday for rain on
Thursday. And he ordains that the rain occurs on Thursday. But importantly,
according to Helm, it makes sense on this view to say that God ordains the
rain on Thursday at least in part because of the petition for rain on Wednesday.
Although both the petition and the fulfilment of that petition are ordained by
God, this does not mean that the one does not happen *because* of the other;
quite the contrary.

To illustrate this point, suppose an author conceives of an entire novel one
day, sitting on the train from London to Manchester. Over some period of
time she writes the whole thing down. In the narrative, as one would expect,
one event follows another, and some events in the beginning of the narrative
have important causal implications for later events in the narrative. Helm's
view seems to be that God's determining all that comes to pass is rather like
an author conceiving of, and executing, a work of imagination. Just because
the author decides all that comes to pass in the novel does not mean (from

39. P. Helm, 'Asking God', *Themelios* 12.1 (1986), p. 24.

the point of view of the reader, at least) that a later event in the novel does not happen because of an earlier event, to which it is intimately connected in the broad sweep of the narrative. If the author conceives of the novel all at once, and commits it to paper without any changes to the narrative, plot and characterization (let us say), then this does sound rather like the sort of deterministic account that Calvin enunciates in his writings. In which case, the divine author of the created order may have ordained my prayer and its fulfilment as two related parts of the one overall 'plotline' of history. He does not just ordain the whole plot. He ordains all the parts thereof, and the sequence in which they occur in the narrative that makes up the whole. In this sense, and on a Calvinian account of impetration, certain events may well obtain *because* I have prayed for them to happen.

But this raises a very real additional problem, having to do with conflicting petitions. These come in many guises, but they need not be instances where one petition is clearly morally inappropriate or otherwise suspect, and therefore unlikely to be answered by God. If I pray that my friend recovers from cancer whilst, unbeknown to me, a second party is praying that my friend dies a horrible death, there are good theological reasons for doubting that God would grant the petition of the second party. However, even in this instance what is interesting is that, on a Calvinian view, the prayer of the second party is also part of the divine design. God has ordained that this second party pray as she does and that her prayer is ineffective because immoral. This also gives us an inkling of how the Calvinian may respond to those situations in which two or more people are impetrating God for different, mutually conflicting outcomes, where none of the petitioners is asking God for things which are immoral or unreasonable. Consider a scenario where I pray that it will be a fine day all day long so that I can enjoy a trip to the exquisite Dyrham Park in Gloucestershire, whilst a local farmer prays that it will rain in the same area, on the same day, during the same period, in order that her crops flourish. God ordains both prayers, on the Calvinian account. But at most only one of the prayers can be answered. Which will it be? Whichever one it is (if either), God will bring about what he does according to his good purposes, all things considered. In this case, it may be for the best that it does rain on the day I asked for sunshine, because God deems the crop flourishing to be the outcome that best comports with his purposes, all things considered. My prayer is not unanswered. It is denied because my request was not in line with what God ordained. So the rain is granted because of the prayer of the farmer. But my prayer is refused. It plays no part in the subsequent meteorological events God has ordained – though it may play a part in subsequent events in other ways. Perhaps God ordains my prayer and its frustration as part of a larger project which involves my coming to see that my prayer life is shallow and selfish, and needs to be more focused on seeking God's will, rather than my own.

Let us take stock. According to Calvin, God ordains all that comes to pass. As such my petitioning God is part of what God has determined will obtain. There is nothing 'open-ended' on Calvin's account of impetration, as if my petitioning God will bring about a change of heart on the part of the Deity, who may, as a consequence of my prayer, change his mind and bring about some state of affairs that would not have obtained without my prayer (e.g. the healing of my friend's cancer). So my prayer is consequentially necessary. That is, it is necessary as a consequence of what God has ordained will come to pass. It is a part of the whole matrix of events that God has ordained that, given Calvin's adherence to a determinist account of the divine nature, cannot include any notion of a two-way contingency. For the sort of two-way contingency philosophers like Geach and Brümmer presume requires a libertarian account of human freedom that Calvin will not countenance. We have seen that, on Calvin's way of thinking, doing something of necessity does not entail compulsion. I may act of necessity without being forced or coerced into so acting. Which is to say his is a version of theological compatibilism: my being determined by divine decree to offer the prayer I do is consistent with my doing so freely. After all, I choose to offer the prayer I do. So my impetration is part of the nexus of events that make up the unfolding of history as God has ordained it. Just as God is not surprised by any other mundane event that takes place, he is not caught off guard by my request. He does not have to deliberate, making changes to his plans in light of my petition. All things, my prayer included, are part of what he has ordained will occur. And this means that the Calvinian must give up the notion of a two-way contingency as an integral component of impetration.

This is a very different understanding of the metaphysics of impetration than that offered by a number of philosophers in the recent literature, including Geach and Brümmer. It is also an account which, I venture to say, will seem counterintuitive to many non-philosophers. But does it render impetration pointless? Not unless one thinks that any given human act that obtains on a determinist account such as that offered by Calvin entails that such action is pointless. The determinist is committed to the idea that every act I perform, from praying for my friend who has cancer to expressing my preference for a tuna sandwich over a chicken sandwich, is determined by God. But this does not necessarily render all such action pointless. Consider a situation in which my child comes to me crying after having fallen from her bicycle. Assume that it is in my nature to be caring and loving towards my offspring, such that I am, in some sense, bound to offer comfort to my injured daughter. Would we think this a pointless act if I cannot help but offer comfort in such a circumstance because it is in my nature so to act? That seems like a very odd thing to say. In fact, the opposite seems to be the case: we typically think that such an act, born out of my natural desire to comfort my child, is very worthwhile, one which will promote the flourishing of my children.

Transpose this reasoning onto a situation of impetration. God brings it about that I impetrate him for my friend with cancer. In one sense, this is determined. But in another sense, it is my voluntary action. Is it pointless because it is determined that I act in this way, pouring out my concern to God? Of course God could bring about the healing of my friend without my prayer. But then, God could bring about numerous logically possible states of affairs without intermediaries. So this is not necessarily an objection to impetration on the determinist account, since almost all parties who have a stake in a doctrine of impetration think God is able to bring about all sorts of events directly and immediately – though, in the normal course of things, he does not. What the Calvinian wants to say is that God has ordained that I pray as part of the nexus of events that obtain in this world, including the outcome of my prayer. My friend will recover or will die according to divine ordination, just as I will pray, or refrain from praying, according to divine ordination. All these things are in the hand of God. But this does not mean I have no reason to pray. And it does not mean my prayer is not a voluntary action.

But does such a Calvinian account of impetration reduce prayer to something merely therapeutic? It makes me feel better, we might think. But does it make any difference beyond that, all things considered? Granted, it is part of the divine plan. This does not necessarily mean it has any efficacy apart from its therapeutic value.

There are several things to say in response to this. First, the therapeutic value of prayer is not to be underestimated. This is a good in and of itself. The issue is whether this is the only good outcome of petitioning God. But what we have seen from Calvin is that this is clearly not the only good outcome. Prayer is a means by which the believer exercises his or her faith. It is also an expression of Christian patience and hope. So, according to Calvin, petitioning God develops certain virtues which are not merely therapeutic in nature. For one thing, they help the believer to rely upon divine grace and trust to God's providential care, even when events seem to run contrary to what we might expect if God does oversee all that takes place. This may have a therapeutic dimension. But it is no more *merely* therapeutic than the trust one places in a lifeguard who throws a drowning man a buoyancy aid.

But also, if impetration is part of the very fabric of the divine plan, then it has a purpose beyond the therapeutic, being something that is ordained in order (ultimately) to bring glory to God. We are assured that God does all things for a good purpose (Rom. 8:28). And we are enjoined to pray that God's will is done 'on earth as it is in heaven', a matter Calvin takes very seriously. Bringing our desires into line with what God desires is no small matter. It may well be a very hard thing to do, as, no doubt, St Paul found when he asked for his 'thorn in the flesh' to be removed, though it was not.

We might put it like this: the Calvinian perspective on impetration means petitioning God is more about bringing my will into line with God's will, than it is seeking to change God's mind. It is about praying that God's will is done, and that we are given the grace to accept that, in the understanding that all things work to the good for those who trust God. But if this isn't reducible to a therapeutic account of impetration, is it a quiescent account of prayer – impetration as resignation, as it were? Not exactly; it is more like impetration as conforming to the divine will, rather than impetration as giving up, 'letting go, and letting God', so to speak. I pray; I bring my desires before God. But I endeavour to ensure that my impetration is framed by values and concerns that are fitting for a Christian seeking to honour God, who, we trust, provides for and sustains his people according to his good plan for them. In this way, Calvin's account of prayer is of a piece with what he says about providence. It is also, I suggest, a reminder that impetration is an aspect of the Christian life that involves self-discipline and the development of Christian virtues. Perhaps it is not too much to characterize Calvin's position on impetration as one concrete way in which the Christian is enjoined to pursue the glory of God in the exercise of patient submission to his will and in the hope of salvation, come what may.[40]

---

40. Thanks to Paul Helm and Ben Myers for helpful comments on a previous draft of this chapter.

# 7. THE SECRET AGENT OF NATURAL CAUSES: PROVIDENCE, CONTINGENCY AND THE PERFECTING WORK OF THE SPIRIT

*David A. Höhne*

It is, indeed, true that the several kinds of things are moved by a secret impulse of nature, as if they obeyed God's eternal command, and what God has once determined flows on by itself.[1]

For it is the Spirit who, everywhere diffused, sustains all things, causes them to grow, and quickens them in heaven and in earth.[2]

These two quotes represent mere hints of possibility in Calvin's theological description of providence in the *Institutes*. The former marks one of the few admissions of a degree of contingency in creation that is appropriate to its distinct ontology.[3] The second quote is an equally atypical naming of the Spirit as the agent of God's sovereign actions in and for creation.[4] The scarcity of language depicting secondary or natural contingency in Calvin's work on creation has led scholars like Colin Gunton to suspect the reformer

---

1. *Inst.* 1.16.4.
2. *Inst.* 1.13.14.
3. Specifically *Inst.* 1.16–19.
4. That is, reference to the Spirit in this fashion in the *Institutes* is certainly uncommon.

of necessitarianism in his doctrine of providence. Gunton's solution to the problem of determinism was an explicitly trinitarian description of God's relations with the world. In this chapter it will be shown that not only was Calvin aware of the need to carefully articulate secondary causality, but also that the reformer was, to an extent, sympathetic towards some of the foundational concepts involved in a more intentionally trinitarian explanation of providence.

The charge of necessitarianism arose from Gunton's concern over the relationship between chance and contingency in Calvin's description of providence. Specifically, Gunton perceived the reformer to be unable to distinguish appropriately between the two. According to Gunton, the overall description of providence given by Calvin is uncomfortably deterministic: 'the unqualified assertion of divine willing is not adequate to escape a tendency to necessitarianism'.[5] This concern over the degree of determinism in Calvin's thought arose in the midst of general praise, on Gunton's part, for the reformer's rejection of Hellenistic intermediary quasi-agencies in a Christian doctrine of creation.[6] Gunton also applauds Calvin's avoidance of scholastic speculation, but wonders whether there is enough space left for a second sense of contingency that is necessary if creation is to have its own distinct existence – distinct, that is, from God's. Calvin is certainly strong on the world's dependence upon God, but what of the world's non-necessity, particularly in relation to its divine source? Gunton wonders whether chance and contingency really should be viewed as the same thing and points to the following as an example of Calvin's indifference on this matter:

> What then? you will ask. Does nothing happen by chance, nothing *by contingency*? I reply: Basil the Great has truly said that 'fortune' and 'chance' are pagan terms, with whose significance the minds of the godly ought not to be occupied.[7]

Is chaos the only alternative to divinely and imminently enforced order in Calvin's thought? This is a question that will be pursed in the first section of this paper.

Schreiner reads Calvin as certainly averse to notions of chance. In her work on Calvin's doctrine of creation she observes:

---

5. C. E. Gunton, *The Triune Creator* (Grand Rapids: Eerdmans, 1998), p. 151.

6. Ibid., pp. 149ff.

7. *Inst.* 1.16.8 (emphasis added).

Articulated in Calvin's doctrine of providence are all those themes that govern his view of creation: the passion for order, the horror of chaos, the power and sovereignty of God, and the faithfulness of God to his creation.[8]

Schreiner's assessment is comprehensive, to be sure; however, as we have noted above, there are hints at least of Calvin allowing for 'the secret impulses of nature' (or what Gunton would refer to as contingency or secondary causality) in his description of providence. It will be through pursuing these hints that this chapter will judge whether the reformer ought to be exonerated from charges of necessitarianism. In addition, and in the second section of this paper, the possibility of Calvin's sympathy towards appropriating to the Spirit a role as mediator in a description of providence will be explored. Of particular interest is the possibility of such a description allowing more conceptual space to discuss secondary causality. Might Calvin have agreed that the Spirit is the secret agent behind nature's impulses, as Gunton proposed?

Gunton maintained that notions of secondary causation require a trinitarian description of mediation to maintain the appropriate relationship between God and the world. He writes:

Secondary causation, without Trinitarian description, is either too strong – producing the redundancy of God in deism – or it is too weak, and the world becomes once again the determined product of divine mono-causality as in Spinoza.[9]

Without a trinitarian description of mediation, something else – matter, or some other feature of the universe – becomes the mediator and thus potentially eternal. Now Calvin himself was a great trinitarian theologian,[10] if not in the specific sense in which the term has been applied in twentieth-century discussions.[11] Furthermore, thanks to Warfield, Calvin has often been described as 'pre-eminently the theologian of the Holy Spirit'.[12] Therefore, by delving into hints of the Spirit in his description of providence, however oblique, this

---

8. S. E. Schreiner, *The Theatre of His Glory* (Durham: Labyrinth, 1991), p. 7.

9. Gunton, *Creator*, p. 152 n. 16.

10. Something openly acknowledged by Gunton: C. E. Gunton, 'Aspects of Salvation: Some Unscholastic Themes from Calvin's *Institutes*', *IJST* 1.3 (1999), pp. 253–265.

11. Gunton's assessment of the renaissance of an intentionally trinitarian description in twentieth-century theology was, 'Suddenly we are all Trinitarians, or so it would seem': C. E. Gunton, *The Promise of Trinitarian Theology*, 2nd edn (Edinburgh: T. & T. Clark, 1997), xv.

12. B. B. Warfield, 'John Calvin the Theologian', p. 484, cited in John Bolt, '*Spiritus*

chapter will also seek the extent to which Calvin's pneumatology might accommodate one of Basil the Great's ideas – the perfecting work of the Spirit. Basil described God's relationship to creation in a distinctly trinitarian fashion:

> And remember foremost that in the creation, the Father is the original cause of all things that are made; the Son is the creative cause; the Spirit is the perfecting cause; so that the angels subsist by the will of the Father, are brought into being by the operation of the Son, and perfected by the presence of the Spirit.[13]

This concept of God perfecting creation by the mediation of the Spirit was a central plank of Gunton's description of the economy of salvation in general and providence in particular.[14] The present chapter will explore ways in which Calvin's highly influential account of providence might be further protected from charges of determinism through developing incipient elements of his theological description of the Spirit.

## The question of contingency

### *God's providence through the sun*
We begin with the question of contingency in Calvin's description of providence. The significance of this doctrine for Calvin can be seen by the extent to which it acted as a scarlet thread running through much of his work.[15] Much has been written in many places and at various times discussing the implications of this fact. However, this chapter will concentrate on some of the more purple patches of Calvin's work on providence that address directly the idea of secondary causation or contingency. These often appear in the form of illustrations from nature and especially the role of the sun:

> The sun rises by day; but it is God that enlightens the earth by his rays. The earth brings forth her fruits; but it is God that giveth bread, and it is God that giveth

---

   *Creator*. The Use and Abuse of Calvin's Cosmic Pneumatology', in *Calvin and the Holy Spirit*, ed. P. De Klerk (Grand Rapids: Calvin Studies Society, 1989), p. 17.

13.   Basil, *Sur Le Saint-Esprit*, trans. Benoît Pruche, 2e édn entièrement ref. ed. (Paris: Cerf, 1968), 16.38.15. (Note the reference to Basil in the above quotation from *Inst.* 1.16.8.)

14.   See Gunton, *Creator*, p. 184. See also C. E. Gunton, *The One, the Three and the Many* (Cambridge: Cambridge University Press, 1993), ch. 7.

15.   P. Helm, *John Calvin's Ideas* (Oxford: Oxford University Press, 2004), pp. 93ff.

strength by the nourishment of that bread. In a word, as all inferior and secondary causes, viewed in themselves, veil like so many curtains the glorious God from our sight (which they too frequently do), the eye of faith must be cast up far higher that it may behold the hand of God working by all these His instruments.[16]

This quote from the 1558 treatise on 'The Secret Providence of God' takes us immediately into Calvin's description of God's providential actions in relation to secondary causes or *media*, as he calls them here. In reference to either the past or the future, Calvin contends that all power is to be ascribed to God in the activity of all things, 'whether viewed with their means [*media*], without their means, or contrary to their mediums'.[17] These sentiments mirror statements in the final edition of the *Institutes*:

> God's providence must be considered with regard to the future as well as the past. Secondly, it is the determinative principle of all things in such a way that sometimes it works through an intermediary, sometimes without an intermediary, sometimes contrary to every intermediary.[18]

In the treatise, the appeal to the workings of the sun in the world is in order to provide us with concrete examples of what Calvin means when he refers to secondary causes of God's providence. That is, whether one points to the power of the sun, the fruits of the earth or the richness of the loaves that could be made from her harvest, God is the one who gives life and strength and nourishment via these instruments. All these secondary causes are mere veils that obscure the true source of all life in the cosmos. None act alone or independently of God, and all obscure our sight of the real cause of anything in the cosmos.[19] Yet the language of 'too frequent veiling' needs to be handled carefully, for it would be a mistake to interpret Calvin's attitude towards the

---

16. J. Calvin, 'A Defence of the Secret Providence of God', trans. by H. Cole, repr. in *Calvin's Calvinism* (Grand Rapids: Reformed Free Publishing, 1987), p. 231.

17. Calvin, 'Secret Providence', p. 230.

18. *Inst.* 1.17.1.

19. Helm opines that Calvin was 'by no means averse to using some of the standard conceptual distinctions of medieval scholasticism'. According to Helm this is clear in the way that the reformer organizes the relationship between primary and secondary causes: 'every event in creation has a primary cause [God] and a secondary cause'. No secondary cause influences the primary cause: P. Helm, 'Calvin (and Zwingli) on Divine Providence', *CTJ* 29 (1994), p. 400.

elements of creation as being somehow derogatory when describing providence. Calvin's attitude towards creation is always positive – he is certainly no
Gnostic.[20]

We can observe clearly the reformer's positive assessment of creation in
an even more expansive reflection on the power of the sun that occurs in the
*Institutes*:

> No creature has a force more wondrous or glorious than that of the sun. For
> besides lighting the whole earth with its brightness, how great a thing is it that by
> its heat it nourishes and quickens all living things! That with its rays it breathes
> fruitfulness into the earth! That it warms the seeds in the bosom of the earth,
> draws them forth with budding greenness, increases and strengthens them,
> nourishes them anew, until they rise up into stalks! That it feeds the plant with
> continual warmth, until it grows into flower, and from flower into fruit! That
> then, also, with baking heat it brings the fruit to maturity! That in like manner
> trees and vines warmed by the sun first put forth buds and leaves, then put forth a
> flower, and from the flower produce fruit! Yet the Lord, to claim the whole credit
> for all these things, willed that, before he created the sun, light should come to
> be and earth be filled with all manner of herbs and fruits [Genesis 1:3, 11, 14].
> Therefore a godly man will not make the sun either the principal or the necessary
> cause of these things which existed before the creation of the sun, but merely the
> instrument that God uses because he so wills; for with no more difficulty he might
> abandon it, and act through himself. Then when we read that at Joshua's prayers
> the sun stood still in one degree for two days [Joshua 10:13], and that its shadow
> went back ten degrees for the sake of King Hezekiah [2 Kings 20:11 or Isaiah 38:8],
> God has witnessed by those few miracles that the sun does not daily rise and set
> by a blind instinct of nature but that he himself, to renew our remembrance of his
> fatherly favour toward us, governs its course.[21]

Calvin's dispute in this section of the *Institutes* is with those who would argue
for chance as a viable explanation of the way things are in the world. Calvin will
have nothing of such talk, pointing out that even in the actions of inanimate
objects it is the ever-present hand of God that moves things on their way. The
'beautiful order' of the creation is clearly visible in Calvin's description of the
sun's work, yet even here it is not the power of the sun – as marvellous as it
is in all its effects as a cause of life – that is on display to the eyes of faith.

---

20. Schreiner, *Theatre of Glory*, p. 8.
21. *Inst.* 1.16.2.

Rather, the power of the sun, *or* life *or* light, which courses through the various *media* mentioned in the above quote, comes from one absolute source – the God who 'holds and continues a peculiar care of every single creature that He has created'.[22] In fact, God is able to do all this without the sun, since life was brought forth in the world before the sun, according to the Genesis account. What is more, so great is God's power over the earth – or so contingent is the sun upon the command of God – that the sun can be held back from its normal course in the heavens, as seen in the cases of Joshua and Isaiah. Whatever we might say about the order of creation, God is not bound by it; but neither do his special interventions compromise it, since all is kept in life by God's providential care.

Should we then agree with Schreiner's evaluation that 'Calvin was ambivalent about the role of secondary causes?'[23] On one hand, we ought to answer yes: to the extent that Calvin was prepared to *concede* their presence only when the issue was raised in polemic situations. In such circumstances it seems reasonable to accept Schreiner's judgment that 'He feared that a full and unqualified recognition of secondary causality would be interpreted as a "blind instinct" by means of which nature could operate independently of God.'[24] Perhaps Calvin feared that to say more about the importance of secondary causes would give away too much to his antagonists. Perhaps, too, the cost of such a decision – particularly considering some of his comments on the Genesis account in the previous quote – is a tendency towards determinism about which Gunton was concerned. After all, to write, 'for with no more difficulty he [God] might abandon it [the sun], and act through himself' makes the creation seem more arbitrary than good and opens the question of just how God would act through himself.[25] Is Calvin's description of mediation appropriately theological?

On the other hand, in non-polemic situations we might want to disagree with Schreiner. The sun comes out again in a number of Calvin's comments on the Psalms. In Ps. 104 the anthropomorphisms of the poetry provide an interesting insight into the balance that Calvin allowed in his description of

---

22. Calvin, 'Secret Providence', p. 224.

23. Schreiner, *Theatre of Glory*, p. 30.

24. Ibid., p. 31. Schreiner's remarks are in reference to the treatise against astrology.

25. Arbitrariness in a description of creation would be completely out of character, given Calvin's refusal to separate the *potentia absoluta* from the *potentia ordinata*: see D. C. Steinmetz, 'Calvin and the Absolute Power of God', in *Calvin in Context* (Oxford: Oxford University Press, 1995).

secondary causation away from polemic contexts.[26] On the psalmist's words, 'the sun knows when to set', Calvin's only remarks are 'I understand it not only of *his daily circuit*', with the 'he' referring not to God but to the sun. Even though it is God who has arranged the heavens, seen in the reference to the moon in the previous clause, Calvin is at ease with a surprising level of independence that the poet ascribes to the sun. In fact, while the image of the sun's daily journey has the star obediently following his course, Calvin adds an even greater level of initiative to the sun when he writes, '*he knows how to regulate his movements* by which to make summer, winter, spring, and autumn'.[27] Again, away from a polemic context we see the reformer's willingness to entertain the poet's style and allow for a significant level of contingency, albeit in the context of metaphor. Later, commenting on verse 22 in reference to the retreat of wild beasts at the rising of the sun, Calvin focuses on the providential care of God for humankind yet not at the expense of the sun's previously acknowledged agency. A further level of importance is added to the sun's role as he wards off or cordons off the activities of the wild animals.[28] Calvin, rightly, interprets this in terms of God's protection of human life, for that is a key theme in this 'long and loud praise of this universal Providence!'[29]

Ps. 19, with its extended recognition of the glory of God in creation, provides another opportunity to consider 'more undoubted proof of the providence of God'.[30] Here again Calvin seems quite happy to attribute an obvious degree of secondary contingency to the sun:

When we see the sun and the moon performing their daily revolutions, – the sun by day appearing over our heads, and the moon succeeding in its turns – the sun ascending by degrees, while at the same time he approaches nearer us, – and afterwards bending his course so as to depart from us by little and little.[31]

The sun's movements, travelling *his* daily course that *he* adjusts seasonally, are testimony to the glory of the God who made the heavens. Secondary contingency fits easily with the primary cause. Furthermore, as the poet portrays

---

26. In vv. 19–23 the psalmist draws particular attention to God's providential ordering of the heavens.

27. *CC* 6, p. 162 (on Psalm 104:19; emphasis added).

28. *CC* 6, p. 163 (on Psalm 104:22).

29. Calvin, 'Secret Providence', p. 224.

30. *CC* 4, p. 310 (on Ps. 19:2). See especially Ps. 19:4–6.

31. Ibid.

God erecting a tent for the sun from which the bridegroom sun ventures as the triumphant champion in the heavens in verses 4–6, we have a perfect picture of primary and secondary causality. Calvin comments, 'He [David] proposes to us three things to be considered in the sun, – the splendour and excellency of his [the sun's] forms – the swiftness with which he [the sun] runs his course, – and the astonishing power of his heat'.[32] Conscious that the poet is giving us metaphors, as opposed to the description of philosophers (or scientists), Calvin shows no hesitancy in affirming the distinct agency of the sun in a contingent role for the glorification of God.

A final example of Calvin's comments on the sun as an agent of contingency comes from Ps. 136, where the poet meditates on the Genesis 1 account of creation.[33] Here the reformer's remarks are more measured in terms of the elements of freedom afforded to the sun, but this seems less a matter of disputatious strategy than obedience to the text. Again conscious of the distinction between poetry and philosophical description, Calvin understands the Spirit to be using simple language to depict cosmic relations, and so Calvin observes:

> The same remark may be made upon what the Psalmist adds regarding God's having assigned the sun and moon their respective parts, making the one to rule the day, and the other to rule the night, by which we are not to understand that they exercise any government, but that the administrative power of God is very manifest in this distribution. The sun in illuminating the earth through the day, and the moon and stars by night, may be said to yield a reverential homage to God.[34]

Significantly, though he may arrange his own affairs in other places, when it comes to exercising any kind of authority over other beings the sun is merely an agent of God's sovereign government. As the Genesis texts demand, the sun's place in the universe is relativized against the sovereignty of God, and the psalmist sees this too. Calvin is not here seeking to stave off the conjecture of a Libertine or Stoic, but rather following the meditations of the poet in his commentary. In comparison with the above quotation from the *Institutes* that cites the same verses,[35] there is little place given to secondary contingency, but that is because a plain reading of the text will not allow it.

---

32. Ibid., p. 316 (on Ps. 19:4).
33. See especially Ps. 136:7–9.
34. *CC* 6, p. 185 (on Psalm 136:7).
35. *Inst.* 1.16.2.

So there is a limited but definite place for contingency in Calvin's description of providence; the chief limit being whether his description occurs in the context of polemic or not. If ambivalence is too strong a claim on Schreiner's part, the reformer's reflection on secondary causation is confined to the scope of Scripture itself. Where Scripture is generous, so is Calvin. The sun is free to go about his business but confined to that, and any talk of greater influence in the cosmos is quickly diverted to adoration of God's sovereignty and the extent to which the sun testifies to this. Furthermore, Calvin's description of providence, especially away from the context of polemic, is quite clearly on the distinction between chance and contingency. As was clear in the instances considered from the Psalms, Calvin's willingness and ease of interaction with the poetry of Scripture on issues of secondary causation showed, at times, a surprising level of freedom accorded to the sun. It may be only a very weak view of contingency, but it is there nonetheless. Perhaps if the media of God's actions were a more essential part of his relationship with creation, as opposed to the occasional nature of various elements of creation, it would be even easier to balance divine sovereignty with creaturely freedom.

### God's providence through the Son?

So far so good: considering what Calvin writes of God working through the sun, it is clear that the reformer is not in two minds about secondary causality. However, what has always been of greatest concern about Calvin's doctrine of providence, for an exponent of God's triune nature, is the extent to which Calvin might be ambivalent about the agency or mediation of the Son in his description of providence. This was Barth's famous complaint:

> We have to take note of the astonishing fact that older Protestant theology was guilty of an almost total failure even to ask concerning the Christian meaning and character of the doctrine of providence, let alone assert it. Even in Calvin (*Inst.* 1.16–18) we seek in vain for a single pointer in this direction.[36]

What Barth meant by a 'Christian meaning of providence' was a description of God's actions towards the world understood 'wholly on the basis of the revelation of God in Jesus Christ'.[37] Barth's remarks have caused no small amount of conjecture, as scholars seek either to defend Calvin's

---

36. K. Barth, *CD* III/3, p. 30.
37. Ibid.

'Christocentrism' on this subject,[38] confirm Barth's denial of it,[39] or even question the appropriateness of 'Christocentric' as a description of Reformation
theology.[40] For the purposes of this chapter, and because secondary causation
requires a trinitarian description of mediation to maintain the appropriate relationship between God and the world, we shall consider an important instance
of Calvin's understanding of Christ Jesus in providence.

In the treatise on 'Secret Providence', and against the Stoic notion of fate,
Calvin considers the following proposition: 'What God hath decreed must
necessarily come to pass; yet so, that what does thus come to pass is not, in
itself, really and naturally a necessity'.[41] Calvin then engages in an intriguing
consideration of the bones of the Lord Jesus as an *illustration* of his point. The
pericope is intriguing for the way in which the meditation on the incarnation
is not so much prescriptive for the relations between primary and secondary
causes as exemplary of them. The thrust of this section is that, even though
Christ Jesus' bones could be broken – since he 'assumed a body in all things
like unto ours' – God's decree was that no part of his body would be broken.[42]
Thus Calvin understands himself not to be describing an absolute necessity in
God's providence, but rather:

---

38. See W. J. Torrance Kirby, 'Stoic and Epicurean? Calvin's Dialectical Account of
    Providence in the *Institutes*', *IJST* 5.3 (2003), pp. 309–22. Torrance Kirby provides
    an engaging discussion of Calvin's interaction with both the Stoics and the
    Epicureans in articulating a Christian doctrine of providence. Regrettably, the
    extent to which Calvin's solution to these two problems can be said to be
    Christocentric in the *Institutes* amounts to special pleading, insofar as Torrance
    Kirby provides no evidence that the discussion of providence ever mentions
    Christ.

39. For a comprehensive study of Calvin's preaching on the subject via the book of
    Job, see D. W. H. Thomas, *Proclaiming the Incomprehensible God: Calvin's Teaching on Job*
    (Ross-shire, Scotland: Mentor, 2004).

40. See R. A. Muller, 'A Note on "Christocentrism" and the Imprudent Use of Such
    Terminology', *WTJ* 68 (2006), pp. 253–60. Cf. R. A. Muller, 'The Place and
    Importance of Karl Barth in the Twentieth Century: A Review Essay', *WTJ* 50
    (1988), pp. 127–156. See also R. A. Muller, 'Karl Barth and the Path of
    Theology into the Twentieth Century: Historical Observations', *WTJ* 51 (1989),
    pp. 25–50.

41. Calvin, 'Secret Providence', p. 235.

42. Ibid.

In this case, therefore, when we are required to look into the law and order of nature as appointed of God, I by no means reject the contingency involved, in my sense and meaning of such contingency.[43]

This section is important for a number of reasons. The first is that the illustration gives us a sense of what Calvin means by contingency in the personal realm. What God has decreed must come to pass; yet not in a way that renders actual events as necessities. Our previous discussion has considered the notion in the non-personal realm, but the appeal to the person of the incarnate Son shows that the same principle of primary and secondary causality holds true. The second reason this passage is important is that Christ Jesus is treated as just another medium for divine sovereignty – like the sun. Unfortunately, the trinitarian relations that make Christ Jesus the perfected medium of God's actions by the Spirit, in creation, for creation are overlooked.[44] To see what such a description could mean for secondary causality in the personal realm we shall turn to the second thread of our investigation: the role of the Spirit in providence.

## The providential and perfecting work of the Spirit

As indicated in its introduction, the second main line of exploration in this chapter will be into Calvin's understanding of the Spirit's work in creation. Gunton expressed a concern that Calvin's explanation of providence was open to the charge of determinism, along with an inability to discern between chance and contingency. We have already indicated that Calvin had no difficulty allowing for a significant level of contingency in his description of providence, and this quite distinct from chance. What needs clarification is the notion of mediation in the reformer's doctrine of providence, in order to clear up the question of determinism. This is the value of an intentionally trinitarian account, a key element of which for Gunton was the perfecting work of the Spirit – especially His relations with Christ Jesus.

For Gunton the perfecting work of the Spirit meant God working by His

---

43. Ibid.

44. Wyatt concurs with our assessment, concluding in relation to secondary causality, 'there is much more to be said for the case that Calvin is simply applying to Christology a general principle identified in the course of his discussion of providence': Peter Wyatt, *Jesus Christ and Creation in the Theology of John Calvin* (Allison Park: Pickwick, 1996), p. 72.

Spirit as the mediator of perfection in creation's relationality. The Spirit perfects, that is, gives ontological direction to the *hypostases* of everything in creation towards the Father, through the Son. This, according to Gunton, allows us
'to develop an ontology of the material particular as that which is destined to
achieve a distinctively finite completeness or perfection in space and through
time'.[45] It is not a static notion of perfection but rather a sense of having come
through a state of fallenness by means of redemption in order to be what they
were meant to be in ongoing relationship with the living Creator.[46] The Spirit's
providential actions can be described thus:

> As a form of enabling action, providential action, the Spirit's action is that which liberates
> things and people to be themselves, as, paradigmatically, the Spirit's leading enabled the
> human Jesus to be truly himself in relation to God the Father and the world.[47]

The focus of divine and creaturely agency is revealed to be pre-eminently in
the person of the Son, Christ Jesus. For here, it is asserted, the perfection of
creation is 'previewed' in time and space *via* the resurrection in the Spirit: 'God
the Father through His Spirit shapes this representative sample of the natural
world for the sake of the remainder of it.'[48] Gunton argues, however, that it
is the perfection of the human life of Jesus as a whole through the mediation
of the Spirit that reveals 'that which he was created to be, his particular *telos*'.
In effect, the perfecting work of the Spirit is to enable secondary causality to
occur in accordance with relational order the Father instigates through His
Son, Christ Jesus. Some scholars have criticized this proposal – especially the
Christological aspects of it – as being 'unreformed',[49] which makes the possibility of Calvin's sympathy for appropriating providence to the Spirit all the
more intriguing.

---

45. Gunton, *The One, the Three and the Many*, p. 206.
46. Elsewhere Gunton writes, 'As the "perfecting cause" the Holy Spirit, the Lord the
    Giver of Life, gives reality to the world by perfecting what the Father does through
    his Son: originating what is truly other': C. E. Gunton, *Intellect and Action*
    (Edinburgh: T. & T. Clark, 2000), p. 104.
47. Gunton, *Creator*, p. 184.
48. C. E. Gunton, 'The Spirit Moved over the Face of the Waters: The Holy Spirit and
    Created Order', *IJST* 4.2 (2002), p. 199.
49. See John Webster, 'Systematic Theology after Barth: Jüngel, Jenson and Gunton',
    in *The Modern Theologians: An Introduction to Christian Theology since 1918*, ed. David
    Ford and Rachel Muers (Oxford: Blackwell, 2005), pp. 249–263.

Let us return to the original citation of Calvin on the Spirit, but include some more of the context:

> For it is the Spirit who, everywhere diffused, sustains all things, causes them to grow, and quickens them in heaven and in earth. Because he is circumscribed by no limits, he is excepted from the category of creatures; but in transfusing into all things his energy, and breathing into them essence, life, and movement, he is indeed plainly divine.[50]

Occurring as it does in the chapter on the oneness of God, this comment is a building block on the way to establishing a description of God's triune nature. Gunton acknowledged Calvin's pedigree in this area but was concerned that the reformer's description of providence was none-the-less insufficiently trinitarian. Without trying to accommodate Calvin to another modern agenda, it will be seen that his theological description was certainly sympathetic towards an explicitly trinitarian explanation of providence.[51]

In the above quotation Calvin quite plainly allows for activities that might otherwise fall under the doctrine of providence to be appropriated to the Spirit. Not only do we read that the Spirit 'sustains all things, causes them to grow, and quickens them in heaven and in earth'; we find in the same chapter a description of the unity of God's works *ad extra* that bears a striking resemblance to Basil's original explanation of the perfecting work of the Spirit:

> Nevertheless, it is not fitting to suppress the distinction that we observe to be expressed in Scripture. It is this: to the Father is attributed the beginning of activity, and the fountain and wellspring of all things; to the Son, wisdom, counsel, and the ordered disposition of all things; but to the Spirit is assigned the power and efficacy of that activity.[52]

Calvin does not acknowledge any debt to Basil, but the resemblance is clear. What is more interesting is the manner of the Spirit's efficacy in terms of the discussion of providence. The Spirit is the agent of 'power and efficacy' in God's actions towards creation. In terms of an explicitly trinitarian description of providence, all that remains to be seen is the sense in which the Spirit effects the order of creation which comes through the Son. That will have to

---

50. *Inst.* 1.13.14.
51. See R. A. Muller, *The Unaccommodated Calvin* (Oxford: Oxford University Press, 2000).
52. *Inst.* 1.13.18.

wait for the moment, as we turn our attention more specifically to the agency of the Spirit.

In commenting on Gen. 1:2, 'the Spirit of God hovered over the waters,'[53] Calvin writes:

> We have already heard that before God had perfected the world it was an undigested mass; he now teaches that the power of the Spirit was necessary in order to *sustain* it. For this doubt might occur to the mind, how such a disorderly heap could stand; seeing that we now behold the world preserved by government, or order. He therefore asserts that this mass, however confused it might be, was rendered stable, for the time, by the secret efficacy of the Spirit.[54]

Once again Calvin seems happy to appropriate a sustaining work to the Spirit or, as in more intentionally trinitarian language, God by His Spirit sustains the world in an orderly state, restraining the forces of chaos.[55] If we combine the intentions of the last two quotations from Calvin, then we must consider the orderliness of creation to be the work of the Son, such that we might say that by His Spirit and through His Son God sustains the cosmos.[56] Again, we shall consider this more closely in due course, but for now it seems quite possible that for Calvin it is the Spirit who is the secret agent of contingency in God's providential work. Calvin offered a careful delineation of the Spirit's spheres of influence in his comment on Rom. 8:14:

> But it is right to observe, that the working of the Spirit is various: for there is that which is universal, by which all creatures are sustained and preserved; there is that also which is peculiar to men, and varying in its character: but what he means here is sanctification, with which the Lord favours none but his own elect, and by which he separates them for sons to himself.[57]

---

53. Author's paraphrase.
54. J. Calvin, *A Commentary on Genesis*, trans. J. King 1847 (repr. London: Banner of Truth, 1965), pp. 73–74 (emphasis added).
55. See also *Inst.* 1.13.14.
56. Harink clarifies what Gunton has not made explicit: namely that the ability to perceive the agency of the Spirit in creation is, in fact, a gift of the Spirit himself that is illuminated only by the Word spoken in Scripture by the Son: D. Harink, 'Spirit in the World in the Theology of John Calvin: A Contribution to a Theology of Religion and Culture', *Didaskalia* 9.2 (1998), p. 69.
57. *CNTC* 8, p. 167 (on Rom. 8:14).

To distinguish a sphere of the Spirit's work as that 'which is peculiar to men, and varying in its character' gives scope to some interesting possibilities for the Spirit's actions outside the church. For one thing, it opens up an intriguing opportunity to consider contingency or secondary causation in the personal realm.

So, in answer to the question 'How does god's impulse come to pass in men?' the reformer writes:

> To sum up, since God's will is said to be the cause of all things, I have made his providence the determinative principle for all human plans and works, not only in order to display its force in the elect, who are ruled by the Holy Spirit, but also to compel the reprobate to obedience.[58]

Given the previous association that Calvin made with the work of creation in general, it would seem churlish not to allow the statements to be read together. That is, Calvin does not isolate the work of God in creation in general and the work of God in the regenerate.[59] In fact, there are a number of occasions where Calvin appropriates God's general actions for humankind to the Spirit. So, in commentary on the spread of human civilization after the fall in Gen. 4:20, we read:

> just as the experience of all ages teaches us how widely the rays of divine light have shone on unbelieving nations, for the benefit of the present life; and we see, at the present time, that *the excellent gifts of the Spirit are diffused through the whole human race.* Moreover, the liberal arts and sciences have descended to us from the heathen. We are, indeed, compelled to acknowledge that we have received astronomy, and the other parts of philosophy, medicines and the order of civil government, from them. Nor is it to be doubted, that God has thus liberally enriched them with excellent favours that their impiety might have the less excuse.[60]

---

58. *Inst.* 1.18.2.

59. See *CNTC* 7, p. 120–121 (on Acts 17:28), and especially *Inst.* 2.2.16: 'Nor is there reason for anyone to ask, What have the impious, who are utterly estranged from God, to do with his Spirit? We ought to understand the statement that the Spirit of God dwells only in believers [Romans 8:9] as referring to the Spirit of sanctification through whom we are consecrated as temples to God [1 Corinthians 3:16]. Nonetheless he fills, moves, and quickens all things by the power of the same Spirit, and does so according to the character that he bestowed upon each kind by the law of creation.'

60. Calvin, *Genesis*, p. 218.

The skills necessary for all human beings to build a culture, great or small, are a gracious gift of God through the Spirit. Again, in description of God's providential care of all life, we find Calvin's comments on Acts 17:28:

> And, therefore, God himself doth separate himself from all creatures by this word Jehovah, that we may know . . . that we have our being in him, inasmuch as by his Spirit he keepeth us in life, and upholdeth us. For the power of the Spirit is spread abroad throughout all parts of the world, that it may preserve them in their state; that he may minister unto the heaven and earth that force and vigour which we see, and motion to all living creatures. Not as brain-sick men do trifle, that all things are full of gods, yea, that stones are gods; but because God doth, by the wonderful power and inspiration of his Spirit, preserve those things which he hath created of nothing.[61]

How might we connect these notions of the Spirit's enabling throughout creation particular in terms of human culture?[62] As Bolt has rightly argued, it is certainly not a matter of confusing the fashions and trends of human culture as a work of the Spirit – however constructive they may be.[63] Bolt reminds us that Calvin saw the Spirit acting as much as a restraint and bridle on the evil acts of the wicked. Thus in the *Catechism of the Church of Geneva* we read:

> Although, he does not govern them (wicked and devils) by his Spirit, yet he checks them by his power [*potestate*] as if with a bridle, so that they are unable to move unless he permits them to do so. Further he even makes them ministers of his will.[64]

So the skills for building a culture are a gift from the Spirit. The *kind* of culture that humans build is that for which they are accountable before God for the good gifts he provides. Such qualifications are important and not especially prominent in Gunton's description.[65] Furthermore, Gunton's rather vague

---

61. *CNTC* 7, pp. 119–120 (on Acts 17:28).
62. See the comment on Matt. 12:18 regarding human rulers: 'It is indeed true that there was never any uprightness in the world which did not proceed from the Spirit of God and remain in being by His heavenly power. In the same way no king can either set up or maintain a legitimate order, save in so far as he is equipped by the same Spirit': *CNTC* 2, pp. 36–37.
63. Bolt, '*Spiritus Creator*', pp. 26f.
64. Ibid., pp. 23ff.
65. D. A. Höhne, *The Spirit and Sonship: Perfecting a Particular Person* (Farnham: Ashgate, forthcoming).

notion of 'liberating things and people to be themselves' needs some of the clarification that is available in Calvin's remarks on human competence:

> What then? Shall we deny that the truth shone upon the ancient jurists who established civic order and discipline with such great equity? Shall we say that the philosophers were blind in their fine observation and artful description of nature? Shall we say that those men were devoid of understanding who conceived the art of disputation and taught us to speak reasonably? Shall we say that they are insane who developed medicine, devoting their labor to our benefit? What shall we say of all the mathematical sciences? Shall we consider them the ravings of madmen? No, we cannot read the writings of the ancients on these subjects without great admiration. We marvel at them because we are compelled to recognize how preeminent they are. But shall we count anything praiseworthy or noble without recognizing at the same time that it comes from God?[66]

The Spirit enables humans to be themselves as creatures living together in God's good creation. They undertake the various activities that make for society and culture, sometimes showing remarkable insight into the workings of the world and each other. There are great discoveries of the truth about nature; great advances in good care for the sick; great masterpieces of the representation of beauty. The greatness of any and all of them is due to the gracious acts of God by his Spirit. It must be acknowledged therefore that here in Calvin's work there is clear space for a concept of secondary causality in the personal realm, just as there was in the non-personal realm examined above. Not only is there no question of confusing chance and contingency, there is also hardly any room for Gunton's charges of determinism, if only for the fact that Calvin's description is so close to that which Gunton himself was trying to achieve.

What is of further interest, and certainly should have been to Gunton, for whom it is so important, is the way that Calvin describes the Spirit's gift of knowledge to all humankind for all these various activities: 'It is no wonder, then, that the knowledge of all that is most excellent in human life is said to be communicated to us through the Spirit of God.'[67] Such a line of thought was integral to Gunton's general theology of revelation. Hence he wrote, 'If there is a revelation of the truth of the world, it is because the Spirit of truth enables it to take place.'[68] Gunton was seeking to establish that the Spirit is

---

66. *Inst.* 2.2.15.

67. *Inst.* 2.2.16.

68. C. E. Gunton, *A Brief Theology of Revelation* (Edinburgh: T. & T. Clark, 1995), p. 34.

the governor of revelation for both theological and non-theological thinking. This does not mean that all knowledge is of the same kind, but it does imply we cannot know anything unless we are taught by that which is other than ourselves, which 'means God the Spirit albeit in diverse mediations'.[69] As we have seen, Calvin's position on the Spirit is, ironically, quite sympathetic towards his modern critic. As we turn, finally, to the centre of Gunton's description of the Spirit's perfecting work, the person and work of Christ Jesus, we shall find Calvin singing from a remarkably similar hymn sheet.

For Gunton, the temptation episode was a prime example of the relationship between divine sovereignty and human freedom. This relationship of primary and secondary causality in the personal realm, perhaps more than any other, is associated with the question of determinism in discussions of providence. According to Gunton, the wilderness experience of Christ Jesus encapsulates the dilemma of 'The right action, when we can recognize it, often seems burdensome and heteronomous.'[70] Following on from the baptism, where Jesus is 'called and empowered by God to enter upon a particular career and to perform it humanly', the temptations are 'meant to indicate the meaning and direction of this particular human life'. For Gunton, the tempter's questioning repetition of God's pronouncement ('If you are the Son of God . . .') suggests ways such a person should behave. They present opportunities for autonomy. The outcome is that Jesus rejects the offers 'in favour of a *kind* of heteronomy'. Jesus is obedient to God and the 'law of his being',[71] that is his creaturehood in relation to God, and thus accepts God's elevation in subordination. Gunton opined that these features are meant to indicate that Jesus was not merely passive but freely obedient to God in the desert. What is more, it was the Spirit's agency that enabled Jesus to be the perfect Son of God fulfilling God's promises to redeem creation.

When we consider Calvin's comments on the wilderness temptation, the actions of the Spirit are integral to the meaning of what transpires. On Matthew's account Calvin noted, 'the Son of God voluntarily endured the temptations, which we are now considering'.[72] One of the burning questions in this section concerns the meaning of such temptations: especially the sense in which it could be said that Christ Jesus was tempted. For if he could not

---

69. Gunton, *Revelation*, p. 35.

70. C. E. Gunton, *Enlightenment and Alienation* (Eugene: Wipf & Stock, 2006), p. 93.

71. Gunton, *Enlightenment*, p. 92. Gunton borrowed this phrase from Wilfrid Mellers. Apparently it originated with Bultmann, but Mellers gives no citation.

72. *CNTC* 1, p. 135.

be tempted, it would be difficult to discern much place for secondary causality in God's providential actions at this point. Noting the importance of the
Spirit's empowering work, Calvin proceeds to explain the phenomenon firstly
by pointing to Hebrews 4:15: 'Christ took upon him our infirmity, but without
sin'. His second defence is quite illuminating, particularly in light of what we
have considered above:

> It detracts no more from his glory, that he was exposed to temptations, than that he
> was clothed with our flesh: for he was made man on the condition that, along with
> our flesh, he should take upon him our feelings.[73]

In the context of the commentary, Calvin is discussing whether or not
Christ Jesus was subject to temptation as consequence of some kind of weakness, because, 'when temptation falls on men, it must always be owing to
sin and weakness.' In terms of our consideration of contingency, we might
wonder whether Christ Jesus' fragility in body extended also to his desires?
It would appear that Calvin was prepared to answer 'yes' to such a question:
'for he was made man on the condition that, along with our flesh, he should
take upon him our feelings'. So how did the sovereign decree of God to save
interact with the contingent aspect of Christ Jesus' desires?

> It is justly reckoned a weakness of human nature, that our senses are affected by
> external objects. But this weakness would not be sinful, were it not for the presence
> of corruption; in consequence of which Satan never attacks us, without doing some
> injury, or, at least, without inflicting a slight wound. Christ was separated from us, in
> this respect, by the perfection of his nature; though we must not imagine him to have
> existed in that intermediate condition, which belonged to Adam, to whom it was only
> granted, that it was possible for him not to sin. We know, that *Christ was fortified by the
> Spirit* with such power, that the darts of Satan could not pierce him.[74]

So the Spirit enables Christ Jesus to overcome the possibility of corruption
despite even the fact that he has taken all our weaknesses. Alternatively, we
might say that the Spirit enables or perfects the contingent aspects of Christ
Jesus' creatureliness to conform to God's will for salvation. Here at the crucial
point, for Gunton, Calvin evinces a description of the Spirit's work that is not
only *illustrative* of God's providential actions in the world but also potentially

---

73. *CNTC* 1, p. 136.
74. Ibid., emphasis added.

*prescriptive.* That is, in the incarnate Son we may perceive the Spirit effecting and perfecting the order of creation that God mediates to creation through the eternal Son. Unlike the sun, Christ Jesus is the *medium* par excellence, because in him the purposes of God in and for creation are achieved redemptively.

## Conclusion

So in order to conclude this reading of Calvin on providence we must first note a number of things from both parts of this chapter. We began with Gunton's allegation of determinism in Calvin's doctrine of providence linked to an inability to distinguish between chance and contingency. After reading Calvin's work in *both* polemical and non-polemical writings, it seems clear that the reformer was more than capable of allowing for a definite sense of contingency, or secondary causality, without ambivalence. The description of the sun's agency in God's providence brooked no question of chance either. The only real concern here was the apparent weakness of Calvin's description of mediation from a theological perspective in general and Gunton's explicitly trinitarian agenda in particular. What emerged, however, was a significant degree of sympathy (or at least empathy) on the part of the reformer for one of his modern critic's central tenets – the perfecting work of the Spirit through the Son. Though it would surely be an overstatement to say that Calvin's doctrine of providence was replete with such language, his description of the Spirit's providential enabling of human culture in general and the saving actions of God through Christ Jesus in particular, at points achieved with great clarity that for which Gunton was arguing.

Therefore, we can conclude, *inter alia,* two things. First, whatever might be said about the character of Calvin's polemical writings on providence, the reformer was not necessitarian when it came to describing God's ongoing relations with creation. Secondly, it is not difficult to enlist Calvin's support for appropriating to the Spirit a perfecting work in creation. A significant reason why Calvin's doctrine of providence is not deterministic lies in the fact that it is easily reconcilable with an explicitly trinitarian description of the economy of salvation.

© David A. Höhne, 2009

## 8. GOD WILLS ALL PEOPLE TO BE SAVED – OR DOES HE? CALVIN'S READING OF 1 TIMOTHY 2:4

*Martin Foord*

## Introduction

When the name John Calvin is mentioned, predestination is likely what comes to mind for many. This is remarkable, given that all the Reformers believed and taught predestination, as did a whole host of medieval theologians. In other words, the doctrine of predestination is not really what makes John Calvin unique. What is it then that makes Calvin's ideas distinctive? Simply studying Calvin himself will not yield the answers. These can only be found, as Richard Muller has so powerfully shown, when we compare Calvin with his contemporaries, and with those forerunners who helped shape the intellectual world he inhabited.[1] Hence, Heiko Oberman broke considerable new ground when he read the Reformers against their own thought world, and especially their medieval predecessors.[2] He discovered a continuity that had hitherto gone

---

1. R. A. Muller, *The Unaccommodated Calvin: Studies in the Foundation of a Theological Tradition* (New York/Oxford: Oxford University Press, 2000).

2. H. A. Oberman, *Masters of the Reformation: The Emergence of a New Intellectual Climate in Europe*, trans. D. Martin (Cambridge: Cambridge University Press, 1981); *The Dawn of the Reformation: Essays in Late Medieval and Early Reformation Thought* (Edinburgh: T. & T. Clark, 1986); *The Impact of the Reformation: Essays* (Grand

unnoticed. Moreover, Oberman's student, David Steinmetz, shed new light on Calvin's distinctives when he compared Calvin's reading of certain biblical texts with those of medieval divines.[3]

Comparing Calvin with others cannot be done in terms of a simple continuity and discontinuity model.[4] This mistake helped skew the so-called 'Calvin and the Calvinists' debate in recent years. The Reformers held certain *loci* in common with their medieval predecessors, even if the former made radical changes in other *loci* such as soteriology and ecclesiology. Thus, comparison must be framed in terms of continuities and discontinuities. In this chapter I hope to make a modest contribution to the discovery of Calvin's uniqueness by comparing his exegesis of 1 Timothy 2:4, 'God wills all people to be saved', with those of his medieval predecessors and fellow Reformers. Why choose 1 Timothy 2:4 as a point of comparison? This verse had become something of a *locus classicus* in the medieval debates about divine predestination.[5] Moreover, Calvin's understanding of 1 Timothy 2:4 has been particularly misunderstood.

## The Medieval Era

An appropriate place to start examining the traditional exegesis of 1 Timothy 2:4 is with the Master of the *Sentences*, Peter the Lombard: for two reasons. The first is because Lombard's *magnum opus*, his *Libri quatuor sententiarum*, became the standard theological textbook in the medieval schools.[6] Indeed, Marcia Colish believes that one could safely map the medieval theological terrain by

Footnote 2 (*cont.*)

   Rapids: Eerdmans, 1994); and *The Two Reformations: The Journey from the Last Days to the New World* (New Haven: Yale University Press, 2003).

3.  D. C. Steinmetz, *Calvin in Context* (New York/Oxford: Oxford University Press, 1995).

4.  R. A. Muller, *After Calvin: Studies in the Development of a Theological Tradition* (New York/Oxford: Oxford University Press, 2003), pp. 63–102.

5.  G. Leff, *Gregory of Rimini: Tradition and Innovation in Fourteenth Century Thought* (Manchester: Manchester University Press, 1961), p. 199.

6.  M. Colish, *Medieval Foundations of the Western Intellectual Tradition* (New Haven/London: Yale University Press, 1996), pp. 282–286; P. W. Rosemann, *The Story of a Great Medieval Book: Peter Lombard's Sentences*, Rethinking the Middle Ages 2 (Toronto: Broadview, 2007).

CALVIN AND I TIMOTHY 2:4

simply examining sequentially the *Sentences* commentaries from that era.[7] In other words, the structure of the *Sentences* helped set the agenda for theological reflection during the Middle Ages. Secondly, Lombard explicitly addresses 1 Timothy 2:4 in the *Sentences*, and hence so did many of the medieval doctors in their *Sentences* commentaries.

### Peter Lombard (c.1100–1160)

Peter Lombard examines 1 Timothy 2:4 in both his *Libri quatuor Sententiarum* (c.1150) and *Collectanea in epistolas sancti Pauli* (c.1155–1158).[8] We begin with the *Sentences*.[9] 1 Timothy 2:4 is addressed in 1 *Sent.* 46 under the question of whether God's will can be annulled.[10] In the previous distinction, 45, he discusses God's will more generally. Here Peter recognized that the word for will, *voluntas*, and its cognates had a variety of meanings in Scripture when attributed to God. These different renderings, he believed, gave rise to a basic distinction in God's will between the *voluntas beneplaciti* ('will of good pleasure') and the *voluntas signi* ('will of the sign' or 'signified will'). The Lombard appears to have derived this distinction from one of his Parisian teachers, Hugo of St Victor.[11]

The 'will of good pleasure' is the fundamental meaning of the *voluntas Dei*. It is God's set purpose or plan for his world that cannot be changed. Peter finds this taught in such texts as the Vulgate's Psalm 113:11 (MT Psalm 115:3), 'Whatever he wills the Lord does' and Romans 9:19, 'who resists his [God's] will?'[12] The Lombard grounds the 'will of good pleasure' in his doctrine of God's essence and simplicity:

---

7. M. Colish, *Peter Lombard*, Studies in Intellectual History 41, 2 vols (Leiden: Brill, 1994), I, 1. For an attempt to examine some of the most important *Sentences* commentaries, see Rosemann, *Story*.

8. For the dating of the works, refer to M. M. Mulchahey, 'Peter Lombard', in *Biographical Dictionary of Christian Theologians*, ed. P. W. Carey and J. T. Lienhard (Westport: Greenwood, 2000).

9. P. Lombard, *Libri quatuor sententiarum* 1.45. The *Sentences* text used in this paper is that taken from Bonaventura's *Sentences* commentary, in *OOSB* 1.

10. Lombard, *Sententiarum* 1.46.1–2; *OOSB* 1, p. 815; *PL* 192, p. 644.

11. Hugo of St Victor, *De Sacramentis* 1.4.1–11 (*PL* 176). For Hugo as Peter's teacher, see P. W. Rosemann, *Peter Lombard*, Great Medieval Thinkers (Oxford: Oxford University Press, 2004), pp. 27–28; and *Story*, pp. 234–239.

12. Lombard, *Sententiarum* 1.45.5; *OOSB* 1, p. 795. The translations are mine, from Peter Lombard's original Latin text.

God's will is truly and properly called that which is his essence; and this is one, and it admits neither multiplicity nor change, and it cannot be unfulfilled.[13]

However, Peter notes that the word *voluntas* in Scripture has five other meanings: God's 'precept, prohibition, counsel, permission, [and] operation'.[14] These are all named the 'will of God', he believes, because 'they are signs [*signi*] of the divine will'. The Master argues that, just as signs of God's anger or love are sometimes simply referred to as anger or love, so the signs of God's will are sometimes called his will. Therefore, the five meanings of God's signified will are not literally God's will; however, each 'is not false but true ... shadowed under the cloud of a trope'.[15] In other words, there is a relationship of metaphor between the signs and God's will.[16] Thus 'precept, prohibition, counsel, permission, [and] operation' are named the *voluntas signi*, the 'will of the sign'. Peter shows how the distinction between the *voluntas beneplaciti* and the *voluntas signi* functions in the story of Abraham's attempt to sacrifice Isaac.[17] God's command to sacrifice Isaac is a precept (the *voluntas signi*), but ultimately God's will was to spare Isaac (the *voluntas beneplaciti*).

Armed with this fundamental distinction concerning God's will, Peter is now able to examine 1 Timothy 2:4 as a verse that suggests the *voluntas Dei* can be thwarted: 'God wills all people to be saved'.[18] This appears to contradict the fact that not all are saved, and the clear statements of Scripture, 'Whatever God wills he does' (Psalm 113:11, VG) and 'Who resists his will?' (Rom. 9:19). In order to explain how 1 Timothy 2:4 does not threaten the immutability of God's will, the Lombard deploys Augustine's explanation in the *Enchiridion*.[19] Augustine read 'who wills all people to be saved' as 'no one is saved except whom he [God] wills to be saved'.[20] Following Augustine, Peter contends that 1 Timothy 2:4 is read in the same way as John 1:9, 'The

---

13. Ibid., 1.45.5.2; *PL* 192, pp. 641–642; *TS* 1:243.

14. Ibid., 1.45.6.1; *PL* 192, pp. 642–643; *TS* 1, p. 244.

15. Ibid.

16. J. L. Halverson, *Peter Aureol on Predestination: A Challenge to Late Medieval Thought*, Studies in the History of Christian Thought 83 (Leiden: Brill, 1998), p. 58.

17. Lombard, *Sententiarum* 1.45.7.1; *PL* 192, pp. 642–643; *TS* 1, p. 245.

18. Lombard, *Sententiarum* 1.46.1–3; *OOSB* 1, p. 814; *PL* 192, pp. 644–645.

19. See Augustine, *Enchiridion* 103; *PL* 40, pp. 280–281; *NPNF1* 3, p. 270.

20. Lombard, *Sententiarum* 1.46.2; *OOSB* 1, p. 815; *PL* 192, pp. 644–645. Again, the translations following this note from John 1:9 and 1 Tim. 2:4 are mine, from Peter Lombard's original Latin text.

true light which lights all people was coming into the world'. Here 'all people' cannot mean every person. Thus, for Peter, when 1 Timothy 2:4 says, 'God wills all people to be saved', God's will is the *voluntas beneplaciti*, not the *voluntas signi*.

Proceeding to Peter Lombard's 1 Timothy commentary, it is clear he is working closely from Augustine's *Enchiridion*.[21] The Master provides three ways to understand 1 Timothy 2:4, none of which call into question God's omnipotence. The first two interpretations follow Augustine. The first is that which Peter deploys in the *Sentences*: those who are saved are saved only through God's will (of good pleasure).[22] The second explanation interprets the words 'all people' distributively as 'all kinds of people', not every single person.[23] Hence, again, God's will is understood as his 'will of good pleasure'. The third interpretation takes God's will as a command (*consulit, hortatur et jubet*): God exhorts all people to be saved. Although the Lombard does not explicitly mention it, this is an example of God's will as the *voluntas signi*. His point is that any of these three readings will preserve God's omnipotence, and that God's will must always be done.

### The rejection of Lombard

We now turn to several significant thinkers of the thirteenth century, the leading lights of the *via antiqua*: Alexander of Hales (1183–1245), Albertus Magnus (1193/1206–1280), Bonaventure (1221–1274) and Thomas Aquinas (1225–1274). One of the texts under examination here is the *Summa Theologica* attributed to Alexander of Hales, which mostly likely contains additions from other authors.[24]

The distinction between God's will of good pleasure and the will of the

---

21. Even the wording is identical: compare *Enchiridion* 103, (*PL* 40, p. 280) with P. Lombard, *Collectanea in epistolas sancti Pauli*, in *PL* 192, pp. 338A–338B (on 1 Tim. 2:3–15).

22. Lombard, *Collectanea*, in *PL* 192, pp. 337B–338D.

23. This point too is made in identical words, except for *hominum* instead of *humane*: compare Lombard, *Collectanea*, in *PL* 192, p. 338C with Augustine, *Enchiridion* 103 in *PL* 40, p. 280.

24. See V. Doucet, 'The History of the Problem of the Authenticity of the Summa', *Franciscan Studies* 7 (1947), pp. 26–41, 274–311; and I. Brady, 'The *Summa Theologica* of Alexander of Hales (1924–1948)', *Archivum Franciscanum Historicum* 70 (1977), pp. 437–447. Despite this difficulty, for the sake of convenience I will speak of Alexander of Hales as the primary author.

sign would become a 'commonplace in Scholastic theology' in this cen-tury.[25] However, these *via antiqua* divines would tread a different path from Peter Lombard when reading 1 Timothy 2:4. Indeed, all of them examine Augustine's explanations but opt for another.[26] For example, Albert believes that Augustine's explanation makes the entirety of salvation rest upon the will of God alone, without the consent and cooperation of the human will.[27] Therefore, these thinkers deploy the distinction between God's *antecedent* and *consequent* will found in John of Damascus' *The Orthodox Faith*. They all believe 1 Timothy 2:4 refers to God's *antecedent* will, which has two aspects. First, it refers to the way in which God prepares all humanity for salvation.[28] Albert the Great, for example, asserts that the antecedent will is partly of nature and partly of grace: it includes God's planting of the law in all people, and his provision of Christ's sufficient sacrifice for the entire human race.[29] In this way, according to Alexander of Hales, God has made all humanity 'savable' (*salvabilem*).[30]

The second aspect of the *voluntas antecedens* in these *via antiqua* authors con-cerns God's own perspective on humans, when he considers them as humans *per se*, without reference to their deeds.[31] In his *Sentences* commentary (which was more influential in the medieval era than his *Summa Theologiae*),[32] Thomas Aquinas explains that the antecedent will is when God considers humans only according to their nature (*natura*), not their circumstances.[33] Hence, from this perspective, God wills all people to be saved, because this is good (*bonum*). Thomas makes the same point in his *Summa Theologiae*, but he also includes an illustration of the antecedent/consequent distinction from the legal sphere.

25. Halverson, *Peter Aureol*, p. 58.
26. Alexander of Hales, *Summa Theologica* (*STAH* 1, p. 373); Albertus Magnus, *Commentarii in I Sententiarum* 1.46.1 (*Opera Omnia* 26, p. 424 col. 1); Bonaventure, *Commentaria*, 1.46.q1.conclusio (*Opera Omnia* 1, pp. 820–821); Aquinas, *Commentaria 1 Tim. 2:1–6a* (*IPAC* 3, pp. 67–68).
27. Albertus, *Commentarii* 1.46.1 (*Opera Omnia* 26, p. 424 col. 2).
28. Alexander of Hales, *Summa* (*STAH* 1, p. 300).
29. Albertus, *Commentarii* 1.46.1 (*Opera Omnia* 26, p. 424 col. 1–2); Bonaventure, *Commentaria* 1.46.q1.conclusio (*Opera Omnia* 1, pp. 820–821).
30. Alexander of Hales, *Summa Theologica* (*STAH* 1, p. 320); Albertus, *Commentarii* 1.46.1 (*Opera Omnia* 26, p. 424 col. 1).
31. Albertus, *Commentarii* 1.46.1 (*Opera Omnia* 26, p. 424 col. 2).
32. Oberman, *Dawn*, pp. 4–5; Rosemann, *Story*, p. 83.
33. Aquinas, *Super Sent.*, lib. 1 d. 46 q. 1 a. 4 co.

A just judge would believe that it is good (*bonum*) for a human *per se* to live, and bad (*malum*) for them to die. However, if a particular human being happens to be a murderer and thus places the public in danger, then it is right for him to die. Hence, a just judge without knowing anything about the man would will *antecedently* that it is wrong for him to die. But when the judge comes to understand all the facts that qualify the man, he would will *consequently* that it is good for him to die. Hence, by analogy (*similiter*), God wills antecedently for all to be saved, but wills consequently that only the elect are saved. The new element in Thomas' explanation in his *Summa* is that he believes the antecedent will may be called a *velleitas*,[34] a 'willingness'[35] or 'wishing' in God.[36] Of course, for Aquinas, this is not 'wishing' in a human manner; his doctrine of God will not allow it. But nonetheless Thomas is happy for this word to be used to describe God's will in 1 Timothy 2:4.

The *via antiqua* divines all understood that the distinction between God's antecedent and consequent will was a further distinction in God's *voluntas beneplaciti*.[37]

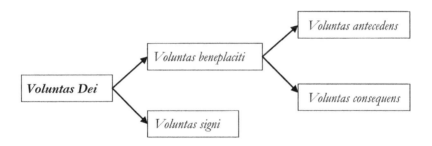

In other words, like Augustine, they believed God's will in 1 Timothy 2:4 was not a reference to the *voluntas signi*, but the *voluntas beneplaciti*.

34. Aquinas, *Summa Theologiae* 1a.19.12.

35. The Fathers of the English Dominican province translated it this way in their 1947 edition. Moreover, Aquinas gives an explanation of *velleitas* for humans in *Summa Theologiae*, 2a.13.5.

36. Francis Cacot and Thomas Tuke rendered the term in this way in their 1606 translation of William Perkins' *A Christian and plaine treatise of the manner and order of predestination and of the largenes of Gods grace*.

37. Alexander of Hales, *Summa Theologica* 1.1.5; I.i.v; Albertus, *Commentarii* 1.46.1 (*Opera Omnia* 26, p. 424 col. 1); Bonaventure, *Commentaria* I.xlvi.q1.conclusio (*Opera Omnia* 1, p. 820).

## Peter Aureol's revision

When we turn to the fourteenth century, the period of 'Franciscan hegemony',[38] a new chapter unfolds in the reading of 1 Timothy 2:4. In the late thirteenth and early fourteenth centuries we find leading divines such as Giles of Rome (c.1243–1316), John Duns Scotus (c.1266–1308) and Durandus of Saint-Pourçain (c.1275–c.1332/4) still reading 1 Timothy 2:4 as referring to God's antecedent will, despite the voluntarist doctrine of God ushered in through Scotus.[39] However, exegesis of 1 Timothy 2:4 would take a drastic turn under the influence of the French Franciscan Peter Aureol (c.1280–1322).[40] James Halverson has cogently demonstrated that Aureol produced a radical revision of God's simplicity and especially God's will.[41] Concerning God's will, Aureol first rejected the distinction between God's antecedent and consequent will. Secondly, he contended that the *voluntas signi* was not, strictly speaking, a sign of God's *beneplaciti* but rather was 'the guiding principle for all acts and operations and beings which effectively depend on him'.[42] God's will, for Aureol, was twofold. Firstly, and fundamentally, it was God's delight (*complacentia*): 'that by which God is pleased in His goodness and in all beings participating in it'.[43] Unlike the medieval tradition hitherto, Aureol believed that this will, God's delight, had no *ad extra* reference. This was because, he reasoned, any *external* willing of God must entail necessity – God's will *ad extra* would demand a fatalistic understanding of human history.[44] Hence God's *complacentia* was purely *ad intra*.[45] The second aspect of God's will for Aureol was what he coined God's 'efficacious will'. It referred to God's workings *ad extra*. However, Aureol believed that it was not actually God's will but merely 'assumes the characteristic of God's will'. God's efficacious activity in the world cannot be attributed to either God's will alone or God's power alone.

38. H.A. Oberman, *Dawn*, pp. 5–8.
39. Giles of Rome, *In libros Sententiarum* I.xlvi.p1.q1; Scotus, *Ordinatio* I.xlvi.q.unica (*Opera Omnia* 6, pp. 379–380); Durandus, *In Petri Lombardi Sententias Theologias Commentarium libri IIII*, I.xlvi.q1.11, p. 119 col. 2.
40. Halverson, *Peter Aureol*, pp. 85–173.
41. Ibid., pp. 13–75.
42. Aureol, *Borghese 329*, f. 508 ra, cited and translated in Halverson, *Peter Aureol*, pp. 60–62.
43. Ibid.
44. Aureol, *Borghese 329*, f. 509 va, cited and translated in Halverson, *Peter Aureol*, p. 65 n. 45 (see the discussion on pp. 64–65).
45. Halverson, *Peter Aureol*, p. 67.

Rather, it refers to *aspects of both* God's will in eternity *and* power realized in time.[46]

Critical in Aureol's theological adjustments was a different reading of 1 Timothy 2:4. He opposed Duns Scotus' teaching on unconditional election precisely because, in his mind, it contradicted 1 Timothy 2:4.[47] How could God will the salvation of some (so Scotus) when the verse explicitly says, 'God wills all people to be saved'?[48] Aureol developed the notion of God's 'general election': God does will the salvation of all people even if all are not ultimately saved.[49] He resolved the seeming incongruity of this by arguing that there is a condition attached to 1 Timothy 2:4: 'God wills that all [people] who do not possess an obstacle to grace be saved'.[50] Hence God's election is general and predestination is ultimately conditioned on human response.

### The New Pelagians versus the Augustinian Renaissance
Aureol's doctrine of general election exerted something of an influence upon significant thinkers after him.[51] It played a part in the development of a new Pelagianism both in England and on the continent, from which arose a reaction Heiko Oberman has dubbed the 'Augustinian Renaissance'.[52] We turn firstly to the 'new English theology' or Oxford 'Pelagians' of the 1330s, against whom Thomas Bradwardine (c.1290–1349) took up his pen.[53] These *Pelagiani moderni* were most likely, and at least, William of Ockham (c.1287–c.1348) and Robert Holkot (c.1290–1349).[54] How did they read 1 Timothy 2:4? William of

---

46. Ibid., pp. 67–70.

47. Ibid., p. 103.

48. Aureol, *Borghese 329*, f. 438 va, cited and translated in Halverson, *Peter Aureol*, p. 103 n. 64.

49. This is Halverson's phrase.

50. Halverson, *Peter Aureol*, p. 83.

51. Ibid., pp. 112–157.

52. Oberman, *Dawn*, pp. 8–12.

53. For a general overview of the 'new English theology', see W. J. Courtenay, *Schools and Scholars in Fourteenth Century England* (Princeton: Princeton University Press, 1987). Concerning Bradwardine, see G. Leff, *Bradwardine and the Pelagians* (Cambridge: Cambridge University Press, 1957); and H. A. Oberman, *Archbishop Thomas Bradwardine: A Fourteenth Century Augustinian* (Utrecht: Drukkerij En Uitgevers, 1957).

54. Oberman, *Bradwardine*, pp. 28–48; Leff, *Bradwardine*, pp. 127–139.

Ockham prefaces his discussion concerning God's will in his *Sentences* commentary with what he believed was the commonly (*communiter*) accepted understanding of God's twofold will: the *voluntas beneplaciti* and *voluntas signi*.[55] He notes that the former is again divided into the antecedent and consequent will and that the latter has five meanings (*à la* Lombard). Ockham then concludes that God's consequent will of good pleasure cannot be impeded, whereas God's antecedent will of good pleasure and his will of the sign can.[56] Hence, when Ockham tackles 1 Timothy 2:4 he concludes uncontroversially that it refers to God's antecedent will.[57] However, when we turn to Robert Holkot we find a reading similar but not identical to Aureol.[58] In his *Sentences* commentary Holkot understands 1 Timothy 2:4 to be speaking not of God's *voluntas beneplaciti* but rather the *voluntas signi*. God, for Holkot, has made all humanity with a capacity for salvation, and he has erected laws so that those who live by them will be saved.[59] Hence 1 Timothy 2:4 speaks of God's general will for all people, not his will of good pleasure.[60]

In Bradwardine's response to the *Pelagiani moderni* codified in his massive *De Causa Dei*, he argues that 1 Timothy 2:4 does not threaten God's sovereign grace in salvation. Bradwardine draws upon two readings from the Fathers which harmonize with God's sovereign grace in salvation.[61] First, he deploys Ambrose. Faced with the fact that not all humanity are saved, Ambrose (according to Bradwardine) believed that 1 Timothy 2:4 had a hidden condition: 'God wills all people to be saved, but if they come to him'.[62] It would be unthinkable, for Ambrose, that God saved people who themselves wished not to be saved. Bradwardine secondly turns to Augustine and notes his explanations. Thus, Bradwardine has shown that 1 Timothy 2:4 has been read

---

55. Ockham's commentary on book I of the *Sentences* is found in *Opera Theologica*. *Scriptum In Librum Primum Sententiarum Ordinatio*, ed. G. Gal, S. Brown, G. I. Etzkorn and F. E. Kelley, referred to hereafter as *OTh* 1–4.

56. Ockham, *Ordinatio* I.xlvi.q1 (*OTh* 4, p. 671).

57. Ockham, *Ordinatio* I.xlvi.q1 (*OTh* 4, p. 676).

58. For discussions on Holkot see Halverson, *Peter Aureol*, pp. 126–127; and H. A. Oberman, *The Harvest of Medieval Theology*, 3rd edn (Grand Rapids: Baker, 1983), pp. 244–245.

59. Holkot, *Super sententias* II.q1.CC.resp.

60. This is also seen in Holkot, *Super libros Sapientiae* Lect. 144 A.

61. Bradwardine, *De Cause Dei contra Pelagium et de virtute causarum ad suos Mertonenses* 1.39 (Savile edition, London, 1618, p. 356).

62. Bradwardine, *De Cause Dei* 1.39 (Savile edn, pp. 356–7).

several ways in the Christian tradition which do not threaten God's grace in salvation.[63]

In Paris during the 1340s, Gregory of Rimini unleashed a powerful assault against certain pelagianizing tendencies, particularly concerning the doctrine of predestination.[64] Peter Aureol's writings influenced Thomas of Strassbourg, who appears to be something of an influence for these Parisian pelagians.[65] Strassbourg reads I Timothy 2:4 in basically the same way as Peter Aureol: God wants all people to be saved as long as there is no obstacle to grace in them.[66] Gregory of Rimini responded to the pelagianizers with an unashamed doctrine of double pre-destination. When addressing I Timothy 2:4, he examines the distinction between God's antecedent and consequent will, as found in Thomas Aquinas, Giles of Rome, Duns Scotus and William of Ockham.[67] Gregory contended that, first, God's will is absolute and unchangeable and secondly, the four divines' use of the antecedent/consequent distinction is unfaithful to John of Damascus himself.[68] Rather, Gregory reads I Timothy 2:4 according to Augustine;[69] 'all humanity' is to be understood distributively as all kinds of humans, not every single human.[70] Hence, for Gregory, God's will in I Timothy 2:4 is his *voluntas beneplaciti*.

In closing this section we briefly mention three more influential think-ers pertaining to I Timothy 2:4. The first is the Franciscan Nicholas of Lyra (c.1270–1349), who authored the first commentary on the entirety of Scripture.[71] In his comments on I Timothy 2:4 he raises the familiar problem of how God could will that all are saved and yet not all are saved. Nicholas provides three explanations of how to read the verse, without mentioning from whom he drew them.[72] The first is the *distributio accommodata*: those who

---

63. Leff reads Ambrose's understanding of I Tim. 2:4 as Bradwardine's own position: Leff, *Bradwardine*, p. 81; and G. Leff, *Gregory of Rimini: Tradition and Innovation in Fourteenth Century Thought* (Manchester: Manchester University Press, 1961), p. 199.

64. Halverson, *Peter Aureol*, pp. 143–157.

65. Ibid., pp. 134–143.

66. Thomas of Strassbourg, *Commentaria in quattuor libros Sententiarum* I.xli.q1, p. 112. For a full discussion of Strassbourg's position in relation to Aureol, see Halverson, *Peter Aureol*, p. 137.

67. Gregory of Rimini, *Lectura* I.xlvi-xlvii.q1 (*LPSS* 3, pp. 514–515).

68. Ibid.

69. Gregory of Rimini, *Lectura* I.xlvi-xlvii.q1 (*LPSS* 3, p. 517.18–20).

70. Gregory of Rimini, *Lectura* I.xlvi-xlvii.q1 (*LPSS* 3, p. 517.27–28).

71. Nicholas of Lyra, *Glossa Ordinaria* 6, pp. 694–695.

72. Ibid., p. 695.

are saved are so because God wills it. The second is the *distributio pro generibus singulorum*: God wills all kinds of people to be saved. And finally the third is that God wills antecedently that all are saved. From our above survey we can see that the first two explanations come from Augustine, and the third from the traditional construal of the Damascene.

The second figure is the 'morning star' of the reformation, John Wyclif (c.1330–1384). He analysed 1 Timothy 2:4 in a rebuttal of Origen's doctrine of *apokatastasis*.[73] Wyclif mentions three ways in which *doctores* have glossed the verse which do not entail universalism. He simply mentions the three positions expounded by Nicholas of Lyra; however, he does note they are derived from Augustine and John of Damascus. The third theologian is the prominent fifteenth-century nominalist Gabriel Biel, who appears to have been an influence upon the young Martin Luther.[74] Biel reads 1 Timothy 2:4 in the same way as the putative wellspring of nominalism, William of Ockham, and the thirteenth-century *via antiqua* fathers: God antecedently wills all people to be saved – John of Damascus again.[75]

Thus we have explored something of the exegesis of 1 Timothy 2:4 in the medieval epoch. In summary, we find five basic explanations of 'God wills all people to be saved':

1. Those who are saved can only be so by God's will (Lombard, following Augustine).
2. 'All people' is a reference to 'all kinds of people', not every single person (Rimini, following Augustine).
3. There is a hidden condition: God wills all people to be saved *if* they come to him (Bradwardine attributes this to Ambrose).
4. God wills the salvation of all according to God's antecedent (not consequent) will of good pleasure (the majority view of those we have examined; it is drawn from John of Damascus).
5. God wills all people to be saved according to the will of the sign not the will of good pleasure (Robert Holkot; but noted as an option by Lombard).
6. God wills all people to be saved if there is no obstacle to saving grace (pioneered by Peter Aureol in his doctrine of general election). This

---

73. Wyclif, *De Veritate Sacrae Scripurae*, trans. R. Buddensieg (London: Wyclif Society, 1907), p. 30.
74. A. E. McGrath, *The Intellectual Origins of the Reformation* (Oxford: Blackwell, 1987), pp. 108–121.
75. G. Biel, *Collectorium circa quattuor libros Sententiarum* I.xlvi.q1, p. 760.

position is similar to point 3, in that there is a condition in God's will. However, we will keep it separate so as to clarify its origins.

It is worth noting here that the *Glossa Ordinaria* comments on 1 Timothy 2:4 are citations from Ambrose (which Bradwardine also quoted) and Augustine's two explanations from the *Enchiridion* 97 and 103.[76] Thus, whilst some medieval theologians followed the *Glossa*, many in our sample did not.

## The Reformation

The Reformation gave rise to two main Protestant traditions: the Lutheran and the Reformed. In the interests of space we will focus upon the Reformed tradition during the Reformation era, and especially how Calvin is located within it. However, we begin with a brief examination of Martin Luther, the pioneer Reformer.

### *Martin Luther*

Martin Luther (1483–1546) has some scattered remarks on 1 Tim. 2:4 in his corpus. He briefly discusses it in his 1515–1516 *Romans* lectures when discussing Romans 8:28 and the doctrine of predestination. Here Luther examines a number of objections by those who deny predestination, the second of which is 1 Timothy 2:4, 'God desires all [people] to be saved'. Luther simply states that 1 Timothy 2:4 and other verses like it pertain 'to the elect only'.[77] He says, 'In an absolute sense Christ did not die for all'. In his letter of 1522 to Hans von Rechenberg Luther again denies that 1 Timothy 2:4 refers to all humanity. Rather, he believes it teaches that no one is saved apart from God's will.[78] He says:

> St. Paul says very correctly that it is God's will that everyone be saved; for without his will this does not happen.[79]

This, of course, is Augustine's *distributio accommodata* explanation; Luther doesn't mention Augustine.

Finally, in his 1527–1528 sermons on *1 Timothy* Luther examines 2:4, again

---

76. *Glossa Ordinaria* 6, pp. 694–695.
77. *LW* 25, p. 377.
78. *LW* 43, p. 54.
79. *LW* 43, p. 54.

wishing to explain how it does not contradict the doctrine of God's unconditional election. And again he follows Augustine's interpretation. When it says
'God wills all people to be saved', it means,

He causes all men to be saved, therefore He is the only Savior.[80]

Thus, Luther has not followed Ockham or Biel but rather the Augustinian
reading of 1 Timothy 2:4.

## The early Reformed tradition

### Heinrich Bullinger (1504–1575)
Heinrich Bullinger wrote commentaries on all of Paul's letters, and thus we are
able to grasp something of how he read 1 Timothy 2:4. The Zürich reformer
believes the statement 'God wills all people to be saved' in its context speaks
of the new salvation historical era ushered in by Jesus. Prior to Christ, God's
special revelation was given to one nation.[81] But since Christ's advent, Bullinger
asserts that the message of salvation is now for all nations.[82] As proof he turns
to the great commission of Mark 16:15, 'Go into all the world and preach the
gospel to all creatures'. Hence, Bullinger believes it is fitting for the church to
pray for all people, because this is God's will and believers should not resist
it. In his highly influential *Decades* Bullinger uses 1 Timothy 2:4 in the same
way; he cites it amidst a raft of other texts to prove that the church's task is to
preach the gospel to all people.[83]

   However, in his commentary Bullinger does tackle the perennially nagging
question: if God wills all to be saved, why are all not saved?[84] He believes that
this question has regularly generated more problems than profit and notes two
erroneous responses.[85] On one hand, some so magnify God's salvific grace
that human responsibility for sin is nullified. But on the other hand, there are
others who so emphasize human responsibility that God is robbed of his gracious work in salvation. Rather, Bullinger avers that the 'ancients' embroiled

---

80.  *LW* 28, p. 261.

81.  H. Bullinger, *Commentarii in omnes Pauli apostoli epistolas* (Zürich: Apud
      Christophorum Froschouerum, 1582), p. 433.

82.  Ibid.

83.  Bullinger, 'Of the Gospel', in *Decades* 4.1 (*DHB* 4, p. 33).

84.  Bullinger, *Commentarii*, p. 433.

85.  Ibid.

in the Pelagian controversy have given a prudent response. Here he turns to the work *De vocatione omnium Gentium*, which Bullinger believes may have been authored by Ambrose, although it most likely comes from Prosper of Aquitaine (c.390–c.455), the fifth-century defender of Augustine.[86] Bullinger cites a passage from *De vocatione* which addresses the question at hand.[87] The author makes three points believers are to confess:[88] firstly, God wills all people to be saved; secondly, salvation is not by one's own merits but by divine grace; and thirdly, humans cannot fathom how God wills the salvation of all but not all are saved, and thus believers should not seek to do so.

Bullinger then refers to two works of Augustine, both of which argue that believers must avoid the Scylla of emphasizing God's gracious saving work so as to relieve humans of responsibility for sin and the Charybdis of emphasizing human responsibility so as to lessen God's complete saving grace.[89] Bullinger himself concludes from all these citations that believers are to hold simultaneously that God wills all people to be saved, and yet the saved are so by grace which ultimately originates in God's unconditional election.[90]

Thus Bullinger raises the difficult question about whether God's will fails, and answers it without reference to the medieval tradition implicitly or explicitly. Indeed, he rests exclusively on Patristic material.

### *Wolfgang Musculus (1497–1563)*

Wolfgang Musculus examines I Timothy 2:4 both in his colossal *Loci Communes* and in his commentary on I Timothy.[91] However, it is worth noting his comments about the doctrine *de voluntate Dei* in the former work.[92] Musculus begins by saying that he hopes to present the topic so that it will lead to godly living

---

86. P. De Letter, 'Introduction', in Prosper of Aquitaine, *The Call of the Nations*, trans. P. De Letter (London: Longman Green, 1952), p. 8.

87. Prosper, *The Call of the Nations*, pp. 89–90 (*De vocatione*, 2.1 in *PL* 51, pp. 685–687).

88. Ibid.

89. The two texts are Augustine, *De Dono Perseverantiae*, 19 in *PL* 45, pp. 1023–1025 and Augustine, *In Evangelium Joannis Tractatus*, 53.18 in *PL* 35, pp. 1777–1778.

90. Bullinger, *Commentarii*, pp. 433–434.

91. Musculus, *Commonplaces of Religion* (London: R. Wolfe, 1563), p. 920 col. 2; Musculus, *In Divi Pauli epistolas [. . .] Commentarii* (Basel: Ex Officina Hervagiana, 1578), pp. 353–355.

92. Musculus, *Loci Communes theologiae sacrae* (Basel: Sebastianum Henricpetri, 1599), pp. 444–452 (§45).

and salvation. He chides the schoolmen for being distracted with questions of needless speculation:

> [To] wade too farre into it [the topic of God's will], by reasonyng over-scrupulously and curiously, is for irreligious and curious Creatures, rather than for Godly disposed persons. As those questions bee of the Schoolmenne, howe there is a will in God: And whether it be all one to hym to will, and to bee: that the will of God shoulde be hys substaunce: & whether he be that which he willeth.[93]

Noting the Lombard's distinction between the *voluntas beneplaciti* and *voluntas signi*, Musculus contends that the fundamental issue concerns the will of God 'towards us', which is twofold: first, how and what God has determined concerning 'our salvation'; and secondly, what God would have us be and do.[94] Hence Musculus grounds God's will in the historical purposes of God for humanity (*pro nobis*) rather than simply a metaphysical analysis of the *voluntas Dei in se*.

In his *Loci Communes* Musculus examines 1 Timothy 2:4 when answering the broader question of whether God's will may be hindered.[95] He firstly notes Ockham's solution: that the *voluntas beneplaciti consequens* cannot be thwarted, whereas the *voluntas beneplaciti antecedens* and the *voluntas signi* can. Secondly, he notes Lombard's solution, which follows Augustine.[96] Musculus, like Bullinger, believes that 1 Timothy 2:4 was written to indicate that God excludes none from coming to salvation.[97] But unlike Bullinger, Musculus argues that 1 Timothy 2:4 is speaking of God's immutable will 'that all humans are saved', which includes the condition 'and come to a knowledge of the truth' (1 Tim. 2:4b). This condition is added, 'to the intente we should not thinke that God would save all without difference'.[98] This, as we have seen, was mentioned by Thomas Bradwardine and found in the *Glossa ordinaria*, both sources attributing it to Ambrose. However, Musculus recognizes that some may not find his reading of 1 Timothy 2:4 convincing. Hence he recommends Augustine's exegesis from the *Enchiridion* 103: God wills all kinds of people to be saved.[99] Either way, Musculus seeks to demonstrate that 1 Timothy 2:4 need not

---

93. Musculus, *Loci Communes*, p. 445 (§ 45); *Commonplaces*, p. 919 col. 2.
94. Musculus, *Loci Communes*, p. 445 (§ 45.1); *Commonplaces*, p. 920 col. 1.
95. Musculus, *Loci Communes*, pp. 451–452 (§ 45.7); *Commonplaces*, pp. 932 col. 1–934 col. 2.
96. Ibid.
97. Ibid.
98. Ibid.
99. Ibid.

be read as proof that God's will is mutable. Finally, in his commentary on 1 Timothy 2:4, Musculus presents an identical argument to the *Loci Communes*: first he propounds his conditional reading, but then if the reader is not persuaded, he recommends Augustine.[100]

### Peter Martyr Vermigli (1500–1562)

The Italian Reformer Peter Martyr Vermigli discusses 1 Timothy 2:4 in his *Loci communes*.[101] Unlike Musculus, Vermigli is happy with the basic distinction of the 'schoolmen' between the *voluntas signi* and the *voluntas beneplaciti* (or *efficacis*).[102] He believes that the *voluntas signi* indicates what believers should do or avoid, and consists in the 'law, commandments, promises, threatenings, and counsels'.[103] We note that these five meanings are not the same five as Lombard's *voluntas signi*. Vermigli explains that humans can thwart God's *voluntas signi*. But this does not mean the five meanings should not be designated God's 'will'. It is because Vermigli finds this usage in Scripture: for example, Matthew 12:50:

> The one who does the will of my Father, he is my mother, my brother, and my sister.[104]

Vermigli then turns to the *voluntas beneplaciti* (*potentis* or *efficacis*), asserting that it cannot be frustrated.[105] For proof he deploys two verses used by the medievals:

> Whatever he wills, he does. (Psa. 135:6) . . . Who is able to resist his [God's] will? (Rom. 9:19)[106]

Vermigli contends that God's two wills differ, in that the *voluntas signi* declares to humanity what is needful for salvation, whereas God's *voluntas beneplaciti* is

---

100. Musculus, *Commentarii*, p. 354.

101. A posthumous compilation by a certain Robert Masson.

102. Vermigli, *Petri Matyris Vermilii Florentini praestantissimi nostra aetate theologi Loci Communes* (London: Ioannis Kyngstoni, 1576), p. 114 (1.14.38); it must be noted that the numbering is different in *The Commonplaces of [. . .] Peter Martyr* (London, 1574), p. 201 col. 1 (1.17.38).

103. Ibid.

104. Ibid.

105. Ibid.

106. Ibid.

hidden from humanity. Like Lombard, Vermigli illustrates the distinction with the example of God's command for Abraham to sacrifice Isaac (God's *voluntas signi*), with the eventual preservation of him (God's *voluntas beneplaciti*).[107]

Later in Vermigli's work, within the *locus* on predestination, he examines 1 Timothy 2:4.[108] Following Augustine, Martyr believes that the will referred to in 1 Timothy 2:4 is God's *voluntas beneplaciti*. Therefore, the 'all people' refers to all kinds of people, not every single individual.[109] Whilst Vermigli agrees with Augustine, he mentions that some take God's will here as a reference to the *voluntas signi* or *voluntas antecedens*.[110] He believes that such a reading is 'very likely and also apt', but prefers Augustine's interpretation.

Thus with Peter Martyr Vermigli we find a Reformer who is comfortable with scholastic distinctions and terminology, and who follows Augustine closely. There is little if any innovation in his exegesis of 1 Timothy 2:4.

## John Calvin (1509–1564)

Before we examine Calvin's exegesis of 1 Timothy 2:4, it is vital to grasp how he understood God's will. In his (1559) *Institutes* Calvin spoke of God's will as one and unified, but when accommodated to humans it appeared twofold: hidden and revealed:

> For since Moses proclaims that the will of God is to be sought not far off in the clouds or in abysses, because it has been set forth familiarly in the law, it follows that he has another hidden will [*voluntas abscondita*] which may be compared to a deep abyss. [111]

To justify this distinction Calvin particularly draws attention to Deuteronomy 29:29, which differentiates between the 'secret things' that belong to God alone, and what is 'written' for Israel.[112] He understands God's hidden will as his incomprehensible plan for creation, and his revealed will as God's revelation in his word, accommodated to finite humans. Having mentioned the

---

107.  Ibid.

108.  Vermigli, *Loci Communes*, p. 466 (3.1.45); *Commonplaces*, p. 31 col. 2 (3.1.45).

109.  Ibid.

110.  Vermigli, *Loci Communes*, p. 466–467 (3.1.45); *Commonplaces*, pp. 31 col. 2–32 col. 1 (3.1.45).

111.  *Inst.* 1.17.2.

112.  Ibid.

accommodated two wills, Calvin was keen to emphasize that they are a unity to the uncreated God.[113] We note that in his *Institutes* Calvin does not explicitly deploy the technical medieval scholastic nomenclature.

Turning now to 1 Timothy 2:4, Calvin discusses this text in a number of his works:[114]

1. *De aeterna dei praedestinatione* (1552), 8.2
2. *Commentarii in priorem epistolam ad Timotheum* (1556, second revised edition).
3. *Commentarii in priorem epistolam Pauli ad Corinthios*, 1:27 (1556, second revised edition).
4. *De Occulta Dei Providentia* (1558), Article I.
5. *Institutio Christianae Religionis* (1559), 3.24.16 (with a minor reference in 3.2.14).
6. *Commentarii in Acta Apostolorum* (1560), 17:11.
7. *Ioannis Calvini Praelectiones in librum prophetiarum Danielis* (1560), 7:27.
8. *Sermons sur les épistres à Timothee et à Tite* (1561), Sermon 13.

Calvin's basic understanding of 1 Timothy 2:4 appears to remain stable throughout these writings. So, rather than expound them chronologically and thereby trudge over the same ground repeatedly, we will focus on the salient features of Calvin's position. Others who have examined Calvin on 1 Timothy 2:4 draw the conclusion that he is simply following Augustine: God wills all kinds of people to be saved.[115] However, such a conclusion is to be questioned. A focus on two issues will clarify Calvin's position: first, how he understands 'all people'; and secondly, how Calvin understands God's willing.

So we first turn to Calvin's reading of the phrase 'all people' in 1 Timothy

---

113. *Inst.* 1.18.3.
114. For the dating of these works see T. H. L. Parker, *Calvin's Old Testament Commentaries* (Edinburgh: T. & T. Clark, 1986), pp. 225–227; *Calvin's New Testament Commentaries*, 2nd edn (Louisville: Westminster John Knox, 1993), pp. 206–216; *Calvin's Preaching* (Louisville: Westminster John Knox, 1992), pp. 153–170.
115. J. H. Rainbow, *The Will of God and the Cross: An Historical and Theological Study of John Calvin's Doctrine of Limited Redemption* (Allison Park: Pickwick, 1990), pp. 136–147; F. Turretin, *Institutes of Elenctic Theology*, trans. G. M. Giger, ed. J. T. Dennison (3 vols; Phillipsburg: P & R, 1994), 3, p. 473 (14.14.38). See also R. Nicole, 'John Calvin's View of the Extent of the Atonement', *WTJ* 47 (1985), pp. 212–214; and F. S. Leahy, 'Calvin and the Extent of the Atonement', *Reformed Theological Journal* 8 (1992), pp. 60–61.

2:4. One could easily think that Calvin is merely following Augustine when he makes statements like these:

> Who does not see that the reference [to 'all'] is to orders of men rather than individual men?[116]

> But since it clearly appears that he is there speaking not of individuals, but of orders of men, let us have done with a longer discussion.[117]

> For it is (so to speak) more certain than certainty itself that the apostle is not, in that passage [1 Tim. 2:4] speaking of individuals at all, but of orders of men in their various civil and national vocations.[118]

Here Calvin believes that 'all' doesn't refer to 'individuals' (*singuli*) but to 'orders' (*ordines*) of people. But what does he mean by these words? As we have seen, Gregory of Rimini followed Augustine by reading 'all people' in the sense of *some* from all kinds of people. However, Calvin's understanding is more subtle. 'All' is a reference firstly to orders (or kinds) of people, but that doesn't necessarily entail some from all kinds. Rather Calvin means *all* from all kinds. We see this in two potentially misleading citations from Calvin's sermon on 1 Timothy 2:4:

> And yet we must marke that Saint Paule speaketh not here of every particular man, but of all sorts, and of all people [*mais de tous estate et de tous peuples*].[119]

> If a man will reade but three lines, he shall easily perceive, that Saint Paule speaketh not here of every particular man [*que sainct Paul ne parle point ici de chacune personne*] (as we have shewed alreadie) but he speaketh of all people, and of all states [*mais il parle de tous peuples, et des estats*].[120]

In both quotations Calvin appears to pit 'every particular man' against 'all sorts/states' and 'all people', when they appear to convey an identical meaning.

---

116. J. Calvin, *Concerning the Eternal Predestination of God*, trans. J. K. S. Reid (Louisville: Westminster John Knox, 1997), p. 109 (§ 8.2).
117. *Inst.* 3.24.16.
118. Calvin, *De Occulta Dei Providentia*, I.
119. J. Calvin, *John Calvin's Sermons on Timothy and Titus*, trans. L. T. (facsimile edn, Edinburgh: Banner of Truth, 1983), p. 149 col. 1 (*CO* 53, p.148).
120. Calvin, *Timothy & Titus*, p. 151 col. 2 (*CO* 53, 149).

The reason why Calvin has been misunderstood, it would seem, is that his phrase 'every particular man' and in his Latin writings the word 'individuals' (*singuli*) have been miscontrued.[121]

We will appreciate this misreading by turning to our second question: how Calvin understands God's willing in 1 Timothy 2:4. Jonathan Rainbow believes that when Calvin speaks of 'individuals' (or 'every particular man'), he simply means every single person.[122] However, the critical point to grasp is this: Calvin's use of 'individuals' (and 'every particular man') refers to *God's hidden will concerning particular individuals*. Thus, when he says that Paul is not speaking of 'individuals', Calvin means 1 Timothy 2:4 speaks of God's *revealed will*. So, in *Concerning the Eternal Predestination of God* he says:

> Who does not see that the reference is to orders of men rather than individual men? Nor indeed, does the distinction lack substantial ground: what is meant is not individuals of nations but nations of individuals. At any rate, the context makes it clear that *no other will of God is intended than that which appears in the external preaching of the gospel.* Thus Paul means that God wills the salvation of all whom He mercifully invites by preaching to Christ.[123]

Indeed, in his Timothy sermons he is more explicit:

> And yet we must marke that Saint Paule speaketh not here of every particular man, but of all sorts, and of all people: Therefore, when he saith, that God will have all men to be saved, we must not thinke that he speaketh here of Peter, or John, but his meaning is this, that whereas in times past he chose out one certeine people for himselfe, he meaneth now to shewe mercie to all the worlde, yea to them that were as it were shutte out from the hope of salvation.[124]

In his Timothy commentary Calvin makes the same point: 'God's will' is not God's hidden plan concerning individuals – it is the 'teaching of the gospel':

> But he is speaking of classes and not of individuals and his only concern is to include princes and foreign nations in this number. *God's will that they also should share the*

---

121.  I am thankful to David Ponter for sharing this observation.

122.  J. H. Rainbow, *The Will of God*, pp. 136–147.

123.  Calvin, *Eternal Predestination*, p. 109, § 8.2 (emphasis added).

124.  Calvin, *Timothy & Titus*, p. 149 col. 1–2 (*CO* 53, p. 148).

*teaching of the Gospel* is clear from the passages already quoted and from others like them.

In other words, the revelation that God wills the salvation of all is to have the effect upon believers of a command to preach the gospel. Another clear indicator that this is what Calvin meant is his use of the word 'sign', which may reflect in Calvin the conceptual similarity of the revealed will to the *voluntas signi*. So in his sermon on 1 Timothy 2:4 he says:

> For we cannot gesse [guess] and surmise what God his will is, unlesse he shewe it [to] us, and give us some signe [*quelque signe*] whereby we may have some perceverance [perception?] of it.[125]

Furthermore, in his commentary on 1 Timothy 2:4 he dismisses those who use the verse to deny predestination, by arguing that God's will does not concern God's secret purpose for specific persons ('individuals'), but concerns 'external signs', and these do not contradict unconditional election:

> They [who deny predestination] argue, 'If God wills all men without distinction to be saved, then it is not true that by His eternal counsel some have been predestined to salvation and others to perdition.' There might be some grounds for holding this if in this passage Paul were concerned with individuals [i.e. God's hidden will for specific individuals], although even then there would still be a good answer [perhaps Augustine's/Rimini's solution is in mind?]. For although it is true that we must not try to decide what is God's will by prying into His secret counsel, when He has made it plain to us by external signs, yet that does not mean that God has not determined secretly with Himself what He wishes to do with every single man.[126]

An argument Calvin repeats in his works to prove that 1 Timothy 2:4 does not refer to God's hidden will is that the gospel hasn't been preached to all people; indeed, in the OT era God's truth was given only to Israel.[127] If the hidden will was in mind, all people would have heard the gospel.

If 1 Timothy 2:4 is a reference to God's revealed will then it would make little sense to limit the word 'all'. And this is precisely what we find Calvin

---

125. Calvin, *Timothy & Titus*, p. 150 col. 1 (*CO* 53, p. 149).
126. *CNTC* 10, p. 208 (on 1 Tim. 2:4).
127. *Inst.* 3.24.16; *Eternal Predestination*, pp. 108–9 (§ 8.2); *Timothy & Titus*, p. 152 cols 1–2.

arguing. Hence, in his commentary on 1 Timothy 2:4 he makes these two statements:

> he [Paul] is showing that God has at heart the salvation of all, for he calls all men to acknowledge his truth.[128]

> for the apostle's meaning here is simply that no nation of the earth or rank of society is excluded from salvation, since God wills [by his revealed will] to offer the Gospel to *all without exception*. Since the preaching of the gospel brings life, he rightly concludes that God regards all men as being equally worthy to share in salvation. But *he is speaking of classes and not of individuals* and his only concern is to include princes and foreign nations in this number.[129]

Calvin explicitly pre-empts a series of questions if 'all' is read universally in 1 Timothy 2:4 and similar verses.[130] First, if God's revealed will is 'the salvation of all people' and his hidden will the election of some, are not these two wills contrary? Calvin believes not. The will of God announced in the gospel, that God's mercy extends to all, is only *provided* that they 'ask for and implore' (*expetunt atque implorant*) it.[131] In other words, God's revealed will contains a condition, which is a similar understanding of 1 Timothy 2:4 as found in Ambrose according to Thomas Bradwardine, and championed by Wolfgang Musculus. But, of course, Calvin argues it is ultimately only the elect who fulfil this condition and respond to the gospel. So he concludes there is no contradiction between the two wills. The second question concerns why the gospel is to be announced to 'all people', namely both elect and non-elect?[132] Calvin believes it is so that the 'godly' may be humbled as they recognize all are sinners, and that the 'wicked' may be without excuse in their rejection of the gospel.

## Conclusions

What conclusions can we draw about Calvin from this study? First, Calvin does not follow the classic Augustinian reading of 1 Timothy 2:4 propagated by the

---

128. *CNTC* 10, p. 208 (on 1 Tim. 2:4).
129. *CNTC* 10, pp. 208–209 (emphasis added).
130. *Inst.* 3.24.17.
131. Ibid.
132. Ibid.

likes of Gregory of Rimini and Peter Martyr Vermigli, which limits the word
'all'. The Genevan reformer believes the verse speaks of the new era ushered
in by Christ, in which the gospel is now to be preached to all nations, having
been confined to one nation in the OT. Some accuse the Reformers of having
little to say about mission.[133] However, Calvin finds 1 Timothy 2:4 teaching
such an idea; indeed, he explicitly says it is God's will that Christ is preached to
*extraneos populos*, 'foreign nations'.[134] Therefore Calvin is a potent reminder for
the contemporary church that world mission is an imperative, and is not only
to be found in the so-called 'Great Commission' (Matt. 28:18–20).

Secondly, Calvin's reading of 1 Timothy 2:4 is not a slavish rendition of any
one divine or school of thought, as with, say, Vermigli. Rather, he draws from
many strands in the Christian tradition, which he weaves into his own unique
formulation. He follows Augustine (and Gregory of Rimini) in believing that
'all people' refers primarily to 'kinds' of people. However, he doesn't follow
them when he construes God's will as revealed, not hidden. In this he is like
the medieval 'pelagian' Robert Holkot. But when resolving God's revealed will
as presented in 1 Timothy 2:4 does not contradict his hidden will, he arrives at
a conclusion similar to Thomas Bradwardine and Wolfgang Musculus (in the
vein of Ambrose).

Thirdly, Calvin has a delicate relation to scholasticism concerning his
reading of 1 Timothy 2:4. Scholasticism we understand fundamentally as a
methodology, not a theology.[135] The scholastic methodology may certainly
influence a resulting theology, but scholasticism is essentially methodological.
We have seen that Peter Martyr Vermigli was happy to introduce and deploy
medieval scholastic terminology. Musculus explained it, but was less content
to use it, and explicitly scolded the 'schoolmen' for getting caught up in arcane

---

133. For example, S. Neill, *A History of Christian Missions*, 2nd edn, rev. H. Chadwick
     (London: Penguin, 1986), p. 189.

134. *CNTC* 10, p. 209.

135. R. A. Muller, 'The Problem of Protestant Scholasticism – A Review and
     Definition', in *Reformation and Scholasticism: An Ecumenical Enterprise*, ed. W. J. van
     Asselt and E. Dekker (Grand Rapids: Baker, 2001); Muller, *After Calvin: Studies in the
     Development of a Theological Tradition* (New York/Oxford: Oxford University Press,
     2003), pp. 25–46; W. J. van Asselt, 'Scholasticism Protestant and Catholic: Medieval
     Studies and Methods in Seventeenth-Century Reformed Thought', in *Religious
     Identity and the Problem of Historical Foundation: The Foundational Character of
     Authoritative Sources in the History of Christianity and Judaism*, ed. J. Frishman, W. Otten
     and G. Rouwhorst (Leiden: Brill, 2004), pp. 457–470.

questions. With Bullinger, scholasticism is all but absent. Calvin doesn't overtly use scholastic terminology, although perhaps it was lurking in the background when he spoke of God's revealed will as a 'sign'. Moreover, his distinction between the hidden and revealed will has conceptual similarities to the medieval scholastic tradition. Scholasticism has been charged with excessive metaphysical speculation. Certainly, as we have seen, the medievals sought to resolve the tension between God's will to save all and the fact that not all are saved with all sorts of distinctions. However, Calvin also desired to resolve the same question with a reasonable solution. Bullinger was the least prepared to explain the tension. Calvin's humanism certainly appears in his discussion of 1 Timothy 2:4, but with small hints of scholastic influence.

## 9. CALVIN ON THE SUPPER: PUZZLING AND PROVOCATIVE

*John McClean*

Calvin's claims about the presence of Christ in the Lord's Supper have been a puzzle and provocation to many of his theological heirs. On this matter Calvin's language is emphatic. In his 'Short Treatise on the Lord's Supper' he argues that 'all benefit which we ought to seek from the Supper is annulled, unless Jesus Christ be there given to us as substance and foundation of all', and that to deny that 'true communication of Jesus Christ is offered to us in the Supper is to render this holy sacrament frivolous and useless'.[1] Even more confronting is Calvin's reference to the communication of the body and blood of Christ. He claims that there is a 'mystical blessing' [*mystica haec benedictio*] which is that 'we are . . . bidden to take and eat the body which was once for all offered for our salvation'.[2] It is Calvin's insistence on union with the body and blood of Christ which is the main problem for many of his Reformed and Evangelical readers. This chapter will focus on this most provocative element of Calvin's teaching on the sacraments in order to gain an insight into more general features of his view of the Lord's Supper and baptism.

Calvin's view of the communion with body and blood of Christ in the Lord's

---

1. J. Calvin, 'Short Treatise on the Lord's Supper', in *Calvin: Theological Treatises*, trans. J. K. S. Reid (Philadelphia : Westminster Press, 1954), p. 146.
2. *Inst.* 4.17.1.

Supper is found in his liturgies and in his more scholarly writings. In liturgies for both Strasbourg and Geneva, Calvin had the following exhortation,

> let us believe those promises which Jesus Christ, who is the unfailing truth, has spoken with His own lips; He is truly willing to make us partakers of His body and blood, in order that we may posses Him wholly and in such a way that He may live in us and we in Him. And though we see but bread and wine, we must not doubt that He accomplishes spiritually in our souls all that He shows us outwardly by these visible signs, namely, that He is the bread of heaven to feed and nourish us unto eternal life.[3]

Calvin presented his view in relation to Rome, Luther and Zwingli in the midst of a controversy which threatened to destroy the Protestant movement. He was a strong critic of the doctrine of transubstantiation and the associated doctrines of Rome and 'the schoolmen'. He happily calls this 'buffoonery'.[4] For Calvin Luther's view of the presence of Christ 'in, with, and under' the elements had not moved far enough from Rome.[5] In the 'Short Treatise' Calvin says that Luther stumbled because 'it is difficult to give an explanation of so high a matter, without using some impropriety of speech'. That criticism did not mean that he stood with Zwingli.[6] He suggests that Zwingli and Œcolampadius 'forgot to define what is the presence of Christ in the supper'.[7] Calvin presented his position as mediating between that of Zwingli and that of

---

3. J. Calvin, 'The Form of Church Prayers', in B. Thompson, *Liturgies of the Western Church* (Philadelphia: Fortress Press, 1980), p. 207.

4. Calvin, 'Short Treatise', pp. 155–163 and *Inst.* 4.17.11–17. He describes the doctrine as 'fictitious' (4.17.14) and those who hold it as 'foully deluded by Satan's tricks' (4.17.15).

5. Luther's insistence on this was based on his commitment to take Jesus' words of institution and his teaching in John 6 seriously and literally. Luther defended his view on the basis of the ubiquity of Christ's human nature because of the communication of the properties in the hypostatic union. See J. Pelikan, *The Christian Tradition : A History of the Development of Doctrine*, vol. 4, *Reformation of Church and Dogma* (Chicago: University of Chicago Press, 1984), pp. 158–160; and M. Wreidt, 'Luther's Theology', trans. K. Gustavs, in *The Cambridge Companion to Martin Luther*, ed. D. K. McKim (Cambridge: Cambridge University Press, 2003), p. 110.

6. Zwingli 'believed in the presence of Christ, but not his bodily presence, nor his presence in his human nature': W. P. Stephens, *Zwingli: An Introduction to His Thought* (Oxford: Oxford University Press, 1992), p. 94.

7. 'Short Treatise', p. 165.

Luther. He argues, with too great an optimism, that although the controversy is fierce there is common ground in that all confess that 'in receiving the sacrament in faith . . . we are truly made partakers of the real substance of the body and blood of Jesus Christ'.[8]

Gerrish summarizes Calvin's view in the following points.[9]

1. The Lord's Supper is a divine gift. It is not merely the reminder of a gift.
2. The gift that is given is Christ himself. In addition, it is the whole Christ that is given.
3. The gift is given through signs, which are intimately connected with the reality that is signified and which guarantee the presence of the reality that is signified.
4. The gift is given by the Holy Spirit. When Calvin says that Christ is 'spiritually present', he means that the body and blood of Christ are made present by the mysterious power of the Holy Spirit.
5. The gift is given to all who communicate, but those who receive the Supper without faith receive it to their condemnation.
6. The gift evokes gratitude, and this is the eucharistic sacrifice of thanksgiving and praise.

For our purposes, points 2–4 are the centre of interest. We will seek to understand why Calvin saw the gift as 'the whole Christ' and why it mattered to him to insist that this included Christ's body and blood. We will also investigate what Calvin meant by Christ being present in this mode by the Spirit.

### Interpretative struggle: is there a difference between Zwingli and Calvin?

Interpreters have struggled to understand the debate between Calvin and Zwingli and to make sense of Calvin's view. Pelikan presents the debate as

---

8. 'Short Treatise', p. 166.
9. B. A. Gerrish, 'John Calvin and the Reformed Doctrine of the Lord's Supper', in *Articles on Calvin and Calvinism*, vol. 10, *Calvin's Ecclesiology: Sacraments and Deacons*, ed. R. C. Gamble (New York: Garland, 1992), pp. 234–236. Mathison uses Gerrish's summary: see K. A. Mathison, *Given for You: Reclaiming Calvin's Doctrine of the Lord's Supper* (Phillipsburg: P&R, 2002), p. 47.

one between 'Reformed and Lutheran' and does not note a difference between Calvin and Zwingli.[10] Grudem sees no great difference between Calvin and Zwingli on the Supper, saying the difference was about 'the nature of the presence of Christ'.[11]

D. B. Knox takes the view that Zwingli and Calvin (and the English Reformers) held the same view of the Supper: that Christ is present 'sacramentally, that is, by way of sign'; that it is 'Christ in his crucifixion' who is present as he is 'remembered', which for Zwingli is no 'mere bare remembrance'.[12] He argues that 'no spiritually-minded believer' (by which he means any true believer, who must have the Spirit) 'can remember the Lord without at the same time being in conscious fellowship with him through the Spirit'. He thus declared it 'extraordinary' that J. K. S. Reid, in introducing Calvin's 'Short Treatise on the Lord's Supper', should state that he taught 'a true and real presence of Christ' in the elements.[13]

Although these commentators cannot see any great difference between the two positions, there are some who can. Schaff's judgment is that 'Zwingli's theory reveals the spiritualizing and rationalizing tendency of his mind', while 'Luther's theory reveals his realistic and mystical tendency'.[14] He also argues that Calvin succeeded in his goal 'to combine the spiritualism of Zwingli with the realism of Luther, and to avoid the errors of both'.[15] Schaff's recognition that there is a real difference between Calvin and Zwingli is correct. At most Zwingli affirms a real communion with Christ which is brought to mind in the Lord's Supper; Calvin affirms the participation of the believer in the body and blood of Christ by means of the Supper. The explanation of what underlies this difference is not straightforward, but the existence of the difference is plain.

---

10. J. Pelikan, *Reformation*, pp. 187–203. Given Pelikan's focus on church doctrine and the eventual production of the Zürich Consensus in 1549, which presented a united Reformed view, his approach is understandable.

11. W. Grudem, *Systematic Theology: An Introduction to Biblical Doctrine* (Leicester: IVP, 1994), p. 995 n. 10.

12. D. B. Knox, *The Lord's Supper from Wycliffe to Cranmer* (Exeter: Paternoster, 1983), pp. 52–53.

13. Ibid., pp. 64–65.

14. P. Schaff, *History of the Christian Church*, vol. 8, *Modern Christianity: the Swiss Reformation* (1910; repr. Grand Rapids: Eerdmans, 1981), p. 86.

15. Ibid., p. 590.

### Rejection of Calvin: the preference for Zwingli

Mathison has shown that Calvin's position was the consensus position of Reformed theology in the sixteenth century.[16] He then finds a gradual, though not uniform, move away from Calvin's position toward that of Zwingli, so that 'by the time we reach mid-eighteenth-century New England, there is little left of the original eucharistic theology of Calvin because the emphases of Zwinglian theology have become dominant'.[17] He highlights the move away from Calvin's view through an examination of the controversy between J. W. Nevin and C. Hodge over Nevin's 1846 work *The Mystical Presence*.[18] Nevin presented Calvin's position as the proper Reformed view, from which later theology had declined; Hodge responded by accusing Nevin of having the theology of Schleiermacher and holding a heretical Christology. Highlighting a key issue in the debate, Hodge claimed that the Reformed doctrine of union with Christ referred only to the reception of the Spirit and did not involve Christ's human nature. Nevin's voluminous response seems to have won the debate over historical theology, though Hodge was far more influential in his own day and subsequently.[19] Mathison shows the same trend in Scottish theology in the nineteenth century and in twentieth-century conservative Reformed theology, though Warfield stands as an exception.[20]

Mathison's observation is confirmed by the fact that many recent authors who generally follow Calvin have found his view of the sacraments problematic and have preferred a view more like that of Zwingli. Charles Hodge presents his views as very similar to those of Calvin.[21] Yet he judges Calvin's view that there is a special benefit in the Supper by which our soul is vivified

16. Mathison, *Given for You*, pp. 49–91.

17. Ibid., p. 128.

18. This has been reprinted as J. W. Nevin, *The Mystical Presence: A Vindication of the Reformed or Calvinistic Doctrine of the Holy Eucharist*, ed. A. Thompson (Eugene: Wipf & Stock, 2000).

19. Mathison, *Given for You*, pp. 136–156.

20. Ibid., 161–176.

21. C. H. Hodge, *Systematic Theology* (1872, 3 vols; London: James Clarke, 1960), III, 646–647 seeks to harmonize Calvin and Zwingli on the question of the presence of the glorified body of Christ offered in the Supper. Calvin affirms this but Zwingli denies it; Hodge comments that Calvin can mean this only as a way of expressing our reception of the benefit of Jesus' death, or else he would be inconsistent.

by the blood and body of Christ 'peculiar'.[22] Likewise Berkhof finds Calvin's view of sacramental union 'not entirely clear' and 'obscure' and 'dubious'. He declares that Calvin 'seems to place too much emphasis on the literal body and blood' and states a preference for Dabney and Hodge, who speak less realistically.[23]

Grudem offers a decidedly Zwinglian account, stating that Christ is 'spiritually present' as we partake of the Supper, which symbolizes the body and blood of Christ. The relation between the elements and the body and blood of Christ is minimal.[24] Erickson is dismissive of Calvin's view. He attributes even a view of Christ's spiritual presence to an inappropriate conservatism among the Reformers and a mystical interpretation of 'a profound encounter with Christ' by participation in the Supper. He states 'the rite is basically commemorative'.[25]

Reymond is wary of Calvin's approach and charges that he

> comes perilously close to suggesting the Godhead's apotheosising of Christ's
> humanity and to transferring, at least in the Lord's Supper, the saving benefits of
> Christ's atoning death directly to his human nature now localised in heaven.[26]

Reymond's critique is probably the most vigorous of any contemporary Calvinist and will demand more attention in the examination of Calvin's position.

### Rejection of Calvin: Radical Orthodoxy

Not all critics of Calvin are Zwinglian. Recently those associated with Radical Orthodoxy have been critical of Calvin's view of the Supper. Graham Ward argues that Calvin's thought is caught in a dualism which distinguishes between a 'carnal' presence and a 'spiritual' presence. According to Ward, this leads Calvin to affirm Christ's absence as the Ascended One and rests on a nominalist view of the creation of meaning in a sign to affirm Christ's presence. Ward recognizes that for Calvin this was a true sign, but argues that Calvin sets the

---

22. Hodge, *Systematic Theology*, III, 630.

23. L. Berkhof, *Systematic Theology* (1939, repr. Edinburgh: Banner of Truth Trust, 1981), pp. 653–654.

24. W. Grudem, *Systematic Theology*, p. 995.

25. M. J. Erickson, *Christian Theology*, rev. edn (Grand Rapids: Baker, 1998), p. 1130.

26. R. Reymond, *A New Systematic Theology of the Christian Faith* (Nashville: Nelson, 1998), p. 963.

stage for modernity, which doubts the truth of the sign of an absent Christ.[27] According to Milbank, Calvin's sacramental theology 'is not really coherent', since 'the idea of the spiritual participation in a body that is in heaven makes very little sense'. He prefers the Thomist view, which affirms that Christ's body if it is to be present must as a body be physical, 'albeit mysteriously physical'.[28]

The Radical Orthodox criticism coheres with the Zwinglian to the extent that both claim that Calvin's assertion of the true presence of Christ does not fit well in his wider theology. The Zwinglian then says that the presence language should be attenuated, while the Radical Orthodox want the wider theology framed in a more 'participatory metaphysics'.[29]

## How Christ saves

In order to assess Calvin's doctrine of the Supper, we have to view it in relation to other themes of his thought. Only once we have seen his doctrine in its proper theological context can we make an assessment of it. Since it is Christ as Saviour who Calvin insists is presented in the sacraments, then we will not understand this view of sacraments unless we understand his account of who Christ is and how he saves.

When Calvin begins his exposition of the person and work of Christ he starts with the assertion that 'it is of greatest importance for us that he who was our Mediator be both true God and true man'.[30] Not only did our separation from God by sin require that he must descend to us, but this descent must take place in such a way that 'his divinity and our human nature might by mutual connection grow together'.[31] Calvin's exposition of Christ's work makes much of the incarnation, with the result that there is no simple distinction between the person of Christ and his work. Redemption required

27. G. Ward, 'Church as the Erotic Community', in *Sacramental Presence in a Postmodern Context*, ed. L. Boevee and L. Leijssen (Louvain: Peeters, 2001), pp. 181–188.

28. J. Milbank, 'Alternative Protestantism', in *Radical Orthodoxy and the Reformed Tradition: Creation, Covenant and Participation*, ed. J. K. A. Smith and J. H. Olthuis (Grand Rapids: Baker, 2005), p. 35.

29. Milbank, 'Alternative Protestantism', p. 35.

30. A more detailed engagement with Calvin's Christology is found in Mark Thompson's contribution to this volume.

31. *Inst.* 2.12.1.

incarnation because of the depth of the human plight. There had to be an exchange and, Calvin asks rhetorically, 'Who could have done this [work] had not the self-same Son of God become the Son of man, and had not so taken what was ours as to impart what was his to us, and to make what was his by nature ours by grace?'[32] Calvin unfolds this necessity, further explaining that since man was lost by his own disobedience it was necessary that man should counter this with obedience and satisfaction of God's judgment. So, 'since neither as God alone could he feel death, nor as man alone could he overcome it, he coupled human nature with divine that to atone for sin he might submit the weakness of the one to death; and that, wrestling with death by the power of the other nature he might win victory for us.'[33] Calvin holds that the work of Christ requires that he take on human nature fully.

When Calvin comes to deal with the relation of the two natures in the God-man he walks the well-established paths of Chalcedonian orthodoxy. In doing so he stresses the unity of the person as the usual concern of the Bible, rather than speculative questions about the two natures. He offers the hermeneutical key that 'those things which apply to the office of the Mediator are not spoken simply either of the divine nature or of the human'.[34] That is, he will explain the work of redemption in terms of what Christ the God-man did, rather than attributing elements of the work to one nature or the other.

As Calvin deals with the work of the Mediator as prophet, priest and king, his exposition emphasizes the priestly work of Christ.[35] Here again Calvin shows the importance of the incarnation as the premise of the life and death and resurrection of the Mediator. So, he says, 'from the time he took on the form of a servant, he began to pay the price of liberation in order to redeem us'. Calvin then takes a tighter focus: 'to define the way of salvation more exactly, Scripture ascribes this as peculiar and proper to Christ's death'.[36] As Calvin deals with Jesus' death it is clear that not only its possibility but also its effectiveness depends upon his humanity. Calvin emphasizes that 'the penalty to which we were subject has been imposed upon this righteous man', and focuses on Jesus' condemnation by Pilate as a demonstration that 'he took

---

32. *Inst.* 2.12.2.

33. *Inst.* 2.12.3.

34. *Inst.* 2.14.3.

35. *Inst.* 2.15.1–6 deals with the threefold office; the following chapters focus particularly on his work of expiation.

36. *Inst.* 2.16.5.

the role of a guilty man and evildoer'.[37] This 'representation', 'transfer' and 'substitution' (as Calvin calls it) depends on Jesus being human. Jesus also took the curse 'as an expiatory sacrifice'.[38] Again this depends upon him taking on human flesh.

When Calvin considers Jesus' burial he sees in it the truth that Christ entered fully into death, in order that he might conquer death for us.[39] In his treatment of Christ's burial Calvin also begins to develop the theme that what Christ experienced in his body believers come to experience in their bodies. He notes there is a second effect of Christ's death: 'by our participation in it, his death mortifies our earthly members so that they may no longer perform their functions; and it kills the old man in us that he may not flourish and bear fruit'.[40]

When Calvin turns to the resurrection he explains that it has three aspects.[41] On the one hand it reveals the accomplishment of the cross, for in it 'his death manifested its power and efficacy in us'.[42] There is also a benefit in the experience of believers in the resurrection itself: 'we are reborn into righteousness through his power'. That is, regeneration or vivification are ours because of Christ's resurrection. The third benefit is still awaited: our physical resurrection.

The hope of physical resurrection is also related to Christ's ascension. Calvin's discussion of the ascension stresses Christ's physical absence and the coming of the Spirit, so that 'as his body was raised up above all the heavens, so his power and energy were diffused and spread beyond all the bounds of heaven and earth'.[43] Christ's physical *absence* from earth is due to his physical *presence* in heaven. Thus the benefits which flow to the Christian from the ascension come by the Spirit, but are related to Christ's body. He has entered heaven 'in our flesh, as if in our name', so in a sense we are already seated with

---

37. Ibid.

38. *Inst.* 2.16.6.

39. '[H]e let himself be swallowed up by death, as it were, not to be engulfed in its abyss, but rather to engulf it that must soon engulf us; he let himself be subjected to it, not to be overwhelmed by its power, but rather to lay it low, when it was threatening us and exulting over our fallen state': *Inst.* 2.16.7. The creedal reference to Christ's descent into hell receives a similar exposition in *Inst.* 2.16.10.

40. *Inst.* 2.16.7.

41. On the bodiliness of the resurrection Calvin says: 'he suffered the same death that other men naturally die; and received immortality in the same flesh that, in the mortal state, he had taken upon himself': *Inst.* 2.16.13.

42. Ibid.

43. *Inst.* 2.16.14.

him (so Eph. 2:6). For Calvin the representative work of Christ is tied to his remaining in human flesh.

This review of Calvin's exposition of the work of Christ highlights the place that he gives to Christ's body. At each point the work of redemption is grounded in the fact that the Son of God has taken on our flesh. The traditional Reformed exposition of the person of Christ in his work has dealt with two states: the state of humiliation and the state of exaltation.[44] Calvin works with three stages in his account of the work of redemption. He speaks of (1) the whole of Christ's life culminating in the cross as the payment for sins; then (2) the resurrection of Christ's body; and then (3) his bodily ascension and absence. In each stage Christ's body is the locus of human redemption.

### How do we share in redemption?

Calvin's answer to the question of how we share in salvation comes in the famous opening words of Book 3 of his *Institutes*. He declares that 'as long as Christ remains outside of us, and we are separated from him, all that he has suffered and done for the salvation of the human race remains useless and of no value to us'.[45] That is, sinners must be united with Christ and participate in him in order to enjoy his benefits. Saving union with Christ rests on the incarnation and the resulting unity of Christ with humanity. The two are not, however, identical. Garcia points out that when Calvin writes to Vermigli about the matter he states that the incarnation union is 'very general and feeble' and that a mystical union with Christ, leading to a spiritual union, is necessary for sinners to enjoy the benefits secured in the incarnation.[46]

There has been considerable discussion about how Calvin's doctrine of 'union with Christ' should be understood. Calvin retains the traditional language of 'mystical union', leading some to conclude that he has a form of mysticism.[47] Others have suggested that Calvin's view of union is more like

---

44. H. Bavinck, *Reformed Dogmatics*, trans. J. Vriend, ed. J. Bolt (4 vols; Grand Rapids: Baker, 2003–2008), III, 406.

45. *Inst.* 3.1.1.

46. M. A. Garcia, *Life in Christ: Union with Christ and Twofold Grace in Calvin's Theology* (Milton Keynes: Paternoster, 2008), pp. 186–187.

47. For Calvin's reference see *Inst.* 3.11.10. For the cautious claim that Calvin's view is mystical see D. E. Tamburello, *Union with Christ: John Calvin and the Mysticism of St. Bernard* (Louisville: Westminster John Knox, 1994), pp. 7, 11.

the Eastern doctrine of *theosis*, in which the *energia* of God fills the redeemed but not his *ousia*. Butin and Billings have argued that Calvin's doctrine is theotic, grounded in a perichorectic union.[48] Neither mysticism nor *theosis* are labels which do justice to Calvin's view of the nature of union with Christ.[49] Calvin gives no formal definition of the concept. Garcia's comment accurately reflects what can be gathered from Calvin's use of the concept:

> communion with Christ is much more than mental but less than baldly physical or essential. It is real and true but not a miracle of ontological oneness but by the blessing of the Spirit's work.[50]

The relationship is ultimately undefinable because it is 'mysterious': that is, beyond human knowing.

However we describe Calvin's view of union, he is clear that it involves union with the whole Christ, including – indeed, especially – Christ's bodily humanity. John 6 was very important for him with regard to the nature of saving union. Jesus' words at Capernaum represent one of many points in John's Gospel at which it becomes clear that incarnational union is not sufficient for salvation. Jesus says that people must eat his flesh and drink his blood in order to have eternal life (John 6:54–56). Calvin recognizes that Jesus' graphic language is a way of describing faith (John 6:29, 35, 40, 47, 69); however he insists that while 'eating' is a metaphor, the reference to Jesus' flesh is not metaphoric. It speaks of 'the uninterrupted communication of the flesh of Christ' which brings salvation. He goes on to say that the passage is not about the Lord's Supper, but that 'there is nothing said here that is not figuratively represented, and actually bestowed on believers, in the Lord's Supper; and Christ even intended that the holy Supper should be, as it were, a seal and

---

48. J. T. Billings, *Calvin, Participation, and the Gift: The Activity of Believers in Union with Christ* (Oxford: Oxford University Press, 2007), pp. 61–66. Billings refers to 'Calvin's doctrine of deification, if we may call it such' and repeats all his qualifications in note 162, see p. 60. See also P. W. Butin, *Revelation, Redemption and Response: Calvin's Trinitarian Understanding of the Divine-Human Relationship* (Oxford: Oxford University Press, 1995), pp. 83, 186 nn. 45, 46.

49. For an assessment of the claims that Calvin's view of union can be described as mysticism, or perichorectic *theosis*, see J. McClean, 'Perichoresis, Theosis and Union with Christ in the Thought of John Calvin', *RTR* (forthcoming).

50. Garcia, *Life in Christ*, p. 258.

confirmation of this sermon'.[51] That is, while John 6 is not about the Lord's Supper, the Supper is about what John 6 is about. That point, however, runs ahead of our discussion at present.

The centrality of union with Christ in Calvin's soteriology is underlined by the opening words of the 'Confession of Faith concerning the Eucharist' composed by Farel, Calvin and Viret around 1537. The statement indicates that salvation comes only as the Spirit brings believers into union with Christ:

> We confess that the spiritual life which Christ bestows upon us does not rest on the fact that he vivifies us with his Spirit, but that his Spirit makes us participants in the virtue of his vivifying body, by which participation we are fed on eternal life.[52]

When Calvin expounds the life of faith in the Spirit in Book 3 of the *Institutes*, the three stages of the work of Christ play an organizing role in his thought, underlining the relation of the incarnation and the Christian life. The traditional motifs of mortification and vivification play an important role in his exposition of repentance and are coupled with a stress on life lived in hope.[53] Mortification aligns with Christ's suffering, vivification with Christ's resurrection and hope with his ascension. Calvin teaches that mortification and vivification happen only 'by participation in Christ'. Because we share in Christ's death and resurrection, our old self is crucified and we are raised into newness of life that the image of God may be restored in us. This course of repentance runs through the whole of the Christian life, until the believer is conformed to the image of God in glory.[54]

Calvin offers an analysis of the psychological experience of suffering, indicating how it teaches and trains believers. Underlying that account is the fact that suffering flows from participation in Christ and brings conformity with Christ. Furthermore, in suffering we experience the power of the resurrection.[55] Sufferings will have this spiritual significance only because we live now in hope of the resurrection. So Calvin concludes, 'if believers' eyes are turned to the power of the resurrection, in their hearts the cross of Christ will at last triumph over the devil, flesh, sin and wicked men'.[56]

---

51. *CNTC* 4, pp. 169–170.
52. 'Confession of Faith concerning the Eucharist', in *Calvin: Theological Treatises*, p. 168.
53. *Inst.* 3.3.5–9.
54. *Inst.* 3.3.9.
55. *Inst.* 3.8.1.
56. *Inst.* 3.9.6.

The connection between Christ's work in his body and our salvation in our bodies is at the heart of Calvin's account of the Christian life. He does not treat sharing in Christ as simply a figure of speech. For example, in his exposition of Romans 6 he deals with Paul's horticultural metaphor that we are 'ingrafted' [*symphytoi*] with Christ in the likeness of his death.[57] He comments that this deals not only with 'our conformity to the example of Christ but also the secret union [*arcanan coniunctionem*] by which we grow together with Him'.[58] He acknowledges the metaphorical aspects of the expression by pointing out two important differences between the metaphor and the reality it describes. Firstly, 'in the grafting of trees the graft draws its nourishment from the root but retains its own natural quality', but in union with Christ 'we not only derive the strength and sap for the life which flows from Christ, but we also pass from our own nature into His'. On the other hand, our death is not the same physical death as his, but rather there is an 'analogy'. Having acknowledged these ways in which the figure is not like the reality, Calvin asserts that the words show that we share in Christ's nature, that is, his physical death and resurrection, and that we experience that sharing in vivification and mortification.

### How do we come to be united with Christ?

Since union with Christ is the way in which believers come to share in his blessings, the next question must be: how do they come to be united with Christ? Calvin's answer to this question is as clear as it is well known. He opens Book 3 of the *Institutes* with the assertion that 'we obtain this by faith', but that there is a higher answer which comes from God's side: 'the secret energy of the Spirit, by which we come to enjoy Christ and all his benefits'.[59] Later, Calvin explains that 'Christ, when he illumines us into faith by the power of his Spirit, at the same time so engrafts us into his body that we become partakers of every

---

57. The word occurs in Rom 6:25 and can have the horticultural meaning which Calvin develops, though Doug Moo comments that it is used in too many other contexts for there to be any degree of probability that the association is present in this passage: D. Moo, *The Epistle to the Romans* (Grand Rapids: Eerdmans, 1996), p. 368 n. 76.

58. *CNTC* 8, pp. 123–124.

59. *Inst.* 3.1.1. See Billings, *Participation*, pp. 100–102, for a discussion of Calvin's introduction of Book 3 and the opening chapter into the 1559 edition of the *Institutes*.

good'.[60] Calvin's doctrine of the union of the believer with Christ by the Spirit is not in distinction from a doctrine of union with the body of Christ. Rather, Calvin holds that the incarnate Christ was anointed with the Spirit as the second Adam that he might share the Spirit with his people and they might be united to him in his incarnation.[61] For Calvin, a union with the body of Christ comes about through the indwelling of the Spirit and the response of faith.

Calvin carefully and consistently ascribes union with Christ to the Spirit and to faith. In this pairing it is clear that the Spirit grants faith and so has a causal priority, since 'faith is the principal work of the Holy Spirit'.[62]

The role of faith in union with Christ relates to Calvin's claim that the gospel mediates this union. Calvin declares that Christ is presented to us 'clothed in his gospel' and it is always through the Word that God draws people to himself.[63] Torrance has argued that Calvin saw that we were offered 'auditory, intuitive knowledge of God' in the Word.[64] That is a knowledge which is not reached by deduction but is a direct personal knowledge of God: 'the Word of God does certainly involve the communication of truths and statements, in and through these God speaks to us directly and confronts us with the majesty and dignity of his Truth'.[65] Torrance's account of how Calvin came to this view is not sustained by the evidence, but his summary of Calvin's view is still helpful.[66]

Deddo explains Torrance's claim in the following terms: 'the Spirit puts us in actual, immediate, intuitive, non-formal, even empirical touch with the actual reality and presence of God himself as the Word, not just externally but internally present to our spirit'.[67] The word 'immediate' is inaccurate,

---

60. *Inst.* 3.2.35. Similarly, 'Perfect salvation is found in the person of Christ . . . that we might become partakers of it "he baptises us in the Holy Spirit and fire" bringing us into the light of faith in his gospel and so regenerating us that we become new creatures': *Inst.* 3.1.4.

61. *Inst.* 3.1.2.

62. See *Inst.* 3.1.4.

63. *Inst.* 3.2.6.

64. T. F. Torrance, *Theological Science* (London: Oxford University Press, 1969), p. 23. For an extended exposition of this, see T. F. Torrance, *The Hermeneutics of John Calvin* (Edinburgh: Scottish Academic Press, 1988), pp. 86–95.

65. Torrance, *Hermeneutics*, p. 93.

66. A. N. S. Lane, 'Recent Calvin Literature: A Review Article', *Themelios* 16.2 (1991), p. 20.

67. G. W. Deddo, 'The Holy Spirit in the Theology of T. F. Torrance', in *The Promise of Trinitarian Theology: Theologians in Dialogue with T. F. Torrance*, ed. E. M. Colyer (Lanham: Rowman & Littlefield, 2001), p. 101.

since Torrance's claim is that the intuitive knowledge is mediated by the word. Deddo is correct to stress that this knowledge is not merely cognitive, either in Calvin or in Torrance's description. For Calvin the declaration of the gospel brings us into an encounter with Christ, and as the Spirit gives faith the Word mediates a union with Christ. This union, as I have stressed, is a union with the whole Christ, particularly with the ascended, incarnate Christ.

## Christ's human nature and union

At this point we can return to Reymond's vigorous criticism of Calvin. He claims that the Reformer holds that the benefits of salvation come from the virtues of the humanity of Christ 'which flow into it from the Godhead'. He believes that the implication of this is that Calvin unintentionally 'comes perilously close to apotheosising' Christ's humanity: that is, making the humanity of Christ divine.[68] This seems to imply that Calvin moved too close to a Lutheran view of the *communicatio idiomatum*, or at least that this language did not properly guard against that. Reymond makes this criticism because Calvin insists that participation in the body and blood of Christ is how the Supper mediated salvation.

We have to keep in view Calvin's whole account of the relation of the two natures in order in order to assess Reymond's criticism. Calvin presents both Christ's divine and human nature as indispensable to his work as Mediator. He states that the life, righteousness, lordship and authority required to swallow up death, conquer sin and rout the powers lie 'with God alone'. At the same time, only man could remedy disobedience with obedience, satisfy God's judgment and pay the penalties for sin.[69] So the Mediator had to be both divine and human, and the two natures had to, as it were, work in concert in order for him to complete his work.

Calvin typically does not refer to the 'natures' working, for it is the person of Christ who works. Calvin explains the communication of the attributes as a way of expressing truths of the incarnation: 'things that he carried out in his human nature are transferred improperly, although not without reason, to his divinity'.[70] In Calvin's exposition of the work of Christ he retains a careful treatment of the union of the two natures but with a focus on the one person

---

68. Reymond, *Systematic Theology*, p. 963.

69. *Inst.* 2.12.3, p. 466.

70. *Inst.* 2.14.2. H. Blocher comments, rightly, that the term 'improper' 'has no negative connotation; it is a philologist's word for a departure from ordinary . . . forms of

of the Mediator. Muller argues that in teaching such a *communicatio idomatum in concerto* with its focus on the concrete person of Christ, Calvin, along with Zwingli, Bucer and Bullinger, 'consistently refused to allow a flow of divine attributes from the divine to the human'.[71]

Calvin is very wary of teaching a direct union with Christ's divine nature, because this was the teaching of Osiander. The point that Calvin rejects in Osiander's teaching on justification is 'that Christ is our righteousness because he is God eternal, the source of righteousness'.[72] Calvin focuses our righteousness in that which comes from Christ's death and resurrection. He acknowledges that our righteousness comes from God, and indeed from the Father. But this righteousness does not become ours by participation in the essential righteousness of God, but rather by our union with Christ the Mediator we participate in the righteousness of his life, death and resurrection. Calvin does not reverse Osiander's position and say that we receive righteousness from Christ's human nature alone. Indeed, he allows that if Osiander had taught that Christ's essence becomes ours as man and 'also in that the divine essence is poured into us', then his position would have been less dangerous and objectionable.[73]

In criticism of Osiander Calvin returns to the theme of Book 2: that Christ's work of redemption required him to be God and man and that he 'carried out all these acts according to his human nature'.[74] In explaining his position Calvin makes explicit reference to the Lord's Supper and John 6. He argues that in both cases our attention is directed to 'the whole Christ', and that we learn that we receive what is his through his flesh. He often uses the trope of a fountain, in that the death and resurrection of Christ make him the source from which flows blessings which 'otherwise would lie unprofitably hidden in that deep and secret spring'. At the conclusion of this discussion Calvin states that when the work of Christ is understood in the terms he has outlined then he would accept Osiander's expression that the 'righteousness of which Christ makes us partakers with himself is the eternal righteousness of the eternal God'.[75]

---

expression': H. Blocher, 'Luther and Calvin on Christology', paper presented to Edinburgh Dogmatics Conference, August 2007, p. 9 n. 92.

71. R. A. Muller, *After Calvin: Studies in the Development of a Theological Tradition* (Oxford: Oxford University Press, 2003), p. 13.

72. *Inst.* 3.11.5.

73. *Inst.* 3.11.6.

74. *Inst.* 3.11.9.

75. Ibid.

Reymond is correct to state that Calvin teaches that the believer receives through Christ's humanity 'virtues which flow into it from the Godhead'. However, this is not a teaching unique to Calvin's view of the sacraments, but is a consistent part of his teaching of the believer's union with Christ. Reymond's claim that Calvin has simply chosen confusing language is not accurate. Calvin explicitly opposes a teaching that we receive righteousness immediately from divine essence, insisting that all that we receive from God comes to us through Christ's human nature. The righteousness which believers enjoy comes from God, and indeed from the Father, but is also that which is achieved by Christ in his death and resurrection and so can never be separated from his flesh.

Reymond's criticism highlights exactly that point of Calvin's theology which informs his view of the Lord's Supper. Salvation lies in the person and work of the incarnate Son. In order to share in salvation we must have a communion with him, and the Lord's Supper offers and sustains that communion. As Horton says, 'if we have trouble with this aspect of Calvin's eucharistic teaching, then we will have difficulty with his entire doctrine of union'.[76]

## The Lord's Supper and participation

Having reviewed Calvin's account of salvation and the place of union with Christ in that, we are now able to understand the importance of his doctrine of participation in the body and blood of Christ in the Lord's Supper. Calvin holds that the Lord's Supper presents the gospel and therefore it presents Christ. In the 'Short Treatise' he states the principle that 'just as God has set all fullness of life in Jesus, in order to communicate it to us by means of him, so he has ordained his Word as instrument by which Jesus Christ, with all his benefits, is dispensed to us'. Then he argues that 'the Lord instituted for us his Supper, in order to sign and seal in our consciences the promises contained in his gospel'.[77] In the *Institutes* Calvin argues that 'the sacrament requires preaching to beget faith'.[78] Wallace shows from a wide range of Calvin's works that he held that the sacraments had no validity or effect without the Word, that the sacraments were representations of the Word and that they

---

76. M. S. Horton, *People and Place: A Covenant Ecclesiology* (Lousiville: Westminster John Knox, 2008), p. 134.

77. 'Short Treatise', pp. 143–144.

78. *Inst.* 4.14.4.

sealed the Word.[79] For Calvin sure knowledge of God as Creator is possible only through the Scriptures.[80] Knowledge of God as Redeemer depends even more entirely upon the Scriptures, for there is Christ presented in his gospel.[81] Calvin's doctrine of the sacraments builds on this view of revelation by the Word. Without the gospel proclaimed, the sacraments have no meaning and so no effect.

At this point Calvin's more general discussion about the sacraments illuminates his understanding of the Supper. Calvin related both Word and sacraments to the presentation of Christ to the believer by drawing in Augustine's theory of signs. As he discusses the Lord's Supper, Calvin states that God shows the incomprehensible mystery of union with Christ 'in visible signs best adapted to our small capacity'.[82] Van der Kooi explains that Calvin's thought about the sacraments reflects a certain view of creation as well as about salvation.[83]

With Augustine, Calvin made the distinction between *signum* ('sign') and *res* ('thing'). Understanding and communication depend on signs which signify things. Words are the most common signs, though there are other types. Words are not natural signs (the way smoke is a natural sign of fire). Rather words are given signs [*signum datum*] in which the meaning must be established and is not inherent. There are physical objects which are also given signs and these can be treated as if they are words, so Augustine calls them 'visible words' [*verba visibilia*]. For Augustine the timeless intelligible realities of God are known when words function as signs and 'help direct our mind's eye to the realities they signify'. These realities and the truth do not exist in the sign; the *signum* must not be confused for the *res*. The sign conveys the truth of the thing, so that the hearer can grasp the truth inwardly. It is in the mind that the truth of things is grasped. This Platonic conception is linked for Augustine with the further need for words to recount for us historical events which are themselves signs of divine truth and are part of God's redemption. Most important of these historical truths is that 'the Word became flesh'.[84] The necessity of historical

---

79. R. S. Wallace, *Calvin's Doctrine of the Word and Sacrament* (Edinburgh/London: Oliver & Boyd, 1953), pp. 137–141.

80. *Inst.* 1.6.1–4.

81. *Inst.* 2.9.2.

82. *Inst.* 4.17.1.

83. C. van der Kooi, *As in a Mirror: John Calvin and Karl Barth on Knowing God, – A Diptych*, trans. D. Mader (Leiden: Brill, 2005), p. 195.

84. T. Williams, 'Biblical Interpretation', in *The Cambridge Companion to Augustine*, ed. E. Stump and N. Kretzmann (Cambridge: Cambridge University Press, 2001), p. 66.

events to reveal God and bring redemptive knowledge of him modifies the Platonism upon which Augustine drew. It does not, however, qualify the fundamental distinction between *signa* and *res*.

Calvin is less enamoured of Platonism than Augustine, and for the sake of this examination we can set aside a discussion of the extent of the Reformer's debt to Plato.[85] However, Calvin embraced the account of the relation of *signa* and *res* which he found in Augustine and, like Augustine, applied it particularly to the sacraments.[86] The power of the view was that it made a distinction between the two without denying that the *signa* mediate the truth of the *res*. So Calvin explains that 'the sacred mystery of the Supper' consists of 'physical signs' and 'spiritual truth', which are 'represented and displayed' by the symbols. He explains that this analysis makes clear why he does not hold that Christ is present 'only by understanding and imagination', but in such a way that believers have 'true participation in him'. [87]

This theory of signs gave Calvin the tools to give a powerful account of the nature of the sacraments. The Supper and baptism are, if understood physically, simply bread and wine and water. However, they are used in actions which God has made into 'given signs' and which are explained by the words of the gospel, in particular the words of institution.[88] Calvin adopts Augustine's definition of a sacrament as 'a visible sign of a sacred thing or of an invisible grace'. His exposition of this definition is that a sacrament 'is a testimony of divine grace toward us, confirmed by an outward sign, with a mutual attestation of our piety toward him'.[89] So Calvin maintains Augustine's distinction

---

85. J. Boisset claims that a Platonic perspective is required to see the unity of Calvin teaching: J. Boisset, *Sagesse et sainteté dans la pensée de Jean Calvin* (Paris, 1959), p. 272, quoted in J. Fitzer, 'The Augustinian Roots of Calvin's Eucharistic Thought', *Augustinian Studies* 7 (1976), p. 69 (repr. in *Articles on Calvin and Calvinism*, vol. 10, *Calvin's Ecclesiology: Sacraments and Deacons*, ed. R. C. Gamble, New York: Garland, 1992, p. 165). Partee responds that 'it seems extremely wayward' to assert any direct influence of Plato on Calvin's view of participation: see C. Partee, *Calvin and Classical Philosophy* (1977; repr. Louisville: Westminster John Knox, 2005), pp. 114–115.

86. T. J. Davis, *This Is My Body: The Presence of Christ in Reformation Thought* (Grand Rapids: Baker, 2008), pp. 147–148, shows the key role of Augustine in shaping Calvin's thought about the Supper in the 1543 edition of the *Institutes*.

87. See *Inst.* 4.17.11.

88. On the importance of the words of institution for Calvin's view of the Supper, see Davis, *This Is My Body*, pp. 67–71.

89. *Inst.* 4.14.1.

between the sign [the *sacramentum rei* or *res significans*] and the invisible reality which is signified and mediated [the *res sacramenti*].[90] When performed in the context of the proclaimed Word, these actions point to Christ and salvation in him. In doing so they mediate an inner knowledge of and participation in that to which they point. This mediation comes about only when the Spirit works to bring about union with Christ and so when faith is present.

Calvin does not claim that his exposition of the sacraments using Augustine's sign theory allows a full explanation of the presence of Christ in the Supper. Indeed, just the opposite is the case. Calvin explains that 'it is a secret too lofty for either my mind to comprehend or my words to declare' and that it is more experienced [*experior*] than understood [*intelligam*].[91] The signs theory allows Calvin to speak of participation in Christ mediated by Word and sacraments.

The Radical Orthodox criticism of Calvin on the sacraments is that he moves too far from the Platonism of Augustine and Thomas and so affirms a true presence but not a real presence. It is true that Calvin's stress on the ascension introduces a note of 'absence' in his account of the presence of Christ in the Supper. However, this may not be simply due to a nominalism which can find only an arbitrary relation between *res* and *signa*. Calvin is certainly careful to maintain the distinction between creature and Creator.[92] However, his insistence on the heavenly location of Christ's body is not simply because he lacks a participationary metaphysic. Rather it is an important affirmation of the importance of the body of Christ, qua body, in redemption. It is not clear how Aquinas' account of Christ's body present but occupying no location, at rest in heaven and only discernible by the intellect is a more adequate account.[93]

## More in the Supper than the Word?

One of the puzzles for some interpreters of Calvin is why he seems to ascribe greater effect to the Supper than he does to the Word. This feature of his view

90.  Van der Kooi, *As in a Mirror*, p. 196.

91.  *Inst.* 4.17.31.

92.  Berkouwer explains that Calvin stood 'on guard against any crossings of creaturely boundary-lines' because 'from the gospel he learned that the riches of Christ consisted in the fact that he redeemed us as one of us'. So he resisted any suggestion that Christ did not remain fully human: G. C. Berkouwer, *The Person of Christ*, trans. J. H. Kok (Grand Rapids: Eerdmans, 1977), p. 282.

93.  *ST* 17, pp. 107–119 (3a, 75 a5–7).

is the point at which the Zwinglian view makes its objection. The Zwinglian critique observes that the Word of God mediates life from God and is the foundation of the sacrament. It asks how there can be any way to ascribe more to the Supper, let alone any reason to ascribe more. Calvin's answer is summed up in his term 'seal'. The Supper, like the Word, is a sign, but it is also a seal. He states that the chief function of the Supper is not 'to extend to us the body of Christ' but 'to seal and confirm that promise by which he testifies that his flesh is food indeed and his blood is drink'.[94] The theory of signification underlies Calvin's account of the sealing dimension of the Supper. As God-ordained and Spirit-empowered signs, the sacraments convey the thing they signify. However, the very physicality of them – the sight, touch and taste of the elements – makes them compelling. As bodily beings we benefit greatly from the physical signs which God gives to confirm the promises he has made. The sacraments do not make God's promise true or more true, so Calvin says that 'God's truth is of itself firm and sure enough, and it cannot receive better confirmation from any other source than from itself'.[95] The sacraments do, however, convey the truth of God's promises to believers in a striking way.

The 'signification' of the sacraments explains why Calvin particularly relates the reception of the body and blood of Christ to the Lord's Supper. As a sign of God's grace the Supper mediates all of Christ and all his blessings, for there is no separating of one blessing from the others. However, the words of institution and the meaning given to the signs refer particularly to the body and blood of Christ. Calvin then aligns the reality mediated by the Supper with the truth that it signifies. This is the point of analogy or *tertium comparationis* which ensures that the relation between the *sacramentum rei* and *res sacramenti* is not arbitrary. The Scriptures make the connection between the Supper and participation in Christ's body and blood. Jesus' own words in the setting of the Last Supper, held during the Passover festival and with the prospect of Jesus' death, establish the connection. Paul asks, 'Is not the cup of thanksgiving for which we give thanks a participation [*koinōnia*] in the blood of Christ? And is not the bread that we break a participation in the body of Christ?' (1 Cor. 10:16). This biblical description of the Supper leads Calvin to affirm that as an effective sign the Supper grants to those who believe that which it signifies.

A summary of the case so far is in order. I have argued that Calvin's view of the Supper rests on his view of the importance of the incarnation in redemption. Christ's body is central to his redemption of embodied humans. Calvin's

94. *Inst.* 4.17.3.

95. *Inst.* 4.14.3.

account of the Christian life is that it involves Spirit-mediated union with the risen and ascended embodied Christ. This union is established and sustained by the Word through which the Spirit presents Christ to believers. The Supper presents to believers a visible and tangible sign of the truth that Christ has died for them, and that they share in Christ's death and resurrection. Thus the Spirit of Christ by the words, actions and elements of the Lord's Supper seals to Christians their union with Christ's body and blood.

## Scriptural basis

Calvin is committed to presenting a theology which answers fully to Scripture. So we can rightly ask if his doctrine of the sacraments is found in Scripture. If we begin with the question of the participation in Christ in the sacraments, Calvin can point to 1 Corinthians 10. There Paul asserts that to eat and drink the Supper is to participate in Christ. Similarly, 1 Corinthians 11:27 speaks of unworthy eating and drinking as 'sinning against the body and blood of the Lord'. The words of institution also play an important part in Calvin's theology.[96] Beyond the references to the Supper, Calvin's theology of the Supper is supported by the biblical emphasis on the importance of the incarnation and union with Christ. John 6 is most important in drawing these themes together.[97]

Calvin's doctrine of the Supper gives a clear insight into his approach to Christian theology. It is grounded in a careful and thoughtful understanding of biblical texts. However, he is not simply collecting and summarizing texts which refer directly to the Supper. Calvin's method is to deal with the many themes of Scripture and to draw those themes together in a theological exposition, with a constant interest in how he can serve Christian piety. As he does this the Supper becomes an important topic in his thought.

## Baptism

Further light may be shed by examining the way Calvin speaks of the other Christian sacrament, baptism. Calvin treats baptism in a similar way to the

---

96. *Inst.* 4.17.20–25.

97. Horton lays out the biblical support for Calvin's view in detail in *People and Place*, pp. 119–123.

Lord's Supper, though with an important difference in emphasis. He describes baptism with similarly realistic language about union with Christ's death and resurrection. He writes that 'those who receive baptism with right faith truly feel the effective working of Christ's death in the mortification of their flesh together with the working of his resurrection in the vivification of the Spirit'.[98] Yet he often is content to speak of what the water of baptism 'represents' (the washing away of sin, sharing in mortification and vivification and union with Christ) with no further discussion of the presence of Christ in the sacrament.[99] The relatively reduced emphasis on the 'real presence' in baptism may be explained in terms of the representation involved. That is, the bread and wine represent Christ's body and blood, while the water represents Christ's Spirit.

Gerrish wonders if there is an incoherence in Calvin's view of baptism. He points out that Calvin can refer the validity of baptism to the past as a sign of the fact that God has already adopted the children of believers.[100] He can relate it to the present, 'in the assurance that the reality is present in and with the sign'.[101] He can also claim that the sacrament will in time bear the fruit of faith.[102] Gerrish argues that Calvin has developed each of these strands in interaction with a different problem and that this introduces a certain tension into his presentation.[103]

There is no need to find an incoherence in Calvin's view at this point. His presentation reflects the subjective and objective elements of his presentation, but applied to the sacrament of entry rather than of sustenance. In dealing with both the Supper and baptism Calvin holds that God truly uses the sacrament and is truly present in it, but that he uses it as a sign and so is present by mediation. This is the objective side of Calvin's view of the sacraments. Calvin

---

98.  *Inst.* 4.15.5.

99.  So Calvin says the Lord 'speaks to us through a sign' and 'performs for our soul within as truly and surely as we see our body outwardly cleansed, submerged and surrounded with water': *Inst.* 4.15.14.

100. 'God declares that he adopts our babies as his own before they are born, when he promises that he will be our God and the God of our descendants after us. Their salvation is embraced in this word': *Inst.* 4.15.20.

101. Gerrish, 'Reformed Doctrine', p. 115.

102. 'Infants are baptized into future repentance and faith, and even though these have not been formed in them, the seed lies hidden without by the secret working of the Spirit': *Inst.* 4.16.20.

103. Gerrish, 'Reformed Doctrine', p. 115.

also teaches that the effect of the sacrament and God's presence depends upon the work of the Spirit, and this work can never be controlled by the church in its celebration of the sacraments. This is the subjective side of his view of the sacraments. Because baptism deals with 'entry' into God's family, the temporal question arises in a way in which it does not with the Lord's Supper, and both the objective and the subjective sides must be included in explaining baptism. So Calvin can say both that in baptism the children of believers are adopted as God's children, and also that through this sign the Spirit brings assurance of adoption and the fruit of union with Christ. This complexity of presentation is consistent with Calvin's view of the sacraments.

Calvin had a great deal of biblical material to lead him toward this view of baptism. The New Testament uses the term over one hundred times, and from Matthew 28 on it is consistently presented as the sign that people have entered into salvation in Christ and so in the church. Peter's sermon at Pentecost calls for repentance and offers baptism in the name of Christ for forgiveness (Acts 2:38). Three thousand baptisms occurred that day, and this continued through Acts (8:12, 36; 9:18; 10:48; 16:15, 33; 18:8; 19:5; 22:16). Christians continued to baptize people as they became disciples (Rom 6:3; 1 Cor. 1:13; Gal. 3:27) and this continued in the post-apostolic era.

It is sometimes suggested that much of the baptism language of the New Testament is metaphorical. However, Leon Morris comments 'that this is a distinction the New Testament never makes'.[104] That is, in most cases there is a reference to water baptism, even if the term has a more extended reference as well (e.g. 1 Cor. 12:13; Col. 2:12). The New Testament writers then routinely relate baptism to a wide range of spiritual blessings. Beasley-Murray repeats and endorses Schlatter's comment that 'there is no gift or power which the Apostolic documents do not ascribe to baptism'.[105]

Because baptism was the common experience of Christians, it is quite likely that there are also allusions to baptism in texts that do not explicitly mention baptism (e.g. Eph. 5:26; Titus 3:5).[106]

Thus Calvin as a biblical theologian had every reason to speak realistically

---

104. L. L. Morris, *New Testament Theology* (Grand Rapids: Zondervan, 1986), p. 81.

105. G. Beasley-Murray, *Baptism in the New Testament* (1962; repr. Exeter: Paternoster, 1972), p. 263.

106. See G. Wainwright, 'Baptism, Baptismal rites', in *Dictionary of the Later New Testament and its Developments*, ed. R. P. Martin and P. H. Davids (Downers Grove: IVP, 1997) for a range of possible allusions to baptism in the later NT and for post-canonical references.

about the connection between salvation and baptism, stating that 'at whatever
time we are baptized, we are once for all washed and purged for our whole
life', and 'through baptism Christ makes us sharers in this death, that we
may be engrafted in it', and 'those who receive baptism with right faith truly
feel the effective working of Christ's death in the mortification of their flesh
together with the work of his resurrection in the vivification of the Spirit'.[107]
As with Calvin's realism about the Supper, his language here about baptism has
troubled some later Reformed writers who want to distance themselves more
fully from baptismal regeneration. Calvin's affirmations depend on his theology of signification. He is not claiming that the water of baptism in itself
brings us into salvation.[108] Rather, as with the Lord's Supper, we have a God-
ordained sign which is a sign of incorporation into Christ and by the Spirit is
used to grant that which it signifies.


## Appreciating Calvin and the sacraments

Can the heirs of Calvin appreciate his view of the sacraments? We can surely
appreciate his Christological emphasis. For Calvin Christ is the material [*mate-
riam*] or substance [*substantiam*] of the sacraments. This is because all their
firmness [*soliditatem*] lies in him and without him they promise nothing. Calvin
states this in order to make the point that it is only as the sacraments lead us
to Christ that they have any value for us. When we find Christ through them
then 'we receive in true faith what is offered there'.[109]

We can appreciate Calvin's theology of the sacraments as part of his vision
of the Christian life. He has an ecclesial vision in which the church is key to
entering into God's salvation. It is a vision of mediated salvation in which the
Word proclaimed in the church and sacraments enacted by the church bring
believers into union with the ascended Christ and so into all his blessings. The
special role of the sacraments is to seal to believers that which they have been
promised in the Word and have grasped by faith. Just because this vision is
often missing in contemporary churches, we can allow Calvin to show us that
the Bible directs us to the church as our mother, and to the Word and sacraments as God's ordained means to create and sustain his church.

We can appreciate that Calvin's emphasis on the sacraments is motivated

---

107. *Inst.* 4.15.3, 5.
108. *Inst.* 4.15.2.
109. *Inst.* 4.14.16.

by his belief that they rank highly among God's blessings for his church. For Calvin the two sacraments alone are ceremonies which 'promise salvation' because they come from God. God alone can determine how he will testify to the truth of his promises, and in his wisdom he has done so in the Lord's Supper and baptism. Only baptism in the context of the gospel preached can mark a person's entry into the faith, and the Lord's Supper is how God determines to offer 'a sort of continual food on which Christ feeds the household of his believers'.[110] For that reason Calvin calls for these ceremonies to be conducted in the church without the addition of further elements or the obscuring effect of other ceremonies. Reformed and evangelical churches in the twenty-first century usually put far less stress on the sacraments than did Calvin. We teach on them rarely, and reduce our celebration of them. As we appreciate Calvin's approach we will place a renewed emphasis on the sacraments.

This chapter has aimed to help us appreciate Calvin's provocative view of the presence of Christ in the sacraments. Calvin insists on this because salvation depends on union with the whole Christ offered to faith by both Word and sacraments. Explanations of the sacraments in evangelical churches routinely speak of what they are not (in order to avoid superstition), but say little of what they are. Calvin reminds us that the Bible uses dramatically realistic language to describe the place of the sacraments in the life of the church. He gives us a theology of the sacraments in which we celebrate God's kind provision for the church, in which he seals to us that which he promises. Calvin claims that not only may Christ be found in the sacraments, but for those who hear his Word and trust in him he *will* be found in them. We may want to seek a different way to describe how baptism and the Lord's Supper mediate union with Christ, perhaps using speech–act theory rather than Augustinian signification theory. As we do, however, we have far more need to learn from Calvin than we have need to correct him.

© John McClean, 2009

---

110. *Inst.* 4.18.19.

## 10. HOW 'ETHICS' WORKS: AN ENGAGEMENT WITH JOHN CALVIN

*Andrew J. B. Cameron*

A chapter about ethics would probably have bored Calvin as much as a chapter about Calvin, because he would not have accepted that right and wrong could be studied as 'ethics'. The subject of our behaviour could not, for Calvin, somehow be separated from an overall picture of Christ's cosmos and our place within it. Nor would he have considered it a particularly useful subject of enquiry, because we turn out not to be very good at it. Even when we half-see what might be right, we then go on to do whatever we wanted to do anyway.

Calvin was more interested in telling a different story. It gives us something to work with when it comes to deciding how to live, yet is not fixated on that. We come to know ourselves in this story; but in a neat judo throw, we receive that knowledge only as we come to know someone else. It explains how we may participate in life alongside this other, so that our surging emotions become something beautiful. Calvin would say that we can only know how 'ethics' works once *this* story becomes real.

Commentators suggest that Calvin's ethic includes many modes and derives from several sources. For Ronald Wallace, there is a broad outlook yet many narrow pronouncements. Calvin may closely attend to particular and specific contexts, or resort to an extreme 'other-worldliness'. The Christian life is sometimes specified as cross-bearing and following Jesus, or sometimes as a response to general ethical principles derived from a natural order.[1] In dialogue with the Western tradition, Calvin attends to the ends of action, to acts in themselves, and to motives for action.[2] Even just the analysis of acts includes 'several notions: nature and natural law, conscience, humanity, equity, the rule of love and moderation', as David Foxgrover puts it.[3] William Keesecker thinks that law is a fundamental concept in Calvin's ethics.[4] It would be easy to conclude that Calvin's complex ethic is an eclectic scrapbook of whatever seemed convenient. (This conclusion particularly commends itself if we have already decided that ethics reduces to some simple tenet, such as a list of rights, or the dictates of 'conscience', or a principle of universality, or a test of satisfied preferences.)

The complexity of Calvin's ethic is compounded by the variety of roles he lived out: pastor to average Christians, theological ambassador for the Reformation, civic leader in Geneva, and 'consultant' to other such leaders. Theologians are not often engaged across such a range of ecclesial and secular responsibilities, and Calvin's various policies, rulings, initiatives and attitudes are on more public display than would be the case for most other pastors, theologians or statesmen.[5] Scholars have examined many of the issues he addressed, including the use and abuse of legal systems; the logic and conduct of marriage and divorce; the proper 'shape' of cultural activities such as dancing, gambling, card-playing, alcohol consumption or the acquisition of luxuries; the evaluation of economic practices, including work, trade and interest payments; the validity and boundaries of war; gender relations in society; and childrearing. An examination of Calvin's normative judgments would be a useful exercise if his conclusions became a laboratory in which to test the workings of our own moral reasoning and view of the world. Unfortunately, the tone of some

1. R. S. Wallace, *Calvin's Doctrine of the Christian Life* (Edinburgh: Oliver & Boyd, 1959), v.
2. D. L. Foxgrover, 'A Scrap of Bread and a Right Conscience', in *Calvin and Christian Ethics: Papers and Responses Presented at the Fifth Colloquium on Calvin and Calvin Studies*, ed. P. De Klerk (Grand Rapids: Calvin Studies Society, 1987), pp. 126, 139 n. 8.
3. Foxgrover, 'Scrap of Bread', p. 128.
4. W. F. Keesecker, 'The Law in John Calvin's Ethics', in *Calvin and Christian Ethics: Papers and Responses Presented at the Fifth Colloquium on Calvin and Calvin Studies*, ed. P. De Klerk (Grand Rapids: Calvin Studies Society, 1987), p. 19.
5. A compendium of Calvin's norms, which also reviews some of the secondary literature, can be found in J. H. van Wyk, 'Calvin on the Christian Life', in *Our Reformational Tradition: A Rich Heritage and Lasting Vocation* (Potchefstroom: Potchefstroom University for Christian Higher Education, 1984), pp. 247–265.

engagements is not like that. Modern declarations against Calvin are not always sensitive to his reasoning in the situation, nor reflective about the processes of modern moral reasoning that drive these pronouncements.

The least we could say for Calvin's ethical complexity is that his theology and lived experience enabled him to recognize why moral deliberation needs to be variegated. His various modes of moral discourse each highlight something that needs to be noticed about morality and reflect the way our experience of our world is complex.

But as Robert C. Doyle puts it, ethics is for Calvin 'ever only a sub-set of the doctrine of God, and therefore of Christology'.[6] This chapter will consider aspects of Calvin's moral complexity from the perspective of 'union' with Jesus Christ, a theological theme now regarded as central to Calvin's thought.[7] Doyle regards this union as Calvin's 'central organizing principle', used by Calvin to 'stabilize' his doctrine and ethics.[8] How does ethics spring from this 'union', and why does it generate some norms rather than others? Theologians can be broad or vague about the normative outcomes of the 'union'. I will try to examine these a little more closely.

Participation in a union with Christ can be hard to understand at first, for it requires some familiarity with the risen Son of God, whose unique person and work cannot be summarized under some generic concept. Also, the applicability to ethics of this union can be hard to understand in a milieu that immerses us in a quite different moral language of autonomous choice and personal 'values'. But, given time and close enough attention, we begin to see how a union with Christ can integrate some disparate ethical themes and is rich enough to generate a 'positive ethic for life in the world'.[9] I will engage

---

6. R. C. Doyle, 'John Calvin, his Modern Detractors and the Place of the Law in Christian Ethics', *RTR* 41.3 (1982), p. 74.

7. See further C. Partee, 'Calvin's Central Dogma Again', *The Sixteenth Century Journal* 18.2 (1987), pp. 194f; online http://www.jstor.org/stable/2541176 (accessed 4 March 2009).

8. R. C. Doyle, 'Decision Making at the Boundaries of Life: How Religious Beliefs Affect Ethical Judgments', in *The Ethics of Life and Death*, ed. Barry G. Webb (Homebush West: Lancer, 1990), p. 69.

9. O. M. T. O'Donovan, *Resurrection and Moral Order: An Outline for Evangelical Ethics* (Leicester: Apollos, 1994), p. 142. I cite O'Donovan because he seeks to outline how Christ, in his universality as Son of Man and in his particularity as the Risen Son of God, restores the 'authority' of creation's moral order to humanity. O'Donovan's optimism about a 'positive ethic' is opposed to the view that '[t]he

with these questions:

1.  What governs humanity's immediate awareness of ethics?
2.  How does 'union with Christ' work for ethics? What does it 'look like', here and now, for those who are 'in Christ'?
3.  Is there a 'natural law' embedded in creation? If so, what relationship does it bear to ethics springing from union with Christ?
4.  What are the laws and commandments of the Old Testament for, and to what extent should those 'in Christ' be guided by them?
5.  If Calvin's ethic is based upon our participation with Christ, why did Calvinism often drift into the over-reliance upon rules that we call 'legalism'?

Much has been written on each of these questions, both in relation to Calvin and more generally. I will not survey all of that writing, nor will I sum up everything Calvin has to say. I simply want to offer a small 'package tour' of Calvin's landscape, traversing it lightly, so that we may begin to see 'how ethics works'. For the story Calvin wishes to tell is that Christ himself reveals and fulfils something about each of these questions and, through a 'participation' with him, humanity can begin to respond to and experience some of what Christ fulfilled and lived.[10]

## Immediate awareness

According to Calvin, our normal state is to be 'blinded and drunk with self-love'.[11] But we ought to spare a thought for the drunk and the blind. What do their values contribute, and what perspectives do they offer?

The blind move through a world that makes coherent and orderly sense for them. So also do drunks, who muddle along well enough despite their difficulties with physics and social relations. To be 'blinded and drunk with self-love' is utterly compelling. After all, there is a lot to love. The self is, as Calvin

---

gospel always bowls' but 'never goes in to bat' (xiv) – that is, the view that a Christian ethic is only able to deconstruct error rather than to supply an alternative moral vision. O'Donovan contends that a constructive, substantive ethic can be found in a proper Christology.

10.  Doyle, 'Detractors', pp. 74–80; Wallace, *Christian Life*, vi and *passim*.
11.  *Inst.* 2.7.6.

puts it, 'a workshop graced with God's unnumbered works . . . a storehouse overflowing with inestimable riches'.[12] Calvin thinks this 'storehouse' should point us to its Creator; but in saying so he also shows why loving ourselves is not particularly inventive or novel. We simply respond to the miracle of our embodied existence, and defend and promote it accordingly. To be 'blinded and drunk' with this love is to live in a way that is self-evidently reasonable to the resident of that embodied existence.

Calvin's metaphor neatly summarizes the Augustinian account of human self-awareness. Self-love is an internally consistent form of rationality, and there is no obvious alternative rationality from which to challenge the self-lover. ('For, since blind self-love is innate in all mortals, they are most freely persuaded that nothing inheres in themselves that deserves to be considered hateful.'[13]) On this basis, Calvin disagrees with a popular local diagnosis of what it is to be human, according to which we all share a general moral rationality, but are sometimes tricked into error by false perceptions. This diagnosis is 'pointless and foolish', for 'not only did a lower appetite seduce [Adam], but unspeakable impiety occupied the very citadel of his mind, and pride penetrated to the depths of his heart.'[14] As a result, 'the whole man is overwhelmed – as by a deluge – from head to foot, so that no part is immune from sin and all that proceeds from him is to be imputed to sin'.[15] This is Calvin's way of describing our rationalizations and self-deceptions – our regular capacity to become blind to the realities that surround us, due to our self-love. (We will see below that Calvin slightly moderates his account of 'general moral rationality'. He concedes that people can sometimes agree about some ethical matters, but the vagaries of self-love make these agreements erratic and unpredictable.)

To modern ears, Calvin's attack is much too extreme. If self-love is an internally consistent rationality for those who rate it among their 'values', who is he to pronounce against it? And should we take 'self-hate' to be preferred? Why should Calvin denigrate 'self-love' in a world where 'self-hate' gives way to self-harm, self-destructive behaviour, abuse of others and suicide? At best, say some, Calvin's anthropology is an overstatement; at worst, it is misanthropic and life-denying.

We could easily 'correct' his excess by discussing what makes for a well-

---

12. *Inst.* 1.5.4.

13. *Inst.* 2.1.2.

14. *Inst.* 2.1.9.

15. Ibid.

lived life. We might discern what makes for human flourishing, from which we could denote a pattern of authentic humanity. In time, we would arrive at a nuanced account of the well-lived life – a life, say, that pays some attention to the people and the world around us, while also paying due regard to the needs of the self. Ethics would then become a set of recommendations based upon this account. These recommendations might be lists of various duties or rights that should generally be respected; or statements of goals that we should act towards; or those settled patterns and habits of action and feeling we call 'virtues'. The Western philosophical tradition, both ancient and modern, has proceeded more or less along these lines – and Calvin is quite aware of it. He opposes Plato's anthropology and is milder towards the Aristotelian version of it, but on the whole he refuses to play the game.[16]

His logic parallels that of the proverbist: 'Like a city whose walls are broken down is a man who lacks self-control' (Prov. 25:28).[17] For him, philosophical descriptions of humanity are highly suspect. The philosophers face 'great obscurity' by 'seeking in a ruin for a building, and in scattered fragments for a well-knit structure'.[18] Calvin does not seek with them a denotative definition of the good human, the good life, or human flourishing. He also believes that those who do are not any further advanced in the task of ethics. Commenting on the corrupted remnants of humanity's ability to distinguish between right and wrong, Calvin agrees with Themistius' observation about the way our self-love sabotages our ethical conclusions (a pattern that can also be argued from recent social psychology and behavioural economics):

[T]he intellect is very rarely deceived in general definition or in the essence of the thing; but . . . is illusory when it goes farther, that is, applies the principle to particular cases. In reply to the general question, every man will affirm that murder is evil. But he who is plotting the death of an enemy contemplates murder as something good. The adulterer will condemn adultery in general, but will privately flatter himself in his own particular adultery. Herein is man's ignorance: when he comes to a particular case, he forgets the general principle that he has just laid down.[19]

Only an external perspective can supply blind drunkards with the news of their alienation from wider reality. What supplies Calvin with his settled

---

16. Cf. *Inst.* 1.15.6–7.

17. Biblical quotations in this chapter are from the NIV.

18. *Inst.* 1.15.8.

19. *Inst.* 2.2.23.

judgment about our blindness, drunkenness and ruin? It comes from an osten-
sive definition of humanity, like that woman who ran, pointing to a figure at a
well, and shouted, 'Come, see a man . . .!' (John 4:29).


## Participation

The self-referential internal consistency of our self-love, and the complacent
ethic it generates, can be offset only when we 'come and see a man' who supplies a countervailing viewpoint (and, we discover eventually, *the* countervailing viewpoint) for how to be truly human. Participation in a union with Christ
begins by simply seeing and responding to the magnetically attractive character
of history's Jesus. He is celebrated as the truest human image of God, offering
epistemic and existential access to those respects in which we ourselves are in
God's image.[20] In Jesus, Calvin sees a man who acts in love, whose emotions
are well ordered, who is moderate in adversity, who perseveres[21] and who 'has
been set before us as an example, whose pattern we ought to express in our
life'.[22]

To mention Christ's 'example' risks wrecking the concept of participation
before it begins. Modern ethics pictures us as autonomous choosers of our
values and destiny. It follows that when Christ and 'imitation' appear in the
same sentence, we immediately imagine ourselves emulating him, 'painfully
seeking by ourselves and in our own strength to shape our lives after his
pattern.'[23]

But Calvin does not believe that moral reality can be accessed like this, 'since
the apostle does not say that [Christ] was sent to help us attain righteousness
but himself to be our righteousness'.[24] To sustain this point, Calvin offers a
cascade of further allusions to Paul's epistles, describing redemption from
condemnation, and reconciliation with and adoption by the Father, so that
'we are already, in a manner, partakers of eternal life, having entered into the
Kingdom of God through hope.'

It seems safe to say that most Reformed Christians can picture and enjoy
Christ as 'our righteousness', effecting freedom into a new relationship with

---

20.  *Inst.* 1.15.4.

21.  Doyle, 'Detractors', p. 75, who cites several of Calvin's commentaries and sermons.

22.  *Inst.* 3.2.3.

23.  Wallace, *Christian Life*, p. 47.

24.  *Inst.* 3.15.5.

the Father. Many can also begin to perceive how 'we are already, in a manner, partakers of eternal life,' although Calvin regularly concedes that this status is somewhat hidden.[25]

But it becomes much harder to picture what Calvin means when he outlines 'yet more' about the nature of our participation with Christ. I will dwell on the existential meaning of this 'yet more', because it is quite hard to understand at first; yet without its logic we cannot understand the way participation in Christ affects Christian ethics:

> Yet more: we experience such participation in him that, although we are still foolish in ourselves, he is our wisdom before God; while we are sinners, he is our righteousness; while we are unclean, he is our purity; while we are weak, while we are unarmed and exposed to Satan, yet ours is [his] power . . . while we still bear about with us the body of death, he is yet our life.[26]

This juxtaposition of opposites has exemplary biblical credentials. But what can it possibly mean? It confronts modern people as a series of incomprehensible riddles. We have become used to conceiving 'ourselves' and 'our identity' as one and the same thing; but this chorus of 'participations' seriously contends that our identity may somehow be formed by another. Modern Western adults even find this concept insulting (although children are more at ease with it); but putting aside whatever makes us despise the notion, how would we proceed? How may I perceive myself as foolish and, simultaneously, see Christ's wisdom as mine? How may I do so with his purity, his power and his life, while at the same time acknowledging that I have none of these?

My intention is not to challenge either Calvin or the theology of a participation with Christ. Rather, I am reminded of David Gouwens' comment that 'the basic task of the theologian is not to make Christianity understandable to moderns, but to train moderns in the capabilities that can allow them to understand the gospel.'[27] Nowhere is this 'training' more necessary than in the matter of a participation with Christ. For it confronts those drunk on self-love in two quite unanticipated ways.

First, we are confronted with the possibility that *whatever 'identity' we currently conceive for ourselves is alienated from reality, if not measured against Christ's 'identity'*

---

25. Wallace, *Christian Life*, pp. 83–86. Cf. Col. 3:3–4.

26. *Inst.* 3.15.5.

27. D. J. Gouwens, *Kierkegaard as Religious Thinker* (Cambridge: Cambridge University Press, 1996), p. 12.

*as the Son of Man*. His humanity is 'universal' in a way that encompasses and 'decodes' everyone's diversity, all journeys, and every vocation.[28] This claim has become deeply shocking to modern minds, and there is no generally available logic by which we can defuse this shock, other than to 'come and see a man' who, as the woman at the well puts it, might be the Christ.

Second, to 'participate' flings us headlong into the deepest logic of personal relationship, whether or not we have learnt it elsewhere. Participation involves sharing, even where we have little to offer in return; for *our participation with Christ consists primarily in his sharing his life with us*. The letter to the Ephesians visualizes the manner of Christ's sharing using human marriage at its best. Calvin reflects on this 'living picture' to conclude that 'not only am I his, but also he is mine, so that his life belongs to me'.[29] What began as an attraction to Jesus culminates in his *sharing with us*, to the extent that *his entire life*, both on earth and while seated at the right hand of the Father, 'belongs to me'.

Calvin also expounds that other facet of Christ's making his life our own, where 'the Holy Spirit is the bond by which Christ effectually unites us to himself'.[30] Those moments when we are psychologically assured of Christ's sharing are Spirit-mediated. But whether or not his sharing is psychologically evident to us, it is always evident to Christ. From his perspective, everything of his becomes ours:

> Christ, having been made ours, makes us sharers with him in the gifts with which he has been endowed. We do not, therefore, contemplate him outside ourselves from afar in order that his righteousness may be imputed to us but because we put on Christ and are engrafted into his body – in short, because he deigns to make us one with him. For this reason, we glory that we have fellowship of righteousness with him.[31]

How does ethics work, once we participate with Christ? How does this

---

28. Intuitively, we think of Christ the Son of God as somehow 'universal' (since God is omnipresent) and Christ the Son of Man as a 'particular' (since Jesus was spatially limited). But in the Bible, Christ the Son of Man is presented as 'universal' humanity, and Christ the Son of God as 'particular' divinity. 'As the one whom God has sent he is irreplaceable; as the new man he is the pattern to which we may conform ourselves': O'Donovan, *Resurrection*, p. 143.

29. Calvin, 'Sermon on Ephesians 5:28–30', cited in Doyle, 'Detractors', pp. 75–76.

30. *Inst.* 3.1.1.

31. *Inst.* 3.11.10.

'fellowship of righteousness' proceed? Near the beginning of his treatise on the Christian life, Calvin gives a *tour de force* on the outcomes of participation, listed in terms of the 'individual parts' of salvation.[32] The list takes the form of six 'ever since' statements, which describe some work of the Father, Son or Spirit, and a correlative 'fitting' response. These six aspects of salvation form 'the most auspicious foundations upon which to establish one's life' and trump the virtues of natural ethics, which 'never rise above the natural dignity of man.'

This list requires our close attention. It is important for ethics, because it lays out a pattern of *fitting responses* to participation. What makes the responses fitting is because in each case, participation expands our horizons beyond self-love. The self-lover may have his or her reasons; but like a blind person beginning to see or a drunkard becoming sober, participation with Christ brings the participant into proper contact with the structures of the universe, and elicits new loves. I will repeat Calvin's list and offer some brief comments on each item:

1.  *'Ever since God revealed himself father to us, we must prove our ungratefulness to him if we did not in turn show ourselves his sons.'* Here is 'family' at its best, where the children cannot resist identifying their membership. The awesome character of an ever-impressive father elicits delighted attention from his children, who trumpet their identification with him using every means possible. Our attachment to this Father, and to his extraordinary character, changes what we love to express. (The term 'must' and the negative phrasing can distract us from Calvin's main point.)

2.  *'Ever since Christ cleansed us with the washing of his blood, and imparted this cleansing through baptism, it would be unfitting to befoul ourselves with new pollutions.'* Our participation in baptism centres our attention on Christ's motive in his work. We begin to see the horror of that from which we have been rescued. The activities of self-love seem entirely reasonable, until we see the lengths taken by Christ to pluck us from this form of life. His rescue highlights the Godhead's evaluation and condemnation of it. Perceiving just a glimmer of his motives causes us to look again at our 'old' selves, in contrast to what this Son of God loves and stands for. We can begin to think, love and act accordingly.

3.  *'Ever since engrafted into his body, we must take especial care not to disfigure*

---

32.  *Inst.* 3.6.3.

*ourselves, who are his members, with any spot or blemish.'* This item relies upon the excellence of Christ's person. Those who have been magnetically attracted to him and then participate with him begin to change who they are in awed deference to him. Our moral failure cannot really diminish Christ's excellence; yet the logic of participation acts as if it could (as least in so far as the watching world is concerned).

4. *'Ever since Christ himself, who is our head, ascended into heaven, it behooves* [sic] *us, having laid aside love of earthly things, wholeheartedly to aspire heavenward.'* Heaven is a kingdom of mutual love relationships,[33] and by ascending there to preside over it, Christ lives out the goal of human being. We 'lay aside love of earthly things' when we stop using them to serve our self-love, and we 'aspire heavenward' as we retrain according to heaven's logic of love. To do all this 'wholeheartedly' indicates that what we love has already begun to change.

5. *'Ever since the Holy Spirit dedicated us as temples to God, we must take care that God's glory shine through us, and must not commit anything to defile ourselves with the filthiness of sin.'* Ironically, this item throws attention upon a new kind of self-love. But this self-love no longer consists in fixation upon immanent natural necessities, or in the ludicrous projection of ourselves onto our world. In our participation with Christ, the Spirit begins to rearrange us into Christ's new pattern for humanity. It is entirely appropriate to love, protect and nurture the new kind of person that the Spirit is enabling us to become. The risks in calling this 'a new kind of self-love' are offset when we remember that the Son of Man is the pattern of new humanity that we love and respect. Effectively, we love him to whom we are becoming conformed.

6. *'Ever since both our souls and bodies were destined for heavenly incorruption and an unfading crown, we ought to strive manfully to keep them pure and uncorrupted until the Day of the Lord.'* This last item combines the previous two. When heaven's absence of 'corruption' begins to mean something to us, we become interested in experiencing it now. Participation with Christ supplies us with an understanding of what will last, and humans usually long for whatever lasts in preference to whatever we know will be destroyed. Calvin therefore pictures a straightforward response to the future.

In this list, participation with Christ brings us into contact with the moral

---

33. I have borrowed this term from M. Hill, *The How and Why of Love: An Introduction to Evangelical Ethics* (Kingsford: Matthias Media, 2002), pp. 79–120.

'order' or 'structure' of the universe. The concept of a 'moral order' or 'moral structure' to the universe is not meant to imply that morality has some existence independent of God. Rather, morality consists (i) in a proper description of the relationships between the Persons of the Godhead, other persons, and things; and (ii) in our proper participation among all those relationships.[34] The Christian ethic is one of response to this 'structure'. As we begin to see those relationships anew, our loves change, and we act accordingly.

The active verbs in Calvin's list ('show ourselves', 'befoul ourselves', 'disfigure ourselves', 'aspire', 'take care [to] shine', 'commit anything to defile ourselves', 'manfully strive') distract a little from the logic of participation. Particularly if we are of an activist bent, these words throw the attention back upon a preoccupation with the operation of human will, which Calvin himself regards as quite feeble.[35] Nonetheless, Calvin more than succeeds in showing how participation with Christ opens out an entire new context from within which to see reality. Discovering Christ's 'interpretation' of reality, we love it differently, and our surprising new reactions are what the biblical authors call 'good works'.

If we do not 'retrain' in this logic of participation, Christian ethics can only go down a few well-worn paths. We have already glimpsed an overemphasis upon the imitation of Christ as the first of these paths. There is a place for imitating Christ, but only within the context of our union with him.[36] The example of Christ is best understood as one means by which Christ gives us a proper view of moral order. Participation with him creates a new and safe 'space' from within which we can regard and then 'experiment with' his example for ourselves. In the logic of participation, nothing hinges upon how successful an imitator we are. We are also freed to respond to the specifics of our situation that differ from those of the incarnate Son of Man.

The second of these paths is legalism. The motives for an over-reliance upon rules cannot all be listed or analysed here, and the place of 'law' will be considered further below. For the moment, I suggest that legalism results from various insecurities. We may doubt our capacity to discern right from wrong, or fear our incapacity to resist the seductions of self-love, or worry about our acceptance by God. Legalism offers to salve these insecurities; but the 'fix' is only ever temporary. Participation with Christ lays each of these insecurities to rest and relegates rules to much lighter roles (such as enabling community order, or transmitting wisdom easily and quickly).

---

34. Cf. O'Donovan, *Resurrection*, pp. 31–35 (and Part One *passim*).

35. *Inst.* 3.7.5.

36. Cf. Wallace, *Christian Life*, p. 47.

The third path is a kind of moral carelessness (as opposed by Paul in Rom. 6:1, 15) where the forensic structure of justification licenses the excesses of self-love. On this view, freedom from legal obligation to God is equated with freedom from the moral structure of reality. Calvin resolutely opposes this notion using spatial language. Those in union with Christ should regard him as being very near, never 'far off'. 'We do not . . . contemplate him outside ourselves from afar in order that his righteousness may be imputed to us but because we put on Christ and are engrafted into his body – in short, because he deigns to make us one with him. For this reason, we glory that we have fellowship of righteousness with him'.[37] 'We ought not to separate Christ from ourselves or ourselves from him. . . . Christ is not outside us but dwells within us. Not only does he cleave to us by an indivisible bond of fellowship, but with a wonderful communion, day by day, he grows more and more into one body with us, until he becomes completely one with us'.[38] Sinning to increase grace becomes impossible to sustain under these conditions of a 'fellowship of righteousness' and a 'wonderful communion'.

### Finding moral order

It is absolutely basic to Calvin's thought that 'ethics' is related to the orderly structure of creation. 'The natural order was that the frame of the universe[39] should be the school in which we were to learn piety'.[40] 'Natural law' describes our proper participation in the order surrounding us and, for Calvin, God's commands often express natural law (see below).

Paul Helm has shown that Calvin accepted and worked with a concept of natural law not unlike that of Thomas Aquinas. Helm therefore opposes the theological voluntarism of some nominalist readings of Calvin, and the resistance among Dutch Reformed commentators even to admit the existence of natural law in Calvin. But Helm also shows how, for Calvin, our *epistemic access* to this moral order is more prone to negligence and error than in the tradition he inherited.[41] I will now revisit the nature of this difficulty from the perspec-

---

37. *Inst.* 3.11.10.

38. *Inst.* 3.2.24.

39. For Battles' summary of Calvin's several Latin terms for this 'frame' or 'structure', see Calvin, *Institutes*, p. 96 n. 2.

40. *Inst.* 1.6.1.

41. Paul Helm, *John Calvin's Ideas* (Oxford: Oxford University Press, 2004), pp. 346–388.

tive of human self-love.

The misleading term 'ethics' does not connote what Calvin meant to include. Loving fellowship with God is essential to the proper consideration of right and wrong. Calvin's engagements with philosophical ethics frequently press the point that human ethical enquiry seems to specialize in excluding fellowship with God as a relevant consideration. In his account of this penchant, human reason is competent for some 'lower' things, such as scientific enquiry, but has lost the ability to penetrate supernatural things. '[T]he natural gifts were corrupted in man through sin, but his supernatural gifts were stripped from him'.[42] Humanity's ethical performance falls halfway between the opacity that characterizes human knowledge of God and the relative clarity enjoyed in scientific enquiry.[43] Therefore 'natural' humanity entirely ignores the 'First Table' of the Decalogue, but has 'somewhat more understanding' of its second:[44]

> Since reason, therefore, by which man distinguishes between good and evil, and by which he understands and judges, is a natural gift, it could not be completely wiped out; but it was partly weakened and partly corrupted, so that its misshapen ruins appear.[45]

Hence Romans 2:14–15 is uncontroversially regarded as evidence that Gentiles are not 'utterly blind as to the conduct of life'.[46] Concerning this conduct,

---

I am thankful to my colleague Dr Mark Thompson for this reference.

42. *Inst.* 2.2.12.

43. *Inst.* 2.2.20, 2.2.13–16.

44. *Inst.* 2.2.24. As I read Battles' translation, Calvin uses the term 'natural' with a morally variable sense. 'Natural order' is morally excellent, referring to God's original design of creation. 'Natural law' is morally good, describing humanity's proper appropriation of created order. Fallen and flawed 'natural humanity' is morally corrupted humanity. 'Natural knowledge' is (sometimes) a morally neutral description of standard human epistemic processes. Further discussion of the term is beyond our scope; but context usually makes Calvin's evaluative intent quite clear.

45. *Inst.* 2.2.12.

46. 'Natural law' and 'natural theology' are commonly confused at this point. Calvin willingly concedes that reason can sometimes discern moral order (i.e. 'natural law'); but it does not follow that people are capable of an adequate natural theology (*Inst.* 1.5.11–12). To put the same point in reverse: Calvin is sure that there

'[t]he human mind sometimes seems more acute . . . than in higher things', and in an interesting engagement with Plato over our access to natural law, Calvin judges (against Plato) that ethical 'ignorance' remains culpable, since '[t]he sinner tries to evade his innate power to judge between good and evil'.[47]

But 'natural' human ethics are conspicuously arbitrary.[48] For Calvin, everyone acts the ethicist, picking and choosing between whatever mode of ethical deliberation suits our self-love. We adhere to principles until specific self-interested cases cause the principle to be forgotten. Conscience is over-ridden by agents fully aware of prospective evil. (Conversely, incontinence temporarily pressures people into a temporary experience of 'ignorance' that is later regretted.)

> Our reason is overwhelmed by so many forms of deceptions [sic], is subject to so
> many errors, dashes against so many obstacles, is caught in so many difficulties, that it
> is far from directing us aright . . . [T]he reason of our mind, wherever it may turn, is
> miserably subject to vanity.[49]

Moral order, then, is intimately connected to creation's Lord and to the structure of his cosmos. No one can dissociate from their human embodiment in a morally structured habitat; therefore aspects of moral order continually become apparent to humanity. Yet, blinded and drunk with self-love, the moral coherence of our habitat hovers beyond our powers of recognition and analysis. In our preoccupation with self-love, we render ourselves unable to participate in proper relationship to whatever or whoever is next to us, unless we deem them to serve our self-love. The divine intervention into this state of affairs is finally effected through participation with Christ, who redeems us not only from the wrath of God, but also from our failed conception of our place in the cosmos. Through him, we begin to participate in the cosmos according to that set of proper relationships that we have called 'moral order'.

Calvin's sixfold list on union with Christ prefaces his brief 'Life of the Christian Man',[50] which does not intend to deal with the fine grain of ethics (such as 'exhortations' and 'virtues') but sets out to summarize an 'ordered life'

---

can be no natural knowledge of God sufficient to save; but there can be some
limited natural discernment of good.

47. *Inst.* 2.2.22.
48. *Inst.* 2.2.25.
49. Ibid.
50. *Inst.* 3.6–10.

according to 'some universal rule'.[51] It is a global overview of Calvin's ethic, although he does go on to show how his 'universal rule' brings new intelligibility to business practice, to the practice of suffering and to the way we handle the onset of death. These act as cameos of how ethical deliberation should proceed in participation with Christ.

The treatise relies upon an affectionate knowledge of Christ that 'possesses the whole soul' and 'finds a seat and resting place in the inmost affections of the heart', in contrast to knowledge that resides in 'memory alone, as other disciplines are'.[52] When such a reordering of the 'inmost affections of the heart' has taken hold, 'we are not our own', since this reordering occurs within the safety of our union with Christ.[53] We should pause to notice Calvin's intense interest in the life of the affections, and their reordering. For humanity's self-love is an affective disorder; therefore to 'do ethics' requires as much attention to the affections as to logical argument.

No denotative definition is offered for 'heart', but, ostensively, it is the domain of commitments, values, 'will' and impulse (modern labels no less mysterious than 'heart'). Calvin's language is consonant with the NT's use of *kardia* and the OT antecedents in *lēb*, terms under which biblical authors gather the intersection of cognitive, emotional and volitional human awareness. In a recurrent contrast between 'knowledge' that either 'flits in the brain' (*cerebrum*) or 'takes root in the heart' (*cor*), Calvin's emphasis upon the latter gives an 'existential' approach to knowledge with clear subjective elements.[54] Indeed, knowledge that is *not* affective is probably not 'of the heart', and therefore suspect. The necessity of reordered affection is seen in polemic against unnamed Christian opponents 'who are content to roll the gospel on the tips of their tongues when its efficacy ought to penetrate the inmost affections of the heart, take its seat in the soul, and affect the whole man a hundred times more deeply than the cold exhortations of the philosophers!'[55]

Calvin's extensive treatment of self-denial shows participants in Christ addressing their own self-love.[56] We are 'quite incapable' of comprehending

---

51. *Inst.* 3.6.1.

52. *Inst.* 3.6.4.

53. *Inst.* 3.7.1; cf. 1 Cor. 6:19–20.

54. *Inst.* 1.5.9. See Battles' note in Calvin, *Institutes*, p. 62 n. 29; and cf. *Inst.* 3.2.8, 3.2.33 and 3.2.36.

55. *Inst.* 3.6.4.

56. *Inst.* 3.7.1–10.

exhortations such as Philippians 2:3 ('consider others better than yourselves') until our affections change, 'such is the blindness with which we all rush into self-love'.[57] But in self-denial, old attachments (such as 'the yearning to possess, the desire for power, and the favour of men') begin to dissolve. Vices are displaced from the heart, and new affections form.

So we regain access to a moral order where the beautiful image of God, 'to which we owe all honour and love', becomes evident in other people and we respond to them accordingly.[58] It becomes possible 'not to consider men's evil intentions but to look upon the image of God in them, which cancels and effaces their transgressions, and with its beauty and dignity allures us to love and embrace them'.[59] On this ground Calvin rejects mere performance of the duties of love. When our affections are reordered, duties can proceed 'from a sincere feeling of love'.[60] Thus business practice ceases to be governed by the consequentialisms of either expansion or necessity.[61] It exists in the service of people.[62]

Robert Doyle has shown how a deeply humanitarian ethic arises from the logic of union with Christ. This form of life excels at regarding and acting upon the good of the other, in radical empathy and mercy. It is attentive to the 'household of faith', but liberally spills over into dealings with everyone.[63] Likewise, for Gunther Haas participation with Christ generates love, with equity the 'rule of thumb' by which love can be implemented.[64] Of course these results would not be ethical 'rocket science' – except that this species so prone to self-love is always surprised when it rediscovers equity and humanity. But because of the moral order of creation, it is no surprise that the Christian finds ethical common cause with others:

> [S]ince man is by nature a social animal, he tends through natural instinct to foster and preserve society. Consequently, we observe that there exist in all men's minds universal impressions of a certain civic fair-dealing and order . . . [W]hile men dispute

---

57. *Inst.* 3.7.4.
58. *Inst.* 3.7.6.
59. Ibid.
60. *Inst.* 3.7.7.
61. *Inst.* 3.7.8–9.
62. For an overview of Calvin's economic ethic, see Keesecker, 'Law', pp. 35–37.
63. Doyle, 'Detractors', pp. 78–80.
64. G. H. Haas, *The Concept of Equity in Calvin's Ethics* (Waterloo: Wilfrid Laurier University Press, 1997), pp. 49–50 and *passim*.

among themselves about individual sections of the law, they agree on the general conception of equity.[65]

## God's law

If the Christian life is constituted by participation in union with Christ, how can Calvin also assert that the Spirit shows us 'how to frame our life according to the rule of his law'?[66] Calvin participates in a longstanding tradition where distinctions between moral, ceremonial and civil laws were used to map the conceptual logic of the biblical material.[67] Calvin's interpretation of biblical law deploys a nuanced version of this threefold set.[68]

Moral law directs our love first to God and then to one another. It is 'the true and eternal rule of righteousness', and is 'a testimony of natural law'.[69] In contrast to today, it was not controversial to suppose that the morality of moral law pivoted upon a conception of the 'natural law'. Natural law is simply a name for the way the structure of the universe impinges upon humanity. As we have seen, Calvin believed that natural law does direct some common ethical agreements, and will go so far as to assert 'that in the arrangement of this life no man is without the light of reason'.[70] Of course, as we have also seen, Calvin also believes that self-love makes people completely error-prone in the use of this reason in relation to morality. Biblical moral law has no such ambiguity, for *it is the natural law according to the word of God.*

---

65. *Inst.* 2.2.13.
66. *Inst.* 2.2.18. For more analysis of Calvin and Luther on biblical law (in reference to the legal material of Exodus), see A. J. Cameron, 'Liberation and Desire: The Logic of Law in Exodus and Beyond', in *Exploring Exodus: Literary, Theological and Contemporary Approaches*, ed. B. S. Rosner and P. R. Williamson (Nottingham: Apollos, 2008), pp. 136–142.
67. Calvin's hermeneutic for distinguishing moral, legal and civil material in the OT is unfortunately beyond our scope.
68. In the *Institutes*, biblical 'law' can refer to the morality of the Decalogue (2.6); or to the various collections within the Pentateuch (4.20.14–16); or simply to everything that Moses said (2.7.1). Each sense is generally made clear by definition or context. (See further Battles, in Calvin, *Institutes*, p. 348 n. 1.)
69. *Inst.* 4.20.15, 4.20.16.
70. *Inst.* 2.2.13.

Biblical *ceremonial* laws spring from moral law, which tutored the Jews in piety to God and toward their eschatological Messiah. Biblical *civil* laws were specific 'formulas of equity and justice, by which they might live together blamelessly and peaceably'.[71] According to Calvin, the ceremonial and the civil both expressed morality among the Jews, instantiating respectively reverent service of God and love for humanity.

Aquinas had already described how divinely ordered moral reality is experienced by humanity as a 'natural law', which is graciously 'republished' for humanity by God in the Bible.[72] Calvin was sufficiently persuaded by this approach to deploy it in broad outline.[73] 'Moral law' expresses 'natural law'; ceremonial law was a specific instance of the moral law to order worship of God; and civil law was a specific instance of the moral law to order human desires and human society. It follows that the specific instances (the ceremonial and civil laws) are no longer directly relevant to Christians (although there remains much to be learnt in them about Christ and about equity). But those in Christ are regaining access to moral order, so moral law remains relevant to them.

Controversy in the Reformation centred on the mode of this ongoing relevance, expressed as a debate about three so-called 'uses' of the law. These more uniquely Reformed distinctions do not easily map onto the older moral-ceremonial-civil divide, and the relationship between the uses and the older formulation can be confusing. This new triad is not discussing the whole Mosaic legal code, as the moral-ceremonial-civil distinction does. Rather, the 'uses' of the law are an argument about how we may take *only the 'moral' component* of biblical law.

In Calvin's terminology, the moral law's first use is a 'theological use': it acts as a 'mirror', convicting everyone of sin and driving us to repent and find grace through faith.[74] Its second use is a 'civil use', a 'bridle' upon wilful sinners, so enabling communities to live in relative harmony.[75] We must note that for Calvin what forms the basis of any modern system of justice is this second use of the biblical *moral* law, *not* the biblical civil law as such. He was quite clear that no biblical *civil* law is binding on later societies. Every nation is free to make whatever laws it considers profitable, as long as these are 'in conformity to [the]

---

71.  *Inst.* 4.20.15.

72.  S. Pinckaers, *The Sources of Christian Ethics*, trans. M. T. Noble (Edinburgh: T. & T. Clark, 1995), pp. 171–185.

73.  See further Helm, *Ideas*, pp. 368–378.

74.  *Inst.* 2.7.6–9.

75.  *Inst.* 2.7.10–11.

perpetual rule of love'.[76] For Calvin, particular societies in specific circumstances rightly enact such laws as are needed, provided they are made within boundaries of equity and natural law, and to promote gentleness and love.[77]

There was a broad Reformation consensus upon these two uses of moral law. Even the antinomian John Agricola could agree to the second, *civil* use of moral law. (His complaint was against its theological use.) In contrast, we would probably find a less clear consensus among Reformed Christians today about either use. (It would be interesting to map the history of the change.)

But the main Reformation dispute was over a so-called 'third use' of the law. Calvin is in no doubt: 'The third and principal use, which pertains more closely to the proper purpose of the law, finds its place among believers . . . Here is the best instrument for them to learn more thoroughly each day the nature of the Lord's will'.[78] Law used in this third way is, in Calvin's startling metaphor, 'a whip to an idle and balky ass' and 'a constant sting' upon the believer (always with the proviso, of course, that no one 'in Christ' can be condemned by law or justified by its works).

What could make intelligible Calvin's wholehearted promotion of this third use? The categories of his thought that we have examined make it so. Biblical moral law is God's own expression of 'natural law' – that is, of moral reality as it pertains to humanity. In that respect it remains 'good', and can function as an aid to self-denial and as an antidote to self-love. It serves to expand the moral horizons of the self-lover. When Calvin asks, 'what would be less loveable than the law if, with importuning and threatening alone, it troubled souls through fear, and distressed them through fright?' he is clearly aware of the potential for the moral law to devastate the conscience of the reader.[79] But it becomes readable and usable beyond its precepts, because of Jesus Christ:

> [T]he Lord instructs by their reading of it those whom he inwardly instils with a readiness to obey. He lays hold not only of the precepts, but the accompanying promise of grace, which alone sweetens what is bitter . . . David especially shows that in the law he apprehended the Mediator, without whom there is no delight or sweetness.[80]

---

76. *Inst.* 4.20.15.

77. *Inst.* 4.20.15–16.

78. *Inst.* 2.7.12.

79. Ibid.

80. Ibid.

In the same way that imitating Christ becomes thinkable within the safety of participation with Christ, so also does the reading of the law. Freed from its 'entire rigour', people 'hear themselves called' in it 'with fatherly gentleness by God'.[81] The moral law becomes another means by which our proper contact with reality is rehabilitated, as we ponder the intent of each command, the features of its opposite and how self-love necessitates its sharp wording.[82]

Unexpectedly (and perhaps unwittingly), Calvin has left the metaphor of 'whip' and 'sting' far behind. In outlining the law's third use, he has almost invented a 'fourth use' for it – as a kind of 'gymnasium' for training our discernment of moral reality.

## Calvinist legalism

It is beyond my competence to judge which 'Calvinisms' were legalistic and when. But if we assume the charge to be correct for some instances, what in Calvin's treatment of ethics could account for this trend?

It would be easy to hold Calvin above the more 'small-minded' of his followers. After all, participation with Jesus Christ is able to settle the insecurities that can drive legalism. This union also generates Calvin's important treatise on Christian freedom,[83] where we are freed by justification from 'law righteousness';[84] freed with 'eager readiness' to respond joyfully to the Father's word;[85] and freed to 'use God's good gifts for the purpose for which he gave

81.  *Inst.* 3.19.5.

82.  *Inst.* 2.8.8–10. For excellent summaries of Calvin's way of reading the law 'in Christ', see Doyle, 'Detractors', pp. 81–82; and D. C. Jones, 'The Law and the Spirit of Christ', in *A Theological Guide to Calvin's Institutes: Essays and Analysis*, ed. D. W. Hall and P. A. Lillback (Phillipsburg: Presbyterian and Reformed, 2008), pp. 313–317.

83.  *Inst.* 3.19.1–16. My engagement with Calvin's ethic is compromised by insufficient attention to this treatise. For a useful summary, see W. Edgar, 'Ethics: The Christian Life and Good Works According to Calvin', in *A Theological Guide to Calvin's Institutes: Essays and Analysis*, ed. D. W. Hall and P. A. Lillback (Phillipsburg: Presbyterian and Reformed, 2008), pp. 344–345.

84.  *Inst.* 3.19.2.

85.  *Inst.* 3.19.4–5.

them to us',[86] according to the rule of love.[87] Surely any legalist 'malfunction' must be the fault of the followers alone.

But without wishing to denigrate Calvin's achievement, we may point to three areas where his followers were likely to stray. The first two of these may be his fault.

1. Calvin's excoriating, ruthless and inexorable attack upon human self-love is one of the most striking features of the *Institutes*. It needed to be said, then as now. Again and again, his psychological descriptions of self-loving humanity evince rueful smiles of self-recognition. Here is a typical example:

> The very vices that infest us we take pains to hide from others, while we flatter ourselves with the pretence that they are slight and insignificant, and even sometimes embrace them as virtues. If others manifest the same endowments we admire in ourselves, or even superior ones, we spitefully belittle and revile these gifts in order to avoid yielding place to such persons. If there are any faults in others, not content with noting them with severe and sharp reproach, we hatefully exaggerate them.[88]

By the time this passage appears, late in the *Institutes*, Calvin has already made dozens of sharp statements against humanity. We do not need more. We need his treatise on the Christian life to push the horizons of our 'moral imagination' beyond our usual self-love. But this passage is so mesmerizing in its accuracy that the main point – how self-denial creates space for a new love toward God and others – is easily lost. Unfortunately, Calvin is so good at this invective that, ironically, it becomes easier to remain fixated upon our self-love.

We might compare with the letter to the Ephesians, where about ten verses describe human sin, perhaps sixty verses describe Christ and our union with him, and roughly eighty verses could be described as the expansion of our moral imagination arising from this union. The comparable ratio in the *Institutes* would be quite different.

In this respect, Calvin is prone to overstatement. His habit is to keep slipping into such invective. In his discussion of neighbour love, Calvin opines that the Lord 'had at hand no more violent or stronger emotion'

86. *Inst.* 3.19.8.

87. *Inst.* 3.19.11–12.

88. *Inst.* 3.7.4.

than our flawed self-love by which to 'express how profoundly we must be inclined to love our neighbours'.[89] For David Jones, 'surely [Calvin] goes wide of the mark. Instead of reading the commandment as "you shall love your neighbour as you [*now sinfully*] love yourself," he could have made his point . . . by reading, "you shall love your neighbour as [*a person like*] yourself."'[90]

I suspect that this aspect of the *Institutes* heightens Christian insecurities about the seductions of self-love. We then rely too heavily on rules in a flawed attempt to curb it (cf. Col. 2:23). The better antidote is to recognize the excellences of God in Christ, of humanity in Christ, of the neighbour and of the good order of the world, so rekindling new love for them.[91] When our affections are reordered in this way, our fixations upon self-love are unmasked as both demented and boring.

2.  A 'third use of the law' is hard to sustain on Calvin's terms of 'whip' and 'sting'. Pastorally, retention of any distinction between third and first use is problematic. The existential experiences of moral instruction under its third use, and theological accusation under its first use, are too similar. In the third use, it comes to the hearer as 'a whip to an idle and balky ass' and as 'a constant sting'.[92] In its first use, 'the wickedness and condemnation of us all are sealed by the testimony of the law'.[93] It is a lot to ask of most Christian people, particularly those weak in the faith, to retain the distinction when the existential similarity is so great. Very little prevents something being 'lost in translation', so that declarations from the law sound, to hearers at least, like 'law righteousness', replete with all the terrors of law that Calvin knows can trouble and distress people. When the first and third uses become confused – surely more often than not – doubts about God's acceptance begin; and the preceding fixation upon law has set in place a paradigm of legalistic response.

    It might be argued that mistakes in pastoral practice do not negate the third use *per se*. It simply sought to extract truth about moral order from the law, as one among many moral truth-bearing sources in Christ. But

---

89.  *Inst.* 2.8.54.

90.  Jones, 'The Law and the Spirit of Christ', p. 313; emphasis and square brackets original.

91.  For an excellent analysis of this new kind of love (in contrast to self-love), see O. M. T. O'Donovan, *The Problem of Self-Love in St. Augustine* (New Haven: Yale University Press, 1980), pp. 18–35 and *passim*.

92.  *Inst.* 2.7.12.

93.  *Inst.* 2.7.8.

the moral truth-bearing value of Old Testament law should be accessed and explained in terms other than 'whip' and 'sting'.[94] I have suggested that Calvin began this project, perhaps inadvertently, by almost inventing a 'fourth use'.

3. Insecurities about how to determine right and wrong may drive an over-reliance upon law to describe the moral order. Legalism may arise for anyone who is yet to discern moral reality in participation with Christ. If Paul can describe this union as a 'profound mystery' (Eph. 5:32), it is no fault of Calvin's that Christians regularly find it hard to comprehend. For Karl Barth, each Christian's vocation consists of knowing and growing in this union. 'How could they be what they are in Christ if they did not continually become it?'[95]

Calvin's understanding of his own union with Christ enabled him to respond to his own self-love, and to moral order, within a context of safety. The same can become true for all of us, and so my first two comments against Calvin need to be made in recognition of the inestimable service he has done to the church by conveying how we may participate with Christ. Christ releases us from our bondage to self-love, shares his own life with us and returns us to our truest humanity. He brings to us the moral structure of reality and enables us to join in fellowship with his Father at the centre of that reality. Calvin's ethic springs from this astonishing news. It is the story he really wanted to tell.

© Andrew J. B. Cameron, 2009

---

94. Andrew Sloane's thesis – that the OT consists of instruction and narrative that alter our 'moral vision' – is an alternative worthy of consideration: A. Sloane, *At Home in a Strange Land: Using the Old Testament in Christian Ethics* (Peabody: Hendrickson, 2008), pp. 143–191, 218.

95. *CD* IV/3.2, p. 547.

## 11. CALVIN AMONG THE STUDENTS: SHAPING THEOLOGICAL EDUCATION

*Peter F. Jensen*

### Introduction

Moore College was described many years ago as 'a narrow Calvinistic seminary'. It was as a graduate of this Calvinistic college that I set tremulous foot in Oxford in 1976. Under the supervision of Professor Patrick Collinson I had completed a thesis on 'Calvinism and the Persecution of Witches in England' and even published an article entitled 'Calvin and Witchcraft' and another one on 'Calvin, Charismatics and Miracles'. And I had read the *Institutes* more than once. But how would Calvin fare in Oxford?

Clearly my *curriculum vitae* alarmed the Moral Tutor assigned to me by my College. Calvin received a negative comment from him in the first moments of our first meeting. The tutor was a kind man and a good scholar, but he intimated that an interest in Calvin was peculiar. I also recollect that in a systematic theology seminar, after an evangelical student had read a fine paper on providence, the Professor observed, with dismissive astonishment, that this was 'Calvinism'. What Calvinists I found were few, though a fellow postgraduate student who belonged to the Roman Catholic Church assured me that Calvin was studied with great respect and intensity amongst the academics of Rome. Furthermore, my new supervisor, Dr B. R. White, had just finished advising R. T. Kendall on his thesis, later published under the title *Calvin and English Calvinism to 1649*. This work has proved somewhat controversial, but I found it a useful guide to my own studies on Elizabethan Protestantism.

My most vivid memory in this connection, however, was when I asked for a recent publication on Calvin from the librarian in the faculty of theology library. Drawing in her breath sharply, she said, 'That awful man!' I demurred: 'Surely some mistake,' I said. 'No doubt you are right,' she rejoined tartly; clearly the best that could be said was that blame for Calvin's warped character could be attributed to his parents. I was startled by this spontaneous animus and wondered who else in the ranks of the theologians and scholars would have evoked it. Had I asked for any other author, would the librarian have taken the liberty to make such a comment? What is there about Calvin to provoke such odium?

Of course, antagonism to Calvin is not an Oxford phenomenon. While I called myself a Calvinist and was happy to do so, amongst English speakers on the whole the word is not intended as a compliment. Calvin is portrayed as one who burned his enemies, ran Geneva as a theocracy with himself as the vicar of God, hated anything beautiful, let loose grasping capitalism on the world, taught a doctrine of God in which God was a despotic and arbitrary tyrant, purveyed a grim and exclusive religion and was himself a dour stranger to joy. The Calvinists who followed him were worse – to this day the names 'Puritan' and 'Reformed' evoke scorn and hatred amongst many – and of course Oliver Cromwell is regarded in some quarters as the quintessential seventeenth-century villain. Calvin and the Calvinists are thought to be intellectually barren and morally flawed.

It would be foolish to suggest that there is only one reason for this hostility, or indeed that only Calvin and his followers suffer from such antagonism. We all label and dismiss one another unfairly. Nor is there much point in demonstrating how wrong-headed the criticism is. Indeed, much of it is based on malice and falsehood unworthy of those who peddle it. But it is still worth contemplating the nature of the reaction and trying to analyse what there is about Calvin and the Calvinists which evokes this particular sort of criticism. At the same time, we ask: is it worth defending Calvin's legacy?

To my mind, the adversaries of Calvin are right in seeing in Calvinism an extraordinarily powerful ideology, one which they do well to be alarmed about. It creates adherents who are bold and assured – or obstinate and arrogant – depending on your point of view. But in my judgment, the nub of the matter is this: John Calvin expounded the Bible in such a clear way that virtually no one else has matched him in showing us what God is like, and therefore what we are like. He is the apostle of the majesty of God. In a world in which human beings are born idolaters, any sight of the majesty and glory of God forces us to scuttle away in fear. Our hostility to Calvin expresses our hostility to the God whom Calvin preached, the God of the Bible. He has given us the real alternative to secularism, Catholicism, Pietism and paganism.

There have been times when Calvin has gone into near obscurity, his reputation at a low ebb. The preface to Auguste Lecerf's book *An Introduction to Reformed Dogmatics* recounts the story that 'In 1930 a visitor knocked at Professor Lecerf's door and introduced himself with these words: "Some friends of mine, hearing that I was passing through Paris, have advised me to come and see you. M. Lecerf is a unique personality, they say. He is in fact the last of the Calvinists and when he dies the type will be extinct. So whatever happens, do not fail to pay him a visit."'[1] And yet, as we know, Lecerf was by no means 'the last of the Calvinists', even in France. As long as the Bible is studied and readers understand that it preaches a God who is the centre of the universe, Calvin will be admired for his witness to the majesty of God. Indeed, on the broader front, the middle of the twentieth century saw a massive re-emergence of reformed theology, of which Karl Barth was only the most significant exponent. Whatever the differences between Barth and Calvin, this much is true: they both spoke in the name of the sovereign God and asserted his priority in creation and redemption in unequivocal terms. In so doing they set themselves against the instincts of human culture, whether in the sixteenth or the twentieth century.

I do not think that it was fair to call Moore College a 'narrow Calvinistic seminary'. Leaving aside the word 'narrow', on the whole it has been evangelical in the English tradition, looking mainly to the English Reformation for its theological inspiration and to the evangelical revival for its piety. Thus 'Calvinistic' may not be accurate. I myself would prefer to be called a 'Cranmerian'. However, in the early 1960s the reading of the *Institutes of the Christian Religion* became compulsory for every student at Moore College and the obligation continues to the present day. I have no doubt that the originator of this monumental requirement was the then principal, David Broughton Knox (Principal 1959–1985), himself a student of the English Reformation, but one who wanted the students to become aware at first hand of the greatness of Calvin.

The obligation involves reading the whole of the *Institutes*, not part thereof. When I once suggested to Knox that it would be better to require set readings in the *Institutes*, he disagreed. To him, such was the importance of this book,

---

1. A. Lecerf, *An Introduction to Reformed Dogmatics*, trans. A. Schlemmer (London: Lutterworth, 1949), p. 7.

as the greatest work of Protestant theology in his estimation, that it should be read in its entirety. He was not recommending books about Calvin. The students of the College should be able to say that they had read at least one great book of Christian theology at first hand from beginning to end before they graduated. This should be the one. Rightly or not, the College has rarely given any tutorial help in this mammoth task; nor have students ever been examined as to their grasp of the teaching of the Reformer. It is enough that they sign a form declaring that they have fulfilled this requirement.

I have been asked to think of Calvin for Today, a topic vague enough for me to choose my own direction. I have therefore taken my start from this counter-cultural Moore College practice. Why did it emerge? What is it intended to achieve? What can we learn from Calvin about the task of an evangelical theological education? Can an interaction with John Calvin be profitable for shaping such theological students and pastors in the twenty-first century? By thinking about this we may assess something of the value of Calvin for today.


## Calvin as a biblical intellectual

What did Knox aim to achieve by introducing Calvin in such a prominent way into the syllabus of Moore College? In the 1960s, it was especially important to hear from Calvin as a counter to two large linked cultural movements, outside and inside the church. From without, there was the whole explicit movement to repudiate Christianity altogether, a movement frequently but inadequately called secularization. In the face of such a major challenge, the evangelical response has in turn been tempted to become anti-intellectual and to rely on religious experience as a means of validating Christian faith. This has resulted in the burgeoning Pentecostal and charismatic movement, a fresh form of Arminian pietism which by the end of the century had captured much of the evangelical heartland. To both movements, Calvin is an antidote.

The anti-Christian tsunami of the 1960s and beyond left the Protestant churches of the West notably outclassed intellectually. One of the disappointing features of the Christian attitude to new movements such as feminism or the sexual revolution has been the *ad hoc* nature of the response. It is as if there is no such thing as a worked-out Christian theology capable of sustaining itself while providing a critique of other movements of thought and practice. Again and again, Christian leadership simply succumbed piecemeal to intellectual fashion. What Harry Blamires memorably referred to as 'The Christian mind' has been notably vacant, as though there is no coherent Christian position. We have indeed reached the point where leaders of significant denominations with a proud history of Christian thought and practice are reduced to appealing to half-remembered theological mantras, to the alleged practice of Jesus and to current slogans such as 'inclusiveness'. Not only has the culture suffered a breathtakingly speedy amnesia about the content of the Christian faith; so too have Christians themselves.

In insisting on the study of Calvin (especially the *Institutes*), what Knox did was to open his students to the fact of Christianity viewed as a set of coherent intellectual commitments. After all, the *Institutes* constitute a comprehensive and ordered account of the Christian faith. Wherever one locates Calvin on the map of Christian history, there is no serious doubt that he is a major theologian and thinker from within that history, that tradition. In relating to him, the reader is aware of the creeds and the Fathers and the Reformers, at least. More than that, however, the architecture of the *Institutes* is a reminder that the parts of the Christian faith relate intimately to one another. For example, the marvellous opening of Book Three has always been a model statement of the way in which the biblical revelation itself coheres, its parts depending on one another and enriching one another. It means that coming to terms with a surrounding culture is not a matter of bartering bits of the faith away without consequence. In short, there is such a thing as an integrated Christianity: it makes demands on the mind and it is worth exploring and defending.

Furthermore, the very assimilation of Calvin is a major intellectual task, itself a reminder that theological study is meant to be rigorous and demanding; that we are not to bring our second best to this exercise. Theological students are intended to think, and in Calvin they have a person whose grasp of the Christian faith will make them think. Here is both a way of doing things and a corpus of work into which they may enter as into a great cathedral, and spend time seeing how it is constructed and what gives it its strength and resilience. Unlike many theologians, Calvin is a thinker worth spending time and effort with. He remains a great doctor of the faith. In the 1960s an increasingly well-educated student body was arising. No matter how sophisticated and impressive the exercise of intellectual life in other disciplines may be, here too in Christian theology we grapple with great ideas. As we spend time with Calvin, we see that the secularizing culture around us does not have the last or even the most important word.

But there is an even deeper reason why Calvin may be regarded as the most suitable theologian for evangelical theological students. Calvin is especially important to evangelicals because he is so consistently biblical. It is clear, of course, that he is thoroughly familiar with the great writings of the Christian and humanist traditions. But it is his encounter with Scripture which shapes and moulds his thought. Difficult though Calvin is for the beginner, there is an access to his thought through the knowledge of the Scriptures. Even the inexperienced student is looking at the same material as the mighty Calvin; reader and author share a common language, the language of Scripture. Properly understood, the reading of Calvin in this context is not, in the end, merely an attempt to grapple with his thought, but an attempt to allow him to teach us what the Bible is saying. Understanding this is crucial to the proper use of Calvin by theological students.

A great difficulty in writing systematic theology is to know how to introduce and appeal to Scripture. In many cases the systematician resolves the difficulty by assuming that the tradition in which he or she is working is sufficient warrant and that to interact with the tradition assumes the witness of Scripture. The work becomes a discussion between theologians, usually within a family, and the differences or novelties are simply course adjustments occurring within a flow of tradition. The normative character of Scripture is lost, and there is little appeal over the heads of other theologians to Scripture itself. This is true in the Reformed traditions much as in others. But it is not true of Calvin.

In contemporary theological education, one of the major contributors to this alarming state of affairs is the academic specialization which has grown up as the main written expressions of Christian theology. Exegetes, philosophers, historians, biblical theologians all have their limited part to play, but no one is assigned to bring the whole together, and the different specialists are wary before they trespass in another's field. The one discipline which may be looked to in order to provide the necessary summation of what theology has to say, systematic theology, has its own internal specializations and its own conversation partners. Its practitioners are wary of offering sustained exegesis on the grounds that this is the preserve of the biblical scholars; the biblical scholars are wary of offering summary statements as they fear that this will compromise their exegesis of particular passages.

The malign effect of this specialization on theological education is obvious: especially on Protestant and evangelical education. Here, the main purpose is to produce preachers who will pastor congregations. The main form in which the Christian faith finds expression is the sermon, intended to be an exposition of the biblical text or passage. The preacher cannot be an academic specialist. The task of the preacher is to bring the word of God to bear on the lives of his congregation. He must be able to call on the whole counsel of God; his education must equip him to be able to bring to bear the whole resources of the Christian faith in one address lasting (usually) less than half an hour. He cannot afford to be a mere specialist. The business of preaching requires intellectual gifts of a high order and thorough training. It is not brought into effective existence by the study of either pietistic meanderings or academic specialists given to atomistic versions of the Christian faith.

In the preparation of preaching pastors, Calvin remains a great teacher. He was a specialist in the whole revelation of God in Scripture. He preached the Bible; he lectured on the Bible; he summarized the teaching of the Bible; he applied the teaching of Scripture. The one person did it all, without feeling that somehow this was trespassing on another's patch. In particular, he understood the normative nature of Scripture and was able to bring Scripture to bear in a way which shows its role in teaching us the faith and sustaining our piety. Fundamental to this unified approach was a unified understanding of Scripture – he saw all of it as the revelation of God, inspired by God, and hence able to be read as a whole. It is especially fruitful for theological students to be ministered to by a scholar who sees the Bible thus and therefore encourages them to interpret each passage in the light of the whole. This means that his commentaries and lectures on the texts of particular books are always suffused with the theology of the whole Bible.

Another thing which the student can see by studying Calvin is the importance of the original languages to the preacher. Calvin takes us back to the sources, refusing to trust himself to translations alone. We can see as a consequence that the encounter with the text in this form promotes genuine exegetical labour. It helps guard against facile interpretations or the over-theologizing of individual passages. It is agreed by all that the acquisition of the relevant languages is the most demanding element in the training of pastors and that which extends the necessary time. But, as well as facility in understanding texts, it also helps the student to understand the intellectual quality demanded in preparing to preach and the foundation of the Christian faith in the ancient history of the world. It is the point most under pressure in the busy programme of the modern seminary. Calvin reminds us to resist the short-cut which the abandonment of the languages would be.

Calvin's commitment to the original language is part of his exegetical and hermeneutical approach. His works are voluminous, but his style is not prolix. He does not pause for long asides. But what is basic to his method is the close attention he pays to the words of the text and a clear belief that these words reflect the reality which they purport to describe. In other words, his is a notably historical approach to the text of Scripture. This enables him to comment far more frequently than modern preachers do on the piety (or impiety) exhibited in the text and its consequences for the contemporary reader. He is not detached from the text, always wondering what the reading behind the words is. He reads the words in the light of the canon as a whole and in the belief that God is speaking through these words. The result is that he is constantly, seriously, feeding faith.

In some quarters, he would be accused of moralism and neglecting the theological flow of the Bible, that is, biblical theology. But this is to miss the theological, whole-of-Bible understanding he constantly exhibits. The interpretation of Scripture requires biblical doctrine as well as biblical theology, so-called. It would be better if his critics were to learn something about the depth of material which then becomes accessible through the Scriptures. The consequence of their rush to a Christological exegesis is paradoxically superficial. Likewise, it is true that he is less aware of what we may call the literary qualities of texts; but once again there is the danger of avoiding the normative content of Scripture via critical conjectures about the way in which texts have been compiled. What he does demonstrate is the value of a biblical doctrine for the task of interpretation. It is via biblical doctrine that he is able to move so quickly to exhortation, rebuke and drawing out the implications of the text for the world which he inhabited.

There is a danger in introducing the inexperienced to Calvin, and I have seen the ill consequence in some cases. The danger is that a student will become fixated with an abstracted form of Calvinism, and that entry into the great cathedral of Calvin's thought will be permanent, uncritical and theologically fatal. For some, the search for certainty and the need for intellectual system proves too compelling and Calvinism becomes their faith. So imposing is the structure that it is possible to spend a lifetime examining parts of it and contending over this or that buttress or column. Everything is answered by reference to Calvin or to what may be deduced from Calvin, and there is no possibility of refuting any part of it. It also becomes less possible to live in the modern world, as everything must be referred to a man who was a pre-modern thinker. It may have been wisdom that, although Knox asked his students to read Calvin, he did not lecture on Calvin and seldom referred to him in class. The *Institutes* was not his textbook.

Indeed, my memory is that Knox used Calvin more often as an adversary than as an ally. This was made possible by his fundamental agreement, especially over the authority and nature of Scripture. He was attracted to Karl Barth in some ways, but could never have used him as a sparring partner in the way he used Calvin, because of the difference concerning Scripture. His disagreements with Calvin were clear to all his students: he did not think that Calvin was right ecclesiologically or sacramentally, for example. He doubted that Calvin held to the doctrine of limited atonement as it was expounded by some later Calvinists. In fact, he distanced himself from that version of it. He preferred the discretion of the Thirty-Nine Articles on the subject of reprobation to the bold logic of Calvin. He certainly did not use predestination as a starting point in his discussion of God, as we see in later Calvinists. He was strongly committed to evangelism and world mission. In short, it was clear that Knox wanted his students to learn from Calvin and to encounter such a seminal thinker at first hand, not just through books about him. But they were to keep their wits about them and to test Calvin against the Scriptures – and the English Reformation as well.

This critical approach helps address one of the obvious problems with using a pre-modern theologian such as Calvin as a central thinker in a modern seminary. It was right, for the reasons given above, to use him as a counter-weight to the theological and cultural movements let loose in the 1960s. After all, theology is a perennial discipline, and we need to beware of the chronological snobbery which consigns the past to irrelevance. For example, the great issues which shook the world during the Reformation deal with matters which will always confront us in our relationship with God, whatever cultural form the issues take. Furthermore, in some ways Calvin is not so much pre-modern as early modern – a fact which keeps his biblical commentaries still in use and referred to by contemporary critical scholars. His methodological commitment to the exposition of Scripture will always keep him within the great Christian – and human – conversation which transcends the centuries. But to become a Calvinist, in the sense of making his theology our theology without critical appreciation, is a mistake which condemns the student to living in the wrong place at the wrong time.

What is it which makes Calvin an excellent theological resource in a post-modern age? It is that he introduces us to the Christian faith in its biblical and historical form at a high level of erudition and intellectual challenge. Thus, in my judgment, Knox's move was a valid one and had beneficent results in the training of contemporary pastors. Indeed, precisely because Calvin is not a member of the contemporary intellectual milieu of the West, he speaks with a different, challenging and confronting voice. The antagonism to him (and the devotion he generates) suggests that his voice retains a singular power even now. But there is more that makes Calvin an excellent conversation partner in the study of theology. I have suggested that this has something to do with him being an apostle of the majesty of God, and I want to explore this idea further. For what Knox tried to do at Moore College was to make the knowledge of God, relationship with God, the central fact of its existence, an aim to which Calvin made a major contribution.

## Really knowing God

One of the dangers of all formal theological education aimed at producing pastors is that it can turn into a deceptive shadow of what it is meant to be.

The syllabus may be the same as ever; the activities very similar; chapels may be held, classes go forward, teachers meet and discuss and assessments be made. But it may fail dismally nonetheless. And chief amongst its failures will be the absence of God.

For the aim of theological education must be the same as the aim of life itself: namely, to know God. We can turn our classes into sessions in learning theology or history or the New Testament without recognizing that if God is not at the centre of the whole enterprise, we are doing damage to the students and to their churches. Frequent chapel is not a substitute for the knowledge of God in the classroom. Indeed, chapel may be the problem. If the teachers of the different subjects do not recognize that their chief business is the knowledge of God, all is lost. Of course, this involves academic methods and rigour. We are still to study Paul to the Romans and the Council of Nicaea and the Book of Judges and the problem of suffering; but the real centre of the curriculum is the knowledge of God, and the teachers must be the exponents of that knowledge within their specialities, or they are simply mechanics of Divinity and will turn out men and women of like disposition to inflict upon the churches.

How does Calvin help us here? By his testimony to God. The famous opening words of the *Institutes*, 'Nearly all the wisdom we possess, that is to say, true and sound wisdom, consists of two parts: the knowledge of God and of ourselves,' capture exactly the essence of that which gives this work its perennial value – and that which provokes the anger and odium of so many.[2] The student who reads Calvin attentively will be instructed in all sorts of ways. But at the centre of this instruction will be the great and necessary gospel issues of who we are meant to be and how we are to come to know God. Or, rather, who God is and who we are, for the emphasis falls without doubt on the necessary priority of the being and the actions of God. If we know him, it is because he has chosen to make himself known to us. Calvin says beautifully, 'We enjoy Christ as we embrace Christ clad in his own promises'.[3] If the seminary experience is not an acceptance of God in the place where God has decreed that he will be found and in the submissive and trusting attitude of mind and heart which is appropriate before God, it only damages the student and the churches. This Calvin shows us.

Consider, first, what Calvin says about human existence. The good life is a life of wisdom, and its wisdom is centred on God. This is the very point he

---

2. *Inst.* 1.1.1.

3. *Inst.* 2.9.4.

makes also at the beginning of the Genevan Catechism, where we are told that the chief end of human life is 'to know God by whom men were created . . . because he has created us and placed us in this world to be glorified in us. And it is indeed right that our life, of which he himself is the beginning, should be devoted to his glory.'[4] This, he says, is 'the highest good of man', and without it, 'our condition is worse than brutes'.[5] The whole being of man is to be centred on God and the glory of God. That is why we exist, and our common experience of being forgetful of God and living under the sway of the human ego and the world is worse than brutish.

There could scarcely be a more profound difference between this world-view and that of the increasingly secular world in which the Western Christians now live. The new atheists are merely giving loudest voice to the opinion of the age. The knowledge of the world now available to the human race through scientific endeavour and rational thought set free from adherence to theology is so great that there no longer exists any place at all for the knowledge of God. In fact, theology is anti-truth, anti-knowledge. In the words of Michel Onfray,

> Monotheism loathes intelligence, that sublime gift defined as the art of connecting what at first and for most people seems unconnected. Intelligence reveals unexpected but undeniable causalities; it produces rational, convincing explanations based on reasoning; it rejects manufactured fiction. With its help, we can spurn myths and fairy tales. We need no posthumous paradise, no salvation or redemption of the soul, no all-knowing, all-seeing God. Properly and rationally directed, intelligence wards off all magical thinking.[6]

The knowledge of God has been relegated to the sphere of superstition. In particular, scientific advance, allegedly rejected by Christians at every point, has dispelled the darkness and enabled us to live without God and with reality, to our very great benefit. 'In science,' Onfray argues, 'the church has always been wrong about everything: faced with epistemological truth, it automatically persecutes the discoverer . . . We can scarcely dare imagine how swiftly the West would have advanced without such sustained brutalization of science!'[7]

A notable thing about the written works of the new atheism is the raucous

---

4. J. Calvin, 'Catechism of the Church of Geneva' (1545), in *Tracts*, 2, p. 37.

5. Ibid., p. 38.

6. M. Onfray, *Atheist Manifesto: The Case against Christianity, Judaism and Islam*, trans. J. Leggatt (New York: Arcade, 2007), p. 67.

7. Ibid., p. 83.

tone of voice adopted by the authors. The rejection of God is not for these authors simply a matter of logical deduction, but of passion, anger, scorn and contempt. In the case of Richard Dawkins, religious enthusiasm is replaced by his enthusiasm for the possibilities inherent in science, which, he says,

> flings open the narrow window through which we are accustomed to viewing the spectrum of possibilities. We are liberated by calculation and reason to visit regions of possibility that had once seemed out of bounds or inhabited by dragons . . . I am thrilled to be alive when humanity is pressing against the limits of understanding. Even better we may eventually discover that there are no limits.[8]

In choosing wisdom as the basis of the knowledge we need to live in this world, Calvin is following the epistemology of the Bible. Wisdom arises from the fear of the Lord; the true wisdom is to know God. He is also aware of the biblical truth that the knowledge of God and the knowledge of ourselves are intimately linked. He completely bypasses philosophical proofs for the existence of God. In thinking about God we are not to objectify him, as though he is an entity like any other entity in the world waiting to be examined, probed and perhaps discounted or, worse, even believed in because of the superior intellect of the thinker. The proper way into this discussion is irreducibly relational and requires an understanding of the nature of God and of ourselves if it is to be prosecuted with success.

The emotive language and passionate tone of the atheists is revealing. They, too, know that there is far more at stake here than merely a set of proofs for the existence or non-existence of God, though Dawkins does offer a treatment of such material. The fundamental issue is the nature of humanity and the question of human freedom. No one could put more clearly nor more crushingly (from one point of view) the demands which being a human creature of God makes upon humans than Calvin does. The whole of life is to be lived in all its parts to the glory of this God. Here is a heavy burden indeed, a slavery which affronts the human spirit. How can we live like that? Onfray prefers 'the solar, affirmative, positive, free, and healthy aspects of the individual standing beyond magical thinking and fables'.[9]

The clash between such a position and that of Calvin is therefore a clash about anthropology. What is the true end of man? What is the 'good life'? Where does human freedom lie? Even the committed Christian will feel the

---

8. R. Dawkins, *The God Delusion* (London: Bantam, 2006), p. 374.

9. Onfray, p. 16.

problem posed by Calvin's powerful delineation of the plight of humans and the majesty of God. Does he leave us any room to be human?

One of the sharpest criticisms of the new atheists is found in Chris Hedges' book *I Don't Believe in Atheists*. He accuses them of utopianism – a charge which makes sense when we read the fevered words of Dawkins. Of course, such utopianism arises from a Pelagian view of human beings.

> The belief that rational and quantifiable disciplines such as science can be used to perfect human society is no less absurd than a belief in magic, angels and divine intervention . . . We have nothing to fear from those who do or do not believe in God; we have much to fear from those who do not believe in sin . . . We discard the wisdom of sin at our peril. Sin reminds us that all human beings are flawed – though not equally flawed. Sin is the acceptance that there will never be a final victory over evil, that the struggle for morality is a battle that will always have to be fought.[10]

What is it that Calvin wishes us to know about ourselves if we are to attain wisdom? He certainly wishes us to acknowledge that 'the mighty gifts with which we are endowed are hardly from ourselves'. But as well as the extraordinary character of the human being, there are the 'ignorance, vanity, poverty, infirmity, and – what is more – depravity and corruption' which lead us to contemplate the contrast between the goodness of God and our own misery. It is in this reciprocal contemplation – of ourselves, of God and then of ourselves in the light of what we know must be true of God – that we begin to attain the wisdom which we need.[11]

How significant is human corruption? So significant that in fact we cannot come to the knowledge of God except by God's own revelation and the Holy Spirit's illumination. When Calvin measures human nature by the law of God, he reveals depravity and corruption and of course denies the power of the will to turn to God even by a fraction. In the Roman Catholic theology of the Council of Trent, sin became culpable with the consent of the will. Calvin, in line with the other Reformers, sees sin as sinful even before the will assents to its desires. Thus in his comments on the tenth commandment he explains the difference between the earlier prohibitions and this one:

> For intent, as we spoke of it under the preceding commandments, is deliberate consent of the will where lust subjects the heart. But covetousness can exist without

---

10. C. Hedges, *I Don't Believe in Atheists* (London: Free Press, 2008), pp. 3, 14.
11. *Inst.* 1.1.1.

such deliberation or consent when the mind is only pricked or tickled by empty and perverse objects. The Lord has previously commanded that the rule of love govern our wills, our endeavours, and our actions. Now he enjoins that the thoughts of our mind be so controlled to the same end that none of them may become depraved or twisted and thus drive the mind in the opposite direction.[12]

Sin beats us before we begin. Not surprisingly, Calvin regards us as being totally unable to turn to God of our own accord.

[T]he mind of man has been so completely estranged from God's righteousness that it conceives, desires and undertakes, only that which is impious, perverted, foul, impure, and infamous. The heart is so steeped in the poison of sin, that it can breathe out nothing but a loathsome stench. But if some men occasionally make a show of good, their minds nevertheless remain enveloped in hypocrisy and deceitful craft, and their hearts bound by an inner perversity.[13]

The truth is that human beings are indeed little more than brutes without the knowledge of God. As the Genevan Catechism explains:

*M:* But are all the works of men so vile and valueless that they cannot merit favour with God?

*S:* First, all the works which proceed from us, so as properly to be called our own, are vicious, and therefore they can do nothing but displease God, and be rejected by him.

*M:* You say then that before we are born again and formed anew by the Spirit of God, we can do nothing but sin, just as a bad tree can only produce bad fruit?

*S:* Altogether so. For whatever semblance works may have in the eyes of men, they are nevertheless evil, as long as the heart to which God looks is depraved.[14]

It would be difficult to surpass the grimness of this account of human nature. We are guilty, vile and helpless, unable to take the first step towards God. But whereas Hedges has insisted on ineradicable human sin in order to warn us against utopianism, Calvin has another motive. He wishes to ensure that we see the bitter truth about ourselves and so have nowhere to turn but to the Lord God himself. He saw that in other systems of Christian thought,

---

12. *Inst.* 2.8.40.

13. *Inst.* 2.5.19.

14. Calvin, 'Catechism', in *Tracts*, 2, p. 54.

notably Tridentine Catholicism, there remains an element of human ability and righteousness, which can form the basis of a move toward salvation; and a salvation which includes the imparting and not simply the imputation of righteousness. As he remarks concerning justification in his 'Antidote to the Sixth Session of the Council of Trent',

> The principal cause of obscurity, however, is, that we are with the greatest difficulty induced to leave the glory of righteousness entire to God alone. For we always desire to be somewhat, and such is our folly, we even think we are.[15]

It is in this context that Calvin refers to the Council of Trent as devising 'a middle way, by which they might not give God the whole in justification, and yet give something'.[16] This is an illuminating remark for understanding Calvin. He was deliberately and definitely not seeking a middle way, which he saw as only corrupting the truth. Arriving at the truth about both God and man required not a middle way, but two 'extremes' – the extremity of the corruption of man, leaving us with absolutely nowhere to turn but to God himself – and the extreme of a sovereign God, the ruler of the world and the one and only Saviour of his people. To fail to embrace both these 'extremes' was to fail to understand the Christian mode of salvation and indeed the relationship between God and man.

In other words, the account of human nature given by Calvin corresponds to his account of the divine nature. God is all-sovereign and all-righteous; human beings are weak and unrighteous, unable to resist sin and unable to save themselves. It is not surprising, therefore, that Calvin's theology has been so vigorously rejected by Roman Catholics, Arminians, liberal Christians and humanists. Its unrelentingly dour picture of humanity steeped in unavoidable and yet culpable sin is not attractive. If anyone on the grounds of the dignity of man wishes to say that salvation to some extent, however small, must lie in the human capacity for choice, they will reject Calvin. Not least they will affirm that sin is only sin when the will intentionally acquiesces; that we cannot be blamed for the unwelcome thoughts of the heart.

In particular, Calvin's account will be strongly resented by those who insist on a version of human freedom which is based on the goodness of human nature and insists that we do not come under the authority of another person, divine or human. In other words, modern individualistic versions of the human

---

15. J. Calvin, 'Antidote to the Sixth Session of the Council of Trent', in *Tracts*, 3, p. 108.
16. Ibid.

person will find the Calvinistic doctrine unbearably confronting and impossible. It cannot lead to their version of salvation, in which we contribute to our own happiness by the exercise of abundant choice. But the rejection of Calvinism will not arise out of new information about human nature; indeed, it could be argued that the history of the twentieth century, supported by the first decade of the twenty-first, only goes to show that Calvin is right. It will arise from a different and more optimistic version of humanity, one more flattering to ourselves and one which gives us licence to fulfil our own desires rather than to centre our lives on a God who demands the totality of our commitment: 'For we always desire to be somewhat, and such is our folly, we even think we are.'

The depravity and helplessness of the human race is matched in Calvin by the majesty of God. The God to be honoured is the one and only God, the Maker of all things and in particular the Creator of the human race and hence our rightful Lord and sovereign. It is integral to Calvin's biblical theology that God be separated from his creatures in power and holiness. His relationship with the created order is not that of some distant potentate, but nor is he involved in a sort of hierarchy of beings whereby his power is shared and relative. God is not first amongst equals, or merely the last resort of the desperate. Calvin is supremely aware that the human heart, as a manufacturer of idols, will create an image of God which brings God down to size; which humanizes him in favour of his creatures. If God is to be honoured, it is essential that we must know him in truth and not in error. And the truth is that he is the sovereign Lord of all things, from the smallest to the greatest. As Calvin says in a lecture on Jonah: 'it is yet ever true that the gnawings even of worms are directed by the counsel of God'.[17]

The God of Calvin is the entirely self-sufficient triune Creator and Ruler of the universe. It is true that he uses angels, humans and even demons to forward his work. But he does not need to do this, and it shows rather more of his power than less. He is not at the mercy of our power, not even of our power to know things. It is true that the works of God reveal a great deal about him – but this is a revelation, not an investigation by human skill and intellect. Indeed, although the revelation through nature exists, human beings are unable because of their moral corruption to understand it and to respond adequately. The fact is that nature responds to his constant government: 'his hand is always engaged in working, so that nothing is done except through Him and by his decree.'[18]

---

17. J. Calvin, *Commentaries on the Twelve Minor Prophets by John Calvin*, trans. J. Owen (5 vols; Edinburgh: Calvin Translation Society, 1846–9), III, 137.

18. Calvin, 'Catechism', in *Tracts*, 2, p. 40.

Just as Calvin's account of human nature creates hostility, it is not surprising that his account of God has not received universal acceptance. For some it is objectionable because it cleans the world out of other spiritual forces and wills which, although not the equal of God, still have a part to play in the spiritual universe. In Calvin, there is only one Will with which men and women have to contend. For others, it makes the laws by which the universe is thought to function into the operations of a person and so threatens their investigation of the cosmos with questions of meaning. For others, the close power of God is inexplicable, given the moral and physical evil which we encounter, and their only explanation, if they are to believe in God, is that he has accepted – or perhaps is unavoidably restricted by – an inability to rule all things. For others – and this indeed gets to the heart of the matter – there is not room in the universe for such a God as Calvin's and for themselves as human beings. He does not leave them enough space, enough personal freedom. Where Calvin rightly sees that the heart of piety must be obedience, they prefer to think that true piety will be a matter of the happy collaboration of partners in the running of the world. If God is not an egalitarian, what use is he?

Paradoxically, the Calvinist account of the world helped lay the foundation of modern science. It did so by laying all the weight of the world's operation on the single will of a good and utterly dependable God and effectively ridding the world of lesser spirits and powers. In the Calvinistic universe, miracles are so rare as to need no special provision to account for them. There is indeed the danger in all this that Calvinism will unwittingly foster atheism by giving us a confidence in the world which in the end will require no explanation beyond itself. On the other hand, the advent of such secularism has also been accompanied by a renewed paganism, as though the vacuum caused by the absence of God from the world must be filled by assorted sprits who still answer the old questions of 'why' and 'who' and 'how' which human beings, confronted by the vagaries and mysteries of nature, have always asked.

In establishing on biblical grounds the depravity of humankind and the majesty of God, Calvin saw himself as making way for the truth of the gospel. Only thus can he establish the 'Godness' of God; his unassailable majesty in his own world. For human beings are saved by the grace of God alone, there being no good thing in human nature which would either attract or deserve salvation, or indeed secure it through any element of human effort. Not only does our salvation depend on the death of Christ as our substitute on the cross; it depends from start to finish on God's grace through his Spirit bringing about regeneration and the new heart which turns to God in faith and repentance. What Calvin sees, of course, is that the fear that we may lose our freedom by turning to God in this way is a sinful and distorted fear. We have been created in such a way that we will find our true happiness – indeed, we will *only* find our true happiness – by so turning to him. When God becomes the very centre of our lives, we are at last free.

This understanding of the gospel dictates Calvin's account of faith. According to him, the hinge on which all of religion turns is this: 'unless you first of all grasp what your relation to God is, and the nature of his judgement concerning you, you have neither a foundation on which to establish your salvation nor one on which to build piety towards God.'[19] To know God is the essence of what it is to be human; that is what we have been created for. The first element of such knowledge is faith, or confidence in God, a confidence which relates us to a God whom we trust because we have become acquainted with his true character. He is our Father and the Author of our salvation. 'When first even the least drop of faith is instilled in our minds, we begin to contemplate God's face, peaceful and calm and gracious toward us. We see him afar off, but so clearly as to know that we are not at all deceived.'[20] All this comes to us from the assurance of the word of God, by which we understand that God is merciful towards us. And it comes by the work of his Holy Spirit, because faith is born of regeneration and illumination, not human effort and reasoning.

Because faith is based on the sure word of God centred on Christ and his work for us, it is in itself assurance. That is not to say that we can achieve perfect faith in this life. Faith will be assailed and accompanied by doubts. But the beauty of Calvin's apprehension of faith is revealed in the idea above: that we see the peaceful, calm and gracious face of God far off, but clearly. Assurance means confidence, boldness, access to God not on the basis of my merits, but on the sound basis of the merits of Jesus Christ alone. It is the aloneness of Christ, the word of God, and the grace of God which secures God's majesty and the joy of our assurance. Anyone who thinks that Calvin was a stranger to joy and peace in his personal religion has never read his writings with attention or sympathy. The faith in the sovereign God, this assurance that the God who rules all things is the Father who cares for us, gave Calvin himself the unassailable confidence to obey God in all circumstances, and inspired the great movement which learned the faith from him not to passivity but to a strenuous activity in the service of the living God.

In my experience, the doctrine of sin is crucial to retaining the integrity of the gospel. When the doctrine of sin weakens, the effect is felt immediately

---

19. *Inst.* 3.11.1.

20. *Inst.* 3.2.19.

in soteriology; for a start, the atoning sacrifice becomes less powerful and human effort is allowed for. In the end, some version of the exemplary theory of the atonement becomes the whole story, and Christianity is reduced to a morality tale. Along the way, before that point is reached, believers are robbed of assurance, since some part of their salvation is dependent on themselves rather than God. The consequence is that assurance is sought in sacraments or in experience (speaking in tongues, prosperity, healing). The glorification of experience becomes the soul of religion, and attention is distracted from the piety of obedience to the unvarnished word of God.

## Conclusion

The virulent attacks on John Calvin have done much to rob the faith of one of its chief and best exponents.[21] I am not suggesting that Calvin become the syllabus of the seminary, or even that it be dominated by whatever variety of Calvinism is the local reigning version. I am saying that the presence of Calvin – in the Moore experience – has been beneficial, but, more to the point, the theology which John Calvin so brilliantly expounded, and especially the theology of the majesty of God (with its concomitant, the depravity of man), should be integral. This theology is the best explanation of the gospel of Jesus Christ and of the world in which we live. It confronts each of the cultural forces which we see around us: the worship of science, the false anthropology, atheism as a protest movement, the idolatry of superstition. Its summons to us to know God in the way in which God has made himself known is exactly what is needed, if we are to have within a seminary not merely an educational institution but an authentic proving ground for shaping those who would preach the gospel and pastor the churches.

I began with references to the way in which Calvin is reviled by many even to this day. And yet it is interesting that in a world which has almost lost touch with Christian things, one of the remnants is John Newton's hymn 'Amazing Grace'. I realize that it is mainly the tune which appeals; yet many people sing the words with gusto. Do they recognize that what they are singing is the Calvinistic gospel? All references to human beings are negative: 'lost', 'blind',

---

21. Since writing these words I have become aware of the two beautiful and brilliant novels by Marilynne Robinson, *Gilead* (London: Picador, 2004) and *Home* (London: Picador, 2008), which incorporate genuinely respectful references to Calvin by characters within the novels, particularly the first.

'wretch'; all references to divine grace are powerful. The wretched are found, kept, brought home; and when they come home, their whole lives are devoted to singing the praises of him who has purchased them. Will the day come again when Newton's old words will be sung by thousands and thousands out of a deep sense of our own helpless unworthiness and the grace which saves? 'I am a great sinner,' said Newton, 'but Christ is a great Saviour.' This should be the glad testimony of every faculty member and every student. Is this not exactly what makes the message of John Calvin relevant to all ages?

© Peter F. Jensen, 2009

12. CALVINISM IN AUSTRALIA 1788–2009:
A HISTORICAL ASSESSMENT

*Colin R. Bale*

The topic of 'Calvinism in Australia' might seem to be an unusual one, given that the first European settlement in Australia occurred in 1788, 224 years after Calvin's death. There is obviously no direct link between the Great South Land and the sixteenth-century Reformer. Moreover, secular historians often claim that the Christian faith, which would necessarily include any form of Protestantism influenced by Calvinism, has had little impact on Australia. Writing in 1999, Bob Ellis, in an article about Australian identity, claimed that Australia was 'the first agnostic society', where 'the forms and ceremonies of religion were served in the bare stone churches and the weatherboard cathedrals in the paddocks on the hills, but none who sang the hymns or took the holy communion truly believed anymore . . . in the Life to come, in waking up from the grave to eternal bliss'.[1] Ellis made quite a leap from acknowledging the physical presence of the Christian faith in Australia to claiming that what transpired in the churches was merely a residue of the faith of previous generations. I disagree with his view-point and other like-minded perspectives, which claim that Christianity has had little impact in Australia. Rather, the Christian faith, especially in its Protestant form, has been an active and significant factor in the development of Australian society and culture. Indeed, there are more than sufficient historical works that

---

1. Bob Ellis, 'Our Place in the Sun', *Sunday Telegraph*, 24 January 1999.

support this contention.[2] It is important, therefore, to consider how Calvinism has shaped and influenced Australian Protestantism.

In 1982, Alexander Barkley published a short assessment of the impact of Calvinism in Australasia.[3] This was a very helpful work and has proved to be a useful overview of the topic. However, it is time to revisit the subject for two reasons. First, twenty-six years have elapsed since the publication of Barkley's chapter, and it is important that the period since 1982 be investigated. Secondly, some aspects of Barkley's assessment need further development and/or nuancing.

In assessing the influence of Calvin's theology on Christianity in Australia, it is surprising to find that very few Australian church history texts in the last twenty-five years have paid much attention to this theme.[4] By and large, there are scant overt references to Calvin or Calvinism in the texts. This may indicate, positively, that the authors understand the importance of Calvinism to Christianity in Australia and, therefore, that it is inferred, or assumed, in the works. However, negatively, it may also be an indication of widespread ignorance among church historians about this important aspect of Australian religious history. My reading of these texts moves me to think that it is more likely to be the latter option.

One exception needs to be made to the above observation. Stuart Piggin's *Evangelical Christianity in Australia: Spirit, Word and World* (1996) treats the issue of Calvinism in Australia with more consideration than his academic contemporaries. In part this is due to Piggin's own theological commitment, for he describes himself as an 'evangelical Calvinist'.[5] As well, as a historian Piggin understands the importance of Calvinism in Australian evangelicalism and its place in the development of Australian identity and values. Thus he seeks to show how Calvinism has been a significant factor in Australian Christianity. However, his

---

2. See R. Thompson, *Religion in Australia: A History* (Oxford: Oxford University Press, 2002); S. Piggin, *Evangelical Christianity in Australia: Spirit, Word and World* (Melbourne and Oxford: Oxford University Press, 1996). Other works are noted at footnote 4 below.

3. A. Barkley, 'The Impact of Calvinism on Australasia', in *John Calvin: His Influence in the Western World*, ed. W. S. Reid (Grand Rapids: Zondervan, 1982).

4. I. Breward, *A History of the Australian Churches* (Sydney: Allen & Unwin, 1993), 4 references; H. Carey, *Believing in Australia* (Sydney: Allen & Unwin, 1996), no references; I. Murray, *Australian Christian Life from 1788* (Edinburgh: Banner of Truth, 1988), 2 references; Thompson, *Religion*, no references. Even the older work by H. Mol, *Religion in Australia* (Nashville: Nelson, 1971) has only one reference.

5. Piggin, *Evangelical Christianity*, p. 157.

work is not an investigation of Calvinism in Australia *per se*, and therefore it has limitations. Moreover, some of his treatment of the subject tends to focus on the negativity of Calvinism in the Australian context, often as perceived by others, so that it does present as narrow and divisive.[6] While this is one element of the story of Calvinism in Australia, there is more that needs to be said.

## Evangelical Anglicans

Barkley notes that Calvinism came to Australia via a number of avenues, but stresses two in particular: Evangelical Anglicans and Scottish Presbyterians.[7] In terms of the former, he mentions the influence of the 'saintly Charles Simeon', who shaped a couple of generations of Cambridge graduates, of whom a number came as Church of England clergy to the Australian colonies.[8] Barkley is right to emphasize the link between Simeon and many evangelical Anglican clergy who came to the Antipodes in the nineteenth century, but Barkley does not indicate anything about the nature of Simeon's Calvinism.

Charles Simeon described himself as a 'moderate Calvinist'. Indeed, he preferred to be known as a biblical Christian rather than a Calvinist. This point of view is all too apparent in the celebrated interview between Simeon and John Wesley that occurred in 1787:

*Simeon:*  Sir, I understand that you are called an Armenian; and I have been sometimes called a Calvinist; and therefore I suppose we are to draw daggers. But before I consent to begin the combat, with your permission I will ask you a few questions. Pray, Sir, do you feel yourself a depraved creature, so depraved that you would never have thought of turning to God, if God had not first put it into your heart?

*Wesley:*  Yes, I do indeed.

*S:*  And do you utterly despair of recommending yourself to God by anything you can do; and look for salvation solely through the blood and righteousness of Christ?

*W:*  Yes, solely through Christ.

*S:*  But, Sir, supposing you were at first saved by Christ, are you not somehow or other to save yourself afterwards by your own works?

---

6. For examples, see Piggin, *Evangelical Christianity*, pp. 18–19, 36–37.

7. Barkley, 'Calvinism', p. 325.

8. Ibid., p. 326.

W:      No, I must be saved by Christ from first to last.

S:      Allowing, then, that you were first turned by the grace of God, are you not in some way or other to keep yourself by your own power?

W:      No.

S:      What then, are you to be upheld every hour and every moment by God, as much as an infant in its mother's arms?

W:      Yes, altogether.

S:      And is all your hope in the grace and mercy of God to preserve you unto His heavenly kingdom?

W:      Yes, I have no hope but in Him.

S:      Then, Sir, with your leave I will put up my dagger again; for this is all my Calvinism; this is my election, my justification by faith, my final perseverance: it is in substance all that I hold, and as I hold it; and therefore, if you please, instead of searching out terms and phrases to be a ground of contention between us, we will cordially unite in those things wherein we agree.[9]

The last lines of the interview reveal Simeon's willingness to be inclusive towards other Protestants, not overly stressing Calvinist doctrine but seeking for theological principles upon which there could be agreement. Kenneth Hylson-Smith argues that this attitude typified many evangelicals in the Church of England at the beginning of the nineteenth century: 'Although the great majority of the Evangelicals were Calvinists, their Calvinism was of a very moderate type, and they did not want it to be a cause of dispute'.[10]

The Reverend Richard Johnson was the first Church of England clergyman in Australia. Johnson and his wife arrived with the First Fleet in 1788 and returned to England in 1800. For the first six years of the convict settlement, he was the only chaplain. Indeed, the Church of England, with a couple of small exceptions, was the only authorized denominational ministry for much of the chaplaincy period until 1820.[11]

---

9.  H. C. G. Moule, *Charles Simeon* (1892; repr. Leicester: IVP, 1965), p. 79.

10. K. Hylson-Smith, *Evangelicals in the Church of England, 1734–1984* (Edinburgh: T. & T. Clark, 1989), p. 52.

11. The Wesleyan Revd Samuel Leigh arrived in Sydney in 1815 and was tolerated by Governor Macquarie on the proviso that Leigh remain subject to the Anglican clergy, especially with regard to the sacraments. Although Roman Catholics comprised one-third of the convict population, their spiritual needs were ignored by the authorities until 1803, when Father James Dixon was allowed to celebrate the Mass. Dixon's permission was withdrawn in the aftermath of the uprising at

Johnson was an evangelical. Although he was probably not directly influenced by Charles Simeon, because Johnson's and Simeon's times at Cambridge overlapped by only one year, it is possible to see similarities in the ministries of both men which were also typical of the ministries of other Anglican evangelicals at the time. It is not easy to discern all the threads of Johnson's evangelicalism, because only one of his sermons has survived, along with letters and journals. The latter tend to give excellent insight into the conditions he experienced, but do not reveal very much about the theological basis of his faith. What can be gleaned from the sources is that Johnson was decidedly Calvinist with regard to the Lord's Supper.[12] Neil Macintosh also notes that Johnson, like other Anglican evangelicals, in speaking of salvation and conversion tended 'to follow a Calvinist approach and emphasise the supremacy of God's call to those who were predestined to salvation'.[13]

In 1794 the Reverend Samuel Marsden joined Johnson.[14] Marsden was to remain in Australia until his death in 1838. With regard to Samuel Marsden, probably the most notable, some may argue notorious, evangelical Anglican clergyman in Australia during the first half of the nineteenth century, his biographer A. T. Yarwood argues that there was a strong Calvinist influence in his theology, particularly evident in his understanding that the elect are a small body chosen for salvation.[15] Yet Marsden's Calvinism often was tempered by an ecumenical attitude to other Protestant ministers, and he worked cooperatively with Wesleyans and Congregationalists. He, like Simeon, could cooperate with Arminians.

Not all Anglican clergy in the early years of the colony adopted this approach. Piggin notes that two Church of England men, William Cowper and John Youll, 'out of their Calvinist commitment' opposed Wesleyan ministry in Sydney.[16] Likewise, some Wesleyans eschewed fellowship with Protestant clergy who were devoted Calvinists.

----

Footnote 11 (*cont.*)

   Castle Hill in 1804 because the Colonial Office feared that allowing the Mass would encourage Irish sedition in Sydney.

12. N. K. Macintosh, *Richard Johnson: Chaplain to the Colony of New South Wales* (Sydney: Ambassador Press, 1978), p. 33.

13. Ibid.

14. The Revd James Bain had arrived in Sydney in 1791 to be the chaplain of the NSW Corps. He departed in 1794. Bain gave little assistance to Johnson.

15. A. T. Yarwood, *Samuel Marsden: The Great Survivor*, 2nd edn (Melbourne: Melbourne University Press, 1996), p. 24.

16. Piggin, *Evangelical Christianity*, p. 19.

The Simeon approach also seems to have characterized some later evangelical Anglicans in Australia. Simeon influenced Frederic Barker, the second bishop of Sydney (1854–1882), at Cambridge. Reading Barker's extant sermons/charges, there appears to be a strong Calvinist theme in these.[17] Moreover, Barker's wife Jane shared his theological position. Jane had been converted in 1820, in no small part due to the influence of an aunt who was 'the incarnation of Calvinism'.[18] This comment by Hartley Coleridge was not intended to be complimentary. Yet, again, like so many of his Anglican evangelical peers, there is also evidence of Barker's openness to working with other Protestant denominations, including those that did not have a Calvinist perspective.

Charles Perry, the first Anglican bishop of Melbourne, was also an evangelical and another Cambridge man. However, it seems he was more influenced by the second generation of 'Simeonites' rather than Simeon himself, although he still bore the marks of Calvinism.[19] Nowhere is this more evident than in the comment he made in 1860 that the Church of England agreed generally with Presbyterianism, except in the matter of episcopal ordination.[20] Perry is speaking, of course, of reformed, evangelical Anglicanism when he speaks of the Church of England.

By the end of the nineteenth century evangelical Anglicanism in Australia was mainly located in two pockets: Melbourne and Sydney. In Melbourne, subsequent diocesan bishops eroded the conservative evangelicalism of Bishop Perry. The third bishop, Field Flowers Goe (1886–1902), although an evangelical, fostered an attitude of tolerance towards other forms of churchmanship in the diocese. His practice dismayed evangelicals. This, in part, lay behind the establishment of Ridley College in 1910 by a group of evangelical clergy and laity, including the bishops of Bendigo and Gippsland. Ridley was independent of the Diocese of Melbourne and it aimed to promote the theological training of evangelicals who maintained a Reformed Evangelical perspective.[21]

---

17. K. Cable, 'Barker, Frederic', in *Australian Dictionary of Biography*, vol. 3 (Melbourne: Melbourne University Press, 1969), pp. 90–94.

18. Murray, *Australian Christian Life*, p. 217.

19. A. de Q. Robin, *Charles Perry* (Perth: University of Western Australia Press, 1967), p. 10.

20. Robin, *Perry*, pp. 124–125. Perry also said that there was a difference between the two denominations with regard to 'universal' redemption: he believed the Presbyterian doctrine was that the Son of God redeemed the elect, while Anglican doctrine was that the Son of God redeemed all mankind but the Holy Spirit sanctified only the elect.

21. Breward, *History*, p. 65.

The college was regarded with hostility by the then Anglican Archbishop of Melbourne, Henry Lowther Clarke, who claimed it had been created in an air of mistrust and suspicion.

Whereas Anglicanism in Melbourne began to resemble the English scene, where dioceses of the Church of England were largely broad and inclusive, the situation in the Anglican Diocese of Sydney was different. This was due in no small part to the growing influence of Moore (Theological) College. From the late nineteenth century until the present, Moore Theological College has played a critical role in maintaining a Reformed, Calvinist, perspective among evangelical Anglicans in Australia, most particularly in Sydney. The college, which was established by Bishop Barker in 1856, struggled in the first few decades. With the appointment of Nathaniel Jones as principal in 1897, things began to look up. Jones was a Calvinist, although he took a position on free will and responsibility that was decidedly un-Calvinist.[22] Jones 'pounded into his students that the Bible, not experience or reason, was the Christian's only and absolute authority. Jones held the doctrine that Scripture was the inspired, full, plenary and authoritative revelation of God'.[23] Under Jones a number of key clergy, men like D. J. Knox, H. S. Begbie and R. B. Robinson, were trained. They provided conservative evangelical leadership in the Sydney Diocese during the first half of the twentieth century.

The years from the death of Nathaniel Jones in 1911 until the appointment of T. C. Hammond as principal in 1936 were lean ones for Moore College. The principal, D. J. Davies, was a liberal evangelical and regarded with some suspicion by more Reformed evangelical clergy. Marcus Loane, a student at Moore in the latter years of Davies' tenure, observed:

> John Calvin and his *Institutes* were virtually terra incognita at the time when I was a student. I never knew another Moore College man or older Anglican clergyman who had read the *Institutes*. What directed my attention to Calvin was Reformation History. It seemed obvious that Calvin was to Protestants all that Thomas Aquinas was to Catholics. So I bought a second hand set of the *Institutes* in three volumes and began to read them in 1933–34.[24]

---

22. John McIntosh, who is currently researching in this area, says that this is evident in Jones's student notes when he was at Oxford. Jones cited the Tractarian Henry Liddon's *Elements of Religion* on the subject.

23. Piggin, *Evangelical Christianity*, p. 77.

24. Cited in M. Cameron, *An Enigmatic Life: David Broughton Knox, Father of Contemporary Sydney Anglicanism* (Sydney: Acorn, 2006), p. 135.

When T. C. Hammond arrived as principal at Moore College in 1936, he found it understaffed, poorly funded and lacking a distinctive direction.[25] He began a vigorous campaign to improve it. Hammond was a Calvinist, but his particular focus was on the English Reformer Thomas Cranmer. John McIntosh thinks that, in part, this emphasis occurred because the big ecclesiastical issues of the time arose from aggressive Anglo-Catholicism.[26] Nevertheless, it is clear from his writings that Hammond was a Calvinist.[27]

In 1954, on the retirement of T. C. Hammond, Marcus Loane was appointed principal of Moore College, with D. B. (Broughton) Knox as vice-principal.[28] Broughton Knox replaced Hammond's emphasis on Cranmer by a new attention to Calvinism, and he introduced a practice that continues until the present: all students were to read Calvin's *Institutes*.[29] In 1959 Knox became principal, a position that he was to hold until his retirement in 1985. Knox argued that Moore College should be a Protestant college rather than an Anglican one.[30] This brought him into conflict in the early 1960s with Hugh Gough, the Anglican Archbishop of Sydney. Gough felt that Knox emphasized 'evangelical' over 'Anglican' at Moore College and that there was 'excessive Calvinism taught at the college'.[31] Knox would not back down, and the Calvinism stayed.

In 1985, Peter Jensen followed Knox as principal of Moore College. He maintained the theological emphases of the College that had marked Knox's tenure. An interview he gave in 2001, when he was elected Archbishop of Sydney, clearly reveals why he believed Calvinism to be so integral in an Anglican theological college:

> The Church of England, when it was reformed in the seventeenth century, fell into the category of churches that owed their theological being to the Swiss Reformation, in other words, Calvinism. And so the Articles and the Prayer Book of our church

---

25. K. Cable, 'Hammond, Thomas Chatterton (1877–1961)', in *Australian Dictionary of Biography*, vol. 14 (Melbourne: Melbourne University Press, 1996), p. 367.

26. Conversation with John McIntosh, 27 February 2009.

27. Hammond contributed an article 'John Calvin on the Atonement' to *RTR* in 1942, and there is a broad Calvinist approach in his book *In Understanding Be Men* (London: IVP, 1936).

28. Broughton was to become principal in 1959 to replace Marcus Loane, who had become an assistant bishop in the Sydney Diocese the previous year.

29. J. R. Reid, *Marcus Loane: A Biography* (Sydney: Acorn Press, 2004), p. 35.

30. Cameron, *Enigmatic*, p. 169.

31. Cameron, *Enigmatic*, p. 105.

are Calvinistic. They're not completely Calvinistic, that is to say they have elements of them, which John Calvin himself may not have gone along with, but in terms of sheer fact, the foundation documents of the Protestant Church of England belong to the Reformed or Calvinistic wing of the church.[32]

The Knox legacy continued with the appointment of John Woodhouse in 2001 as principal to succeed Peter Jensen. As the training college of the Anglican Diocese of Sydney, its theological emphasis continues to be Reformed and evangelical. This has allowed it to train ministry candidates not only for the Anglican Church, but also for the Presbyterian, Baptist and Congregational denominations.


## Scottish Presbyterians

The most obvious strand of Calvinism to come to Australia was that of Scottish Presbyterianism. The Westminster Confession, adopted by Presbyterians as their rule of faith, is where Calvinism is most apparent. However, this detailed theological statement hasn't guaranteed unity among Presbyterians. Currently there are some twenty-five Presbyterian and Reformed denominations spread throughout Australia. Therefore, when assessing Presbyterianism in Australia, note must be made of the divisions amongst those who affirm the Westminster Confession.

Presbyterianism in the Sydney colony was unorganized until the early 1820s. In 1802 a small band of Scots had settled at Portland Head (Ebenezer) on the Hawkesbury River. They formed a small congregation under the leadership of a layman, James Mein, and in 1809 built the first Presbyterian Church building in Australia.[33] The Wesleyan Samuel Leigh, on his circuit in Sydney's west, reported in 1817 'a few Presbyterians had erected a small house in the wood (near Portland), in which they assembled on the Lord's Day for reading the scriptures and prayer'.[34] The Scottish settlers entreated Leigh to give them a sermon, which he did. The practice of welcoming preachers from other Protestant denominations at Portland Head continued until the denomination was more organized in the 1820s.

---

32. Revd Dr Peter Jensen interview, *Religion Report*, ABC Radio, 13 June 2001.
33. M. Prentis, *The Scots in Australia* (Randwick: University of New South Wales Press, 2008), p. 175.
34. Murray, *Australian Christian Life*, p. 66.

Official Presbyterian ministry in Australia started only in 1822 with the arrival of Archibald McArthur in Hobart. John Dunmore Lang arrived in Sydney in May 1823 to begin formal Presbyterian ministry in that colony. Lang proved to be a controversial figure throughout his long years of ministry (1823–1878), but he never wavered from the Calvinism he had been taught in Scotland. Although he could be divisive and disputatious, Lang worked hard to build the Presbyterian Church in Australia. The most notable contribution he made to Presbyterianism, apart from maintaining his Reformed theological emphasis, was his activity in migration ventures. He made nine voyages to Britain to encourage Scottish migrants to come and settle in the Australian colonies.[35] Many Scots migrants did come and settle in rural areas, notably the Western District of Victoria and the Monaro and New England regions of New South Wales. Robert Campbell, the Sydney Merchant, employed seventy Scottish families at Duntroon (Canberra) on his large sheep run. They were committed Presbyterians, 'whose days began with prayer, who kept the Lord's Day, and whose graves bore such texts as, *For here have we no continuing city, but seek one to come*'.[36]

By 1872 Lang reported that there were seventy-two Presbyterian ministers in the colony of New South Wales, and that 120 churches/chapels had been constructed. This figure placed the Presbyterian Church in fourth position in the colony in terms of numbers of ministers and buildings.[37] The situation was even better for Presbyterianism in Victoria, where it was second in size only to the Church of England, with 15.3% of the population counted as adherents.

However, although there had been remarkable physical growth in the Presbyterian Church in the Australian colonies by the 1870s, the denomination, like all the Protestant churches, was beset by attacks from both within and without on its theological orthodoxy. Darwinism and other scientific theories had become a major challenge to evangelical Christianity. As well, biblical criticism was testing traditional views about the Bible. None of this was unique to Australia. Indeed, the colonies lagged behind Europe and North America, from where the latest in theological thinking was imported.

David Bebbington has noted how the 'erosion of Calvinism proceeded apace' in both Western Europe and the United States 'in the middle years of

---

35.  D. W. A. Baker, 'Lang, John Dunmore (1799–1878)', *Australian Dictionary of Biography*, vol. 2 (Melbourne: Melbourne University Press, 1967), p. 77.

36.  Murray, *Australian Christian Life*, p. 114.

37.  J. D. Lang, *An Historical and Statistical Account of NSW* (updated), cited in Murray, *Australian Christian Life*, p. 126.

the [19th] century'.[38] He argues that the 'principle of free enquiry increasingly seemed to require the elimination of the assumed premises of any doctrinal scheme'.[39] Accordingly, those who maintained an orthodox position were not only challenged by the new views but by attacks on the basis of their scholarship. This was also the case in Australia.

The situation that confronted the Presbyterian Church in Australia in the late nineteenth century is well illustrated by the Strong Affair. Charles Strong was a Scot who came to Victoria in 1875 to be the minister of Scots Church, Melbourne. He had studied at the University of Glasgow, where he rejected much of orthodox Calvinism and had adopted a liberal, Broad Church theology.[40] Presbyterian conservatives in the colony regarded him with suspicion and were worried that he 'did not hold the basic facts of redemption and that his actual beliefs were subversive to them'.[41] Essays written and published by Strong in 1878 and 1879 intensified this suspicion. Matters came to a head with the publication of an article on the Atonement by Strong in 1880.[42] A committee established by the Melbourne Presbytery examined the printed article. The report of the committee was critical of Strong for 'the negative character of the teaching' in his paper, especially 'the absence from it of all direct mention of the Divine person of the Lord Jesus Christ as the Mediator, and Reconciler, working out the Atonement'.[43]

The committee urged Strong to make the central facts of the Christian faith, namely 'the incarnation, the atoning life and death and the resurrection and ascension of our Lord', more prominent in his preaching.[44] Strong declined to comment and announced that he intended to leave Scots Church in August 1881. However, his supporters persuaded him to reconsider this action. He decided to take six months' leave of absence from Scots Church and then return for at least another year. At the congregational meeting

---

38. D. W. Bebbington, *The Dominance of Evangelicalism: The Age of Spurgeon and Moody* (Leicester: IVP, 2005), p.125.

39. Ibid.

40. C. R. Badger, 'Strong, Charles (1844–1942)', in *The Australian Dictionary of Biography*, vol. 6 (Melbourne: Melbourne University Press, 1976), p. 208.

41. R. Ward, *The Bush Still Burns: The Presbyterian and Reformed Faith in Australia 1788–1988* (Sydney: Globe Press, 1989), p. 255.

42. *Victorian Review*, October 1880.

43. R. Hamilton, *A Jubilee History of the Presbyterian Church of Victoria* (Melbourne: Presbyterian Church of Victoria, 1888), p. 403.

44. Ibid.

where this action was decided, one elder, J. C. Stewart, in an attempt to support Strong gave a speech that was extremely critical of the Westminster Confession of Faith and those who claimed to adhere to it, arguing 'that the men who pretend to assert, maintain, and defend all the doctrines contained in the Confession are dishonest men'.[45] Stewart was later censured for his outburst.

With the threat of a charge of heresy hanging over him, Strong decided to leave Victoria. He sailed for Britain on 15 November and next day the assembly declared him to be no longer a minister of the Presbyterian Church of Victoria. Strong returned to Melbourne in 1885 and founded the Australian Church, which he stated was 'comprehensive, non-dogmatic, and liberal'.[46]

The Strong Affair revealed the theological fault-lines running through the Presbyterian Church. Traditional Calvinism as exemplified in the Westminster Confession was under attack. For the next ninety years the denomination would be beset by tension between those who wished to hold firm to its traditional theological Reformed formularies and those who wished to revise them in accordance with modern, liberal thinking. In the 1880s the conservatives prevailed.

Another very public dispute in the Presbyterian Church occurred in the 1930s with the attempt to censure the Revd Dr Samuel Angus for his liberal theological teaching. Angus was Professor of New Testament at St Andrew's College in Sydney, which was the training institution for Presbyterian ministers. Notes of his lectures indicated that his theology diverged from that of the Westminster Confession on a number of points.[47] He was quite radical and questioned the historicity of the virgin birth, the physical resurrection of Jesus, the reality of the ascension and traditional interpretations of the atonement.[48] An attempt to charge him with heresy did not proceed because it was clear that Angus was widely supported and that the Presbyterian Church in New South Wales was deeply divided. In Victoria, Dr Charles Strong 'noted with dry satisfaction that the failure to convict him (Angus) of heresy indicated that the Presbyterian Church had at last caught up with his 1883 position'.[49]

---

45. Ward, *Bush*, p. 257.

46. C. R. Badger, *The Reverend Charles Strong and the Australian Church* (Melbourne: Abacada, 1971), p. 104.

47. Breward, *History*, p. 129.

48. A. Dougan, 'Angus, Samuel (1881–1943)', *Australian Dictionary of Biography*, vol. 7 (Melbourne: Melbourne University Press, 1979), p. 74.

49. Breward, *History*, p. 129.

By the 1960s it was clear that the Presbyterian Church, along with all the major Protestant denominations, was in decline. The number of Presbyterians in Australia had slipped from a high of 11.72% in 1921 to 9.29% of the population in 1961. This would drop to 6.64% in 1976.[50] Decreasing numbers of migrants from Scotland intensified the problem, but the influence of liberal theology was also a factor. Rowland Ward estimates that by the mid-1970s in Victoria and New South Wales the number of evangelical Presbyterian clergy had declined to about 40% of the total.[51] The answer for many in the Presbyterian Church was for the denomination to unite with the Congregationalists and Methodists. Thus the Uniting Church came into being in 1977. However, approximately one-third of Presbyterian parishes declined to join the union, insisting that they would remain Presbyterian.

The 'rump' Presbyterian Church had a number of leaders 'who were determined to create a church purified of liberalism and true to the Westminster Confession'.[52] Breward notes that this was easier to achieve in the states other than New South Wales, where many remaining Presbyterians were connected to the Church of Scotland rather than the Free Church of Scotland with its more strict confessional Presbyterianism.[53] Nevertheless, the Presbyterian Church in Australia post-Union, although small, began to look more discernibly Reformed. By 1989 Rowland Ward was estimating that the percentage of evangelicals in parish ministry was about 80% and that most of the new ministers since 1977 were Calvinistic.[54]

The three Presbyterian training colleges in New South Wales, Queensland and Victoria were critical in achieving this change. All the colleges have witnessed an increase in candidates training for Presbyterian ministry since the 1980s and this led to a renewed emphasis upon Calvin in Australian Presbyterianism. So much so, that the three colleges have joined together in 2009 to stage a conference to celebrate the 500th anniversary of Calvin's birth. The conference, titled 'Discendi Studio – Zeal to Learn', states that Presbyterians in Australia 'are committed to continue his [Calvin's] heritage of building a church which is ruled by God through the Scriptures and taught by pastors who have a love of God and his word and a zeal for learning'. The statement would please Calvin.

---

50. Australian Bureau of Statistics, 1976 Census.
51. Ward, *Bush*, p. 466.
52. Breward, *History*, p. 183.
53. Ibid.
54. Ward, *Bush*, p. 466.

## Congregationalism

Congregationalism has been another important vehicle for Calvinism in Australia. As it developed in the seventeenth century, Congregationalism emphasized the absolute sovereignty of God and claimed that only the elect who are predestined can achieve salvation, and that the elect can do nothing to save themselves without divine aid.[55] The most unique aspect of Congregationalism is its ideas on church government. Power rests with individual congregations rather than with any denominational structure or hierarchy. Individual churches choose their own minister and regulate their own internal discipline. Any external body, such as a Congregational Union, has only an advisory relationship with individual congregations.

Congregationalism never comprised more than about 2% of the Australian population from its formal beginnings in 1822 until the disappearance of most Congregational churches with the formation of the Uniting Church in 1977.[56] However, although it was a small denomination, it was characterized by an active membership. The number of members attending on a regular basis in the nineteenth century remained high. For example, in 1871 it is estimated from census data that there were twenty-five Congregational Churches in New South Wales catering for 5,985 regular members, an average figure of 239 people per congregation.[57]

However, the years 1870 to 1914 were particularly difficult ones for Congregationalism. As indicated already, Australian Christianity imbibed the intellectual and theological discussions abounding in Britain and the United States of America. Ian Breward notes that major components of evangelical Christianity were the subject of discussion and revision: 'creation; the humanity of Jesus; atonement and original sin; the nature of heaven, hell and future life'.[58] The independent nature of Congregationalism and the willingness within the movement to consider the new intellectual ideas caused Congregational churches to move away from Calvinism.

Pat Jalland argues that biblical criticism and new scientific theories not only affected ministers but laity as well.[59] Her study of the language of the

---

55. Information on Congregationalism as it originated in Britain can be found on the website: philtar.ucsm.ac.uk/encyclopedia/christ/esp/congreg.html.

56. Mol, *Religion*, p. 5.

57. Murray, *Australian Christian Life*, p. 126.

58. Breward, *History*, p. 93.

59. P. Jalland, *Australian Ways of Death: A Social and Cultural History 1840–1918* (Oxford: Oxford University Press, 2002), p. 159.

condolence letters sent to the relatives of a deceased person reflected the impact of these factors. She noted that from 1880 onwards 'the content, tone, and emphasis' of such letters changed and they 'lost the familiar (or traditional) Christian language of comfort which once flowed so readily'.[60] The new ideas created uncertainty, which developed into indifference, so that increasing numbers of people did not seek to express their written condolences in the language or images of the faith.

The current Fellowship of Congregational Churches (Australia) website acknowledges this development at the end of the nineteenth and beginning of the twentieth centuries: 'unfortunately, as with many denominations, liberalism, modernism and growing materialism influenced many in the Congregational church. Sadly, many Congregationalists turned from their heritage, away from the truth of Scripture, from the authority of God's word and in doing so, lost their spiritual fervour and their missionary zeal. Consequently, many churches went into decline'.[61]

The number of Congregationalists dropped from 1.95% of the population in 1901 to 0.39% in 1976, the year before the establishment of the Uniting Church of Australia.[62] The decrease in numbers was due in part to the inroads of liberal theology and secularism but, especially after World War 2, also to the decline in the number of migrants coming to Australia from the British Isles, the natural constituency of Congregationalism. In 1977 a few Congregational churches, mainly in New South Wales, chose to stay out of the Union.[63] Although Congregationalism was now a much-reduced presence in Australia, the saving grace of the Union was that the remaining Congregational churches in Australia reclaimed their Calvinist heritage, as is evident in the statement of faith currently affirmed by them.


## Baptists

There has also been a strong Calvinist influence among those who identify themselves as Baptists in Australia. Within the growth of Baptist churches in England in the seventeenth century, two strands developed over the issue of

---

60. Ibid.
61. Fellowship of Congregational Churches (Australia) website: www.fcc-cong.org/ history.asp.
62. H. Carey, *Believing in Australia* (St Leonards, Sydney: Allen & Unwin, 1996), pp. 197–205.
63. Twenty-seven Congregational churches in NSW did not join the Uniting Church.

particular redemption. General Baptists insisted that Christ died for all people, whereas Particular Baptists insist that Christ died only for the elect.[64] The Particular Baptists were the largest and most active of the Baptist groups in England in the nineteenth century, but this was not the case in Australia.[65]

The Baptists started later in Australia than most of the other Protestant denominations. In the 1828 census conducted in New South Wales, only one person was identified as a Baptist. However, as many people in the census chose to identify themselves as Protestants rather than using a denominational descriptor, it is most probable that other Baptists were not clearly identified. The first Baptist service occurred in Sydney in April 1831. The minister who conducted the service was one John McKaeg, 'whose unsatisfactory behaviour led to the collapse of the cause until the arrival of John Saunders in December 1834'.[66] From that point Baptist numbers in Australia increased significantly. By 1871 there were 1,912 regular members at twenty-four Baptist churches in New South Wales.[67] Matched to these were an additional 525 Particular Baptists in three churches.

In the 1860s the two strands of Baptists began to come together and Baptist Unions were formed in each of the Australian colonies: Victoria in 1862, South Australia in 1863, New South Wales in 1868 and Queensland in 1877. Some Particular Baptist churches did not join these associations, rather maintaining their theological distinctiveness, forming the Particular Baptist Association of Australia. However, the isolation of the Particular Baptists witnessed a further decline in their numbers. The history of the Baptist Union of New South Wales comments that the Particular Baptist 'doctrine of Particular Redemption (that the atonement was not made for all men, but only for those whom God had chosen for salvation) had a lessening appeal with the passing of the years'.[68] The comment is also an ironic indication of the reality that a significant number of churches within the colonial Baptist Unions were moving to a more Arminian position on redemption.

The most influential figure among the Baptists in the nineteenth century was the English Baptist C. H. Spurgeon. In many ways he was an unashamed Calvinist:

---

64. P. J. Hughes, *The Baptists in Australia* (Canberra: Australian Government Publishing Service, 1996), p. 3.

65. A. C. Prior, *Some Fell on Good Ground* (Sydney: Baptist Union of NSW, 1966), p. 90.

66. Breward, *History*, p. 28.

67. Murray, *Australian Christian Life*, p. 126.

68. Prior, *Good Ground*, p. 98.

There is no soul living who holds more firmly to the doctrines of grace than I do, and if any man asks me whether I am ashamed to be called a Calvinist, I answer – I wish to be called nothing but a Christian; but if you ask me, do I hold the doctrinal views which were held by John Calvin, I reply, I do in the main hold them, and rejoice to avow it.[69]

Spurgeon also resisted the contemporary pull of Arminianism that Baptist churches were experiencing in the English-speaking world:

And what is the heresy of Arminianism but the addition of something to the work of the Redeemer? Every heresy, if brought to the touchstone, will discover itself here. I have my own private opinion that there is no such thing as preaching Christ and Him crucified, unless we preach what nowadays is called Calvinism. It is a nickname to call it Calvinism; Calvinism is the gospel, and nothing else.[70]

Spurgeon was very aware of the inherent dangers in the second half of the nineteenth century to orthodox Christianity from Darwinism, Higher Criticism and other new theological ideas. He was alarmed at reports of Baptist ministers embracing this liberal thinking and leading their congregations into error.[71] Spurgeon proposed that Baptists adopt a statement of faith: 'one that plainly enunciated the evangelical position – and that acceptance of it be the basis on which membership of a church or a person in the Union would be continued'.[72] However, Spurgeon's call was rejected.

In 1887 he supported a series of articles appearing in his church magazine *Sword & Trowel* under the heading 'The Down Grade', which was a direct reference to what Spurgeon saw as the tendency within the Baptist Union to downgrade the Bible and *sola scriptura*.[73] What surfaced in the ensuing dispute was an attack by liberal critics not only on Spurgeon but on the Calvinism he held dear. The Revd T. R. Stevenson, a member of the Baptist Union Council, wrote to the *Derby Daily Telegraph*: 'Much of his (Spurgeon's) theology is unworthy of him. It is out of joint with the Bible: it is also opposed to the best instincts of humanity . . . To be plain, Calvinism has had its day . . . the world has outgrown

---

69. C. H. Spurgeon, *Autobiography of Charles H. Spurgeon* (Cincinnati: Curts & Jennings, 1889), p. 172.

70. Ibid.

71. A. Dallimore, *Spurgeon: A New Biography* (Edinburgh: Banner of Truth, 1985), p. 204.

72. Ibid.

73. D. W. Bebbington, *Evangelicalism in Modern Britain: A History from the 1730s to the 1980s* (London: Routledge, 1989), p. 145.

it'.[74] Spurgeon decided to withdraw from the Baptist Union, which drew much criticism from fellow ministers.

The Downgrade controversy indicates something of the pragmatism within Protestant churches at the end of the nineteenth century. Iain Murray explains that it 'showed a readiness on the part of many ministers to justify their lack of firm action' in standing against encroaching liberalism 'on the grounds of the greater good to be gained by a more accommodating policy'.[75] This was the attitude of those who sympathized with Spurgeon's concern but regretted his withdrawal, as they balanced it over against the possible good that he might have done had he stayed in the Union. Spurgeon rejected this because he believed that any churches or denominations that 'bound the unorthodox with the orthodox' were 'Confederacies of Evil'.[76]

The influence of Spurgeon on Baptist churches in both the nineteenth century and the twentieth was immense. Between 1863 and 1892 the majority of Baptist ministers who came to Australia from Britain had trained at Spurgeon's College. Indeed, more young ministers went to Australia and New Zealand from Spurgeon's College than to the United States or South Africa.[77] Spurgeon's sermons also were widely read in Australia. So highly were they valued that one man paid for them to be published in several of the Australian papers week by week as advertisements, in order to reach as many people as possible.[78]

Australian Baptists in the twentieth century were generally more resistant to the inroads of liberal theology than other denominations. Nevertheless, a more liberal evangelicalism developed in Victorian and South Australian Baptist churches, compared with Baptists in New South Wales and Queensland, where a more conservative view prevailed.[79] In 1991, the Baptist Union of Victoria conducted a survey among member churches about what was important in being a Baptist. As was expected, the most strongly affirmed item was believers' baptism. Moreover, many Baptists in Victoria still identified with a 'general theological orientation of evangelicalism', but most traces of the Particular Baptist emphases had disappeared.[80] The difference between

--------

74. I. Murray, *The Forgotten Spurgeon* (Edinburgh: Banner of Truth, 1973), p. 180.

75. Murray, *Spurgeon*, p. 160.

76. Bebbington, *Evangelicalism*, p. 145.

77. Piggin, *Evangelical Christianity*, p. 58.

78. C. H. Spurgeon, *Autobiography: The Full Harvest*, vol. 2 (Edinburgh: Banner of Truth, 1973), p. 353.

79. Breward, *History*, p. 95.

80. Hughes, *Baptists*, p. 29.

Baptists in Victoria and in New South Wales is illustrated by the willingness of the Baptist College of Victoria to engage in the Melbourne College of Divinity, even though this meant joining with the Roman Catholics. In New South Wales, the Baptists withdrew from the Sydney College of Divinity over the very same issue.[81] Stuart Piggin also notes this conservatism in the New South Wales Union, where the issue of biblical inerrancy drove a number of Baptist ministers to Victoria in the 1980s.[82]

The theological range of Baptist churches in Australia today is quite diffuse. This was acknowledged in a paper delivered by Dr Ken Manley, the Principal of Whitley College (the Baptist College of Victoria), titled 'Shapers of our Australian Baptist Identity' to the Baptist World Alliance Congress in 2000. The paper argued that fundamentalism continues to 'shape the identity of at least some significant parts of the Baptist community'. By 'fundamentalism' Manley seems to be thinking of those churches within the respective state Baptist Unions that continue to hold to a conservative Calvinist position. To what extent this is the case is not easy to determine.

**Calvinistic Methodists**

Although Calvinism in Australia is most discernible through the influence of a number of the major Protestant denominations, other, smaller, churches should also be included in any assessment. A snapshot of two different Calvinistic churches/denominations will show both the diversity of these groups and yet their common commitment to the Calvinist heritage. It should also be noted that clearly identifying these groups is never easy, as often more than one label can be applied to the smaller churches. For example, Calvinistic Methodists can also be identified as Welsh Presbyterians or even Presbyterians. Often the main distinguisher between the various groups is a particular ethnic identity.

Calvinistic Methodists were one early group to come to the colony of New South Wales. Calvinistic Methodists were those in the eighteenth-century revival who adhered to the doctrinal emphases of George Whitfield and Howell Harris. The church seems to have been associated with Wales more than with other parts of the British Isles, and this Welsh identity is also reflected in their activity in Australia. In 1811 the group was officially recognized in Britain as

---

81. Breward, *History*, p. 215.
82. Piggin, *Evangelical Christianity*, p. 184.

the Calvinistic Methodist Connexion. They adopted a Confession of Faith which contained forty-four articles based on the Westminster Confession as 'Calvinistically construed'.[83]

The Calvinistic Methodists were one of the main religious groups responsible for the founding of the non-denominational Missionary Society (renamed the London Missionary Society in 1818) in 1795. In 1796 the Missionary Society sent the first party of missionaries to Tahiti to establish a station there. Within eighteen months relations with the Tahitians had become so poor that the missionaries were evacuated to Sydney. Three members of the party, William Crook, John Youl and Rowland Hassall, who were Calvinistic Methodists, were the first known members of the denomination in Australia.[84]

At Sydney, William Crook (1775–1846) involved himself in schooling in the colony before returning to the mission field. At the time of Governor Bligh's deposition in 1808 Crook was once again in Sydney. As the mutineers had removed the Revd Henry Fulton from his position in the colony and Samuel Marsden was in Britain, Crook was appointed as an acting chaplain, even though he was neither an Anglican nor ordained.[85] He was discharged from the position when normality prevailed, but he continued as an itinerant evangelist, preaching in many centres in Sydney's west. Then followed another stint on the mission field of the South Pacific, in 1816. He returned to Australia in 1830 and was eventually appointed deacon of the first Congregational church in Sydney.

Rowland Hassall is another early colonial figure closely associated with Calvinistic Methodism. Given some support by the Revd Samuel Marsden when he fled to Sydney in 1798, Hassall worked as an itinerant lay-preacher in the colony. By 1806 he was ministering 'to the Calvinistic Methodist and Presbyterian settlers at Portland Head on the Hawkesbury, and in 1808 he helped them to build a Dissenting chapel (since 1824 exclusively Presbyterian)'.[86] We know that he also preached in the Liverpool area and that he held regular services in his own barn ('the chapel') at Parramatta on Sunday

83. A. S. Wood, 'Calvinistic Methodism', in *The New International Dictionary of the Christian Church*, ed. J. D. Douglas (Grand Rapids: Zondervan, 1978), p. 182.

84. Crook has often been labelled a Congregationalist as well as a Calvinistic Methodist.

85. N. Gunson, 'Crook, William Pascoe', in *Australian Dictionary of Biography*, vol. 1 (Melbourne: Melbourne University Press, 1966), p. 259.

86. N. Gunson, 'Hassall, Rowland', in *Australian Dictionary of Biography*, vol. 1 (Melbourne: Melbourne University Press, 1966), p. 521–522.

and Friday evenings. He did much to stamp the character of 'Calvinistic Methodism' on the Liverpool district, which proved a source of embarrassment to his son-in-law Walter Lawry and the other Wesleyan preachers. However, Hassall always welcomed the Wesleyan ministers, even though they were Arminians, and they, in turn, refrained from undermining his theological influence until after his death.[87]

After the colonial period ended, it is not easy to trace the progress of the Calvinistic Methodists in Australia because there are so few extant sources about them. As they were very close to the Presbyterians in theology, it is likely that members of the denomination joined Presbyterian churches. However, some Calvinistic Methodists clung to both their theological and Welsh identity. The biographical details of one Calvinistic Methodist minister in the second half of the nineteenth century illustrate this feature. William Meirion Evans was a Welsh miner who migrated to Australia in 1849.[88] He made a small fortune on the goldfields and returned to Britain. However, he came to Australia again in 1863 and started a Calvinistic Methodist Church the following year at Ballarat. He also edited numerous journals and articles, many written in Welsh. He died in 1883 and was buried in Ballarat. The church at Ballarat continues in the present as the Carmel Welsh Presbyterian Church.

Like William Meirion Evans, many Welsh people came to Australia during the gold rushes of the 1850s and 1860s. Mostly they came to the Victorian goldfields, with one group moving to Melbourne in the 1860s, where they founded a Welsh Calvinistic Church.[89] This church still exists in Melbourne. An associated website claims that there were originally sixteen of these Welsh churches in Victoria, but that this has dwindled to two congregations.[90]

Very little information is available about the Calvinistic Methodists in the first part of the twentieth century. We know that there was at least one church, because there is an annual report of the Welsh Calvinistic Church from 1944 lodged in the National Library of Australia. However, there are no other annual reports in the collection and there are no explanations in the Library's

---

87. Ibid.

88. R. Ward, 'Evans, William Meirion', in *Australian Dictionary of Evangelical Biography*, ed. B. Dickey (Sydney: Evangelical History Association, 1994), p. 106.

89. Sion Hughes, the current minister of the church, supplied information about the Welsh Calvinistic Methodist Church in Melbourne.

90. The church does not have its own website. Information was obtained from www. gomelbournecity.com/listing.asp?lid=279&page=Melbourne%20Welsh%20 Church.

files about why and how the annual report came into the collection.[91] What is apparent is that the annual report is from the Welsh Calvinistic Church in Melbourne. In 2009, this church is linked with Carmel Welsh Presbyterian Church at Sebastopol near Ballarat. Together they form the Welsh Calvinistic Methodist Connexion in Victoria.


## Reformed churches

The second group of smaller Calvinist churches are those that identify themselves as 'Reformed'. Most of these churches have been established in the second half of the twentieth century. After World War 2, a number of people of the various Reformed Churches of the Netherlands migrated to Australia. They were mainly members of the *Gereformeerde Kerken* (GKN). They should not be confused with migrants from the Dutch Reformed Church, who tended to join the Presbyterian Church.[92] In 1949–1950 the GKN sent the Revd J. Kremer to Australia to investigate the spiritual and church life of the various Reformed groups that had settled in Australia. As a consequence of this visit, the Free Presbyterian Church of St Kilda extended a 'call' to a GKN minister in the Netherlands to work among the Dutch migrants.[93] The arrival of a GKN minister met the needs of the Dutch congregation, but it also highlighted the problems of a GKN church cohabiting with a Free Presbyterian Church. The difference between the culture of the Australian-Scottish Presbyterians and the Reformed Netherlanders was a factor, but the real problem was that the Dutch migrants were uncomfortable with the liturgical restrictions of the Free Church (no organs, no hymns). As other denominations were perceived as too liberal, the Dutch migrants decided in December 1951 to organize a separate denomination.[94] This led to the formation of the 'Reformed Churches of Australia' (CRC).

The CRC is the biggest group in the Reformed sector. It comprises fifty-four churches spread throughout all the states of Australia. Its doctrinal position is set by four confessional standards: the Heidelberg Catechism, the Belgic Confession, the Canons of Dort and the Westminster Confession. There is a

---

91. Reformed online: www.reformiert-online.net/weltweit/7_eng.php.
92. R. Julian, 'The Reformed Church', *The Companion to Tasmanian History*, ed. A. Alexander (Hobart: University of Tasmania, 2005), p. 304.
93. Barkley, 'Calvinism', p. 333.
94. Barkley, 'Calvinism', p. 334.

strong commitment to Calvinism, with the *Institutes* regarded as 'the greatest dogmatic work of the Reformation', and that Calvin himself was 'a brilliant organizer, having formulated the Presbyterian type of church government that we (CRC) still use in the Reformed Church of Australia today'.[95]

The Presbyterian Reformed Church was established in 1967. It has congregations in all the mainland states, except Western Australia. It adheres to five-point Calvinism: total depravity, unconditional election, limited atonement, irresistible grace and the perseverance of the saints.[96] The church runs its own small theological college, funds its own overseas missionaries and sells Reformed books via a mail distribution system.

The Evangelical Presbyterian Church is another group that falls under the Reformed banner. It was established in 1961 and has five congregations along the east coast of Australia, including Tasmania. It holds to the Westminster Confession of Faith and notes on its website that the original members have come from the main Protestant denominations (Anglican, Presbyterian, Methodist, Congregational, Baptists, etc.) because these denominations were tolerating spiritual compromise.[97] As a denomination the Evangelical Presbyterian Church holds to basic Christian truths and stands against the tide of humanism, modernism and liberal theology.

All the religious denominations have involved themselves in the education of children and youth by establishing schools. The Reformed churches have seen schools as a way to combat the influence of humanism in the state education systems. Reformed schools are parent controlled and unashamedly teach Reformed doctrines to the children. For example, the Free Reformed School Association operates the John Calvin Primary Schools in five locations, as well as one secondary school. The association stresses that the 'heritage of the schools can be traced to the time of the Reformation and it owes its name and emblem to a man used by God to lead the people back to Biblical truth: John Calvin (1509–1564), a Frenchman, sought to highlight the preeminence of God in all of life'.[98]

The work of Alexander Barkley in assessing the Reformed churches is revealing. Barkley himself was a member of a Reformed church and was foundation Principal of the Reformed Theological College in Victoria. In

---

95. Taken from the website of the Perth Christian Reformed Church: www.crcperth. org.au/hist.CRCA.htm.

96. Presbyterian Reformed Church website: www.prc.org.au.

97. Website for Evangelical Presbyterian Church: www.epc.org.au.

98. Free Reformed Schools Association website: www.frsa.asn.au.

his assessment of Calvinism in Australia, apart from positively noting the continuing adherence of Reformed churches to Calvinism, Barkley believed that the work of the Reformed Theological College in supplying graduates to Reformed churches, including the various Presbyterian churches in Australia, was the movement's other great strength. However, Barkley recognized a great weakness in the Reformed churches – they were not united. He believed that this factor inhibited their effective outreach in the Australian community because they appeared divisive.[99] This is a sobering assessment from someone inside the movement.

## Conclusion

As is evident from the preceding survey of many of the Protestant churches, Calvinism has been an important theological factor in the types of Protestantism that migrants brought to Australia. In many ways the story of Calvinism in Australia over the last 221 years matches that of Calvinism in other Western countries. It has been challenged by secularism, which has seen churches of all theological persuasions markedly decline in numbers and influence. It has been impacted by new ways of thinking that have attacked its theological foundations. Yet, in spite of these developments, the current situation for Calvinism in Australia is very positive. There remains an overt desire in at least five Protestant denominations, or parts thereof, to name Calvinism as their theological basis. Correspondingly, this commitment to their doctrinal identity has given those respective churches the ability not only to resist the pressures upon them but also to grow in response. A further audit on the five hundred and fiftieth anniversary of Calvin's birth will reveal how well they have done so.

© Colin R. Bale, 2009

---

99. Barkley, 'Calvinism', p. 334.

# BIBLIOGRAPHY

## Calvin

'A Defence of the Secret Providence of God' (1558), trans. H. Cole, London, 1856, repr. as pp. 223–350 in *Calvin's Calvinism*, Grand Rapids, MI: Reformed Free Publishing, 1987.

'Ad Quaestiones Georgii Biandrata responsum Ioannis Calvini' (1559), *CO*, 9, pp. 325–332.

'Adversus Petri Caroli Calumnias' (1545), *CO*, 7, pp. 293–340.

'Antidote to the Sixth Session of the Council of Trent' (1547), pp. 18–188 in *Tracts and Treatises*, vol. 3, trans. H. Beveridge, Edinburgh: Calvin Translation Society, 1849.

'Catechism of the Church in Geneva' (1545), pp. 34–94 in *Tracts and Treatises*, vol. 2, trans. H. Beveridge, Edinburgh: Calvin Translation Society, 1849.

'Confession of Faith concerning the Eucharist' (1537), pp. 168–169 in *Calvin: Theological Treatises*, ed. J. K. S. Reid, Philadelphia: Westminster, 1954.

'Consilium contra Mennonem' (1556), *CO*, 10/1, pp. 167–176.

'Defensio orthodoxae fidei de sacra Trinitate contra prodigiosos errores Michaelis Serveti Hispani' (1554), *CO*, 8, pp. 453–644.

'Expositio impietatis Valentini Gentilis' (1561), *CO*, 9, pp. 365–384.

'Last Admonition to Joachim Westphal' (1557), pp. 346–494 in *Tracts and Treatises*, vol. 2, trans. H. Beveridge, Edinburgh: Calvin Translation Society, 1849.

'Letter 15 – To Simon Grynee (May 1537)', pp. 31–32 in *Letters of John Calvin*, trans. D. Constable, ed. J. Bonnet, Edinburgh: Thomas Constable, 1855.

'Letter to the Physicians of Montpellier, 8 February 1564', in *Calvin's Selected Works: Tracts and Letters*, trans. H. Beveridge and J. Bonnet, repr. 4 vols, Grand Rapids, MI: Baker, 1983.

'Reply to Sadolet' (1539), pp. 221–256 in *Calvin: Theological Treatises*, trans. J. K. S. Reid, Philadelphia: Westminster, 1954.

'Responsio ad Nobiles Polonos et Franciscum Stancarum Mantuanum' (1561), *CO*, 9, pp. 349–358.

'Short Treatise on the Lord's Supper' (1541), pp. 142–166 in *Calvin: Theological Treatises*, trans. J. K. S. Reid, Philadelphia: Westminster, 1954.

'The Form of Church Prayers' (1542), pp. 197–224 in *Liturgies of the Western Church*, ed. B. Thompson, Philadelphia: Fortress, 1980.

'True Partaking of the Flesh and Blood of Christ' (1561), pp. 496–572 in *Tracts and Treatises*, vol. 2, trans. H. Beveridge, Edinburgh: Calvin Translation Society, 1849.

*Biblical Commentaries*, Albany, OR: AGES Software, 1997.

*Calvin's Commentary on Seneca's De Clementia, with Introduction, Translation and Notes*, ed. F. L. Battles and A. M. Hugo, Leiden: Brill, 1969.

*Commentaries of John Calvin*, 46 vols, Edinburgh: Calvin Translation Society, 1844–1855, repr. Grand Rapids, MI: Baker Book House, 1979.

*Commentaries on the Prophet Jeremiah and the Lamentations*, trans. J. Owen, repr. in 5 vols, Grand Rapids, MI: Eerdmans, 1950.

*Commentaries on the Twelve Minor Prophets*, trans. J. Owen, 5 vols, Edinburgh: Calvin Translation Society, 1847.

*Commentary on Genesis*, trans. J. King, 1847; repr. London: Banner of Truth, 1965.

*Commentary on the Book of Psalms*, trans. J. Anderson, Edinburgh: Calvin Translation Society, 1845.

*Concerning the Eternal Predestination of God* (1552), trans. J. K. S. Reid, London: James Clarke, 1961.

*Institutes of the Christian Religion, 1536 Edition*, trans. F. L. Battles, Grand Rapids, MI: Eerdmans, 1975.

*Institutes of the Christian Religion*, trans. F. L. Battles, ed. J. T. McNeil, Library of Christian Classics 20–21, Philadelphia: Westminster Press, 1969.

*Institutes of the Christian Religion*, trans. Henry Beveridge, 2 vols, repr. Grand Rapids, MI: Eerdmans, 1995.

*Ioannis Calvini in Novum Testamentum Commentarii*, 6 vols, ed. A. Tholuck, Berolini: Apud Gustavum Eichler, 1833–1834.

*Ioannis Calvini Opera quae supersunt Omnia*, Brunswick: Schwetschke, 1893.

*Ioannis Calvini Opera Quae Supersunt Omnia*, vols 1–59 [*Corpus Reformatorum*, vols 29–87], ed. G. Baum, E. Cunitz and E. Reuss, Brunsvigae: Apud C. A. Schwetschke et Filium, 1863–1900.

*Ioannis Calvini Opera Selecta*, 5 vols, ed. P. Barth et. al., Munich: Chr. Kaiser, 1926–1936.

*John Calvin's Sermons on Timothy and Titus*, trans. L. T., London 1579, repr. in facsimile, Edinburgh: Banner of Truth, 1983.

*Sermons of Maister John Calvin, upon the Book of Job*, trans. A. Golding, London, 1574, repr. in facsimile, Edinburgh: Banner of Truth, 1993.

*Sermons on Deuteronomy*, trans. A. Golding, London 1583, repr. in facsimile, Edinburgh: Banner of Truth, 1987.

*Sermons on the Acts of the Apostles*, trans. R. R. McGregor, Edinburgh and Carlisle: Banner of Truth, 2008.

*Sermons on the Epistle to the Ephesians*, trans. A. Golding, London 1577, rev. and repr. Edinburgh: Banner of Truth, 1973.

*On the Bondage and Liberation of the Will*, trans. G. I. Davies, ed. A. N. S. Lane, Grand Rapids, MI: Baker, 1996.

*Calvin's Theological Treatises*, trans. J. K. S. Reid, London: SCM, 1954.


## Other primary sources

ALBERTUS MAGNUS, *Commentarii in I Sententiarum* (*Opera Omnia*, 26).

ALEXANDER OF HALES, *Summa Theologica*, 6 vols, ed. Quaracchi, Grottaferrata: Collegii S. Bonaventurae ad Claras Aquas, 1924–1948.

AQUINAS, T. 'On the Divine Simplicity, Disputed Question of the Power of God, 7', trans. R. McInerny, pp. 290–342 in *Thomas Aquinas: Selected Writings*, London: Penguin, 1998.

——, *In Omnes D. Pauli Apostoli Epistolas Commentaria*, Liège: H. Dessain, 1858.

——, *Scriptum super Sententiis in Sancti Thomae Aquinatis Opera Omnia*, Parmae: Typis Petri Fiaccadori, 1858.

——, *Summa Theologiae*, ed. C. Ernst, 61 vols, London: Blackfriars, 1964–1980.

ATHANASIUS, 'Against the Arians', pp. 303–447 in *St Athanasius: Select Works and Letters*, ed. P. Schaff and H. Wace, Grand Rapids, MI: Eerdmans, 1891.

——, 'Against the Heathen', *NPNF2*, 4.

——, 'Defence of the Nicene Definition', *NPNF2*, 4.

——, 'On Luke 10:22', *NPNF2*, 4, pp. 87–90.

AUGUSTINE, 'On the Holy Trinity', trans. A. W. Haddan, *NPNF1*, 3, pp. 17–228.

——, 'Answer to Maximus', pp. 231–336 in *Arianism and Other Heresies, The Works of Saint Augustine: A Translation for the 21st Century*, trans. R. J. Teske, ed. John E. Rotelle, New York: New City, 1995.

——, *Confessions*, trans. H. Chadwick, Oxford: Oxford University Press, 1992.

——, *De Dono Perseverantiae*, 19 in *PL*.

——, *Enchiridion*, *NPNF1*, 3.

——, *In Evangelium Joannis Tractatus*, *PL* 35.

——, *Soliloquies*, trans. C. C. Starbuck, *NPNF1*, 7, pp. 537–560.

AUREOL, P., *Scriptum Super Primum Sententiarum*, 2 vols, ed. E. M. Buytaert, St Bonaventure: The Franciscan Institute, 1953–1957.

BASIL, *Sur Le Saint-Esprit*, trans. Benoît Pruche, 2e éd. entièrement ref. ed., Paris: Cerf, 1968.

BIEL, G., *Collectorium circa quattuor libros Sententiarum, Prologus et Liber primus*, ed. W. Werbeck and U. Hofman, J. C. B. Mohr, 1973.

BONAVENTURE, *Commentaria*, in *Opera Omnia*, vol. 1, repr. Grottaferrata: Ad Claras Aquas, 1882.

BRADWARDINE, T., *De causa Dei contra Pelagium et de virtute causarum ad suos Mertonenses, libri tres*, ed. H. Savile, London, 1618.

BULLINGER, H., *Heinryci Bullingeri commentarii in omnes Pauli apostoli epistolas, atque etiam in epistolam ad Hebraeos*, Zürich: Apud Christophorum Froschouerum, 1582.

——, *The Decades of Henry Bullinger*, ed. T. Harding, 3 vols, Cambridge University: Parker Society, 1849–1852.

CICERO, *The Nature of the Gods*, trans. H. C. P. McGregor, London: Penguin, 1972.

DUNS SCOTUS, J., *Opera Omnia*, ed. C. Balic, Vatican City, 1950–.

DURANDUS OF SAINT-POURÇAIN, *In Petri Lombardi Sententias Theologias Commentarium libri IIII*.

GILES OF ROME, *In Libros Sententiarum*, Frankfurt, 1969.

GREGORY OF NAZIANZUS, 'Epistle 101', trans. C. G. Browne and J. E. Swallow, in *NPNF2*, 7, pp. 439–443.

——, 'Orations', trans. C. G. Browne and J. E. Swallow, in *NPNF2*, 7, pp. 203–434.

GREGORY OF RIMINI, *Lectura super primum et secundum Sententiarum*, 7 vols, ed. Damasus Trapp and Venicio Marcoline, Berlin, 1979.

HOLKOT, R., *In Quatuor Libros Sententiarum Quaestiones*, Lugdini, 1518, repr. Unveränderter Nachdruck, Frankfurt: Minerva GMBH, 1967.

——, *Robertus Holkoti super libros Sapientiae*, Basilea, 1506.

HYPERIUS, A., *In Epistolas D. Pavli Ad Timothevm, Titum, Philemonem, & D. Iudae*, Tigvri: Apvd Chistophorvm Froschovervm, 1582.

LUTHER, M., *Luther's Works*, 56 vols, ed. Jaroslav Pelikan and Helmut Lehman, St Louis/ Philadelphia: Concordia/Fortress, 1955–1986.

MUSCULUS, W., *In Divi Pauli epistolas ad Philippenses, Colossenses, Thessalonicenses ambas, & primam ad Timotheum, commentarii*, Basel: Ex Officina Hervagiana, 1578.

——, *Loci communes theologiae sacrae, ut sunt postremo recogniti & emendati*, Basel: Per Sebastianum Henricpetri, 1599 [*Commonplaces of Religion*, London: R. Wolfe, 1563].

NICHOLAS OF LYRA, *Bibliorum Sacrorum Cum Glossa Ordinaria [. . .] Et Postilla Nicolai Lyrani Additionibus Pauli Burgensis, ac Matthiae Thoryngi Replicis*, Tomus Sextus, Venetiis, 1601.

OSIANDER, A., *An filius Dei fuerit incarnandus*, in *Gesamtausgabe Andreas Osiander*, ed. G. Müller, Gütersloh: Gütersloh Verlaghaus, 1975–1997, IX.

PETER LOMBARD, 'Sententiarum Quatuor Libri', in *Opera Omnia S. Bonaventurae*, vol. 1, repr. Grottaferrata: Ad Claras Aquas, 1882.

——, *The Sentences: Book 1, The Mystery of the Trinity*, trans. Giulio Silano, Crescent East: Pontifical Institute of Medieval Studies, 2007.

PROSPER OF AQUITAINE, *The Call of the Nations*, trans. P. De Letter, Westminster: The Newman Press; London: Longman Green and Co., 1952.

SIMONS, M., 'Brief Confession on the Incarnation (1544)', pp. 422–454 in *The Complete Writings of Menno Simons c.1496–1561*, trans. L. Verduin, ed. J. C. Wenger, Scottdale, PA: Herald, 1956.

——, 'Reply to Martin Micron (1556)', pp. 838–913 in *The Complete Writings of Menno Simons c.1496–1561*, trans. L. Verduin, ed. J. C. Wenger, Scottdale, PA: Herald, 1956.

——, 'The Incarnation of Our Lord (1554)', in *The Complete Writings of Menno Simons c.1496–1561*, trans. L. Verduin, ed. J. C. Wenger, Scottdale, PA: Herald, 1956.

THOMAS OF STRASSBOURG, *Commentaria in quattuor libros Sententiarum*, Venetiis, Stellae, Iordani Ziletti, 1564.

TURRETIN, F., *Institutes of Elenctic Theology*, trans. G. M. Giger, ed. J. T. Dennison, 3 vols, Philipsburg, NJ: Presbyterian & Reformed, 1992–1997.

——, *Opera*, 4 vols, Edinburgh: Lowe, 1847.

VERMIGLI, P. M., *Petri Martyris Vermilii Florentini praestantissimi nostra aetate theologi, loci communes*, London: Ex typographia Ioannis Kyngstoni, 1576.

——, *The Commonplaces of [. . .] Peter Martyr*, London, 1574.

WILLIAM OF OCKHAM, *Guillelmi de Ockham Opera philosophica et theologica ad fidem codicum manuscriptorum edita*, St Bonaventure, 1976–1985.

WYCLIF, J., *De Veritate Sacrae Scripturae*, trans. R. Buddensieg, ed., London: Wyclif Society, 1907.

## Secondary material

ADAM, P. (1996), *Speaking God's Words: A Practical Theology of Preaching*, Leicester: IVP.

—— (2004), *Hearing God's Words: Exploring Biblical Spirituality*, Leicester: Apollos.

—— (2008), *Written for Us: Receiving God's Words in Scripture*, Leicester: IVP.

ANDERSON, M. (1989), 'John Calvin, Biblical Preacher', *Scottish Journal of Theology* 42.2, pp. 167–181.

ASSELT, W. J. VAN (2004), 'Scholasticism Protestant and Catholic: Medieval Sources and Methods in Seventeenth-Century Reformed Thought', in J. Frishman, W. Otten and G. Rouwhorst (eds.), *Religious Identity and the Problem of Historical Foundation: The Foundational Character of Authoritative Sources in the History of Christianity and Judaism*, Jewish and Christian Perspectives Series, VIII, Leiden: Brill, pp. 457–470.

AUERBACH, E. (1953), *Mimesis: The Representation of Reality in Western Literature*, trans. W. R. Trask, Princeton, NJ: Princeton University Press.

AYRES, L. (2000), '"Remember That You Are Catholic" (Serm. 52.2): Augustine on the Unity of the Triune God', *Journal of Early Christian Studies* 8.1, pp. 39–82.

BADGER, C. R. (1971), *The Reverend Charles Strong and the Australian Church*, Melbourne: Abacada.

—— (1976), 'Strong, Charles', in B. Nairn (ed.), *Australian Dictionary of Biography*, vol. 6, Melbourne: Melbourne University Press.

BAKER, D. W. A. (1967), 'Lang, John Dunmore', in D. Pike (ed.), *Australian Dictionary of Biography*, vol. 2, Melbourne: Melbourne University Press, pp. 76–83.

BARKLEY, A. (1982), 'The Impact of Calvinism on Australasia', in W. S. Reid (ed.), *John Calvin: His Influence on the Western World*, Grand Rapids, MI: Zondervan, pp. 325–337.

BARNES, M. R. (1995), 'Augustine in Contemporary Trinitarian Theology', *Theological Studies* 56, pp. 237–250.

BARTH, K. (1960), *Church Dogmatics III/3: The Doctrine of Creation*, trans. G. W. Bromiley and R. J. Ehrlich, ed. G. W. Bromiley and T. F. Torrance, Edinburgh: T. & T. Clark.

—— (1956), *Church Dogmatics IV/1: The Doctrine of Reconciliation*, trans. G. W. Bromiley, ed. G. W. Bromiley and T. F. Torrance, Edinburgh: T. & T. Clark.

—— (1961), *Church Dogmatics IV/2: The Doctrine of Reconciliation*, trans. G. W. Bromiley, ed. G. W. Bromiley and T. F. Torrance. Edinburgh: T. & T. Clark.

—— (1995), *The Theology of John Calvin*, trans. G. W. Bromiley, Grand Rapids, MI: Eerdmans.

BATTLES, F. L. (1977), 'God was Accommodating Himself to Human Capacity', *Interpretation* 31, pp. 19–38.

BAVINCK, H. (2003–2008), *Reformed Dogmatics*, 4 vols, trans. J. Vriend, ed. J. Bolt, Grand Rapids, MI: Baker.

BEACH, M. J. (1999), 'The Real Presence of Christ in the Preaching of the Gospel: Luther and Calvin on the Nature of Preaching', *Mid-American Journal of Theology* 10, pp. 77–134.

BEASLEY-MURRAY, G. R. (1962), *Baptism in the New Testament*, repr. Exeter: Paternoster, 1972.

BEBBINGTON, D. W. (1989), *Evangelicalism in Modern Britain: A History from the 1730s to the 1980s*, London: Routledge.

—— (2005), *The Dominance of Evangelicalism: The Age of Spurgeon and Moody*, Leicester: IVP.

BECKWITH, R. (2001), 'The Calvinist Doctrine of the Trinity', *Churchman* 115.4, pp. 308–315.

BERKHOF, L. (1939), *Systematic Theology*, repr. Edinburgh: Banner of Truth, 1981.

BERKOUWER, G. C. (1977), *The Person of Christ*, trans. J. H. Kok, Grand Rapids, MI: Eerdmans.

BILLINGS, J. T. (2007), *Calvin, Participation and the Gift: The Activity of Believers in Union with Christ*, Oxford: Oxford University Press.

BLOCHER, H. (1987) 'The "Analogy of Faith" in the Study of Scripture', in N. M. de S. Cameron (ed.), *The Challenge of Evangelical Theology: Essays in Method and Approach*, Edinburgh: Rutherford House, pp. 17–38.

—— (2007), 'Luther and Calvin on Christology', paper presented to the 12th Edinburgh Dogmatics Conference, August 2007.

BLUNT, J. H. (1874), *Dictionary of Sects, Heresies, Ecclesiastical Parties and Schools of Religious Thought*, London: Rivingtons.

BOBZIEN, S. (1998), *Determinism and Freedom in Stoic Philosophy*, Oxford: Clarendon.

BOLT, J. (1989), '*Spiritus Creator*: The Use and Abuse of Calvin's Cosmic Pneumatology', in P. De Klerk (ed.), *Calvin and the Holy Spirit*, Grand Rapids, MI: Calvin Studies Society, pp. 17–34.

BOUWSMA, W. J. (1988), *John Calvin: A Sixteenth Century Portrait*, New York/Oxford: Oxford University Press.

BRADY, I. (1977), 'The *Summa Theologica* of Alexander of Hales (1924–1948)', *Archivum Franciscanum Historicum* 70, pp. 437–447.

BRAY, G. (1993), *The Doctrine of God*, Leicester: Inter-Varsity Press.

BREWARD, I. (1993), *A History of the Australian Churches*, Sydney: Allen & Unwin.

BRÜMMER, V. (1984), *What Are We Doing When We Pray?* London: SCM.

BUTIN, P. W. (1994), *Reformed Ecclesiology: Trinitarian Grace According to Calvin*, Princeton, NJ: Princeton Theological Seminary.

—— (1995), *Revelation, Redemption and Response: Calvin's Trinitarian Understanding of the Divine-Human Relationship*, Oxford: Oxford University Press.

CABLE, K. (1969), 'Barker, Frederic', in D. Pike (ed.), *Australian Dictionary of Biography*, vol. 3, Melbourne: Melbourne University Press, pp. 90–94.

—— (1996), 'Hammond, Thomas Chatterton', in J. Ritchie (ed.), *Australian Dictionary of Biography*, vol. 14, Melbourne: Melbourne University Press, pp. 367–368.

CAMERON, A. J. (2008), 'Liberation and Desire: The Logic of Law in Exodus and Beyond', in B. S. Rosner and P. R. Williamson (eds.), *Exploring Exodus: Literary, Theological and Contemporary Approaches*, Nottingham: Apollos, pp. 123–153.

CAMERON, M. (2006), *An Enigmatic Life: David Broughton Knox, Father of Contemporary Sydney Anglicanism*, Sydney: Acorn.

CAREY, H. (1996), *Believing in Australia*, Sydney: Allen & Unwin.

CARROLL, T. K. (1984), *Preaching the Word*, The Message of the Fathers of the Church 11, Wilmington, DE: Michael Glazier.

CHILDS, B. S. (1992), *Biblical Theology of the Old and New Testaments: Theological Reflection on the Christian Bible*, London: SCM.

COLISH, M. (1994), *Peter Lombard*, 2 vols, Studies in Intellectual History 41, Leiden: Brill.

—— (1996), *Medieval Foundations of the Western Intellectual Tradition*, New Haven, CT, and London: Yale University Press.

COURTENAY, W. J. (1987), *Schools and Scholars in Fourteenth-Century England*, Princeton, NJ: Princeton University Press.

CREEL, R. (1986), *Divine Impassibility: An Essay in Philosophical Theology*, Cambridge: Cambridge University Press.

DALLIMORE, A. (1985), *Spurgeon: A New Biography*, Edinburgh: Banner of Truth.

DAVIS, T. J. (2008), *This Is My Body: The Presence of Christ in Reformation Thought*, Grand Rapids, MI: Baker.

DAWKINS, R. (2006), *The God Delusion*, London: Bantam.

DE GREEF, W. (1993), *The Writings of John Calvin: An Introductory Guide*, trans. L. D. Bierma, Grand Rapids, MI: Baker.

DE KOSTER, L. (2004), *Light for the City: Calvin's Preaching, Source of Life and Liberty*, Grand Rapids, MI, and Cambridge: Eerdmans.

DE LETTER, P. (1952), 'Introduction', in Prosper of Aquitaine, *The Call of the Nations*, trans. P. De Letter, London: Longman Green, pp. 3–20.

DEDDO, G. W. (2001), 'The Holy Spirit in the Theology of T. F. Torrance', in E. M. Colyer (ed.), *The Promise of Trinitarian Theology: Theologians in Dialogue with T. F. Torrance*, Lanham, MD: Rowman & Littlefield, pp. 81–114.

DEVRIES, D. (1996), *Jesus Christ in the Preaching of Calvin and Schleiermacher*, Louisville, KY: Westminster John Knox.

DOUCET, V. (1947), 'The History of the Problem of the Authenticity of the Summa', *Franciscan Studies* 7, pp. 26–41, 274–311.

DOUGAN, A. (1979), 'Angus, Samuel', in B. Nairn (ed.), *Australian Dictionary of Biography*, vol. 7, Melbourne: Melbourne University Press, pp. 73–74.

DOYLE, R. C. (1981), 'The Context of Moral Decision Making in the Writings of John Calvin: The Christological Ethics of Eschatological Order', unpublished PhD thesis, University of Aberdeen.

—— (1982), 'John Calvin, his Modern Detractors and the Place of the Law in Christian Ethics', *RTR* 41.3, pp. 74–83.

—— (1990), 'Decision Making at the Boundaries of Life: How Religious Beliefs Affect Ethical Judgments', in Barry G. Webb (ed.), *The Ethics of Life and Death*, Homebush West: Lancer, pp. 49–82.

EDGAR, W. (2008), 'Ethics: The Christian Life and Good Works According to Calvin', in D. W. Hall and P. A. Lillback (eds.), *A Theological Guide to Calvin's Institutes: Essays and Analysis*, Phillipsburg, NJ: Presbyterian & Reformed, pp. 320–346.

EDMONDSON, S. (2004), *Calvin's Christology*, Cambridge: Cambridge University Press.

—— (2005), 'Christ and History: Hermeneutical Convergence in Calvin and its Challenge to Biblical Theology', *Modern Theology* 21.1, pp. 3–35.

EDWARDS, P. (1967), 'Common Consent Arguments for the Existence of God', in

P. Edwards (ed.), *The Encyclopaedia of Philosophy*, London: Macmillan, vol. 2, pp. 147–155.

ELLIOTT, M. (2007), 'Gabler, Johan Philipp', in D. K. McKim (ed.), *Dictionary of Major Biblical Interpreters*, Downers Grove, IL: IVP, pp. 452–457.

ELLIS, BOB (1999), 'Our Place in the Sun', *Sunday Telegraph*, Sydney, 24 January.

EMMEN, E. (1935), *De christologie van Calvijn*, Amsterdam: Paris.

ERICKSON, M. J. (1998), *Christian Theology*, revised edn, Grand Rapids, MI: Baker.

FINK, D. (2006), 'Review of S. Edmondson, *Calvin's Christology*', *Trinity Journal* 27, pp. 331–332.

FITZER, J. (1976), 'The Augustinian Roots of Calvin's Eucharistic Thought', *Augustinian Studies* 7, pp. 69–98; repr. 1992 in R. C. Gamble (ed.), *Articles on Calvin and Calvinism*, vol. 10, *Calvin's Ecclesiology: Sacraments and Deacons*, New York: Garland, pp. 165–194.

FLINT, T. P. (1991), *Divine Providence*, Ithaca, NY: Cornell University Press.

FOXGROVER, D. L. (1987), 'A Scrap of Bread and a Right Conscience', in P. De Klerk (ed.), *Calvin and Christian Ethics: Papers and Responses Presented at the Fifth Colloquium on Calvin and Calvin Studies*, Grand Rapids, MI: Calvin Studies Society, pp. 125–44.

FREI, H. W. (1974), *The Eclipse of Biblical Narrative: A Study in Eighteenth and Nineteenth Century Hermeneutics*, New Haven, CT, and London: Yale University Press.

FRYE, R. M. (1990), 'Calvin's Theological Use of Figurative Language', in T. George (ed.), *John Calvin and the Church: A Prism of Reform*, Louisville, KY: Westminster John Knox, pp. 172–194.

GAMBLE, R. C. (1994), 'Current Trends in Calvin Research 1982–90', in W. H. Neuser (ed.), *Calvinus Sacrae Scripturae Professor: Calvin as Confessor of Holy Scripture*, Grand Rapids, MI: Eerdmans, pp. 91–112.

GANOCZY, A. (1964), *Calvin Théologien de l'Eglise et du Ministère*, Paris: Cerf.

GARCIA, M. (2008), *Life in Christ: Union with Christ and Twofold Grace in Calvin's Theology*, Milton Keynes: Paternoster.

GEACH, P. T. (1969), *God and the Soul*, London: Routledge.

—— (1977), *Providence and Evil*, Cambridge: Cambridge University Press.

GERRISH, B. A. (1969), 'John Calvin and the Reformed Doctrine of the Lord's Supper', *McCormick Quarterly* 22, pp. 85–98; repr. 1992 in R. C. Gamble (ed.), *Articles on Calvin and Calvinism*, vol. 10, *Calvin's Ecclesiology: Sacraments and Deacons*, New York: Garland, pp. 227–240.

GILES, K. (2006), *Jesus and the Father: Modern Evangelicals Reinvent the Doctrine of the Trinity*, Grand Rapids, MI: Zondervan.

GOUWENS, D. J. (1996), *Kierkegaard as Religious Thinker*, Cambridge: Cambridge University Press.

GRAHAM, W. F. (1971), *The Constructive Revolutionary: John Calvin and his Socio-Economic Impact*, Richmond, VA: John Knox.

GREENE-MCCREIGHT, K. (1998), '"We Are Companions of the Patriarchs" or Scripture

Absorbs Calvin's World', in L. G. Jones and J. J. Buckley (eds.), *Theology and Scriptural Imagination*, Oxford: Blackwell, pp. 51–62.

GRILLMEIER, A. (1965), *Christ in the Christian Tradition*, vol. 1, *From the Apostolic Age to Chalcedon (451)*, trans. J. Bowden, Atlanta: John Knox.

GRUDEM, W. (1994), *Systematic Theology: An Introduction to Biblical Doctrine*, Leicester: Inter-Varsity Press.

GUNSON, N. (1966), 'Crook, William Pascoe', in D. Pike (ed.), *Australian Dictionary of Biography*, vol. 1, Melbourne: Melbourne University Press, pp. 259–261.

—— (1966), 'Hassall, Rowland', in D. Pike (ed.), *Australian Dictionary of Biography*, vol. 1, Melbourne: Melbourne University Press, pp. 521–522.

GUNTON, C. E. (1993), *The One, the Three and the Many*, Cambridge: Cambridge University Press.

—— (1993), *A Brief Theology of Revelation: Warfield Lectures 1993*, Edinburgh: T. & T. Clark, 1995.

—— (1997), *The Promise of Trinitarian Theology*, 2nd edn, Edinburgh: T. & T. Clark.

—— (1998), *The Triune Creator*, Grand Rapids, MI: Eerdmans.

—— (1999), 'Aspects of Salvation: Some Unscholastic Themes from Calvin's *Institutes*', *IJST* 1.3, pp. 253–265.

—— (2000), *Intellect and Action*, Edinburgh: T. & T. Clark.

—— (2001), 'Being and Person: T. F. Torrance's Doctrine of God', in E. M. Colyer (ed.), *The Promise of Trinitarian Theology: Theologians in Dialogue with T. F. Torrance*, Lanham, MD: Rowman & Littlefield, pp. 115–137.

—— (2002), 'The Spirit Moved over the Face of the Waters: The Holy Spirit and Created Order', *IJST* 4.2, pp. 190–204.

—— (2006), *Enlightenment and Alienation*, repr. Eugene, OR: Wipf & Stock.

HAAS, G. H. (1997), *The Concept of Equity in Calvin's Ethics*, Waterloo: Wilfrid Laurier University Press.

HALVERSON, J. L. (1998), *Peter Aureol on Predestination: A Challenge to Late Medieval Thought*, Studies in the History of Christian Thought 83, Leiden: Brill.

HAMILTON, R. (1888), *A Jubilee History of the Presbyterian Church of Victoria*, Melbourne: Presbyterian Church of Victoria.

HAMMOND, T. C. (1936), *In Understanding Be Men*, London: Inter-Varsity Press.

—— (1942), 'John Calvin on the Atonement', *RTR* 2.2, pp. 3–12.

HARINK, D. (1998), 'Spirit in the World in the Theology of John Calvin: A Contribution to a Theology of Religion and Culture', *Didaskalia* 9.2, pp. 61–81.

HEDGES, C. (2008), *I Don't Believe in Atheists*, London: Free Press.

HELM, P. (1986), 'Asking God', *Themelios* 12.1, pp. 22–24.

—— (1992), 'Prayer and Providence', in M. Sarot, G. van den Brink and L. van den Brom (eds.), *Christian Faith and Philosophical Theology: Essays in Honour of Vincent Brümmer*, Kampen: Kok Pharos, pp. 103–115.

—— (1994), 'Calvin (and Zwingli) on Divine Providence', *CTJ* 29, pp. 308–405.

—— (2004), *John Calvin's Ideas*, Oxford: Oxford University Press.

—— (forthcoming), *Calvin at the Centre*, Oxford: Oxford University Press.

HILL, M. (2002), *The How and Why of Love: An Introduction to Evangelical Ethics*, Kingsford: Matthias Media.

HODGE, C. H. (1872), *Systematic Theology*, 3 vols, repr. London: James Clarke, 1960.

HÖHNE, D. A. (forthcoming), *The Spirit and Sonship: Perfecting a Particular Person*, Farnham: Ashgate.

HOLDER, R. W. (2006), 'Calvin as Commentator on the Pauline Epistles', in D. McKim (ed.), *Calvin and the Bible*, Cambridge: Cambridge University Press, pp. 224–256.

HOLMES, S. R. (2008), 'Calvin on Scripture', in N. B. MacDonald and C. Trueman (eds.), *Calvin, Barth and Reformed Theology*, Milton Keynes: Paternoster, pp. 149–162.

HORTON, M. S. (2008), *People and Place: A Covenant Ecclesiology*, Louisville, KY: Westminster John Knox.

HUGHES, P. J. (1996), *The Baptists in Australia*, Canberra: Australian Government Printing Service.

HUNT, A. (1998), 'The Art of Hearing: English Preachers and their Audiences, 1590–1640', unpublished PhD thesis, University of Cambridge.

HYLSON-SMITH, K. (1989), *Evangelicals in the Church of England, 1734–1984*, Edinburgh: T. & T. Clark.

JALLAND, P. (2002), *Australian Ways of Death: A Social and Cultural History 1840–1918*, Oxford: Oxford University Press.

JASPER, D. (2004), *A Short Introduction to Hermeneutics*, Louisville, KY: Westminster John Knox.

JONES, D. C. (2008), 'The Law and the Spirit of Christ', in D. W. Hall and P. A. Lillback (eds.), *A Theological Guide to Calvin's Institutes: Essays and Analysis*, Phillipsburg, NJ: Presbyterian & Reformed, pp. 301–319.

JONES, S. (1995), *Calvin and the Rhetoric of Piety*, Columbia: Columbia Theological Seminary.

JULIAN, R. (2005), 'The Reformed Church', in A. Alexander (ed.), *The Companion to Tasmanian History*, Hobart: University of Tasmania, pp. 304–305.

KEESECKER, W. F. (1987), 'The Law in John Calvin's Ethics', in P. De Klerk (ed.), *Calvin and Christian Ethics: Papers and Responses Presented at the Fifth Colloquium on Calvin and Calvin Studies*, Grand Rapids, MI: Calvin Studies Society, pp. 19–49.

KNOX, D. B. (1983), *The Lord's Supper from Wycliffe to Cranmer*, Exeter: Paternoster.

KOOI, C. VAN DER (2005), *As in a Mirror: John Calvin and Karl Barth on Knowing God – A Diptych*, trans. D. Mader, Leiden: Brill.

KRAUS, H.-J. (1977), 'Calvin's Exegetical Principles', *Interpretation* 31, pp. 8–18.

KRUSCHE, W. (1957), *Das Wirken des Heiligen Geistes nach Calvin*, Göttingen: Vandenhoeck & Ruprecht.

LAMPE, G. W. H. (ed.) (1969), *The Cambridge History of the Bible*, vol. 2, *The West from the Fathers to the Reformation*, Cambridge: Cambridge University Press.

LANE, A. N. S. (1991), 'Recent Calvin Literature: A Review Article', *Themelios* 16.2, pp. 17–24.

LEAHY, F. S. (1992), 'Calvin and the Extent of the Atonement', *Reformed Theological Journal* 8, pp. 54–64.

LECERF, A. (1949), *An Introduction to Reformed Dogmatics*, trans. A. Schlemmer, London: Lutterworth.

LEFF, G. (1957), *Bradwardine and the Pelagians*, Cambridge: Cambridge University Press.

—— (1961), *Gregory of Rimini: Tradition and Innovation in Fourteenth Century Thought*, Manchester: Manchester University Press.

LEITH, J. H. (1989), 'Reformed Preaching Today', *The Princeton Seminary Bulletin* 10.3, pp. 224–257.

—— (1990), 'Calvin's Doctrine of the Proclamation of the Word and its Significance Today', in T. George (ed.), *John Calvin and the Church: A Prism of Reform*, Louisville, KY: Westminster John Knox, pp. 206–229.

MACINTOSH, N. K. (1978), *Richard Johnson: Chaplain to the Colony of New South Wales*, Sydney: Ambassador.

MATHESON, P. (1998), *The Rhetoric of the Reformation*, Edinburgh: T. & T. Clark.

—— (2001), *The Imaginative World of the Reformation*, Minneapolis: Fortress Press.

MATHISON, K. A. (2002), *Given for You: Reclaiming Calvin's Doctrine of the Lord's Supper*, Phillipsburg, NJ: P. & R.

McCLEAN, J. (forthcoming), 'Perichoresis, Theosis and Union with Christ in the Thought of John Calvin', *RTR*.

McCORMACK, B. L. (1993), 'For Us and Our Salvation: Incarnation and Atonement in the Reformed Tradition', *Studies in Reformed Theology and History* 1.2.

McGRATH, A. E. (1987), *The Intellectual Origins of the Reformation*, Oxford: Blackwell.

—— (1990), *A Life of John Calvin: A Study in the Shaping of Western Culture*, Oxford: Blackwell.

MILBANK, J. (2005), 'Alternative Protestantism', in J. K. A. Smith and J. H. Olthuis (eds.), *Radical Orthodoxy and the Reformed Tradition: Creation, Covenant and Participation*, Grand Rapids, MI: Baker, pp. 25–41.

MOL, H. (1971), *Religion in Australia*, Nashville: Nelson.

MOLTMANN, J. (1970), *The Crucified God*, trans. R. A. Wilson and J. Bowden, London: SCM.

MOO, D. (1996), *The Epistle to the Romans*, Grand Rapids, MI: Eerdmans.

MORRIS, L. L. (1986), *New Testament Theology*, Grand Rapids, MI: Zondervan.

MOULE, H. C. G. (1892), *Charles Simeon*, repr. Leicester: Inter-Varsity Press, 1965.

MULCHAHEY, M. M. (2000), 'Peter Lombard', in P. W. Carey and J. T. Lienhard (eds.), *Biographical Dictionary of Christian Theologians*, Westport, CT: Greenwood, pp. 416–418.

MULLER, R. A. (1981), 'Christ in the Eschaton: Calvin and Moltmann on the Duration of the *Munus Regium*', *Harvard Theological Review* 74.1, pp. 31–59.

—— (1986), *Christ and the Decree: Christology and Predestination in Reformed Theology from Calvin to Perkins*, Studies in Historical Theology 2, Durham, NC: Labyrinth.

—— (1988), 'The Place and Importance of Karl Barth in the Twentieth Century: A Review Essay', *WTJ* 50, pp. 127–156.

—— (1989), 'Karl Barth and the Path of Theology into the Twentieth Century: Historical Observations', *WTJ* 51, pp. 25–50.

—— (1990), 'The Hermeneutics of Promise and Fulfillment in Calvin's Exegesis of the Old Testament Prophecies of the Kingdom', in D. C. Steinmetz (ed.), *The Bible in the Sixteenth Century*, Durham, NC, and London: Duke University Press, pp. 68–82.

—— (1996), 'Biblical Interpretation in the Era of the Reformation: The View from the Middle Ages', in R. A. Muller and J. L. Thompson (eds.), *Biblical Interpretation in the Era of the Reformation: Essays Presented to David C. Steinmetz in Honor of his Sixtieth Birthday*, Grand Rapids, MI, and Cambridge: Eerdmans, pp. 3–22.

—— (2000), *The Unaccommodated Calvin: Studies in the Foundation of a Theological Tradition*, Oxford Studies in Historical Theology, New York and Oxford: Oxford University Press.

—— (2001), 'The Problem of Protestant Scholasticism – A Review and Definition', in W. J. van Asselt and E. Dekker (eds.), *Reformation and Scholasticism: An Ecumenical Enterprise*, Texts and Studies in Reformation and Post-Reformation Thought, Grand Rapids, MI: Baker, pp. 45–64.

—— (2003), *After Calvin: Studies in the Development of a Theological Tradition*, Oxford Studies in Historical Theology, New York and Oxford: Oxford University Press.

—— (2003), '*Ad fontes argumentorum*: The Sources of Reformed Theology in the Seventeenth Century', in *After Calvin: Studies in the Development of a Theological Tradition*, Oxford Studies in Historical Theology, New York: Oxford University Press, pp. 47–62.

—— (2006), 'A Note on "Christocentrism" and the Imprudent Use of Such Terminology', *WTJ* 68, pp. 253–260.

MURRAY, I. (1973), *The Forgotten Spurgeon*, Edinburgh: Banner of Truth.

—— (1988), *Australian Christian Life from 1788*, Edinburgh: Banner of Truth.

NEILL, S. (1986), *A History of Christian Missions*, 2nd edn, revised by Henry Chadwick, London: Penguin.

NEUSER, W. H. (1986), 'The Development of the Institutes 1536–1559', in B. J. van der Walt (ed.), *John Calvin's Institutes: His Magnum Opus*, Potchefstroom, South Africa: Potchefstroom University for Christian Higher Education, pp. 33–54.

NEVIN, J. W. (2000), *The Mystical Presence: A Vindication of the Reformed or Calvinistic Doctrine of the Holy Eucharist*, ed. A. Thompson, repr. Eugene, OR: Wipf & Stock.

NICOLE, R. (1985), 'John Calvin's View of the Extent of the Atonement', *WTJ* 47, pp. 197–225.

NIESEL, W. (1956), *The Theology of Calvin*, trans. H. Knight, Philadelphia: Westminster.

OBERMAN, H. A. (1957), *Archbishop Thomas Bradwardine: A Fourteenth Century Augustinian*, Utrecht: Drukkerij En Uitgevers.

—— (1970), 'The "Extra" Dimension in the Theology of Calvin', *Journal of Ecclesiastical History* 21.1, pp. 43–64.

—— (1981), *Masters of the Reformation: The Emergence of a New Intellectual Climate in Europe*, trans. D. Martin, Cambridge: Cambridge University Press.

—— (1983), *The Harvest of Medieval Theology*, 3rd edn, Grand Rapids, MI: Baker.

—— (1986), *The Dawn of the Reformation: Essays in Late Medieval and Early Reformation Thought*, Edinburgh: T. & T. Clark.

—— (1994), *The Impact of the Reformation: Essays*, Grand Rapids, MI: Eerdmans.

—— (2003), *The Two Reformations: The Journey from the Last Days to the New World*, New Haven, CT: Yale University Press.

O'DONOVAN, O. M. T. (1980), *The Problem of Self-Love in St. Augustine*, New Haven, CT: Yale University Press.

—— (1994), *Resurrection and Moral Order: An Outline for Evangelical Ethics*, Leicester: Apollos.

OLD, H. O. (1999), *The Reading and Preaching of the Scriptures in the Worship of the Christian Church*, vol. 3, *The Medieval Church*, Grand Rapids, MI, and Cambridge: Eerdmans.

—— (2002), *The Reading and Preaching of the Scriptures in the Worship of the Christian Church*, vol. 4, *The Reformation*, Grand Rapids, MI, and Cambridge: Eerdmans.

ONFRAY, M. (2007), *Atheist Manifesto: The Case against Christianity, Judaism, and Islam*, trans. J. Leggatt, New York: Arcade.

PARKER, G. W. H. (1965), *The Morning Star: Wycliffe and the Dawn of the Reformation*, Grand Rapids, MI: Eerdmans.

PARKER, T. H. L. (1947), *The Oracles of God: An Introduction to the Preaching of John Calvin*, London and Redhill: Lutterworth.

—— (1969), *Calvin's Doctrine of the Knowledge of God*, 2nd edn, Edinburgh: Oliver & Boyd.

—— (1986), *Calvin's Old Testament Commentaries*, Edinburgh: T. & T. Clark.

—— (1992), *Calvin's Preaching*, Edinburgh: T. & T. Clark.

—— (1993), *Calvin's New Testament Commentaries*, 2nd edn, Louisville, KY: Westminster John Knox.

PARSONS, M. (2006), *Calvin's Preaching on the Prophet Micah: The 1550–1551 Sermons in Geneva*, Lewiston/Queenston/Lampeter: Edward Mellen.

PARTEE, C. (1975), 'Calvin and Determinism', *Christian Scholars Review* 5, pp. 123–128.

—— (1977), *Calvin and Classical Philosophy*, repr. Louisville, KY: Westminster John Knox, 2005.

—— (1987), 'Calvin's Central Dogma Again', *The Sixteenth Century Journal* 18.2, pp. 191–200.

—— (1988), 'Prayer as the Practice of Predestination', in W. H. Neusner (ed.), *Calvinus Servus Christi*, Budapest: Presseabteilung des Raday Kollegiums, pp. 245–256.

PELIKAN, J. (1984), *The Christian Tradition: A History of the Development of Doctrine*, vol. 4, *Reformation of Church and Dogma*, Chicago: University of Chicago Press.

PIGGIN, S. (1996), *Evangelical Christianity in Australia: Spirit, Word and World*, Melbourne and Oxford: Oxford University Press.

PINCKAERS, S. (1995), *The Sources of Christian Ethics*, trans. M. T. Noble, Edinburgh: T. & T. Clark.

PRENTIS, M. (2008), *The Scots in Australia*, Kensington: University of New South Wales Press.

PRIOR, A. C. (1966), *Some Fell on Good Ground*, Sydney: Baptist Union of New South Wales.

PUCKETT, D. L. (1995), *John Calvin's Exegesis of the Old Testament*, Columbia Series in Reformed Theology, Louisville, KY: Westminster John Knox.

QUISTORP, H. (1955), *Calvin's Doctrine of the Last Things*, trans. H. Knight, Richmond, VA: John Knox.

RAHNER, K. (1970), *The Trinity*, repr. New York: Crossroad, 1997.

RAINBOW, J. H. (1990), *The Will of God and the Cross: An Historical and Theological Study of John Calvin's Doctrine of Limited Redemption*, Allison Park: Pickwick.

REID, J. R. (2004), *Marcus Loane: A Biography*, Sydney: Acorn Press.

REID, W. S. (1992), 'Calvin and the Founding of the Academy in Geneva', in R. C. Gamble (ed.), *Calvin's work in Geneva*, New York: Garland, pp. 237–270.

REYMOND, R. L. (1998), *A New Systematic Theology of the Christian Faith*, Nashville: Thomas Nelson.

ROBIN, A. de Q. (1967), *Charles Perry*, Perth: University of Western Australia Press.

ROBINSON, M. (2004), *Gilead*, London: Picador.

—— (2008), *Home*, London: Picador.

ROGERS, K. A. (2000), *Perfect Being Theology*, Edinburgh: Edinburgh University Press.

ROSEMANN, P. W. (2004), *Peter Lombard*, Great Medieval Thinkers, Oxford: Oxford University Press.

—— (2007), *The Story of a Great Medieval Book: Peter Lombard's Sentences*, Rethinking the Middle Ages 2, Toronto: Broadview.

SCHAFF, P. (1910), *History of the Christian Church*, vol. 8, *Modern Christianity: The Swiss Reformation*, repr. Grand Rapids, MI: Eerdmans, 1981.

—— (ed.) (1983), *The Creeds of Christendom*, rev. D. S. Schaff, 3 vols, Grand Rapids, MI: Baker.

SCHREINER, S. E. (1986), 'Through a Mirror Dimly: Calvin's Sermons on Job', *CTJ* 21, pp. 175–193.

—— (1991), *The Theatre of His Glory*, Durham, NC: Labyrinth.

—— (2006), 'Calvin as an Interpreter of Job', in D. K. McKim (ed.), *Calvin and the Bible*, Cambridge: Cambridge University Press, pp. 53–84.

SLOANE, A. (2008), *At Home In a Strange Land: Using the Old Testament in Christian Ethics*, Peabody, MA: Hendrickson.

SPURGEON, C. H. (1889), *Autobiography of Charles H. Spurgeon*, Cincinnati: Curts & Jennings.

—— (1973), *Autobiography*, vol. 2, *The Full Harvest*, Edinburgh: Banner of Truth.

STEINMETZ, D. C. (1981), *Reformers in the Wings*, Grand Rapids, MI: Baker.

—— (1982), 'John Calvin on Isaiah 6: A Problem in the History of Exegesis', *Interpretation* 36, pp. 156–170.

—— (1995), *Calvin in Context*, New York and Oxford: Oxford University Press.

—— (1995), 'Calvin and the Absolute Power of God', in *Calvin in Context*, New York: Oxford University Press, pp. 40–52.

—— (2006), 'John Calvin as an Interpreter of the Bible', in D. K. McKim (ed.), *Calvin and the Bible*, Cambridge: Cambridge University Press, pp. 282–291.

STEPHENS, W. P. (1992), *Zwingli: An Introduction to his Thought*, Oxford: Oxford University Press.

STRONG, C. (1880), 'The Atonement', *Victorian Review*, October.

SWINBURNE, R. (1993), *The Coherence of Theism*, revised edn, Oxford: Oxford University Press.

TAMBURELLO, D. E. (1994), *Union with Christ: John Calvin and the Mysticism of St. Bernard*, Louisville, KY: Westminster John Knox.

TAYLOR, C. (2007), *A Secular Age*, Cambridge, MA, and London: Harvard University Press.

THOMAS, D. W. H. (2008), 'The Mediator of the Covenant', in D. W. Hall and P. A. Lillback (eds.), *Theological Guide to Calvin's Institutes: Essays and Analysis*, Phillipsburg, NJ: P. & R., pp. 205–255.

—— (2004), *Proclaiming the Incomprehensible God: Calvin's Teaching on Job*, Ross-shire: Mentor.

THOMPSON, B. (1996), *Humanists and Reformers: A History of the Renaissance and Reformation*, Grand Rapids, MI: Eerdmans.

THOMPSON, M. D. (2009), 'Calvin and the Cross of Christ', in S. W. Chung (ed.), *John Calvin and Evangelical Theology: Legacy and Prospect*, Louisville, KY: Westminster John Knox, pp. 107–127.

THOMPSON, R. (2002), *Religion in Australia: A History*, Oxford: Oxford University Press.

TORRANCE, T. F. (1969), *Theological Science*, London: Oxford University Press.

—— (1988), *The Hermeneutics of John Calvin*, Edinburgh: Scottish Academic Press.

—— (1990), 'Calvin's Doctrine of the Trinity', *CTJ* 25, pp. 165–193.

—— (1993), *The Trinitarian Faith: The Evangelical Theology of the Ancient Catholic Church*, Edinburgh: T. & T. Clark.

—— (1994), *Trinitarian Perspectives: Toward Doctrinal Agreement*, Edinburgh: T. & T. Clark.

—— (1996), *The Christian Doctrine of God, One Being Three Persons*, Edinburgh: T. & T. Clark.

—— (2008), *Incarnation: The Person and Life of Christ*, ed. R. T. Walker, Milton Keynes: Paternoster.

TORRANCE KIRBY, W. J. (2003), 'Stoic and Epicurean? Calvin's Dialectical Account of Providence in the *Institutes*', *IJST* 5.3, pp. 309–322.

TYLENDA, J. N. (1973), 'Christ the Mediator: Calvin versus Stancaro', *CTJ* 8.1, pp. 5–16.

—— (1973), 'The Controversy on Christ the Mediator: Calvin's Second Reply to Stancaro', *CTJ* 8.2 pp. 131–157.

—— (1975), 'Calvin's Understanding of the Communication of Properties', *WTJ* 38.1, pp. 54–65.

—— (1977), 'The Warning that Went Unheeded: John Calvin on Giorgio Biandrata', *CTJ* 12.1, pp. 24–62.

VANHOOZER, K. J. (1998), *Is There a Meaning in this Text?* Leicester: Apollos.

WAINWRIGHT, G. (1997), 'Baptism, Baptismal Rites', in R. P. Martin and P. H. Davids (eds.), *Dictionary of the Later New Testament and its Developments*, Downers Grove, IL: IVP, and Leicester: Inter-Varsity Press, pp. 112–124.

WALLACE, R. S. (1953), *Calvin's Doctrine of the Word and Sacrament*, Edinburgh and London: Oliver & Boyd.

—— (1959), *Calvin's Doctrine of the Christian Life*, Edinburgh: Oliver & Boyd.

—— (1988), *Calvin, Geneva, and the Reformation: A Study of Calvin as Social Reformer, Churchman, Pastor and Theologian*, Edinburgh: Scottish Academic Press.

WALT, A. G. P. VAN DER (1984), 'John Calvin and the Reformation of Preaching', in [no editor named], *Our Reformational Tradition: A Rich Heritage and Lasting Vocation*, Potchefstroom, South Africa: Potchefstroom University for Christian Higher Education, pp. 192–201.

—— (1986), 'Calvin on Preaching', in B. J. van der Walt (ed.), *John Calvin's Institutes: His Magnum Opus*, Potchefstroom, South Africa: Potchefstroom University for Christian Higher Education, pp. 326–334.

WARD, G. (2001), 'Church as the Erotic Community', in L. Boevee and L. Leijssen (eds.), *Sacramental Presence in a Postmodern Context*, Louvain: Peeters, pp. 167–204.

WARD, P. (2005), 'Coming to Sermon: The Practice of Doctrine in the Preaching of John Calvin', *Scottish Journal of Theology* 58.3, pp. 319–332.

WARD, R. S. (1989), *The Bush Still Burns: The Presbyterian and Reformed Faith in Australia 1788–1988*, Sydney: Globe Press.

—— (1994), 'Evans, William Meirion', in B. Dickey (ed.), *Australian Dictionary of Evangelical Biography*, Sydney: Evangelical History Association, p. 106.

WARFIELD, B. B. (1909), 'Calvin's Doctrine of God', repr. in Warfield, *Calvin and Augustine*, ed. S. G. Craig, Philadelphia: Presbyterian & Reformed, 1980.

—— (1909), 'Calvin's Doctrine of the Trinity', repr. in Warfield, *Calvin and Augustine*, ed. S. G. Craig, Philadelphia: Presbyterian & Reformed, 1980.

—— (1956), *Calvin and Augustine*, Philadelphia: Presbyterian & Reformed.

WATSON, F. (1994), *Text, Church and World: Biblical Interpretation in Theological Perspective*, Edinburgh: T. & T. Clark.

WEBSTER, J. B. (2005), 'Systematic Theology after Barth: Jüngel, Jenson and Gunton', in D. Ford and R. Muers (eds.), *The Modern Theologians: An Introduction to Christian Theology since 1918*, Oxford: Blackwell, pp. 249–263.

WENDEL, F. (1963), *Calvin*, trans. P. Mairet, London: Collins.

WILCOX, P. (1993), 'Restoration, Reformation and the Progress of the Kingdom of Christ: Evangelisation in the Thought and Practice of John Calvin 1555–1564', unpublished DPhil thesis, University of Oxford.

—— (2006), 'Calvin as Commentator on the Prophets', in D. K. McKim (ed.), *Calvin and the Bible*, Cambridge: Cambridge University Press, pp. 107–130.

WILKINSON, J. (2001), *The Medical History of the Reformers: Luther, Calvin and John Knox*, Edinburgh: Handsel.

WILLIAMS, T. (2001), 'Biblical Interpretation', in E. Stump and N. Kretzmann (eds.), *The Cambridge Companion to Augustine*, Cambridge: Cambridge University Press, pp. 59–70.

WILLIS, E. D. (1966), *Calvin's Catholic Christology: The Function of the So-Called Extra Calvinisticum in Calvin's Theology*, Leiden: Brill.

WOLTERSTORFF, N. (1988), 'Suffering Love', in T. V. Morris (ed.), *Philosophy and the Christian Faith*, Notre Dame, IN: University of Notre Dame Press, pp. 196–239.

WOOD, A. S. (1978), 'Calvinistic Methodism', in J. D. Douglas (ed.), *The New International Dictionary of the Christian Church*, Grand Rapids, MI: Zondervan, pp. 182–183.

WREIDT, M. (2003), 'Luther's Theology', trans. K. Gustavs, in D. K. McKim (ed.), *The Cambridge Companion to Martin Luther*, Cambridge: Cambridge University Press, pp. 86–119.

WYATT, P. (1996), *Jesus Christ and Creation in the Theology of John Calvin*, Allison Park: Pickwick.

WYK, J. H. van (1984), 'Calvin on the Christian Life', in [no editor named] *Our Reformational Tradition: A Rich Heritage and Lasting Vocation*, Potchefstroom, South Africa: Potchefstroom University for Christian Higher Education, pp. 231–278.

YARWOOD, A. T. (1996), *Samuel Marsden: The Great Survivor*, 2nd edn, Melbourne: Melbourne University Press.

ZACHMAN, R. C. (2006), *John Calvin as Teacher, Pastor, and Theologian*, Grand Rapids, MI: Baker.

# INDEX OF REFERENCES TO CALVIN'S WORKS